Language Variation

Editors: Elena Anagnostopoulou, Mark Baker, Roberta D'Alessandro, David Pesetsky, Susi Wurmbrand

In this series:

1. Bailey, Laura R. & Michelle Sheehan (eds.). Order and structure in syntax I: Word order and syntactic structure.

2. Sheehan, Michelle & Laura R. Bailey (eds.). Order and structure in syntax II: Subjecthood and argument structure.

Order and structure in syntax II

Subjecthood and argument structure

Edited by

Michelle Sheehan

Laura R. Bailey

Michelle Sheehan & Laura R. Bailey (ed.). 2017. *Order and structure in syntax II: Subjecthood and argument structure* (Open Generative Syntax 2). Berlin: Language Science Press.

This title can be downloaded at: http://langsci-press.org/catalog/book/115
© 2017, the authors
Published under the Creative Commons Attribution 4.0 Licence (CC BY 4.0):
http://creativecommons.org/licenses/by/4.0/
ISBN: 978-3-96110-028-6 (Digital)
       978-3-96110-029-3 (Hardcover)
DOI:10.5281/zenodo.1115573
Source code available from www.github.com/langsci/115
Collaborative reading: paperhive.org/documents/remote?type=langsci&id=115

Cover and concept of design: Ulrike Harbort
Typesetting: Birgit Jänen, Alec Shaw, Iana Stefanova, Felix Kopecky, Sebastian Nordhoff, Michelle Sheehan
Proofreading: Antonio Machicao y Priemer, Daniela Kolbe-Hanna, Eran Asoulin, George Walkden, Ikmi Nur Oktavianti, Lea Schäfer, Natsuko Nakagawa, Neal Whitman, Melanie Röthlisberger, Steve Pepper, Teresa Proto, Timm Lichte, Valeria Quochi
Fonts: Linux Libertine, Arimo, DejaVu Sans Mono
Typesetting software: XǝLᴬTᴇX

Language Science Press
Unter den Linden 6
10099 Berlin, Germany
langsci-press.org

Storage and cataloguing done by FU Berlin

Language Science Press has no responsibility for the persistence or accuracy of URLs for external or third-party Internet websites referred to in this publication, and does not guarantee that any content on such websites is, or will remain, accurate or appropriate.

This book is dedicated to Anders Holmberg in recognition not only of his significant contribution to the field of syntax, but also of his support, guidance and friendship to the editors and the contributors to this volume.

Contents

Introduction: Order and structure in syntax
Laura R. Bailey and Michelle Sheehan   vii

I   Papers

1   On the softness of parameters: An experiment on Faroese
Höskuldur Thráinsson   3

2   The role of locatives in (partial) pro-drop languages
Artemis Alexiadou & Janayna Carvalho   41

3   Expletives and speaker-related meaning
Ciro Greco, Liliane Haegeman & Trang Phan   69

4   Places
Tarald Taraldsen   95

5   Flexibility in symmetry: An implicational relation in Bantu double object constructions
Jenneke van der Wal   115

6   Defective intervention effects in two Greek varieties and their implications for φ-incorporation as Agree
Elena Anagnostopoulou   153

7   First Person Readings of MAN: On semantic and pragmatic restrictions on an impersonal pronoun
Verner Egerland   179

8   Who are we – and who is I? About Person and SELF
Halldór Ármann Sigurðsson   197

9	New roles for Gender: Evidence from Arabic, Semitic, Berber, and Romance Abdelkader Fassi Fehri	221
10	Puzzling parasynthetic compounds in Norwegian Janne Bondi Johannessen	257

II Squibs

11	On a "make-believe" argument for Case Theory Jonathan David Bobaljik	277
12	Semantic characteristics of recursive compounds Makiko Mukai	285
13	Expletive passives in Scandinavian – with and without objects Elisabet Engdahl	289
14	The null subject parameter meets the Polish impersonal -NO/-TO construction Małgorzata Krzek	307
15	Ellipsis in Arabic fragment answers Ali Algryani	319
16	Anaphoric object drop in Chinese Patrick Chi-wai Lee	329
17	Icelandic as a partial null subject language: Evidence from fake indexicals Susi Wurmbrand	339
Index		347

Introduction: Order and structure in syntax

Laura R. Bailey and Michelle Sheehan
University of Kent and Anglia Ruskin University

Hierarchical structure and argument structure are two of the most pervasive and widely studied properties of natural language.[1] The papers in this set of two volumes further explore these aspects of language from a range of perspectives, touching on a number of fundamental issues, notably the relationship between linear order and hierarchical structure and variation in subjecthood properties across languages. The first volume focuses on issues of word order and its relationship to structure. This second volume focuses on argument structure and subjecthood in particular. In this introduction, we provide a brief overview of the content of the 10 papers and seven squibs relating to argument structure and subjecthood, drawing out important threads and questions which they raise.

Many of the contributions in this volume deal with subjects other than canonical referential DPs, such as expletives with some referential meaning, non-DP subjects, pronouns in pro-drop languages, or impersonal subjects of one kind or another. Together they provide a snapshot of cross-linguistic variability in subjecthood. Thráinsson's contribution considers evidence from Faroese that the possibility of quirky subjects is parametrically connected to other surface properties by a deep parameter, and ultimately argues that parameters must be 'soft'. Greco, Haegeman & Phan consider the status of overt expletives in Vietnamese and what this implies for the null subject parameter. Their expletives are not like the canonical ones as they have some discourse meaning. 'Non-expletive' expletives also appear in the contribution from Alexiadou & Carvalho, who argue that locative subjects in some partial pro-drop languages are expletive-like, while in

---

[1] All of the papers in this volume were written on the occasion of Anders Holmberg's 65th birthday in recognition of the enormous contribution he has made to these issues.

Laura R. Bailey & Michelle Sheehan. 2017. Introduction: Order and structure in syntax. In Michelle Sheehan & Laura R. Bailey (eds.), *Order and structure in syntax II: Subjecthood and argument structure*, vii–ix. Berlin: Language Science Press.

others they are referential. Taraldsen's chapter also discusses locative subjects, arguing that the PP subjects found in Norwegian are genuine subjects and move to canonical subject position. Similarly, Anagnostopoulou uses her contribution to argue for a difference between Movement and Agree, arguing that some phenomena which have been argued to involve Agree actually involve movement of the subject to Spec,TP.

Both Egerland and Sigurðsson and the squibs from Engdahl and Krzek focus on the interpretation of certain kinds of subjects. Sigurðsson discusses those instances of *we* that cannot be said to include the speaker, and argues for a version of Ross's performative hypothesis, similar to that defended by Wiltschko (vol. 1). Egerland focuses on first-person impersonal pronouns such as German *man* and Italian *si* and argues that a plural interpretation is lexically specified in some languages, and must be the interpretation in certain contexts. Krzek returns to null subject languages with a squib on null impersonal subjects in Polish, while Engdahl discusses expletive passive constructions and (un)expected word orders in the Scandinavian varieties. Wurmbrand's squib focuses on the status of Icelandic in relation to the null subject parameter. Based on the behaviour of fake indexicals, she argues that Icelandic is indeed a partial null subject language, despite its exceptional behaviour in certain respects.

A number of the contributions focus on object arguments rather than subjects. Van der Wal presents data from Bantu languages and shows that they differ with respect to their symmetry and case-licensing properties in ditransitive constructions. She further proposes a novel implicational hierarchy to capture the observed patterns and provides a formalization of this in terms of sensitivity to topicality. It is the absence of ditransitives that fuels Bobaljik's squib, as he notes that Icelandic does not allow ECM distransitives despite lacking the adjacency condition supposed to ban them. This in turn means that Case Theory cannot explain this systematic gap. Lee's squib deals with object drop in Chinese, and returns to the theme of non-specific arguments with indefinite antecedents. Algryani combines the themes of ellipsis and answers to questions with a proposal for fragment answers in Arabic. Fassi Fehri focuses on the role of gender features on all arguments, arguing that a combination of properties means that gender has a range of meanings including diminutive and evaluative, among others.

Lastly, two of the squibs are about the properties of compounds: recursive ones in the case of Mukai, while Johannessen discusses the class of parasynthetic compounds in Norwegian of the type *brown-eyed*, whose heads do not surface alone as adjectives.

1 Introduction: Order and structure in syntax

This volume, like the first, provides new data and analysis based on a wide range of languages. In all these papers, the influence of the work of Anders Holmberg can be observed, from the typology of null subject languages and the status of expletive, locative and generic subjects to the syntax of ditransitives and the status of V2.

Part I

Papers

Chapter 1

On the softness of parameters: An experiment on Faroese

Höskuldur Thráinsson
University of Iceland

> This chapter evaluates the proposal, originally made by Anders Holmberg and Christer Platzack (e.g. 1995), that several syntactic differences between Insular Scandinavian (ISc) on the one hand and Mainland Scandinavian (MSc) on the other can be accounted for by postulating a single parameter that has one setting in ISc and another in MSc. While Faroese was originally supposed to belong to the ISc group, together with Icelandic, it has turned out that there is more variation in Faroese than in Icelandic with respect to the relevant syntactic phenomena. In this paper it is argued that it is exactly this variation within Faroese that makes it an interesting testing ground for hypotheses about parametric variation. It is then shown that while there is extensive intra-speaker variation in Faroese, there is some correlation between speakers' evaluation of sentences containing oblique subjects, Stylistic Fronting, null expletives and the transitive expletive construction, all supposedly typical ISc-phenomena. Although this correlation is not as strong as predicted by the standard parametric approach, it is intriguing and calls for an explanation. It is then suggested that a grammar competition account along the lines of Kroch (1989) and Yang (2002) provides a way of accounting for the observed data.

1 Introduction

Comparative Scandinavian syntax took a giant leap forwards in the late 1980s and early 1990s with the work of Christer Platzack and Anders Holmberg, joint and disjoint. The importance of their work on the nature and limits of syntactic variation in the Scandinavian languages in the late 1980s and early 1990s (see Holmberg & Platzack 1995 with references) can hardly be overestimated. The parameters they proposed guided research on Scandinavian syntax for a long time

Höskuldur Thráinsson. 2017. On the softness of parameters: An experiment on Faroese. In Michelle Sheehan & Laura R. Bailey (eds.), *Order and structure in syntax II: Subjecthood and argument structure*, 3–40. Berlin: Language Science Press.

and also had a more general effect on research into syntactic variation. Several researchers set out to test the predictions made by the proposed parameters and the general ideas behind them, or tried to refine them in different ways. As a result, various kinds of syntactic facts were discovered and syntacticians learned a lot about the nature of variation in general and in Scandinavian syntax in particular.

Gradually, however, the whole parametric approach came under criticism, leading to a lively debate (see e.g. Newmeyer 2004; 2005; 2006, Haspelmath 2008, Boeckx 2011 vs. Holmberg 2010, Holmberg & Roberts 2009, Roberts & Holmberg 2005; see also Berwick & Chomsky 2011 and H. Á. Sigurðsson 2011). This particular debate mainly centered around the place and role (if any) of parameters in linguistic theory. The arguments were partly empirical (e.g. "Is there any evidence for the clustering of properties predicted by parameter A?") and partly conceptual (e.g. "Is the concept of parameters compatible with the minimalist approach to language?"). Parallel to this debate, a different kind of discussion of the nature of parameters also emerged. In that discussion, one of the main issues is whether parameter values are acquired instantly (the TRIGGERING APPROACH, cf. e.g. Gibson & Wexler 1994, Lightfoot 1999) or gradually (the VARIATIONIST APPROACH, cf. e.g. Yang 2002; 2004; 2010). Under the variationist approach to parametric setting, the child acquiring language will try out various possible grammars that are defined by the innate Universal Grammar (UG) and these grammars will "compete" in the sense of Kroch (1989; 2001). In the ideal situation, the target grammar will eliminate other possible grammars because these will only be compatible with some of the input but not all of it. This competition may take some time, depending on the amount and uniformity of relevant input, or as described by Yang:

> [...] the rise of the target grammar is gradual, which offers a close fit with language development [...] non-target grammars stick around for a while before they are eliminated [...] the speed with which a parameter value rises to dominance is correlated with how incompatible its competitor is with the input (Yang 2004: 454)

Although most of Yang's work on parameters has revolved around the question of parameter settings by children during the acquisition period, his approach also has implications for the study of language variation, as he has pointed out:

> In addition, the variational model allows the grammar and parameter probabilities to be values other than 0 and 1 should the input evidence be inconsistent; in other words, two opposite values of a parameter must coexist in a

1 On the softness of parameters: An experiment on Faroese

mature speaker. This straightforwardly renders Chomsky's UG compatible with the Labovian studies of continuous variations at both individual and population levels [...] (Yang 2004: 455)

It is tempting to relate this idea to Chomsky's famous statement about the "ideal speaker-listener":

Linguistic theory is concerned primarily with an ideal speaker-listener, in a completely homogenous speech-community, who knows its language perfectly ... (Chomsky 1965: 3)

Under the standard assumption that linguistic parameters are binary,[1] we can then say that ideal speakers will have set all their parameter values to either + or − (1 or 0 if you will), but some speakers may not have fixed the setting for certain parameters. Instead they may be leaning towards either + or −, with different probabilities. In that sense their parameters can be said to be "soft".[2]

It seems, however, that this approach to variation has been largely absent from studies of syntactic variation in Scandinavian (but see Thráinsson 2013b, Nowenstein 2014). Yet it would seem that comparative Scandinavian syntax does in fact provide an ideal testing ground for ideas of this kind. One reason to believe so is the fact that inter- and intra-speaker variation seems much more prevalent in Scandinavian syntax than previously assumed. This may be especially true of Faroese, as will be discussed in the following sections.

The present paper reports on the results of a study of syntactic variation in Faroese, referred to below as FarDiaSyn (for Faroese Dialect Syntax). Because this study was much more extensive than any other research on Faroese, both in terms of the number of speakers consulted and the number of constructions involved, it makes it possible to experiment with certain statistical methods to test parametric predictions. The study included the following phenomena among others: oblique subjects, Stylistic Fronting (SF), null expletives and the Transitive Expletive Construction (TEC). All of these phenomena have been said to be related by Holmberg and Platzack's Agr parameter, as discussed below. As will be

---

[1] Although this is the standard (and strongest) assumption, other values have also been proposed. But as Roberts & Holmberg (2005: 541) state: "The only really substantive claim behind a binary formulation of parameters is that the values are discrete: there are no clines, squishes or continua." This issue will be discussed in §5.

[2] The formalization of this idea is a non-trivial issue. Saying that the relevant parameters are unspecified or have not yet been set is not a satisfactory description of the situation because the observed variation is not random, as we shall see. We will return to this issue in Sections 4 and 5 below.

demonstrated, the results of FarDiaSyn are typically incompatible with the standard concept of strictly binary parameters because of the extensive intra-speaker variation observed. It will be argued that the variational approach suggested by Yang offers a more adequate account, to the extent that the results can be said to support any kind of parametric approach.

The paper is organized as follows: In §2, Holmberg and Platzack's Agr-parameter is reviewed, together with a selected set of facts that it is supposed to account for. In §3 I present data from Faroese illustrating extensive inter- and intra-speaker variation with respect to evaluation of sentences involving oblique subjects, SF, null expletives and TEC. §4 then shows that despite the extensive variation, speaker judgments of these constructions correlate to some extent, although the correlations are not as general nor as strong as Holmberg & Platzack (1995) would have led us to expect. §5 is the conclusion.

2 Holmberg and Platzack's Agr-parameter revisited

As is well known, the Principles and Parameters (P&P) approach to language variation goes back to Chomsky's *Lectures on Government and Binding* (1981). The basic prediction of the P&P approach is that "[i]nsofar as linguistic variation is due to variation with regard to parameters [...] we should find clusters of surface effects of these deep-lying parameters in the languages of the world" (Holmberg 2010: 4). If such a cluster consists of, say, four properties, every language should in principle either have all four of them or none of them, "all else being equal" (Holmberg 2010: 5).

Holmberg's paper just cited was partially a reaction to the claim advanced by several researchers, including Newmeyer (2004; 2005), Haspelmath (2008) and Boeckx (2011), that proposed parametrically conditioned clusters of surface effects "invariably fail to hold up when a wider range of languages are taken into account" (Holmberg 2010: 12). In an attempt to refute this claim, Holmberg sets out to reconsider the effects of the so-called Agr-parameter proposed in various works by himself and Christer Platzack in the late 1980s and early 1990s. This parameter was supposed to account for a number of syntactic differences between Insular Scandinavian (ISc) on the one hand and (MSc) on the other. In earlier work by Holmberg and Platzack (henceforth H&P) the parameter was believed to account for up to ten differences between ISc and MSc but Holmberg (2010: 13–14) reduces it to the following seven:

(1) Holmberg's reduced list of Agr-related differences: ISc MSc
    1. Rich subject-verb agreement   +   –
    2. Oblique subjects   +   –
    3. Stylistic Fronting   +   –
    4. Null expletives   +   –
    5. Null generic subject pronoun   +   –
    6. Transitive expletives   +   –
    7. Heavy subject postposing   +   –

Although H&P included Old Norse and Faroese in the ISc group together with Icelandic, Holmberg only contrasts Icelandic with MSc in this later paper (2010) "to simplify the presentation". It would obviously complicate the comparison to include a dead language like Old Norse, although we now have more sophisticated tools to study that language than before (see e.g. Rögnvaldsson & Helgadóttir 2011; Rögnvaldsson et al. 2011; Thráinsson 2013a). About the exclusion of Faroese from the ISc vs. MSc comparison in the paper, Holmberg makes the following remark:

> Faroese is an interesting case in this connection, since it is undergoing changes that seem to crucially involve the parameter discussed in the text below. (Holmberg 2010:13n)

If true, this indeed makes Faroese especially interesting for the following reasons among others:

(2) 1. If Faroese is "undergoing changes that seem to crucially involve the parameter" in question, this means that speakers acquiring Faroese, growing up and living in the modern Faroese society will be exposed to variable linguistic input.

2. Under Yang's variationist approach to parametric setting (2004), this predicts that we should not only find extensive inter-speaker variation in Faroese with respect to the relevant syntactic constructions but also considerable intra-speaker variation since the variationist model "allows the grammar and parameter probabilities to be values other than 0 and 1 should the input evidence be inconsistent" (cf. Yang 2004: 455).

3. Under the triggering approach to parametric setting described above (see e.g. Gibson & Wexler 1994, Lightfoot 1999 and later work), the observed variation in the Faroese linguistic community should be the

result of different parametric settings by speakers acquiring the language. Because the input is inconsistent, it will trigger the parametric value 1 for some speakers but 0 for others. Extensive intra-speaker variation in the relevant constructions is not predicted by the triggering approach.

4. If the constructions under discussion are related by a single parameter, there should be a very strong correlation between judgments of all the relevant constructions under the triggering approach to parametric setting. Under the variationist approach we would also expect some correlation between the judgments, although not necessarily particularly strong because various grammar-external factors may influence the judgments when there is optionality.[3] If the constructions under discussion are unrelated and governed by language-particular rules (e.g. in the sense of Newmeyer 2004; 2005), it is less clear what kind of correlations to expect, if any (more on this in Sections 4 and 5 below).

In the next section I will present some results from FarDiaSyn that can be used to test these predictions. This particular part of FarDiaSyn only included a subset of the constructions on Holmberg's reduced list of Agr-related differences in (1) above, namely the following:

(3) Agr-related differences tested in FarDiaSyn: ISc   MSc
    1. Oblique subjects   +   –
    2. Stylistic Fronting   +   –
    3. Null expletives   +   –
    4. Transitive expletives   +   –

H&P have illustrated the Icelandic vs. MSc differences as follows (these examples are mainly taken from Holmberg 2010 but (4a,b) and (6c,d) are taken from H&P's book 1995: 11):

(4) Oblique subjects

    a. ***Hana*** *vantar peninga.*   (Ice)
        her.ACC lacks money.
        'She needs money.'

---

[3] Such "grammar-external factors" would include stylistic differences and issues having to do with pragmatics and discourse phenomena, which some speakers may be more sensitive to than others.

b. * ***Henne*** *saknar pengar.* (Sw)
   her lacks money

c. ***Mér*** *voru gefnir peningar.* (Ice)
   me.DAT were given money
   'I was given money.'

d. * ***Mej*** *blev givet/givna pengar.* (Sw)
   me was given.SG/PL money.PL

(5) Stylistic Fronting (SF)

   a. *[Þeir sem **í Osló** hafa búið] segja að það sé finn bær.* (Ice)
      those that in Oslo have lived say that it is nice town
      'Those that have lived in Oslo say that it's a nice town.'

   b. * *[De som **i Oslo** har bott] säger att det är en fin stad.* (Sw)
      those that in Oslo have lived say that it is a nice town

(6) Null expletives

   a. *Nú rignir (***það**).* (Ice)
      now rains it
      'Now it's raining.'

   b. *Nu regnar *(**det**).* (Sw)
      now rains it

   c. *Í gær var (***það**) dansað á skipinu* (Ice)
      yesterday was there danced on the-ship

   d. *Igår dansades *(**det**) på skeppet.* (Sw)
      yesterday was-danced there on the-ship

(7) Transitive Expletive Construction (TEC)

   a. *Það hefur einhver köttur étið mýsnar.* (Ice)
      there has some cat eaten the-mice

   b. * *Det har ein katt eti mysene.* (No)
      there has a cat eaten the-mice

As can be seen, the MSc data come from Swedish and Norwegian, but Danish data could just as well have been used.

3 The Faroese experiment

3.1 The elicitation methods of FarDiaSyn

As mentioned above, recent studies of Faroese indicate that there is considerable variation in Faroese syntax. This means that in order to get reliable and statistically significant results about possible covariation of particular constructions, the study has to be quite extensive (see also the discussion in Thráinsson 2017). Under Yang's variationist approach, one would assume that probability of a given parameter setting for the relevant parameter for each speaker should predict how the speaker would judge sentences that are related by that particular parameter, "all else being equal". But because other things are not always equal (e.g. because of lexical differences, different sensitivity to stylistic or pragmatic phenomena, etc.), these predictions are most reliably tested in studies that involve a reasonably large sample of the relevant sentences and a large number of speakers from different age groups and with a varying background.

In the study reported on here, 334 speakers of Faroese were asked to evaluate selected sentences. The speakers came from different parts of the Faroes, they ranged in age from approximately 15–70 and there was an even split between male and female speakers (for a more detailed description of the population see Thráinsson 2017). The evaluation method was typically one where the speakers were asked to check one of three possibilities on a written questionnaire as illustrated in Figure 1 (the instructions were given in Faroese, of course, but here they have been translated into English).

Put an X in the appropriate column:
yes = A natural sentence. I could very well have said this.
? = A doubtful sentence. I could hardly say this.
no = An unnatural or impossible sentence. I could not say this.

	yes	?	no	Comments
Teir sjey dvørgarnir vóru í øðini. The seven dwarfs were upset.				
Tað hevði onkur etið súreplið. there had somebody eaten the-apple				

Figure 1: Questionnaire

In addition, the subjects were also asked to choose between two (or sometimes three) alternatives in a setup like in Figure 2 (again, the instructions have been translated from Faroese).

> In the following examples you are asked to compare two possible alternatives in each sentence. Check the most natural one. Check both if you find them equally natural.
>
> *Tað regnar ongantíð í Sahara.*
> it rains never in Sahara
>
> *Í Havn* ☐ *regnar* *ofta.*
> in Tórshavn rains often
> ☐ *regnar tað*
> rains it

Figure 2: Multiple choice test

Although the speakers were given the possibility to select both alternatives in this kind of task, they very rarely did so.

We now present the results for each of the constructions under consideration.

3.2 Oblique subjects

Modern Icelandic is famous for its oblique subjects, which can occur in the Accusative, Dative and Genitive. Nominative is obviously the default or structural subject case in Icelandic, Genitive subjects are very rare, Acc subjects arguably irregular (quirky) in many instances but Dat subjects sometimes thematically related: Experiencer subjects often show up in the Dat in Icelandic and some verbs previously taking Acc subjects now take Dat subjects in the language of many speakers (the (in)famous Dative Substitution or Dative Sickness, see e.g. Zaenen et al. 1985, Thráinsson 2007: 224). Gen subjects have completely disappeared in Faroese and Acc subjects have also virtually died out (see e.g. Thráinsson et al. 2012: 252–251, Jónsson & Eythórsson 2005, Eythórsson 2015). A few verbs still take Dat subjects but in many instances there is variation between Dat and Nom.[4]

---

[4]Barnes claims (1992: 28) that Nom is replacing Dat as a subject case in spoken Faroese, especially among younger people. In our study younger speakers were somewhat less likely to accept Dat subjects in the examples we tested. Although the correlation between judgments and age was rather weak, it was statistically significant for three of the four verbs listed in (8) (it was not significant in the case of the loan verb *mangla* 'need, lack').

Hence both variants were tested in FarDiaSyn as shown in the following examples:

(8)   a1. *Bilurin hjá Óla hevur verið til sýn.*
'Óli's car has been inspected.'
Honum tørvar *ikki at hugsa meira um   tað.*
him.DAT needs   not to think   more about that
'He doesn't have to think more about that.'

   a2. *Hans veit ikki nógv um fiskiskap.*
'Hans doesn't know much about fishing.'
Hann tørvar *ikki at hava svar   til alt.*
he.NOM needs   not to have answer to everything
'He doesn't have to have answers to everything.'

   b1. *Turið hevur sæð nógvar filmar.*
'Turið has seen many films.'
Henni dámar *at hyggja í   sjónvarp.*
her.DAT likes   to look   at TV
'She likes to watch TV.'

   b2. *Sára fer á konsertina í kvøld.*
'Sára going to the concert tonight.'
Hon   dámar *at lurta   eftir tónleiki.*
she.NOM likes   to listen after music
'She likes to listen to music.'

   c1. *Kári hevur nógv at gera.*
'Kári has a lot to do.'
Honum manglar *at gera   húsini   liðug.*
him.DAT needs   to make the-houses ready
'He needs to finish the house.'

   c2. *Anton reypar av at vera góður kokkur.*
'Anton brags about beeing a good cook.'
Hann   manglar *at prógva tað í   verki.*
he.NOM needs   to prove   it   in work
'He needs to prove it in action.'

1 On the softness of parameters: An experiment on Faroese

d1. *Stjórin hjá Súsannu ar altíð ov seinur til arbeiðis.*
'Súsanna's boss always comes too late to work.'
Henni nýtist ikki at hugsa um klokkuna.
her.DAT needs not to think about the-clock
'She doesn't have to think about the clock.'

d2. *Elin kennir øll tey ríku og kendu.*
'Elin knows all the rich and famous.'
Hon nýtist ikki at standa í bíðirøð.
she.NOM need not to stand in line
'She doesn't have to stand in line.'

The evaluation of these examples is shown in Table 1 (percentages for the more positively evaluated variant highlighted by boldface):

Table 1: Evaluation of Dat and Nom subjects with selected verbs in FarDiaSyn.

#	Example	Yes		?		No	
		N	%	N	%	N	%
(8a1)	**Honum tørvar** ikki at hugsa meira um tað.	238	**73.0**	36	11.0	52	16.0
(8a2)	**Hann tørvar** ikki at hava svar til alt.	89	27.6	89	27.6	145	**44.9**
(8b1)	**Henni dámar** at hyggja í sjónvarp.	287	**86.7**	24	7.3	20	6.0
(8b2)	**Hon dámar** at lurta eftir tónleiki.	208	**62.8**	55	16.6	68	20.5
(8c1)	**Honum manglar** at gera húsini liðug.	196	**60.1**	62	19.0	68	20.9
(8c2)	**Hann manglar** at prógva tað í verki.	241	**73.7**	31	9.5	55	16.8
(8d1)	**Henni nýtist** ikki at hugsa um klokkuna.	246	**75.0**	36	11.0	46	14.0
(8d2)	**Hon nýtist** ikki at standa í bíðirøð.	210	**64.4**	49	15.0	67	20.6

Interesting descriptive facts revealed by this table include the following:

1. For three out of the four verbs, Dat is more generally accepted than Nom.

2. There is clearly some intra-speaker variation in subject case assignment for at least three of these verbs (*dáma*, *mangla* and *nýtast*) since the proportion of speakers accepting a Dat subject plus the proportion of speakers accepting a Nom subject is way over 100% for these verbs. In other words, some speakers, but not all, accept both a Dat and a Nom subject for these verbs.

3. The only verb where Nom is more generally accepted than Dat is the Danish loanword *mangla* 'need, lack' in (8c). Since this verb is a (possibly rather recent) loan from Danish,[5] this is perhaps not so surprising. It is in fact more interesting that 60% of the speakers accept it with a Dat subject since this shows that assignment of Dat to subjects is still alive in Faroese (or was at the time when this verb was adopted into the language) and not just an old relic.

This last point is consistent with the general belief that assignment of Dat case to subjects in Faroese is not (or has not been) irregular or quirky.

While the facts summarized in Table 1 indicate considerable variation in the evaluation of Dat and Nom subjects, this method of presenting the data does not really show very clearly to what extent this is inter-speaker variation and to what extent the judgments of the same speaker may vary (intra-speaker variation). But Figure 3 shows that considerable intra-speaker variation is involved in the evaluation of Dat subjects. Here the answers to the questionnaire have been coded as follows (cf. the illustration in Figure 1 above): *yes* = 3, ? = 2 and *no* = 1. This means that if a speaker accepted all four Dat subject examples, (s)he would get the average score (or "grade") of 3, if (s)he rejected all of them the score would be 1, etc.

As shown here, 145 out of 334 speakers accepted all the Dat subject sentences and only four rejected all of them. But more than half accepted some and rejected others, or found the examples doubtful. If acceptance of Dat subjects were governed by a strictly binary setting of a parameter, we would expect a more clear cut result than this.

---

[5] The Faroese-Faroese dictionary Føroysk orðabók (Poulsen et al. 1998) states that it is "colloquial" or belongs to the spoken language (Fa. *talað mál*).

1 On the softness of parameters: An experiment on Faroese

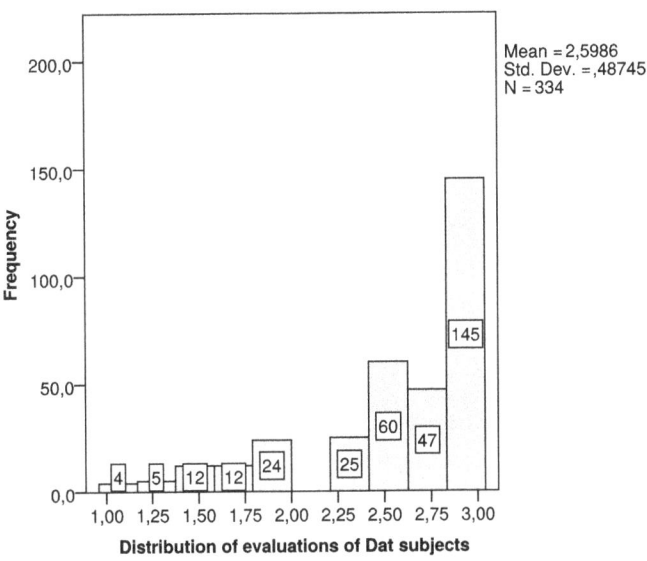

Figure 3: Judgments of Dat subject sentences.

3.3 Stylistic Fronting

As originally described by Maling (1980), Stylistic Fronting (henceforth SF) fronts a constituent in a clause with a "subject gap". There has been some controversy as to whether all fronting of constituents in such clauses should be considered SF or whether SF only fronts heads and fronting of a maximal projection (e.g. a PP) is a case of Topicalization, also when a subject gap is involved (for a review of the issues see Thráinsson 2007: 368–374). As pointed out by H&P and discussed by several linguists (e.g. Barnes 1992, Vikner 1995, Thráinsson et al. 2012, Angantýsson 2011), SF also occurs in Faroese, as it should if it is related to a positive setting of H&P's Agr-parameter and Faroese is a true ISc language. In FarDiaSyn the following examples were used to test the speakers' acceptance of SF (fronted elements in boldface):

(9) a. *Studentarnir fingu summarfrí í gjár.*
  'The students got summer vacation yesterday.'
  Skúlastjórin helt talu fyri teimum, sum **liðug** vóru við skúlan.
  the-principal held speech for those that done were with the-school
  'The principal gave a speech for those who were graduating.'

15

b. *Olga hevur ikki vaskað sær í fleiri dagar.*
'Olga hasn't washed for several days.'
Hon fer ikki í baðikarið, um **har** hava verið mýs.
she goes not in the-bathtub if in-that-place have been mice
'She doesn't go into the bathtub if there have been mice there.'

c. *Fjórða barnið er á veg hjá Róa og Poulu.*
'Rói and Paula are expecting their fourth child.'
Tey vilja keypa ein bil, sum **vælegnaður** er til eina barnafamilju.
they want buy a car that well-suited is for a family-with-children
'They want to buy a car that is suitable for a family with children.'

d. *Kokkurin hevði ikki gjørt nóg mikið av mati.*
'The cook hadn't prepared enough food.'
Øll, sum **einki** høvdu etið, vóru svong.
all that nothing had eaten were hungry
'Everybody who hadn't eaten anything was hungry.'

e. *Kommunuval var í Føroyum í gjár.*
'Municipal elections were held in the Faroes yesterday.'
Tillukku til øll, sum **vald** vórðu.
congratulations to all that elected were
'Congratulations to all who were elected.'

f. *Samráðingar verða í annaðkvøld.*
'There will be negotiations tomorrow night.'
Lønarhækking er tað, sum **ovast** er á breddanum.
salary-raise is that which topmost is on the-page
'Salary raise is at the top of the agenda.'

g. *Eg fari til Prag í Kekkia í næstu viku.*
'I'm going to Prague in the Czech Republic next week.'
Kennir tú onkran, sum **verið** hevur í Kekkia?
know you anybody that been has in Czech-Republic
'Do you know anybody that has been to the Czech Republic?'

As can be seen from this list, the sentences contain fronted elements of different kinds, mostly in relative clauses, but for the reasons described above we avoided examples with fronted constituents that would unambiguously be analyzed as maximal projections (these could arguably involve Topicalization rather

Table 2: Evaluation of Stylistic Fronting in FarDiaSyn.

		Yes		?		No	
#	Example	N	%	N	%	N	%
(9a)	Skúlastjórin helt talu fyri teimum, sum **liðug** vóru við skúlan.	182	**55.3**	73	22.2	74	22.5
(9b)	Hon fer ikki í baðikarið, um **har** hava verið mýs.	155	**47.3**	65	19.8	108	32.9
(9c)	Tey vilja keypa ein bil, sum **vælegnaður** er til eina barnafamilju.	102	31.1	77	23.5	149	**45.4**
(9d)	Øll, sum **einki** høvdu etið, vóru svong	231	**70.4**	48	14.6	49	14.9
(9e)	Tillukku til øll, sum **vald** vórðu.	170	**52.1**	72	22.1	84	25.8
(9f)	Lønarhækking er tað, sum **ovast** er á breddanum.	170	**52.5**	67	20.7	87	26.9
(9g)	Kennir tú onkran, sum **verið** hevur í Kekkia?	128	39.0	52	15.9	148	**45.1**

than SF). The evaluation of these examples is illustrated in Table 2 (the highest percentages for each sentence in boldface):

Again, we find considerable variation, but more speakers accept than reject most of the examples (examples 9c and 9g are an exception). The reason for this extensive variation could be that SF is probably stylistically marked, i.e. it may not belong to the colloquial style that the subjects were asked to have in mind when evaluating the examples.

As before, we can check how the judgments spread, e.g. whether any of the speakers accept all of the SF-examples or reject all of them. This is shown on Figure 4.

As shown here, very few subjects accept all of the SF-examples (only 15) and very few reject all of them (only 8). Most speakers accept some — typically more than half of them. This is somewhat unexpected if the acceptance of SF is governed by a binary parameter. But note that SF is an optional operation: In relative clauses the subject gap can be left "empty" as it were and subject gaps can also

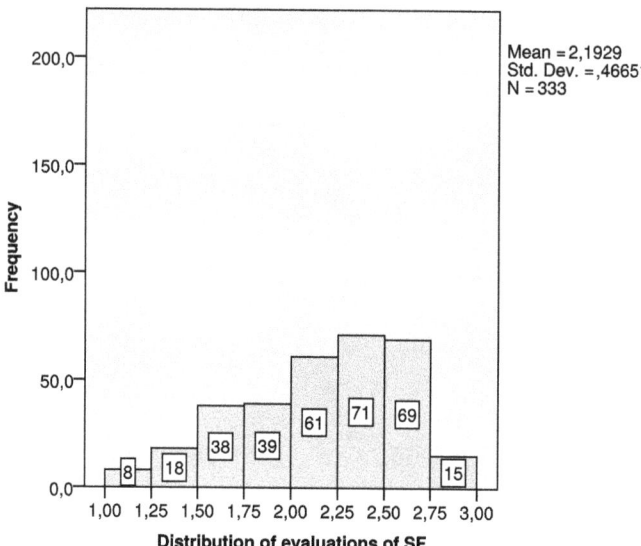

Figure 4: Judgments of Stylistic Fronting.

be "filled" with an expletive, e.g. in examples like (9b).[6] The choice between the alternatives is probably "stylistic" in nature to some extent (hence the name

---

[6]Holmberg has in fact argued (2000) that the element fronted in SF serves the same function as an expletive. One problem with his analysis is the fact that SF-elements and the expletive *það* 'there' do not have the same distribution in Icelandic: SF-elements can fill certain "subject gaps" that the expletive *það* cannot (see e.g. Thráinsson 2007: 351):

(i) a. Þetta er mál   sem __ hefur verið rætt.
        this is matter that   has been discussed

   b. Þetta er mál sem **rætt** hefur verið __

   c. * Þetta er mál   sem **það** hefur verið rætt.
        this is matter that there has been discussed

Similar subject gaps can either be filled with an SF-element or an expletive in Faroese so in that sense Holmberg's suggestion arguably works better for Faroese than Icelandic (see e.g. Angantýsson 2011: 170):

(ii) a. Hetta eru mál   sum __ hevur verið tosað um.
         these are matters that   has been talked about

   b. Hetta eru mál sum **tosað** hevur verið __ um.

   c. Hetta eru mál sum **tað** hevur verið tosað um.

1 On the softness of parameters: An experiment on Faroese

Stylistic Fronting). Thus it is not given a priori that somebody will find a particular example of SF appropriate even if SF is in principle possible in his or her grammar.

3.4 Null expletives

As discussed by many researchers, Icelandic is famous for its null expletives (see e.g. Thráinsson 1979: 477–484, Thráinsson 2007: 309–313, H. Á. Sigurðsson 1989: Chapter 6.3) and H&P originally assumed that Faroese works essentially the same way, as an ISc language should. Since linguists do not always mean the same thing when they talk about null expletives, the discussion here is limited to null expletives of the kind illustrated by H&P with examples like those in (6), namely ones where some non-subject (or the finite verb) is fronted in a main clause and an overt expletive would be obligatory in MSc but impossible in Icelandic. Because it had been pointed out previously that there is some optionality in constructions of this sort in Faroese (i.e. that the expletive can either be overt or non-overt, cf. e.g. Vikner 1995:227, Thráinsson et al. 2012: 285–288), we tested both options, sometimes in pairs of sentences that differed only minimally. The relevant examples are shown in (10–12). The first set contains impersonal passives with and without an overt expletive:

(10) a. *Fyrr í tíðini vóru ongar teldur og einki sjónvarp.*
  'In the old days there were no computers and no TV.'
  Tá varð nógv dansað heima við hús.
  then was much danced home with house
  'Then there was a lot of dancing at home.'
 b. *Fyrr sótu fólk í roykstovuni og arbeiddu.*
  'Previously people would sit in the living room and work.'
  *Tá varð **tað** tosað saman um kvøldarnar.*
  then was there talked together during the-evenings
  'Then people would talk during the evening.'
 c. *Stórt brúdleyp var í Nólsoy.*
  'There was a big wedding in Nólsoy.'
  *Í fleiri dagar varð **tað** etið og drukkið.*
  in many days was there eaten and drunk
  'People were eating and drinking for several days.'

The second type is a weather expression which is a direct yes/no-question with a fronted verb and without an overt weather expletive:

(11) *Abbin var blivin eitt sindur dølskur og spurdi:*
 'Grandpa had become a bit slow and asked:'
 Regnaði í gjár?
 rained yesterday
 'Did it rain yesterday?'

Then there were two examples where the subjects were asked to choose between a variant without the overt expletive and one with it. One of them was a weather expression and the other an Expletive Passive:

(12) a. *Tað regnar ongantíð í Sahara.*
 'It never rains in Sahara.'
 *Í Havn   regnar / regnar **tað** ofta.*
 in Tórshavn rains rains   it   often
 'In Tórshavn it often rains.'
 b. *Tað hendir nógv í Íslandi.*
 'Many things happen in Iceland.'
 *Fríggjadagin bleiv / bleiv **tað** skotin ein hvítabjørn har.*
 the-Friday was   was there shot a polar bear there
 'Last Friday a polar bear was shot there.'

The results of the evaluation of the variants in (10–11) are shown in Table 3 (highest percentages for each example in boldface).

In the first set of examples (the impersonal passives in 10) the variant without the overt expletive (the *a*-example) gets a more positive evaluation than the ones with the overt expletive (examples *b* and *c*). The weather expression in (11) does not have an overt expletive and it does not get as positive evaluation as (10a), which also has a null expletive, albeit of a different kind. This suggests that there might be a difference between "true" expletives (*there*-expletives) and weather expletives (*it*-expletives) in this respect. This would not be surprising since it has been argued that the weather expletive is more argument-like than the true expletive (Vikner even claims (1995: 228–229) that weather expletives are true arguments). But the test sentences where the subjects were asked to choose between overt and non-overt expletives in a weather expression on the one hand and in an Expletive Passive on the other did not show a clear diffence

1 On the softness of parameters: An experiment on Faroese

Table 3: Evaluation of examples with and without an overt expletive.

#	Example	Yes N	Yes %	? N	? %	No N	No %
(10a)	Tá varð nógv dansað heima við hús.	293	89.3	21	6.4	14	4.6
(10b)	Tá varð **tað** tosað saman um kvøldarnar.	229	69.4	47	14.2	54	16.4
(10c)	Í fleiri dagar varð **tað** etið og drukkið.	220	67.7	58	17.8	47	14.5
(11)	Regnaði í gjár?	188	56.8	61	18.4	82	24.8

between the two types, although a third of the speakers found that both variants are possible in the case of the weather expression but very few in the case of the Expletive Passive. This is shown in Table 4 (the most popular choice in boldface).

Here we can also investigate how the the judgments spread, e.g. whether any of the speakers accept both instances of empty expletives or reject both of them (i.e. 10a and 11 — we leave out the examples in 12 because here the elicitation method was different). This is shown in Figure 5, where the value 3 on the X-axis indicates that the relevant speakers found both of the examples with null expletives natural and the value 1 means that they rejected both of them.

Here almost half of the speakers found both examples natural, very few (only 8) rejected both of them but a considerable number found them doubtful or liked one and not the other.

Table 4: Selection between alternatives in expletive constructions.

#	Example	without *tað* N	without *tað* %	both variants N	both variants %	with *tað* N	with *tað* %
(12a)	Í Havn regnar / regnar **tað** ofta.	83	25.4	108	33.0	136	**41.6**
(12b)	Fríggjadagin bleiv / bleiv **tað** skotin ...	111	34.9	28	8.8	179	**56.3**

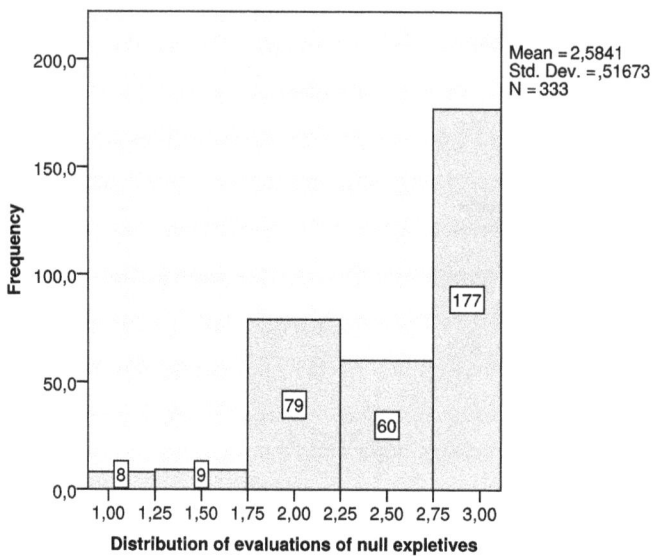

Figure 5: Judgments of empty expletives.

3.5 Transitive expletives

Let us finally look at the so-called Transitive Expletive Construction (TEC). Here the Icelandic and MSc facts seem relatively clear cut: Speakers of Icelandic find TECs fine whereas speakers of MSc typically reject them. But whereas Vikner (1995: 189) maintained that TECs are not accepted in Faroese, Thráinsson et al. (2012: 282) argued that they are accepted "by some speakers" and Angantýsson (2011: 173) found that the majority of his subjects found TEC-examples to be natural. In several discussions of comparative Scandinavian, TECs have played a major role (see e.g. Bobaljik & Thráinsson 1998, Thráinsson 2007: 333–340, Thráinsson 2017). The TEC-examples evaluated by participants in FarDiaSyn are shown in (13):

(13)   a. *Teir sjey dvørgarnir vóru í øðini.*
         'The seven dwarfs were upset.'
         Tað hevði onkur   etið súreplið.
         there had somebody eaten the-apple
         'Somebody had eaten the apple.'

b. *Fleiri hús á Signabø vóru til sølu.*
  'Several houses in Signabo were for sale.'
  Tað keypti onkur húsini hjá Róa.
  there bought somebody the-houses of Rói
  'Somebody bought Rói's house.'

c. *Eg mátti ganga til hús.*
  'I had to walk home.'
  Tað hevði onkur tikið súkkluna hjá mær.
  there had somebody taken the-cycle of me
  'Somebody had taken my bike.'

d. *Hendan bókin er ógvuliga drúgv.*
  'This book is extremely long.'
  Tað hevur helst eingin lisið hana til enda.
  there has probably nobody read her to end
  'Probably no-one has read it to the end.'

An overview of the evaluations can be seen in Table 5 (highest percentages for each example in boldface as before).

Table 5: Evaluation of transitive expletives in FarDiaSyn.

#	Example	Yes N	Yes %	? N	? %	No N	No %
(13a)	Tað hevði onkur etið súreplið.	80	24.4	58	17.7	190	**57.9**
(13b)	Tað keypti onkur húsini hjá Róa.	51	15.5	71	21.6	207	**62.9**
(13c)	Tað hevði onkur tikið súkkluna hjá mær.	82	25.2	65	19.9	179	**54.9**
(13d)	Tað hevur helst eingin lisið hana til enda.	148	**45.4**	62	19.0	116	35.6

More speakers reject than accept the first three examples but more speakers accept than reject the last one. Three of the examples contain an auxiliary verb and the one where the finite verb is a main verb (the *b*-example) was less positively evaluated.[7]

Given what we have already seen, we would expect that the picture showing the spread of the judgments to look rather different from the pictures previously presented. This prediction is borne out, as shown on Figure 6.

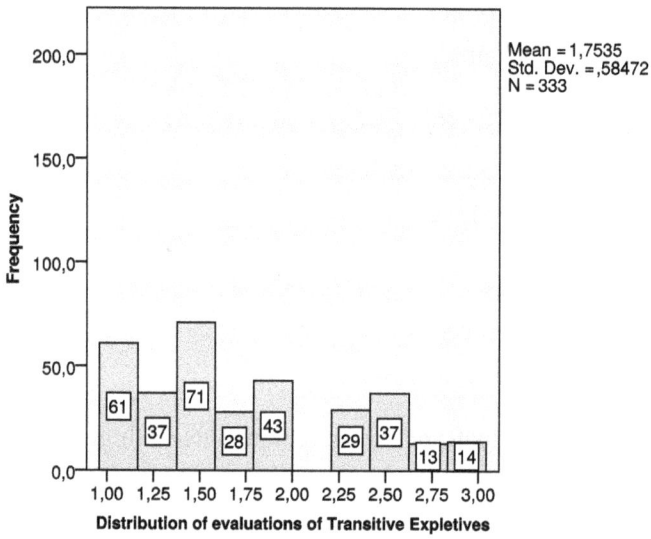

Figure 6: Judgments of Transitive Expletives.

As Figure 6 shows, very few speakers accept all the TEC-examples (only 14) and a considerable number of subjects reject all of them. As explained in the preceding footnote, the relatively low acceptance of TECs in this study compared to that of Angantýsson (2011), for instance, is probably due to an unfortunate choice of logical subject. But in any case, the judgments here indicate considerable intra-speaker variation similar to what we have seen before: Speakers typically accept some of the examples and not all of them.

---

[7] Angantýsson (2011: 173) presents the evaluation results for two TEC-examples in Faroese, one with an auxiliary and one without. His subjects also found the one with the auxiliary more acceptable. — It is also interesting to note that the acceptance rate of the TECs is considerably lower in the FarDiaSyn study reported on here than in Angantýsson's study. A likely reason for this difference is the fact that the logical subject in examples (13a–c) is the simple indefinite pronoun *onkur* 'somebody' whereas corresponding examples in Angantýsson's study contained the more complex subject *onkur útlendingur* 'some foreigner', which might sound more natural in an expletive construction.

4 Comparison of the constructions

4.1 Some correlations

Having gone through the data concerning the individual constructions under discussion, we can now investigate whether there is any correlation between the judgments of the four different constructions. In the ideal world (or for ideal speakers) there should be a very strong correlation between these if the constructions are all related by a single parameter, such as H&P's Agr-parameter, "all else being equal". But because of the extensive intra-speaker variation in the judgments observed in the preceding sections, it is not entirely clear a priori what to expect here. So let us look at Table 6 (the two strongest correlations highlighted by boldface).

Table 6: Correlation between the evaluations of the four constructions under investigation.

	Stylistic Fronting	Null expletives	Transitive Expletives
Oblique subjects	$r = 0.470$ **$p < 0.001$** $N = 333$	$r = 0.330$ $p < 0.001$ $N = 333$	$r = 0.297$ $p < 0.001$ $N = 333$
Stylistic Fronting	xxxx	$r = 0.354$ $p < 0.001$ $N = 333$	$r = 0.371$ **$p < 0.001$** $N = 333$
Null expletives	xxxx	xxxx	$r = 0.168$ $p = 0.002$ $N = 333$

As shown here, the correlations are typically only of medium strength.[8] The only one that could possibly be called strong is the correlation between judgments of examples involving oblique subjects and Stylistic Fronting ($r = 0.470$). Yet the correlations are all highly significant so it might seem tempting to say something like the following: "Look, there is a highly significant correlation between the evaluations of all the constructions – p is nowhere higher than 0.002,

---

[8] The correlation coefficient r can range from −1.0 to +1.0, where −1.0 is a perfect negative correlation, +1.0 a perfect positive correlation and 0.0 indicates no correlation at all. It is often said that if the correlation coefficient r is around ±0.10, the correlation is weak, if it is around ±0.30 the correlation is of medium strength and it is strong if it reaches ±0.50 in studies of this kind.

which in statistical terms should mean that there should be at most 2‰ chance that these correlations are an accident. So H&P were right – these constructions are all related by a single parameter."

Unfortunately, things are not as simple as this for several reasons, including the following:

1. First of all, correlations can never be interpreted as a proof of a causal relationship.

2. Second, if all the constructions considered here were accepted by the majority of the speakers consulted, there should be some correlation between the speakers' evaluation of them: If a speaker is likely to accept construction A (s)he will also be likely to accept construction B because most speakers do, "all else being equal". This need not mean that they are parametrically related.

3. Since all the constructions investigated here were supposedly also found in Old Norse, and thus in older stages of Faroese, it is possible that the correlations observed are basically a reflection of some sort of conservatism in the language: If you are a conservative speaker of Faroese you are likely to accept all these constructions even if they are not related by a single parameter.

So let us look more closely at the data with these possibilities in mind.

As shown in Tables 1, 2, 3 and 4, the acceptance of the example sentences varied considerably but we could "rank" their acceptability as shown in Table 7.

Table 7: Acceptability ranking of the constructions under investigation.

Construction	Speakers finding the examples "natural" (%)	Mean "grade"
Oblique subjects	73.7	2.60
Null expletives	73.1	2.20
Stylistic Fronting (SF)	49.7	2.19
Transitive Expletives (TEC)	27.6	1.75

As shown in the middle column, an average of over 73% of the speakers found the examples involving oblique subjects and null expletives natural whereas about half of the speakers found the SF examples natural and only a little more than 27% found the TEC examples natural. But since the speakers were using a three point scale (natural, doubtful, unnatural/ungrammatical) we can also assign a "mean grade" to each class of examples, where 3 would mean "all subjects found all the examples natural" and 1 would mean "all subjects found all the examples unacceptable". These grades are shown in the rightmost column. Here we see that the "acceptability ranking" of the constructions remains the same regardless of the ranking method (although there is virtually no difference between null expletives and Stylistic Fronting).

Keeping this ranking (or popularity) of the constructions in mind, we might have expected the strongest correlations to hold between oblique subjects and null expletives since these were the two most "popular" constructions. But this is not what we find. Instead the strongest correlation ($r = 0.470$) is between the evaluations of examples containing an oblique subject and examples containing SF. The next-highest correlation is between the judgments of the TEC and SF.

In order to determine whether the observed correlations are simply a reflection of some general conservatism, we can look for a clear innovation and see if or how it relates to the other constructions. FarDiaSyn included a study of the so-called New (Impersonal) Passive (or New Impersonal Construction), first made famous by Joan Maling and Sigríður Sigurjónsdóttir (cf. Sigurjónsdóttir & Maling 2001, Maling & Sigurjónsdóttir 2002 and much later work). The New Impersonal Passive (henceforth NIP) arguably comes in a couple of different guises as partly illustrated by the Icelandic examples in (14c) and (15c):

(14) a. *Einhver lamdi mig.*
somebody hit me.ACC

b. *Ég var laminn.* (Canonical Passive)
I.NOM was hit.M.SG

c. *Það var **lamið mig**.* (NIP)
there was hit.N.SG me

(15) a. *Einhver lofaði henni tölvu.*
somebody promised her.DAT computer.ACC

b. *Henni var lofað tölvu.* (Canonical Passive)
her.DAT was promised.N.SG computer.ACC

c. *Það var lofað **henni** tölvu.* (NIP)
there was promised.N.SG her.DAT computer.ACC

The NIP in (14c) differs from the canonical passive in (14b) in that the argument (the patient) shows up in the Acc instead of Nom and hence there is no agreement with the participle. Besides, the argument can occur in an expletive construction of sorts although it is definite (an apparent violation of the Definiteness Constraint).⁹ The NIP in (15c) only differs from the canonical passive in (15b) in that the definite Dat argument *henni* occurs postverbally (i.e. in an object position). Definite subjects in the canonical passive cannot occur in that position.

It is generally assumed that this NIP is a recent innovation in Icelandic since it was first noticed by linguists towards the end of the last century (for a detailed discussion of the NIP, possible origin and review of the arguments see E. F. Sigurðsson 2012). It does not seem to occur in MSc. But while the subjects in FarDiaSyn rejected the variant corresponding to (14c), a number of them accepted examples corresponding to (15c). These are listed in (16):

(16) a. *Gentan hevði hjálpt beiggjanum alla vikuna.*
 'The girl had helped her brother the whole week.'
 *Tað **bleiv lovað** henni eina teldu.*
 there was promised her.DAT a computer.ACC

 b. *Hanus fekk onga læknaváttan.*
 'Hanus didn't get any doctor's certificate.'
 *Tað varð **rátt** honum frá at fara við skipinum.*
 there was advised him.DAT against to go with the-ship

 c. *Tvíburarnir fyltu 7 ár.*
 'The twins turned 7 years old.'
 *Tað bleiv **givið** gentuni eina dukku.*
 there was given the-girl.DAT a doll.ACC

 d. *Drotningin kom at vitja tey eldru fólkini á ellisheiminum.*
 'The queen came to visit the people in the old people's home.'
 *Tað bleiv **vaskað** teimum væl um hárið.*
 there was washed them.DAT well about the-hair

 e. *Rógvarin Katrin Olsen stóð seg væl í Olympisku Leikunum.*
 'The rower KO did well at the Olympics.'
 *Tað bleiv **róst** henni í bløðunum.*
 there was praised her.DAT in the-newspapers

---

⁹It is generally assumed that this argument is not a subject in the NIP. If so, then it is not to be expected that the Definiteness Effect plays any role.

f. *Bókasavnið hevði framsýning.*
   'The library had an exhibition.'
   *Tað bleiv **víst gestunum** nógv tilfar um Heinesen.*
   there was shown the-guests.DAT much material on Heinesen

The subjects' evaluation of these examples are shown in Table 8 (highest percentages for each example highlighted).

Table 8: Evaluation of New Impersonal Passive examples (w. Datives) in FarDiaSyn.

#	Example	Yes N	Yes %	? N	? %	No N	No %
(16a)	Tað bleiv lovað henni eina teldu.	167	**50.6**	70	21.2	93	28.2
(16b)	Tað varð rátt honum frá at fara við skipinum.	263	**79.7**	32	9.7	35	10.6
(16c)	Tað bleiv givið gentuni eina dukku.	65	19.9	65	19.9	197	**60.2**
(16d)	Tað bleiv vaskað teimum væl um hárið.	87	26.4	65	19.8	177	**53.8**
(16e)	Tað bleiv róst henni í bløðunum.	66	20.2	62	19.0	199	**60.9**
(16f)	Tað bleiv víst gestunum nógv tilfar um Heinesen.	203	**62.1**	55	16.8	69	21.1

Here we see considerable variation: Some of the examples are found to be natural by a majority of the subjects, others are rejected by a majority of the subjects. On the average only about 43% of the subjects find the examples natural. Since this construction must be an innovation in Faroese, it is of some interest to see how the judgments of it correlate with judgments of the constructions under discussion. The r- and p-values are shown in Table 9 (the one non-significant correlation highlighted).

Interestingly, there is considerable correlation (almost "strong") between the evaluations of the innovative NIP-examples (with a Dat argument) and the "old" constructions under investigation, except for null expletives. This kind of correlation can hardly be due to some general conservatism.

Table 9: Correlations between judgments of New Impersonal Passive examples and other constructions in FarDiaSyn.

	Oblique subjects	Stylistic Fronting	Null expletives	Transitive Expletives
NIP (Dat)	r = 0.482 p < 0.001 N = 333	r = 0.464 p < 0.001 N = 333	**r = 0.069** **p = 0.209** N = 333	r = 0.426 p < 0.001 N = 333

4.2 Comparison of the variation

Finally, let us return to the distribution of the variation shown in Figures 3–6, repeated here for convenience.

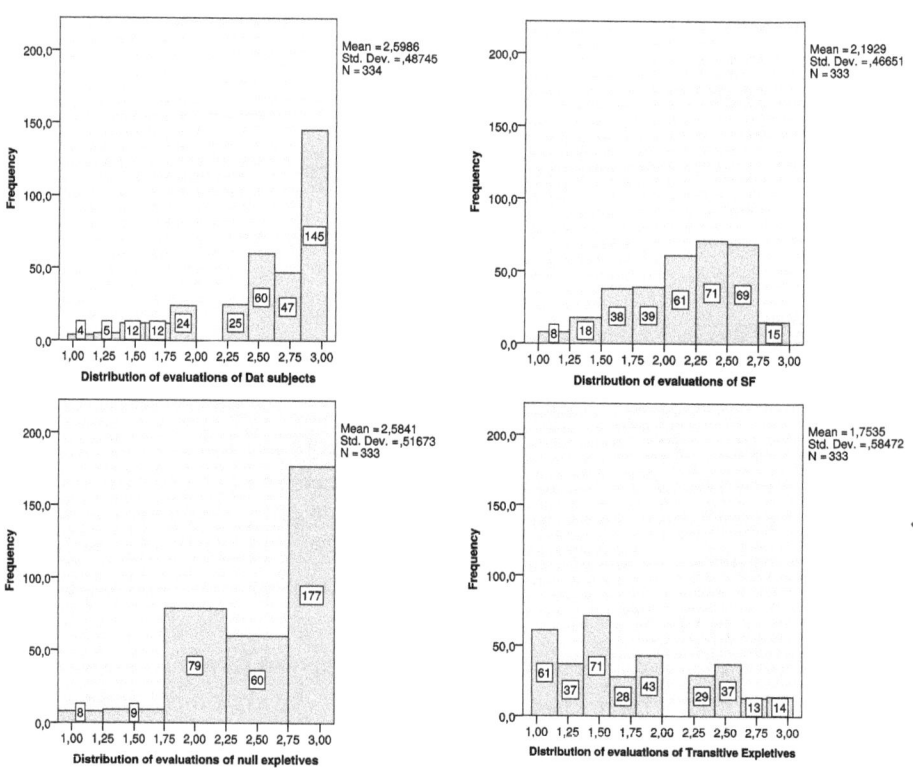

Figure 7: Judgments of examples of the four constructions investigated.

If the four constructions are related by a single parameter, we might have expected greater similarity between the evaluations than these figures reveal, even if we assume that the parameter settings can be "soft" (i.e., their probabilities ranging from 0 to 1). But maybe the figures are not as different as they seem. First, there is considerable similarity between the figures for Dat subjects and null expletives: Many speakers accept all the examples, very few speakers reject all of them and some speakers are in between. This would seem compatible with the concept of soft parameter settings. Second, we could argue that the figure for SF in fact reveals a similar situation: Very few speakers reject all the SF examples, most speakers find most of the examples natural and the reason why so few speakers find all the SF examples perfect might have to do with their stylistic value. But the figure for the TEC is clearly out of line since so many speakers find all the TEC examples unacceptable. This clearly calls for an explanation. A likely reason for this high rejection rate is the unfortunate choice of logical subjects in the TEC examples used (cf. fn. 7), which seems to have had the effect that many more speakers rejected the TEC examples in FarDiaSyn than the TEC examples used in Angantýsson's study. The relatively high correlation between the judgments of the TEC and judgments of some of the other constructions investigated (cf. Table 6) suggests that the TEC might in fact be related to the others in some fashion despite the different acceptability patterns revealed by the figures above.

5 Conclusion and discussion

5.1 Summary of the evidence

The main points of this paper can be summarized as follows:

- As Holmberg pointed out (2010: 13n), Faroese offers an extremely interesting test case for the parametric approach to syntactic variation in general and in Scandinavian in particular. The reason is the extensive inter- and intra-speaker variation found in Faroese syntax in areas where it has been maintained that parameters play a role.

- Because FarDiaSyn was such an extensive study that included a number of supposedly related constructions and involved a large number of speakers, it offers a unique opportunity to test parametric predictions in a new fashion by applying statistical methods.

- While this paper has shown that one has to be very careful in drawing conclusions about linguistic knowledge based on statistical data from syntactic performance (mostly evaluation of sentences in this case), the results from FarDiaSyn cannot be said to support the claim that the acquisition of oblique subjects, Stylistic Fronting, null expletives and the Transitive Expletive Construction is simply governed by a single binary parameter, as originally suggested by H&P.

One possible objection to the main conclusion above might be that the arguments in this paper are for the most part based on data elicited by having the subjects evaluate examples and pass acceptability judgments. The idea would then be that the extensive intra-speaker variation reported on here is a consequence of the methodology and not "real". But several recent studies have found evidence for similar intra-speaker variation using a variety of elicitation techniques and comparing the results to production data (see e.g. Thráinsson 2013b: 184–186, Nowenstein 2014 and references cited by these authors; cf. also Jónsson & Eythórsson 2005). Intra-speaker variation in syntax (and phonology) is much more pervasive than we have often assumed. It is difficult to reconcile this fact in principle with the concept of binary parameters fixed once and for all, ideally quite early in the acquisition period.

5.2 The remaining options

So what are we left with? The P&P approach is a bold and interesting attempt to solve the so-called "logical problem of language acquisition": How can most children come to know their native language very rapidly and in a fairly uniform fashion although the input (the "primary linguistic data", PLD) is supposedly both limited and at times inconsistent and misleading (the standard "poverty of the stimulus" argument)? This is understandable if there is very little to learn, as maintained by the P&P approach. The children ideally just have to set a few parameters and they only need very limited evidence to do so. This is presumably the main reason why so many linguists have embraced the P&P approach. The data reviewed here suggest, however, that language acquisition may not always proceed as simply and quickly as the standard P&P approach would predict if the relevant grammatical properties are parametrically related. So what are the options we are left with?

One alternative, of course, is that there are no parameters, just language-particular rules that speakers have to acquire. This is the account proposed by Newmeyer (2004; 2005; 2006). His main reason for doing so comes from typological evidence: He maintains that the clustering of properties predicted by the standard P&P approach never holds when a large enough sample of languages is considered. Assuming (with H&P) that ISc typically has oblique subjects, Stylistic Fronting, null expletives and the TEC whereas MSc does not, one could then say that ISc has one set of rules accounting for the relevant properties whereas MSc has another. In their reply to Newmeyer's original article (Newmeyer 2004), Roberts and Holmberg claim, however, that while such an account would be "observationally adequate", it "makes no predictions whatsoever regarding the correlation of the properties" (2005: 551). So if such a correlation holds for the properties under discussion, as they assume, the P&P account proposed by H&P is superior to Newmeyer's rule-based account, according to Roberts and Holmberg. To this Newmeyer replies in turn (2006: 7) that "It has been known since the earliest days of transformational grammar that rules are both abstract and often shared by more than one language (just as parameter 2 [= Holmberg & Platzack's Agr-parameter 1995 or its equivalent] is probably best interpreted as a rule shared by the ISC languages)". This statement suggests, however, that the difference between "rules" in Newmeyer's sense and typical P&P parameters is smaller than we might have thought.

But now recall that H&P were originally trying to account for cross-linguistic (or cross-dialectal) differences and similarities. In that sense they were concerned with INTER-SPEAKER VARIATION, i.e. differences between speakers (or groups of speakers, rather). The same is true of the arguments presented in the debate between Newmeyer, Holmberg and Roberts. Thus Newmeyer states (2004: 183) that "language-particular differences are captured by differences in language-particular rules" (and in 2006 he also maintains that cross-linguistic similarities can be captured by assuming similar rules, as we have just seen), whereas Roberts & Holmberg (2005: 538) state that they intend to defend the "principles-and-parameters model of crosslinguistic variation". In the present paper we have argued, on the other hand, that INTRA-SPEAKER VARIATION is an important part of speakers' competence and that it is much more prevalent than typically assumed. This means that it has to be taken seriously and not just brushed aside as some sort of shallow and uninteresting performance phenomenon. But how can it be accounted for?

First, it is important to note that we do not seem to be dealing with variation that is syntactically free and simply conditioned by some non-linguistic factors like social situation. The data reported on here were elicited under the same social conditions and we also find variation in production by individual speakers, e.g. in the case marking of subjects, under the same circumstances and within seconds in spontaneous speech (see e.g. Jónsson & Eythórsson 2005: 236, Nowenstein 2014: 7). Even more importantly, though, the Faroese speakers reported on here typically show intra-speaker variation *to a different extent*. Thus some of them are more likely to show ISc-like judgments than others, as shown by Figures 3–6 above. This is something that needs to be accounted for.[10]

One proposal compatible with extensive intra-speaker variation is the grammar competition approach advocated by Kroch (1989; 2001). It is possible to think of grammar competition in two ways. On the one hand we could say that during a period of linguistic change two "grammars" compete within a given linguistic community: An innovative construction (generated by the new grammar) then eventually (or ideally) drives out a conservative construction (generated by the old grammar). Their relative frequencies within the community shift, typically following an S-shaped curve. We could call this an E-language description of grammar competition as it focuses on the relevant linguistic community as a whole. More interestingly for our purposes, we could also say that for a given individual exhibiting a intra-speaker variation there are two grammatical options within the same internal language. Grammar competition is then a part of the competence of individual speakers, a kind of bilingualism, and it is reflected in the speakers' production or performance. We could call this an I-language description (if by I-language we mean the internalized language of individual speakers and not just the invariant universal language faculty, as in some usages of the term (for relevant discussion see e.g. H. Á. Sigurðsson 2011)).

Yang's variational model (2002 and later) is designed to account for this kind of situation and it can be thought of as an attempt to formalize Kroch's grammar competition approach. Assuming that the task of the child acquiring language is to select the grammar[11] that best accounts for the data encountered by the child (the "primary linguistic data", PLD), it is clear that when there is extensive variability of the relevant kind in the PLD, none of the grammars will account for all the data. Yang suggests that the child will then reinforce (or reward) a particular choice of grammar if the PLD (s)he encounters fit that grammar but otherwise (s)he will penalize it (make it less probable). Since the PLD encountered by different children will vary to some extent, the probability assigned to a given grammar by different children may vary. The variability in the PLD may

---

[10] As shown by Thráinsson (2013b: 182–184), this kind of intra-speaker variation also has its parallels in phonological production. So it is clearly not an artifact of the methodology of FarDiaSyn.

[11] Following Yang and others, I will mostly use the term "grammar" in the following discussion of competition and acquisition and return to the issue of parameters vs. rules at the end of the paper.

1 On the softness of parameters: An experiment on Faroese

also have the effect that it could take children a long time to settle on a particular "choice of grammar" and they may actually never rule one choice out although another option is favored to some extent. This will result in stable variation and give the appearance of "soft parameter settings".[12]

An approach to intra-speaker variation along these lines receives a general support from various acquisition studies: The more unambiguous evidence there is in the PLD, the easier it is for children to acquire the relevant grammatical property. Thus it has been reported, for instance, that there is a direct correlation between the length of the so-called root infinitive stage in Spanish, French and English and the amount of unambiguous evidence that Spanish, French and English children get for a "[+Tense] grammar" (see Legate & Yang 2007). The proportion of unambiguous evidence of this sort is highest in child-directed speech in Spanish and lowest in English and the root infinitive stage is shortest for children acquiring Spanish and longest for those acquiring English. In general, there is growing evidence for the claim that there is an interesting interaction between universal principles of grammar and the statistical properties of the PLD in language acquisition (for a balanced overview see Lidz & Gagliardi 2015).

Finally, three comments are in order. First, Yang wants his model to account for various kinds of acquisition, both the acquisition of various kinds of rules (e.g. in morphology) and of parametric settings where appropriate, as can be seen from the quotes in the Introduction above. Hence his general approach could both be adopted by those who believe in rules and have given up on parameters and by those who believe that parameters still have a chance. Second, recall that despite the intra-speaker variation reported on in this paper, we have shown that there is an interesting correlation between the judgments by the speakers of the four constructions under consideration. While this correlation is not as strong as predicted in the ideal world of binary parameters that are set early and easily, it is still intriguing and calls for an explanation. Roberts & Holmberg (2005) would obviously say that this correlation is incompatible with the language-particular rule approach advocated by Newmeyer (e.g. 2004), but this is not so clear if the relevant parameter can also be expressed as a rule, as maintained by Newmeyer (2006: 7). Newmeyer would point out in turn that the correlation is nowhere near as strong as the standard P&P approach would predict.

---

[12]While one might want to propose that a possible way to express this "softness" would be to say that parametric settings could take on values between 0 and 1, e.g. 0.4 and 0.7 to indicate varying closeness to, say, typical MSc vs. ISc settings, this would not be allowed under the standard assumption that "the values [of parameter settings] are discrete: there are no clines, squishes or continua" (Roberts & Holmberg 2005: 541).

The third and final comment is somewhat more complex. Recall that under Yang's approach the selection of a given grammar (or rule or parameter setting) is penalized if the PLD do not fit. Now assume that for a child acquiring Faroese an ISc-type grammar and an MSc-type grammar are the options. The ISc-type grammar allows oblique subjects, null expletives, Stylistic Fronting and TEC but the MSc-type grammar does not. Now assume that the child encounters data of the following kind (cf. the discussion around examples 8–13 above):

(17) a. **Hon** *dámar at lurta eftir tónleiki.*
 she.NOM likes to listen after music
 'She likes to listen to music.'
 b. *Í fleiri dagar varð* **tað** *etið og drukkið.*
 in many days was there eaten and drunk
 'People were eating and drinking for several days.'
 c. *Kennir tú onkran, sum* **hevur verið** *í Kekkia?*
 know you anybody that has been in Czech-Republic
 'Do you know anybody that has been to the Czech Republic?'
 d. **Onkur** *hevði etið súreplið.*
 somebody had eaten the-apple
 'Somebody had eaten the apple.'

All of these examples are compatible with an MSc-type grammar: The verb *dáma* 'like' takes a Nom subject in (17a) and not an oblique one, the expletive is overt in (17b) and not null, there is no Stylistic Fronting in (17c) and there is no TEC in (17d). Interestingly, however, only (17a,b) are incompatible with an ISc-type grammar. For speakers of ISc-type languages, Stylistic Fronting is optional. Thus the non-occurrence of Stylistic Fronting in an environment where it *could* occur (or could be applied, cf. 9g above) is perfectly compatible with such a language or grammar. Hence the counterpart of (17c) is fine in Icelandic — and (17c) should be fine for all speakers of Faroese, even those who have internalized the most ISc-like grammar. Similarly, TEC is always optional and hence (17d) is perfectly compatible with an ISc-type grammar although TEC could also occur there (cf. 13a). Thus the counterpart of (17d) is fine in Icelandic.

So why is this last comment important? It is because it demonstrates that if we assume Yang's variational acquisition account, ISc-type grammars will never be penalized for the non-occurrence of Stylistic Fronting or TEC in contexts where they could occur. Yet some speakers of Faroese do not seem to like Stylistic Fronting or TEC. Under a parametric account where the availability vs. non-availability of Stylistic Fronting and TEC follows from something else in the grammar, such as a particular parametric setting (or the likelihood of such a setting (in Yang's terms), or its equivalent in the form of an abstract rule, as suggested by Newmeyer 2006) this is understandable. Otherwise it is a puzzle.

Acknowledgements

The research reported on in this paper was supported by the Icelandic Research Fund to the project "Variation in Faroese Syntax" (or "Faroese Dialect Syntax", henceforth FarDiaSyn for short), PI Höskuldur Thráinsson, co-applicants Jóhannes Gísli Jónsson and Thórhallur Eythórsson. This project was a part of the Scandinavian research networks Scandinavian Dialect Syntax (ScanDiaSyn) and Nordic Center of Excellence in Microcomparative Syntax (NORMS, for information see http://norms.uit.no). Many thanks to our Scandinavian colleagues in these networks and in particular to our co-workers on the Faroese project, who included Ásgrímur Angantýsson, Einar Freyr Sigurðsson, Helena á Løgmansbø, Hlíf Árnadóttir, Lena Reinert, Per Jacobsen, Petra Eliasen, Rakul Napóleonsdóttir Joensen, Tania E. Strahan and Victoria Absalonsen. I would also like to thank the editors of this volume and two anonymous reviewers of this paper for very useful comments.

References

Angantýsson, Ásgrímur. 2011. *The syntax of embedded clauses in Icelandic and related languages*. Reykjavík: University of Iceland dissertation.
Barnes, Michael P. 1992. Faroese syntax — achievements, goals and problems. In Jonna Louis-Jensen & Jóhan Hendrik W. Poulsen (eds.), *The Nordic languages and modern linguistics 7*, 17–37. Tórshavn: Føroya Fróðskaparfelag. Also in *Scripta Islandica* 43, 28–43 and in Barnes (2001).
Berwick, Robert C. & Noam Chomsky. 2011. The biolinguistic program: The current state of its development. In Anna Maria Di Sciullo & Cedric Boeckx (eds.), *The biolinguistic enterprise. New perspectives on the evolution and nature of the human language faculty*, 19–41. Oxford: Oxford University Press.
Bobaljik, Jonathan D. & Höskuldur Thráinsson. 1998. Two heads aren't always better than one. *Syntax* 1. 37–71.
Boeckx, Cedric. 2011. Approching parameters from below. In Anna Maria Di Sciullo & Cedric Boeckx (eds.), *The biolinguistic enterprise. New perspectives on the evolution and nature of the human language faculty*, 205–221. Oxford: Oxford University Press.

Chomsky, Noam. 1965. *Aspects of the theory of syntax*. Cambridge, MA: MIT Press.
Chomsky, Noam. 1981. *Lectures on government and binding*. Dordrecht: Foris.
Eythórsson, Thórhallur. 2015. The insular Nordic experimental kitchen. Changes in case-marking in Icelandic and Faroese. In Matthew Whelpton, Guðrún Björk Guðsteinsdóttir, Birna Arnbjörnsdóttir & Martin Regal (eds.), *An intimacy of words – innileiki orðanna. Essays in honour of Pétur Knútsson*, 328–352. Reykjavík: Stofnun Vigdísar Finnbogadóttur í erlendum tungumálum & Háskólaútgáfan.
Gibson, Edward & Kenneth Wexler. 1994. Triggers. *Linguistic Inquiry* 25. 355–407.
Haspelmath, Martin. 2008. Parametric versus functional explanations of syntactic universals. In Theresa Biberauer (ed.), *The limits of syntactic variation*, 75–108. Amsterdam: John Benjamins.
Holmberg, Anders. 2000. Scandinavian stylistic fronting: How any category can become an expletive. *Linguistic Inquiry* 31. 445–483.
Holmberg, Anders. 2010. Parameters in minimalist theory. The case of Scandinavian. *Theoretical Linguistics* 36. 1–48.
Holmberg, Anders & Christer Platzack. 1995. *The role of inflection in the syntax of the Scandinavian languages*. Oxford: Oxford University Press.
Holmberg, Anders & Ian Roberts. 2009. Introduction: Parameters in minimalist theory. In Theresa Biberauer, Anders Holmberg, Ian Roberts & Michelle Sheehan (eds.), *Parametric variation: Null subjects in minimalist theory*, 1–57. Cambridge: Cambridge University Press.
Jónsson, Jóhannes Gísli & Thórhallur Eythórsson. 2005. Variation in subject case marking in Insular Scandinavian. *Nordic Journal of Linguistics* 28. 223–245.
Kroch, Anthony S. 1989. Reflexes of grammar in patterns of language change. *Language Variation and Change* 1. 199–244.
Kroch, Anthony S. 2001. Syntactic change. In Mark Baltin & Chris Collins (eds.), *The handbook of contemporary syntactic theory*, 699–729. Oxford: Blackwell.
Legate, Julie Anne & Charles Yang. 2007. Morphosyntactic learning and the development of tense. *Language Acquisition* 14(3). 315–344.
Lidz, Jeffrey & Annie Gagliardi. 2015. How nature meets nurture: Universal grammar and statistical learning. *Annual Review of Linguistics* 1. 333–353.
Lightfoot, David. 1999. *The development of language. Acquisition, change and evolution*. Oxford: Blackwell.
Maling, Joan. 1980. Inversion in embedded clauses in Modern Icelandic. *Íslenskt mál* 2. 175–193. Also published in Joan Maling & Annie Zaenen (eds.), *Modern*

Icelandic syntax, 71–91. Syntax and semantics 24. San Diego: Academic Press, 1990.

Maling, Joan & Sigríður Sigurjónsdóttir. 2002. The 'new impersonal' construction in Icelandic. *Journal of Comparative Germanic Linguistics* 5. 97–142.

Newmeyer, Frederick J. 2004. Against a Parameter-Setting approach to language variation. In Pierre Pica, Johan Rooryck & Jeroen van Craenenbroek (eds.), *Linguistic variation yearbook*, vol. 4, 181–234. Amsterdam: John Benjamins.

Newmeyer, Frederick J. 2005. *Possible and probable languages*. Oxford: Oxford University Press.

Newmeyer, Frederick J. 2006. A rejoinder to "On the role of parameters in Universal Grammar: A reply to Newmeyer" by Ian Roberts and Anders Holmberg. https://www.researchgate.net/publication/254719548.

Nowenstein, Iris. 2014. Intra-speaker variation in subject case: Icelandic. *University of Pennsylvania Working Papers in Linguistics* 20(28). 1–10.

Poulsen, Jóhan Hendrik W., Marjun Simonsen, Jógvan í Lon Jacobsen, Anfinnur Johansen & Zakaris Svabo Hansen (eds.). 1998. *Føroysk orðabók [Faroese dictionary]*. Tórshavn: Føroya Fróðskaparfelag.

Roberts, Ian & Anders Holmberg. 2005. On the role of parameters in universal grammar. A reply to Newmeyer. In Hans Broekhuis, Norbert Corver, Martin Everaert & Jan Koster (eds.), *Organising grammar. A festschrift for Henk van Riemsdijk*, 538–553. Berlin: Mouton de Gruyter.

Rögnvaldsson, Eiríkur & Sigrún Helgadóttir. 2011. Morphosyntactic tagging of Old Icelandic texts and its use in studying syntactic variation and change. In Caroline Sporleder, Antal van den Bosch & Kalliopi A. Zervanou (eds.), *Language technology for cultural heritage: Selected papers from the LaTeCH workshop series, theory and applications of natural language processing*, 63–76. Berlin: Springer.

Rögnvaldsson, Eiríkur, Anton Karl Ingason, Einar Freyr Sigurðsson & Joel Wallenberg. 2011. Creating a Dual-Purpose treebank. *Journal for Language Technology and Computational Linguistics* 26(2). 141–152.

Sigurðsson, Einar Freyr. 2012. *Germynd en samt þolmynd. Um nýju þolmyndina í íslensku* ['Active but yet passive. On the New Passive in Icelandic']. Reykjavík: University of Iceland MA thesis.

Sigurðsson, Halldór Ármann. 1989. *Verbal syntax and case in Icelandic*. Lund: University of Lund dissertation. Reprinted by the Linguistic institute at the University of Iceland 1992.

Sigurðsson, Halldór Ármann. 2011. Uniformity and diversity. A minimalist perspective. *Linguistic variation* 11(2). 189–222.

Sigurjónsdóttir, Sigríður & Joan Maling. 2001. Það var hrint mér á leiðinni í skólann: þolmynd eða ekki þolmynd? ['"There was pushed me on my way to school": passive or not passive?'] *Íslenskt mál* 23. 123–180.

Thráinsson, Höskuldur. 1979. *On complementation in Icelandic*. New York: Garland. (Cambridge, MA: Harvard University dissertation) [Republished 2014 as vol. 48 in the series Routledge library editions: Linguistics.]

Thráinsson, Höskuldur. 2007. *The syntax of Icelandic*. Cambridge: Cambridge University Press.

Thráinsson, Höskuldur. 2013a. Full NP object shift: The Old Norse puzzle and the Faroese puzzle revisited. *Nordic Journal of Linguistics* 36. 153–186.

Thráinsson, Höskuldur. 2013b. Ideal speakers and other speakers. The case of dative and other cases. In Beatriz Fernández & Ricardo Etxepare (eds.), *Variation in datives. A micro-comparative perspective*, 161–188. Oxford: Oxford University Press.

Thráinsson, Höskuldur. 2017. On quantity and quality in syntactic variation studies. In Höskuldur Thráinsson, Caroline Heycock, Hjalmar P. Petersen & Zakaris Svabo Hansen (eds.), *Syntactic variation in Insular Scandinavian* (Studies in Germanic Linguistics 1), 19–52. Amsterdam: John Benjamins.

Thráinsson, Höskuldur, Hjalmar P. Petersen, Jógvan í Lon Jacobsen & Zakaris S. Hansen. 2012. *Faroese: A handbook and reference grammar*. 2nd edn. Tórshavn & Reykjavík: Faroese University Press & Linguistic Institute, University of Iceland.

Vikner, Sten. 1995. *Verb movement and expletive subjects in the Germanic languages*. Oxford: Oxford University Press.

Yang, Charles. 2002. *Knowledge and learning in natural language*. Oxford: Oxford University Press.

Yang, Charles. 2004. Universal grammar, statistics or both? *Trends in Cognitive Sciences* 8. 451–456.

Yang, Charles. 2010. Three factors in language variation. *Lingua* 120. 1160–1177.

Zaenen, Annie, Joan Maling & Höskuldur Thráinsson. 1985. Case and grammatical functions: The Icelandic passive. *Natural Language and Linguistic Theory* 3. 441–483. Also published in Joan Maling and Annie Zaenen (eds.), *Modern Icelandic Syntax*, 95–136. San Diego: Academic Press, 1990, and in Miriam Butt and Tracy Holloway King (eds), *Lexical semantics in LFG*, 163–207. Stanford, CA: CSLI Publications, 2006.

Chapter 2

The role of locatives in (partial) pro-drop languages

Artemis Alexiadou
Humboldt-Universität zu Berlin/Leibniz-Center General Linguistics (ZAS)

Janayna Carvalho
Universidade de São Paulo

It is usually assumed that a difference between pro-drop and non-pro-drop languages is the presence of overt expletives in the latter group, but not in the former (cf. Rizzi 1982; 1986; Alexiadou & Anagnostopoulou 1998). Compared with this two-way classification, partial pro-drop languages, i.e. languages in which the distribution of pro is more restricted, are intriguing case studies. Unlike in English, for example, the satisfaction of EPP can be done in several ways in this group of languages. Fruitful strategies include remerging deictic elements, such as locatives and temporal adjuncts, or raising of internal arguments. As locatives are elements usually employed by all the languages that fall into this category as a means to satisfy the EPP, our comparison will focus on the use of these elements in two partial pro-drop languages, namely Brazilian Portuguese (BP), and Finnish, and Greek, a full pro-drop language. A comparison with a full pro-drop language will show that the behavior of locatives in partial pro-drop languages is one further characteristic that groups them together in opposition to pro-drop ones, apart from the more constrained distribution of pro. We will be concerned with some structures that contain an overt locative in all three languages, either interpreted as impersonals (null impersonals) or not. We will first compare BP to Finnish, and show that while locatives lack an argumental status and simply satisfy the EPP in Finnish as pure expletives, this is not the case in BP. In this language, locatives can both be argumental and expletive-like. By contrast, in Greek, locatives never check the EPP, i.e. they are never expletive-like. Rather they are referential/deictic elements, which perform a function similar to what has been discussed for English locative inversion.

Artemis Alexiadou & Janayna Carvalho. 2017. The role of locatives in (partial) pro-drop languages. In Michelle Sheehan & Laura R. Bailey (eds.), *Order and structure in syntax II: Subjecthood and argument structure*, 41–67. Berlin: Language Science Press.

Artemis Alexiadou & Janayna Carvalho

1 Introduction

Locatives have received a considerable amount of attention within generative grammar over the decades. Unlike other circumstantial PPs, it has been shown that these elements have grammatical functions in several languages and constructions. For example, Stowell (1981) noticed that PPs in locative inversion behave as subjects with respect to some tests but not others (see Rizzi & Shlonsky 2007 for a reinterpretation of the data). Freeze (1992) claimed that predicative locative sentences (*The book is on the bench*) and existential sentences (*There is a book on the bench*) are the byproduct of a same underlying structure in which a locative is one of the selected arguments of a complete functional complex, a head that selects both an argument and a specifier (Chomsky 1985). Recently, Kayne (2008) argued that expletive *there* in English is a deictic modifier of the associate, merging low in the structure. Richards (2007); Deal (2009), and Alexiadou & Schäfer (2011) reached similar conclusions independently.

In this paper, we explore the role of locatives in Brazilian Portuguese (BP), Finnish, and Greek. By studying these three languages, we provide evidence that the role taken by locatives in different languages is tied to the properties of T in the respective languages. In both BP and Finnish, locatives can satisfy the EPP. However, in BP, locatives behave as arguments in null impersonals, a fact that has not been noticed until now. Greek is very different from these two languages in not using locatives to satisfy the EPP. We relate this to the full pro-drop nature of this language. Full pro-drop languages satisfy the EPP through V-raising (Alexiadou & Anagnostopoulou 1998) and locatives are associated with the CP domain.

The paper is organized as follows. In §2, we discuss the status of 3rd person subjects in partial pro-drop languages. As in other partial pro-drop languages, in BP and Finnish, 3rd definite subject pronouns can be null in embedded clauses, but not in root clauses. In impersonal sentences, however, 3rd generic subject can be null (cf. Holmberg 2005; HNS 2009, henceforth HNS; Holmberg 2010 and Holmberg & Phimsawat 2015; for analyses of BP data, see, e.g., Cavalcante 2007; Galves 2001; Figueiredo-Silva 1996; Kato 1999; Duarte 1995; Nunes 1990; among many others). In §3, we compare Finnish and BP null impersonals, showing that a generic null pronoun is present in the former language but not in the latter.

In order to understand the differences between null impersonals in the two languages, in §4 we deal with the distribution of locatives in these languages. The comparison shows that while locatives are only licensed if T is specified for either generic or definite 3rd person in BP, they behave as pure expletives in

2 The role of locatives in (partial) pro-drop languages

Finnish, being licensed whenever EPP has to be satisfied. In §5, we briefly turn to Greek and show that locatives in this language share properties with English locative alternation. §6 ties the properties illustrated throughout the paper to properties of T in these three languages. §7 concludes the paper.

2 Third person in partial pro-drop languages

As in other partial pro-drop-languages, Finnish and Brazilian Portuguese 3rd definite subject pronouns cannot be null in root clauses, as shown in (1) and (2), whereas 3rd impersonal pronouns can be null, cf. (3) and (4).[1]

(1) Finnish (Holmberg 2005: 539)
 * *(Hän) puhuu englantia.*
  (s/he) speak:3 English:PAR
 'S/he speaks English.'

(2) Brazilian Portuguese
 * *(Ele) fala inglês.*
  (he) speak:3 English:PAR
 'He speaks English.'

(3) Finnish (Holmberg 2005: 548)
 Tässä istuu mukavasti.
 here sit:3 comfortably
 'One can sit comfortably here.'

(4) Brazilian Portuguese
 Aqui vende camisa.
 here sell:3 shirt.
 'T-shirts are sold here.'

However, 3rd definite subject pronouns can be null in embedded clauses, if there is no topic or locative PP intervening between the null subject and the root clause, see (5) from Finnish. (6) shows that BP follows the same pattern.

---

[1] A few remarks are in order about the examples. Unless otherwise stated, Greek examples are due to the first author and BP examples due to the second. The verbal endings glossed as '1, 2, 3' are all singular. The plural verbal endings are indicated in the relevant examples.

(5) Finnish (Holmberg 2005: 539)
 Pekka$_i$ väittää [että hän$_{i/j}$/Ø$_i$/$_j$ puhuu englantia hyvin].*
 Pekka claim:3 that 3SG/Ø   speak:3 English well
 'Pekka claims that he speaks English well.'

(6) Brazilian Portuguese
 João afirma que ele$_{i/j}$/Ø$_i$/$_j$ fala inglês bem.*
 João claim:3 that he/Ø   speak:3 English well
 'John claims that he speaks English well.'

If a locative PP is fronted, the null subject in the embedded clause can only be interpreted as an impersonal sentence, having a generic subject, both in BP, example (7), and Finnish, example (8).

(7) Brazilian Portuguese
 João afirma que no Brasil fala inglês muito bem.
 John claim:3 that in.the Brazil speak:3 English very well
 'John claims that in Brazil people speak English very well.'

(8) Finnish (HNS 2009: 73)
 Jari sanoo että tässä istuu mukavasti.
 Jari say:3 that here sit:3 comfortably
 'Jari says that one can sit comfortably here.'

Although there is no overt generic pronoun in the embedded clauses in the sentences (7) and (8), one can entertain the hypothesis that a generic pronoun is present in these sentences. Indeed, as Holmberg (2005; 2010) argues in detail, a covert generic pronoun must be present in Finnish. In the next section, we draw a quick comparison between Finnish and BP null impersonals in order to investigate whether BP null impersonals also features a generic null pronoun.

3 Null impersonals in BP and Finnish

A first piece of evidence for the presence of a generic pronoun in Finnish null impersonals is that such pronoun can function as an antecedent for an anaphor.[2]

(9) Finnish (Holmberg 2005: 550)
   Nyt täytyy pestä auntonsa.
   Now must:3 wash car:POSS;RFL
   'One must wash one's car now.'

Moreover, the object is assigned accusative Case, even though there is no other overt DP, see (10).[3]

(10) Finnish (Holmberg 2005: 549)
   Täällä voi   ostaa auton   / auto.*
   Here   can:3 buy   car:ACC / car:NOM
   'You can buy a car here.'

Subject-oriented adverbials and purpose clauses are licensed, as shown in (11) and (12).

(11) Finnish (Holmberg 2005: 548)
   Tässä istuu mukavasti.
   Here sit:3 comfortably
   'One can sit comfortably here.'

(12) Finnish (Holmberg 2010: 205)
   Tänne tulee   mielellään   [PRO ostamaan keramiikkaa].
   here   come:3 with.pleasure PRO buy.INF   pottery
   'It is nice to come here to buy pottery.'

---

[2] An anonymous reviewer, a native speaker of Finnish, informs us that this sentence is not completely natural. According to the reviewer an overt subject should be used, e.g.: *Nyt jokaisen [each-one-GEN] täytyy pestä autonsa* 'Now everyone must wash their cars' or leave the possessive suffix out: *Nyt täytyy pestä auto* 'Now it is necessary to was the/a car.' The reviewer comments that: "it may be that the reason has something to do with the fact that the subject of *täytyy* is lexically case marked with genitive. The same goes for other modals with a genitive subject *täytyy, pitää, kuuluu*, all meaning 'must'. The permissive modal verbs 'may' (*saa, voi*) have a nominative subject and they work much better in this context."

[3] As Holmberg (2005) points out, in some modal constructions, the subject is assigned genitive Case and the object nominative Case. Only with these verbs the object can have nominative Case in null impersonals.

However, even though this analysis has been extended to other partial pro-drop languages, it does not seem to work for the canonical BP null impersonal data examined in the literature, i.e. null impersonals with generic time reference.[4] First, as shown in (13), anaphors are not licensed in BP null impersonals.[5]

(13) Brazilian Portuguese
  * *Aqui ensina a si mesmo.*
  here teach:3 to se:OBL self.
  'Here one teaches oneself.'

Also, null impersonals in BP do not license inalienable possessors, which require a human antecedent in Romance. In (14), we observe that an inalienable body part '*a mão*' is interpreted as possessed if c-commanded by a human antecedent. Both a definite DP (*João*) and the impersonal morphology (*se*) warrant this interpretation if they c-command an inalienable body part.

(14) Brazilian Portuguese
  João/se levantou a mão na sala para fazer pergunta.
  John/one raised:3 the hand in.the classroom to ask:INF question
  'John/one raised his hand to ask questions in the class.'

In (15), however, this reading does not obtain as no human DP c-commands the inalienable body part.

(15) Brazilian Portuguese
  ?* *Na sala de aula levanta a mão para fazer pergunta.*[6]
  in.the classroom raise:3 the hand to make:INF question
  'In classrooms, one raises his hand to ask questions.'

---

[4]For some comments on other types, see footnote 11 and §6.2.

[5]As Charlotte Galves (p.c) points out, the test in (9) is not replicable in BP, since *seu*, the former possessive generic/3rd pronoun, is nowadays an almost exclusive 2nd definite possessive pronoun, due to changes in the pronominal paradigm. Hence, a version of (9) into BP leads to the interpretation that a generic entity will wash a car possessed by a definite person. (9') *Agora pode lavar seu carro.* Now can:3 wash:INF your$_{def}$ car.

[6]Three of four speakers judged this sentence as ungrammatical. One speaker judged it as grammatical under a contrastive reading, something along the lines of: 'In the classroom, one raises his hand to ask questions, not to argue with the teacher.' Crucially, under a neutral reading, this sentence is not grammatical for any of our consultants.

2 The role of locatives in (partial) pro-drop languages

Furthermore, subject-oriented adverbials such as *com maestria/com atenção* are not licensed, as we see in (16), and nor are purpose clauses, as (17) shows.[7]

(16) Brazilian Portuguese
* *Naquela escola de culinária prepara doce com maestria/ com*
in.that school of culinary prepare:3 sweet with mastery/ with
atenção.
attention
'One prepares sweets with mastery/with attention in that culinary school.'

(17) Brazilian Portuguese
* *Naquela escola de culinária prepara doce para alimentar criança.*
in.that school of culinary prepare:3 sweet to feed:INF child.
'One prepares sweets to feed the children in that culinary school.'

Given these contrasts, it seems that we cannot maintain Holmberg's analysis for BP, while arguably this captures very nicely the Finnish data. The question that arises then is: what ensures the impersonal reading of these sentences in BP?

Before we offer an answer to this question, note that null impersonal sentences in BP are subject to a number of constraints, which further support our conclusion that they differ from their Finnish counterparts. As shown in (18), unaccusative verbs are out in BP null impersonals. In addition, BP null impersonals do not tolerate other circumstantial PPs: a generic reading for the subject is possible only in the presence of a locative element.[8]

---

[7]Charlotte Galves (p.c.) offers as a counterexample the sentence in (i):

(i) No Brasil só trabalha pra ganhar dinheiro.
In.the Brazil only work:3 to earn money
'In Brazil one only works to earn money.'

This sentence is indeed grammatical to the second author of this paper and other speakers consulted. However, without the contrastive/emphatic adverb *só*, the judgments are not so sharp. As the discussion in footnote 6 suggests, contrastive contexts improve the grammaticality of the relevant sentences.

[8]The only apparent counterexample to this generalization is *hoje em dia* 'nowadays', as in the sentence *Hoje em dia usa saia* (lit. Nowaday wear:3 skirt), discussed in Galves (2001). As this is the only temporal element licensed in BP null impersonals, it cannot be said that temporal as locative PPs satisfy the EPP in BP null impersonals.

(18) Brazilian Portuguese
 * *Naquele hospital nasce com saúde.*
 in.that hospital born:3 with healthy
 Intended: 'One who is born in that hospital is healthy.'

By contrast, these constraints are not found in Finnish. Unaccusative verbs appear in null impersonals and a generic null subject is generally available, no matter what element satisfies the EPP. For example, in (19), the expletive *sitä* satisfies the EPP.[9]

(19) Finnish (Roberts 2015)
 Sitä huolestuu helposti.
 EXPL get.worried easily
 'One gets worried easily.'

(20) exemplifies a further constraint in BP null impersonals. Individual-level verbs do not form null impersonals in BP, but they do in Finnish, as (21) indicates.[10]

(20) Brazilian Portuguese
 * *Naquela casa teme a morte.*
 In.that house fear:3 the death
 Intended: 'One fears the death in that house.'

(21) Finnish (Roberts 2015)
 Sitä ei tiedä milloin kuolee.
 EXPL not know:3 when die:3
 'One doesn't know when one dies.'

Table 1 summarises the differences between BP and Finnish null impersonals discussed above.

---

[9] As BP does not have lexical expletives, (19) has the sole purpose of illustrating that this reading is not dependent on locatives in Finnish, but it is in BP.

[10] One reviewer argues that the psych verb *temer* in (20) may fall under the same generalization proposed for examples (18) and (19), since psych verbs are usually analyzed as unaccusatives. Note, however, that *temer* (fear) is usually taken to represent the class of transitive psych verbs in which the experiencer is a 'deep subject', hence it is analyzed as a transitive sentence (Belletti & Rizzi 1988).

Table 1: Differences between Finnish and BP null impersonals

Test	Finnish	BP
Anaphors	yes	no
Subject-oriented adverbials	yes	no
Purpose clauses	yes	no
Unaccusative verbs	yes	no
Individual-level verbs	yes	no

To summarize, we have presented evidence that i) BP null impersonals do not pass any of the tests for the presence of an implicit agent in their structure; ii) only a subset of transitive stage-level verbs is allowed in BP null impersonals. More precisely, the verb at hand must include an agentive external argument in transitive sentences.

While we recognize that the licensing of a subset of transitive stage-level verbs is not a conclusive piece of evidence in favour of the claim that Finnish and BP are drastically different, the fact that BP null impersonals do not pass any of the tests for the presence of an implicit argument is quite suggestive of a difference between null impersonals in these two languages.[11]

Recall our question above: what ensures the impersonal reading of the BP examples? We propose that it is the locative element that is responsible for this. Crucially, the locative element in the above sentences cannot be analyzed as a topic (contra Barbosa 2011; to appear) or a pure expletive satisfying the EPP (contra Buthers 2009; Avelar & Cyrino 2008) as the tests from (13) to (17) show that a pronoun is not responsible for the human reading in BP null impersonals. Specif-

---

[11] A reviewer reminded us of the two classes of impersonals in Italian discussed in Cinque (1988). In tensed contexts, several types of verbal classes are licensed (transitives, unergatives, unaccusatives, copulas, and the like). In untensed contexts, however, transitive and unergative verbs are the only ones licensed in some constructions. The reviewer then suggests that BP null impersonals can be a silent counterpart of untensed Italian *se*-impersonals. If this were the case, we should be able to detect the presence of this silent pronoun. The tests from (13) to (17), however, show that BP null impersonals lack an element responsible to license agentive-like elements.

ically, we propose that, at least for BP, the locative is the element responsible for deriving the existential interpretation. This proposal is reminiscent of Freeze's (1992) idea that, in several languages, a locative is a subject that generates existential meanings in existential sentences. Likewise, Brody (2013) notes the crucial role of locatives in generating generic readings with personal pronouns. According to this author, locatives have a silent *semantic* person that do not enter into syntactic operations, but contribute to the semantic interpretation of some sentences. In order to demonstrate this, consider the contrast between (22a) and (22b). Whereas (22a) can have an impersonal reading, meaning that people in general like to take a nap in the afternoon when in Italy, (22b) cannot. In other words, as the locative is absent, (22b) can only mean that a definite group of people like to take a nap in the afternoon.

(22) EnglishBrody 2013: 34–35

    a.   In Italy they like to take a nap in the afternoon.

    b.   They like to take a nap in the afternoon.

As we have been arguing that a pronoun is absent in BP null impersonals and it is usually assumed that locatives can give rise to a generic reading, we claim that the locative element is the external argument in these sentences. Under this analysis, we can explain some of the characteristics of BP null impersonals witnessed above, namely: the verbal restriction' and the behavior in respect to agentive tests.

Recall that neither individual-level nor unaccusative verbs form null impersonals in BP. Individual-level verbs are argued to lack the event argument, a spatiotemporal argument above vP responsible for, among other things, the licensing of locatives in stage-level but not individual-level verbs (Kratzer 1995). In addition, the impossibility of forming BP null impersonals with unaccusative stage-level verbs is quite revealing. Note that nothing would forbid the licensing of unaccusative stage-level verbs in BP null impersonals if the locative in this construction were a mere adjunct. As transitive stage-level verbs, unaccusative stage-level verbs like *nascer* 'born', in (18), are endowed with an event argument. However, as noted, the reason why this class of verbs is not licensed in BP null impersonals is that this locative can only be in complementary distribution with an argument that is merged on the same region the locative is: above vP.

Finally, concerning the behavior of BP null impersonals in respect to agentive tests, they corroborate an analysis of locatives as having a silent semantic, but not syntactic, person. The opposite behavior of Finnish in respect to verbal classes licensed and the agentive tests makes it clear that in this language a null pronoun must be present, as argued extensively in Holmberg's work.[12]

If the analysis for BP null impersonals in on the right track, we may be able to detect a specific characteristic of BP syntax that allows an external argument to be a locative in these contexts. We turn to this question in the next section.

4 Locatives as arguments and expletives

Given the contrasts seen in the above section, we can say that locatives have an expletive function when their only purpose is to satisfy the EPP in restricted environments, and are arguments when they yield generic meaning in null impersonals in BP. In Finnish, on the other hand, locatives only satisfy the EPP, as pure expletives (Holmberg & Nikanne 2002). In what follows, we provide evidence for this view by showing that in several 3rd person contexts locatives satisfy the EPP in BP. By contrast, in Finnish, they can remerge to Spec of TP whenever necessary, i.e. there is no constraint regarding the specification of T in this language for the satisfaction of the EPP by locatives.

The order VS in BP is degraded (cf. Berlinck 1988 for its loss throughout the centuries). This is a possible order, however, if either locative or temporal elements are fronted. If the temporal or locative element is overt, even unergative verbs can be licensed in VS order (cf. Avelar & Cyrino 2008; Avelar 2009; Avelar & Galves 2011).

(23) Brazilian Portuguese
Na semana passada entrou um cara na minha casa.
In.the week last enter:PST.3 a man in.the my house
'Last week a man (= a thief) entered my house.'

---

[12] Anders Holmberg (p.c) observes that the theta-criterion has to be abandoned if this analysis for BP null impersonals is right. Although we will not fully develop this idea here, we believe that a constructionist view for argument structure is the adequate one to explain these facts. Under the view that the argument structure is syntax and, therefore, depends on the specific formatives a language has, theta-criterion is nothing but an epiphenomenon. Finally, adopting the idea that several elements besides verbs have external arguments, including prepositions (Svenonius 2010), Wood & Marantz (2017) argue for the existence of a single argument introducer i*, which will be interpreted differently depending on the projection it merges with. This proposal can successfully derive the agentive interpretation in BP null impersonals if we assume that i* can s-select for a PP when merging with a vP in this language. Hence, null impersonals in BP would have a quirky subject. For more details, see Carvalho (2016).

If the locative or temporal element is covert, the interpretation is more constrained. In (24), the only possible interpretation is that the event happened recently, most likely on the same day (see Pilati 2006; Pilati & Naves 2013).

(24) Brazilian Portuguese
Morre   Maria da Silva.
Die.PRS:3 Maria da Silva.
'Maria da Silva died today.'

Consequently, sentence (25), in which an event that took place some years ago is described, is odd.

(25) Brazilian Portuguese
Você lembra   o   que aconteceu há   10 anos?
You remember:2 the what happened there.is 10 years
* *Morreu a   Maria da   Silva.*
Died:3 the Maria of.the Silva
'Do you remember what happened 10 years ago? Maria da Silva died.'

With unaccusative verbs, locatives can be non-canonical subjects (Pontes 1987; Galves 2001; Lunguinho 2006; Rodrigues 2010, among many others), as in the possessor raising data below shows.[13]

(26) Brazilian Portuguese
Cabe muita camisa nessas   gavetas.
Fit:3 a.lot T-shirt in.these drawers

(27) Brazilian Portuguese
[Essas gavetas] cabem muita camisa.
These drawers fit:3PL a.lot   T-shirt
'It fits a lot of things in these drawers.'

A characteristic that unifies all these phenomena is the fact that these locative strategies are fruitful only with 3rd person. Consider, for example, a version of (23) with a 1st person subject. In a neutral context, locatives satisfying the EPP in BP are ungrammatical if T bears 1st or 2nd person features.

---

[13] Nunes (2015) shows that the the object is assigned inherent Case in possessor raising constructions.

(28) Brazilian Portuguese
*Na semana passada entrei eu na minha casa nova.
In.the week last enter:PST.1 I in.the my house new
'I entered my new house last week.'

Even though there is a restriction regarding the grammatical person, locative elements in BP can be said to satisfy EPP in VS constructions, for example. Observe, however, that this does not seem to be the case in either null impersonals or in possessor raising constructions. For null impersonals, we have demonstrated that the locative PP is in complementary distribution with an agentive external argument (cf. the ungrammaticality of 18 and 20). In possessor raising cases, exemplified in (27), the assignment of nominative Case to the locative is poorly understood, but cannot be solely attributed to a means of satisfying the EPP. A more canonical option would be moving the entire DP rather than a part of it.

In Finnish, locatives seem to play a different role. They function, as Holmberg (2005) points out, as pure expletives. Hence, they do not occupy Spec,TP only in 3rd person contexts, but whenever the EPP needs to be satisfied. (29) shows that a locative is satisfying the EPP in a context where T is specified for 1st person. We come back to this issue in §6.2.

(29) Finnish (Holmberg 2005: 547)
Pariisissa minä olen käynyt (mutten Roomassa).
Paris:INE I be:1 visited but.not Rome:INE
'I've been to PARIS (but not Rome).'

Therefore, our original question of why locatives play a central role in BP null impersonals, but not in Finnish, seems to be related to the crucial role of locatives in different types of 3rd person constructions in the first grammar, but not in the second. This question will be discussed in §6.

5 Greek locatives

Contrasting with Finnish and BP, in pro-drop languages locatives only have a discourse function, i.e. they do not satisfy the EPP of this type of language. In Greek, VS orders are generally acceptable with all sorts of subjects, definite, indefinite, all persons, as well as bare plurals. It has, however, been noted in the literature, that VS orders are degraded with unergative predicates. However, as in other pro-drop languages, in Greek, VS orders with certain unergative predicates become acceptable when a locative adverbial is added to the sentence (Torrego 1989; Rigau 1997; Borer 2005; Alexiadou 2010):

(30) Greek
edo pezun pedja.
here play:3PL child:PL
'Children play here.'

Alexiadou (2010) shows that this type of inversion is mainly possible with certain unergative predicates and a sub-class of unaccusatives. This is very different from Finnish, where locatives remerge to spec of TP regardless of the type of verb, showing, again, the different role of locatives in these two grammars.

Alexiadou (2010) argues in detail that the locative does not occupy the Spec,TP position, and that the single DP argument is the external argument of the predicate. For instance, in (31), taken from Alexiadou (2010), we see that the predicate retains its agentive characteristics: it is compatible with agentive/instrumental adverbials just like any other unergative predicate.

(31) Greek
edo epezan pedia prosektika / me ti hrisi bala / epitides
here played:3PL child:PL carefully / with the golden ball / on purpose
'Children play here carefully/with the golden ball/on purpose.'

Instead, Alexiadou (2010) adopts an analysis, according to which the locative is a *stage topic* in Cohen & Erteschik-Shir's (2002) terms. It is situated in the CP domain, the area in the clause structure that is responsible for discourse features (see Rizzi 1997). The presence of a locative in the CP area leads to a focus interpretation of the elements following it. Thus full pro-drop languages lack expletive locatives. We will maintain that for these languages V-raising always satisfies the EPP, and no XP is required to appear in TP for EPP reasons, as has been argued for in great detail by Alexiadou & Anagnostopoulou (1998).

Below, we offer a syntactic structure for a sentence like (30) in Greek (Alexiadou 2010: 72, (19')). This structure will be compared with BP and Finnish later on.

(32)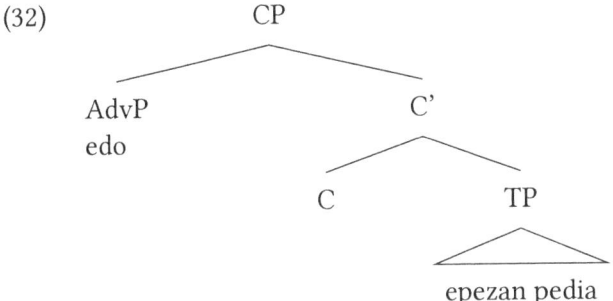

6 Towards an analysis

6.1 The D feature

In Holmberg's (2005) and HNS's (2009) analysis, a crucial difference between pro-drop and partial-pro-drop languages is the feature D in T.[14] D stands for definiteness and its presence in the former group of languages, but not in the latter, accounts for the possibility of having null definite subjects only in pro-drop languages.

In the two aforementioned analyses, both definite and generic 3rd person are treated as instances of the same category. Both start out the derivation as phi-pronouns, pronouns smaller than DPs, having only phi-features as their constituents, following Déchaine & Wiltschko's (2002) typology. After entering into the derivation, the φP pronoun merges as an external argument at some point. The phi-features in T then agree with the bunch of phi-features merged as external argument. Observe, however, that T, besides also having a bunch of phi-features, corresponding to the verbal morphology, has the feature D in contexts in which the interpretation of the subject is definite (3rd referential person, for example) and information about the time of the utterance, as represented in (33). The features in T are then a superset of the features merged as an external argument. Therefore, by means of chain reduction, the features in T will end up being the ones pronounced, i.e. the lower chain will be deleted (35). See the steps of the derivation below, from HNS 2009: 70.

(33) case of external argument to be valued
[T, D_k, uφ, NOM] [vP [3SG, uCase] v...]

---

[14] The feature D is T is inherently specified in Holmberg (2005), but uninterpretable in HNS (2009). In the latter account, D in pro-drop languages is valued by an A-topic in the C domain and, in its turn, value the external argument.

(34) case of external argument is valued
[T, D_k, 3SG, NOM] [vP [3SG, NOM] v...]

(35) chain reduction
[T, D_k, 3SG, NOM] [vP [~~3SG, NOM~~] v...]

In partial pro-drop languages, by contrast, the D feature is not present since definite subjects are not null. Nonetheless, recall that 3rd definite person can be null in both languages if they are the subject of an embedded clause. See examples (5) and (6) from both languages repeated below as (36) and (37).

(36) Finnish (Holmberg 2005: 539)
Pekka$_i$ väittää [että hän$_{i/j}$/ Ø$_{i/*j}$ puhuu englantia hyvin]
DP   claim:3 that he/   Ø   speak:3 English

(37) Brazilian Portuguese
João afirma que ele$_{i/j}$ / Ø$_{i/*j}$ fala inglês bem.
DP   claim:3 that he / Ø   speak:3 English well
'John claims that he speaks English well.'

HNS point out that an alternative derivation must be responsible for the licensing of 3rd person embedded subject in this specific context. Following Holmberg's (2005) analysis, the idea is that the 3rd person definite subject checks EPP, because this reading is only available if there is no intervening element between the subject of the embedded clause and the next clause up, as (38) from Finnish and (39) from BP exemplify.

(38) Finnish (HNS 2009: 73)
Jari sanoo että (hän) istuu mukavasti tässä.
Jari say:3 that (he) sit:3 comfortably here
'Jari says that he sits comfortably here.'

(39) Brazilian Portuguese (Rodrigues 2004: 142)
João$_1$ me contou que (ele$_1$) vende cachorro quente na praia.
João$_1$ me tell:PST.3 that (he$_1$) sell:3 hot   dog   in.the beach
'João told me that he sells hot dogs at the beach.'

If an adverb checks the EPP, for example, the generic reading arises (40) for Finnish and (41) for BP.

(40) Finnish (HNS 2009: 73)
Jari sanoo että tässä istuu mukavasti.
Jari say:3 that here sit:3 comfortably
'Jari says that one can sit comfortably here.'

(41) Brazilian Portuguese (Rodrigues 2004: 142)
João me contou que na praia vende cachorro quente.
João me tell:PST.3 that in.the beach sell:3 dog hot
'João told me that hot dogs are sold at the beach.'

The generalization then is that subjects can have a definite interpretation only if the subject of the embedded clause is c-commanded by the subject of the matrix clause, whereas the generic reading arises if another constituent, either a PP in both Finnish and BP or the object in Finnish, are situated in Spec,TP. The generic reading is thus obtained if the bunch of phi-features remain inside the vP.

In BP, however, we have seen that locatives seem to be responsible for the generation of an impersonal sentence rather than a covert pronoun. Hence, although *tässä* (here), in (40), and *na praia* (at the beach), in (41), satisfy the EPP and preclude the subject of the root clause to control the subject of the embedded one, these two locative elements differ in the sense that *tässä* is non-argumental and *na praia* is argumental. Positing this difference between BP and Finnish null impersonals leads us to consider how the valuation of features between T and the locative in the external argument position will take place in BP. If a locative merges as external argument in BP null impersonals, the derivation should crash since PP locatives do not have syntactic person features, as the BP data have shown. Alternatively, it could be the case that there are other features on T in BP null impersonals and the use of locatives as arguments reflect this. We explore this possibility in §6.2.

6.2 Another type of INFL in BP

Following Ritter & Wiltschko (2014), we assume that in BP locatives anchor the event. In BP, referential T can have a defective set of phi-features (cf. Ferreira 2000; Nunes 2008; Cyrino 2011, among others). Thus, it can be the case that T is devoided of phi-features in BP null impersonals. Null impersonals in this language, we claim, are cases in which INFL is specified for location, hence the mandatory presence of a locative, rather than tense. The examples below show the differences on the interpretation when the locatives are present or not. Crucially, whenever T is episodic, locatives are dispensable. In contrast, under a generic tense, they are obligatory in BP null impersonals. In other words, we propose that INFL has a location specification in BP when T would have default specification (3rd person, generic tense).

Ritter & Wiltschko (2014) claim that two different INFL values cannot coexist as distinctive. As BP null impersonals exemplified above are awkward or entirely out if T is [+past], it seems that location and specified time cannot coexist in BP INFL.

(42) Brazilian Portuguese
 * *Aqui vendeu camisa.*
 here sell:PST.3 T-shirt
 'One sold T-shirts here.'

(43) Brazilian Portuguese
 ?* *Na escola de culinária preparou doce.*
 in.the school of culinary prepare:PST.3 sweet
 'At the culinary school someone prepared sweets.'

Interestingly, as pointed out by Rozana Naves (personal communication) and Charlotte Galves (personal communication), these sentences improve if expressions such as *por muito tempo* (for a long period of time) or *já* (once) are added. (42) becomes grammatical with the addition of these elements.

(44) Brazilian Portuguese
 Aqui já / por muito tempo vendeu camisa.
 here once / for much time sell:PST.3 T-shirt
 'One sold T-shirts here for a long period of time/once.'

Observe, however, that an episodic reading for these sentences is not available. They are generic events that stretched for a period of time in the past.

In cases in which a true episodic reading is available, null impersonals are possible, but locatives are not fronted, i.e. they do not have the same role in sentences in which T is not specified, as examples (45) and (47), from Lunguinho & Medeiros Junior (2013), indicate. If locatives are fronted, as in (46) and (48), they are at least awkward.

(45) Brazilian Portuguese (Lunguinho & Medeiros Junior 2013: 16)
 Matou um rapaz no show do Zezé di Camargo e Luciano
 Killed:PST.3 a guy in.the show of.the Zezé di Camargo e Luciano

ontem.
yesterday
'A guy was killed at Zezé di Camargo e Luciano's show yesterday.'

(46) Brazilian Portuguese
?* **No show do Zezé di Camargo** matou um rapaz.

(47) Brazilian Portuguese (Lunguinho & Medeiros Junior 2013: 16)
Telefonou   aí   da   CEB pra você.
Telephone:PST.3 there of.the CEB to you

'Someone from CEB called you.'

(48) Brazilian Portuguese
* **Aí** telefonou da CEB pra você.

Furthermore, some contrasts found by Holmberg & Phimsawat (2015) between radical pro-drop languages and Finnish null impersonals are replicable in BP. The authors noticed that the alleged null pronoun in languages like Mandarin and Thai can refer to either human or non-human beings if the predicate allows it. Consider example (49) that demonstrates this possibility in Thai.

(49) Thai (Holmberg & Phimsawat 2015: 61)
Rúguo néng huò dé gèng duo de yi´ng yǎng, nà me huì   zhǎng de gèng
if   can get of more   of nutrition, (that) (will) grow of more
kuài.
fast
'If one gets a lot of nutrition, one will grow fast.'

The same interpretation is available for the translation of (49) into BP: *Se pode ter mais nutrição, vai crescer mais rápido.* The null element in both clauses can refer to either plants or humans. Holmberg & Phimsawat (2015) argue that, in the languages in which both interpretations are available, the null pronoun has a referential index – rather than a human feature – that is bound by a generic feature located in C. In languages in which T has phi-features, the null pronoun has a human feature, besides a referential index. This warrants that only a human interpretation will be available and that T must enter into an agree relation with the null pronoun, otherwise the derivation clashes.

Abstracting away from the details of Holmberg & Phimsawat's (2015) analysis, the possibility of having a non-human reading in BP for sentence (49) is intriguing, especially taking into consideration that null impersonals in BP have an

59

INFL specified for location rather than tense, as we have been arguing. Observe, however, that this reading arises when a subordinate clause is present. Subordinate clauses have operators whose primary function is the temporal binding of the sentence (Guéron 1982). Therefore, we can couple (49) with (45) and (47). In these three cases, temporality is involved and a locative, if present, is not INFL related.

In addition, note that an unaccusative verb, *grow* in (49), can be used when temporality is involved, showing, once more, that null impersonals with fronted PP locatives and the cases in which there is a temporal interval and this reading is obtained, are different derivations. Remember that unaccusative verbs cannot form null impersonals in BP when locatives are fronted (cf. Table 1). Given the differences, we believe that the reading of a generic entity in (46), (48) and the BP counterpart of (49) is obtained by operator-binding in BP, which explains two factors: i) as long as the verb allows it, the reading of a human entity is not the only one available; ii) unaccusative verbs are licensed. When locatives are related to INFL, by contrast, unaccusative verbs are out, because the locative is a scene-setting modifier that will merge above the vP, as an external argument, and a semantic human reading is the only one that this element can contribute.

To summarize, we have seen that other types of null impersonals in BP depend on the specification of tense. BP null impersonals with generic reference need a locative as an external argument because the specification of INFL in this type of data is location rather than tense. This explains the characteristics of BP null impersonals we have witnessed throughout the discussion.

At this point, we can present two derivations for BP and Finnish null impersonals.

(50) BP null impersonals (3rd person, generic tense)

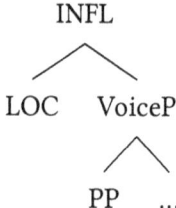

(51) Finnish null impersonals

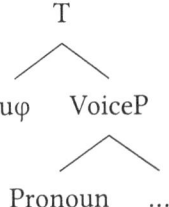

7 Conclusion

We have compared the role of locatives in Finnish, BP, two partial pro-drop languages, and Greek, a pro-drop language. The use of locatives in Finnish and BP, despite sharing a substantial number of properties, do not overlap. One of the crucial differences is the role of locatives in null impersonals. In BP, these elements behave as arguments, whereas in Finnish they are expletive-like elements. The reason why null impersonals in BP and Finnish seem so alike, yet are so different in terms of constituency can be explained in terms of the INFL each language has. BP can specify 3rd non-referential person with a locative feature in INFL, hence locatives can be arguments and expletives in this language. In Finnish, locatives satisfy the EPP, i.e. are pure expletives, as T bears no specification for location regardless of time or person specification.

Importantly, the difference between null impersonals in the two languages shows that partial pro-drop languages cannot be thought as a coherent group. These languages share some properties, such as the behavior of 3rd person, as discussed in §2, but they seem to have chosen different ways of becoming non-pro-drop languages. In particular, BP has chosen a different value to INFL in 3rd non-referential contexts. Even when INFL is specified for time, as seen in (46) and (48), no phi-features seem to be present and operator-binding generates the generic reading for an argument. Finnish, on the other hand, employs tense in null impersonals and locatives only satisfy EPP. In Greek, a full pro-drop language, none of these options is available, V-raising being the main way to satisfy the EPP. The differences among the three languages are summarized in Table 2.

Table 2: Summary of the properties of locatives in the three languages

	Language		
	Greek	Finnish	BP
Function	Focusing adverb	EPP	EPP, argument
Nodes to which locatives are associated with in the language	vP adjunct - CP	vP adjunct – TP	vP adjunct, TP; external argument, TP

Abbreviations

PART partitive

Abbreviations used in this article follow the Leipzig Glossing Rules' instructions for word-by-word transcription, available at: https://www.eva.mpg.de/lingua/pdf/Glossing-Rules.pdf.

Acknowledgements

We are indebted to the comments of two anonymous reviewers that greatly improved the readability of this paper. Many thanks to Anders Holmberg for discussions and for being a constant source of inspiration through the years. The authors would also like to acknowledge the support received from the DFG (grant AL 554/8) awarded to the first author and CNPq (grant #142048/2012-7 and #229746/2013-6) awarded to the second author.

References

Alexiadou, Artemis. 2010. Post-verbal Nominatives: An unaccusativity diagnostic under scrutiny. In Rafaela Folli & Christina Ulbrich (eds.), *Interfaces in linguistics: New research perspectives*, 56–77. Oxford: Oxford University Press.

Alexiadou, Artemis & Elena Anagnostopoulou. 1998. Parametrizing AGR: Word order, V-movement and EPP-checking. *Natural Language & Linguistic Theory* 16. 491–539.

Alexiadou, Artemis & Florian Schäfer. 2011. An unaccusativity diagnostic at the Syntax-Semantics interface: There-insertion, indefinites and restitutive again. In Ingo Reich, Eva Horch & Dennis Pauly (eds.), *Proceedings of Sinn & Bedeutung 15*, 101–115. Saarland: Saarland University Press.

Avelar, Juanito. 2009. Inversão locativa e sintaxe de concordância no português brasileiro [Locative inversion and the syntax of agreement in Brazilian Portuguese]. *Matraga* 24. 232–252.

Avelar, Juanito & Sônia Cyrino. 2008. Locativos preposicionados em posição de sujeito: Uma possível contribuição das línguas Bantu à sintaxe do português brasileiro [Preposed locatives in subject position: A possible contribution of Bantu languages to Brazilian Portuguese syntax]. *Revista de Estudos Linguísticos da Universidade do Porto* 3. 55–75.

Avelar, Juanito & Charlotte Galves. 2011. Tópico e concordância em português brasileiro e português europeu [Topics and agreement in Brazilian and European Portuguese]. In *Textos seleccionados do XXVI encontro nacional da associação portuguesa de linguística*, 49–65.

Barbosa, Pilar. 2011. Partial pro-drop as null NP-anaphora. In Lena Fainleb, Nicholas LaCara & Yangsook Park (eds.), *Proceedings of NELS 41*, 71–84. Amherst: GLSA Publications.

Barbosa, Pilar. to appear. *Pro as a minimal NP: Towards a unified theory of pro-drop*. Forthcoming.

Belletti, Adriana & Luigi Rizzi. 1988. Psych verbs and θ-theory. *Natural Language and Linguistic Theory* 6(3). 291–352.

Berlinck, Rosane. 1988. *A ordem VSN no português do Brasil: Sincronia e diacronia*. Campinas: University of Campinas dissertation.

Borer, Hagit. 2005. *Structuring sense*. Oxford: Oxford University Press.

Brody, Michael. 2013. Silent people. In Johan Brandtler, Valéria Molnár & Christer Platzack (eds.), *Papers from the 2011 Lund conference* (Approaches to Hungarian 13), 33–43. Amsterdam: John Benjamins Publishing.

Buthers, Christiane. 2009. *Emergência da ordem 'XP V (DP)' no PB Contemporâneo e o parâmetro do sujeito nulo: uma abordagem minimalista [The emergence of XP V (DP) in contemporary Brazilian Portuguese and the null subject parameter: A minimalist approach]*. Belo Horizonte: Federal University of Minas Gerais MA thesis.

Carvalho, Janayna. 2016. *A morfossintaxe do português brasileiro e sua estrutura argumental: Uma investigação sobre anticausativas, médias, impessoais e a alternância agentiva [Brazilian Portuguese morphosyntax and its argument struc-*

ture: An investigation of anticausatives, middles, impersonals and the agentive alternation]. São Paulo: University of São Paulo dissertation.

Cavalcante, Sílvia. 2007. O sujeito nulo de referência indeterminada na fala culta carioca [The null indeterminate subject in Rio de Janeiro educated speech]. *Diadorim* 2. 63–82.

Chomsky, Noam. 1985. *Knowledge of language: Its nature, origin, and use.* New York: Praeger.

Cinque, Guglielmo. 1988. On *Si* constructions and the theory of *Arb*. *Linguistic Inquiry* 19. 521–581.

Cohen, Ariel & Nomi Erteschik-Shir. 2002. Topic, focus, and the interpretation of bare plurals. *Natural Language Semantics* 10. 125–165.

Cyrino, Sônia. 2011. On complex predicates in Brazilian Portuguese. *Iberia: An International Journal of Theoretical Linguistics* 2. 1–21.

Deal, Amy Rose. 2009. The origin and content of expletives: Evidence from selection. *Syntax* 12. 285–323.

Déchaine, Rose-Marie & Martina Wiltschko. 2002. Decomposing pronouns. *Linguistic inquiry* 33. 409–442.

Duarte, Maria Eugênia. 1995. *A Perda do Princípio "Evite pronome" no Português Brasileiro [The loss of "Avoid Pronoun" principle in Brazilian Portuguese].* Campinas: University of Campinas dissertation.

Ferreira, Marcelo. 2000. *Argumentos nulos em português brasileiro [Null arguments in Brazilian Portuguese].* Campinas: University of Campinas dissertation.

Figueiredo-Silva, Maria Cristina. 1996. *A posição sujeito no português brasileiro: frases finitas e infinitivas [The subject position in Brazilian Portuguese: Finite and infinitive sentences].* Campinas: Ed. da UNICAMP.

Freeze, Ray. 1992. Existentials and other locatives. *Language* 68. 553–595.

Galves, Charlotte. 2001. *Ensaios sobre as gramáticas do português [Essays on Portuguese grammars].* Campinas: Editora da Unicamp.

Guéron, Jacqueline. 1982. Les opérateurs: Contribution à une théorie de traits syntaxiques. In Jacqueline Guéron & Tim Sowley (eds.), *Grammaire transfonnationnelle. theorie et methodologies*, 185–219. Paris: Univ. de Paris VIII.

Holmberg, Anders. 2005. Is there a little pro? Evidence from Finnish. *Linguistic Inquiry* 36(4). 533–564.

Holmberg, Anders. 2010. The null generic pronoun in Finnish: A case of incorporation in T. In Theresa Biberauer, Anders Holmberg, Ian Roberts & Michelle Sheehan (eds.), *Parametric variation: Null subjects in minimalist theory*, 200–230. Oxford: Oxford University Press.

Holmberg, Anders, Aarti Nayudu & Michelle Sheehan. 2009. Three partial null-subject languages: A comparison of Brazilian Portuguese, Finnish and Marathi. *Studia Linguistica* 63. 59–97.

Holmberg, Anders & Urpo Nikanne. 2002. Expletives, subjects, and topics in Finnish. In Peter Svenonius (ed.), *Subjects, expletives, and the EPP*, 71–106. Oxford: Oxford University Press.

Holmberg, Anders & On-Usa Phimsawat. 2015. Generic pronouns and phi-features: Evidence from Thai. *Newcastle and Northumbria working papers in Linguistics* 21(1). 55–71. http://www.ncl.ac.uk/linguistics/research/working-papers/archive/.

Kato, Mary. 1999. Strong pronouns and weak pronominals in the null subject parameter. *Probus* 11. 1–37.

Kayne, Richard S. 2008. Expletives, datives, and the tension between morphology and syntax. In Theresa Biberauer (ed.), *The limits of syntactic variation*, 175–217. Amsterdam: John Benjamins.

Kratzer, Angelika. 1995. Individual level predicates vs. Stage level predicates. In Gregory Carlson & Francy Pelletier (eds.), *The generic book*, 125–175. Chicago: Chicago University Press.

Lunguinho, Marcus. 2006. Partição de constituintes no português brasileiro: Características sintáticas [Phrase splitting in Brazilian Portuguese: Syntactic characteristics]. In Denise Garcia da Silva (ed.), *Língua, gramática e discurso*, 133–146. Goiânia: Cânone.

Lunguinho, Marcus & Paulo Medeiros Junior. 2013. Inventou um tipo novo de sujeito: características sintáticas e semânticas de uma estratégia de indeterminação do sujeito no português brasileiro [A new type of subject: syntactic and semantic characteristics of an indeterminacy strategy in Brazilian Portuguese]. *Interdisciplinar-Revista de Estudos em Língua e Literatura* 9. 7–21.

Nunes, Jairo. 1990. *O famigerado se: Uma análise sincrônica e diacrônica das construções com se apassivador e indeterminador [The clitic se: Synchronic and diachronic analyses of passive-se and indeterminate-se constructions]*. Campinas: University of Campinas MA thesis.

Nunes, Jairo. 2008. Inherent case as a licensing condition for A-movement: The case of hyper-raising constructions in Brazilian Portuguese. *Journal of Portuguese Linguistics* 7. 83–108.

Nunes, Jairo. 2015. *Breaching phi-features*. Handout delivered at LSRL16.

Pilati, Eloísa. 2006. *Aspectos sintáticos e semânticos das orações com ordem verbo-sujeito no português do Brasil [Syntactic and semantic aspects of verb-subject sentences in Brazilian Portuguese]*. Brasília: University of Brasília dissertation.

Pilati, Eloísa & Rozana Naves. 2013. Desenvolvendo a hipótese da cisão da categoria pronominal no português brasileiro [Developing the hypothesis of pronominal splitting in Brazilian Portuguese]. In Denida Moura & Marcelo Sibaldo (eds.), *Desenvolvendo a hipótese da cisão da categoria pronominal no português brasileiro [Developing the hypothesis of pronominal splitting in Brazilian Portuguese]*, 233–254. Maceió: EDUFAL.

Pontes, Eunice. 1987. *O tópico no português do Brasil [The category topic in Brazilian Portuguese]*. Campinas: Pontes Editores.

Richards, Marc. 2007. On object shift, phases, and transitive expletive constructions in Germanic. *Linguistic variation yearbook* 6. 139–159.

Rigau, German. 1997. Locative sentences and related constructions in Catalan, 395-421. In Amaya Mendikoetxea & Myriam Uribe-Etxebarroa (eds.), *Theoretical issues at the Morphology-Syntax interface*, 395–421. Bilbao: Universidad del País Basco.

Ritter, Elizabeth & Martina Wiltschko. 2014. The composition of INFL. *Natural Language & Linguistic Theory* 32. 1331–1386.

Rizzi, Luigi. 1982. *Issues in Italian syntax*. Berlin: Walter de Gruyter.

Rizzi, Luigi. 1986. Null objects in Italian and the theory of pro. *Linguistic Inquiry* 17. 501–557.

Rizzi, Luigi. 1997. The fine structure of the left periphery. In Liliane Haegeman (ed.), *Elements of grammar: Handbook in generative syntax*, 281–337. Dordrecht: Kluwer.

Rizzi, Luigi & Ur Shlonsky. 2007. Strategies of subject extraction. In Uli Sauerland & Hans-Martin Gärtner (eds.), *Interfaces + recursion = language? Chomsky's Minimalism and the view from Syntax-Semantics*, 115–116. Berlin: Mouton de Gruyter.

Roberts, Ian. 2015. *Null subjects and null arguments*. Handout delivered at MPhil Seminar.

Rodrigues, Cilene. 2004. *Impoverished morphology and A-movement out of case domains*. Maryland: University of Maryland dissertation.

Rodrigues, Cilene. 2010. Possessor raising through thematic positions. In Norbert Hornstein & Maria Polinsky (eds.), *Movement theory of control*, 119–146. Amsterdam: John Benjamins.

Stowell, Tim. 1981. *Origins of phrase structure*. Massachusetts: Massachussets Institute of Technology dissertation.

Svenonius, Peter. 2010. Spatial p in English. Mapping spatial PPs. In Guglielmo Cinque & Luigi Rizzi (eds.), *The cartography of syntactic structures*, vol. 6, 127–160. Oxford: Oxford University Press.

Torrego, Esther. 1989. Unergative-unaccusative alternations in Spanish. *MIT Working Papers* 10. 253–272.

Wood, Jim & Alec Marantz. 2017. The interpretation of external arguments. In Roberta D'Alessandro, Irene Franco & Ángel Gallego (eds.), *The verbal domain*, 255–278. Oxford: Oxford University Press.

Chapter 3

Expletives and speaker-related meaning

Ciro Greco
Ghent University

Liliane Haegeman
Ghent University

Trang Phan
Ghent University/University of Hai Duong

> In our paper, we investigate a set of pronominal forms that have lost their referential meaning and might at first sight be analyzed as expletives. First, we discuss the case of Finnish, which, though a pro-drop language, displays an element *sitä* with expletive function; and the case of Dominican Spanish, another pro-drop language which seems to have an expletive *ello* but in which, unlike Finnish, the expletive conveys a speaker-related meaning. In addition, we also examine the case of Vietnamese, a radical pro-drop language which also seems to deploy an expletive *nó* with discourse value, and the case of the Flemish element *tet*, which has lost its referential value and also has a discourse function. From these data it emerges that independently of the satisfaction of formal EPP-requirements, some languages can employ expletive or expletive-like elements for discourse-related reasons in those contexts where regular expletives are required in languages like English. The data discussed here lead to a more complex picture of the nature of expletives and their function in the grammar.

1 Introduction: expletives as formal devices

1.1 Characterizing expletives

Traditionally, expletives have been defined as elements inserted at some point in the structure to satisfy purely formal requirements, such as, for instance, the

EPP, which requires subject position to be filled in finite clauses (Chomsky 1981; 1995). Under this conception, expletives are a *last resort* device deployed whenever no regular (overt) subject is available to satisfy the formal requirement in question, either because there is no overt subject argument, as with weather or impersonal constructions, or because the relevant argument fails to attain the canonical subject position, as in existential and presentational sentences. Some patterns for English are illustrated in (1–3): in each example set, the (b) sentence illustrates the pattern in which the contentful subject argument does not reach its canonical position and an expletive element is inserted: in the existential patterns in (1b) and (2b) the expletive is *there*, with an extraposed clausal subject in (3b) the expletive is *it*:

(1) a. *Many students are arriving from Italy.*
    b. *There are now many students arriving from Italy.*

(2) a. *A workable solution to this problem does not exist.*
    b. *There does not exist a workable solution to this problem.*

(3) a. *That the students accepted the new regulations is surprising.*
    b. *It is surprising that the students accepted the new regulations.*

From the literature it emerges that cross-linguistically, canonical expletives share a number of properties. (i) Being inserted to satisfy a formal requirement, they are obligatory in the relevant contexts because, in their absence, the specific formal requirement would not be satisfied, leading to ungrammaticality. For instance, in English omission of the expletive subjects in the (b)-examples above leads to ungrammaticality because the canonical subject position has to be filled in English, i.e. SpecTP, or SpecSubjP in a cartographic approach (Rizzi & Shlonsky 2007). (ii) Though expletive elements usually have the form of an existing contentful element (e.g. 3rd person pronoun, locative adverb), expletives are taken to be semantically empty, at least when deployed as formal devices satisfying subject-related grammar requirements. For instance, though originally a locative adverb, English *there* in (1b) and (2b) does not contribute any locative or other semantics.[1] Being semantically empty, expletives cannot be focused or contrasted. For instance, they typically are prosodically reduced, and cannot receive focal stress. Moreover, expletives do not undergo A'-movement to the left

---

[1] Weather expletives might differ from other types of expletives with respect to their semantic content (Bolinger 1977). For a (controversial) example of a meaningful use of an expletive, *er*, in Dutch, see Mohr (2005).

periphery since this type of movement is specialized for the encoding of scope-discourse functions.[2]

(iii) The picture outlined above leads to a crosslinguistic prediction: pro-drop languages should not display overt expletives, because in these languages the EPP can be satisfied through some alternative mechanism (for proposals see, a.o. Rizzi 1982; Alexiadou & Anagnostopoulou 1998; Holmberg & Roberts 2009). Thus, the contrasts between English and Italian illustrated in (4–5) have been traced back to the availability of an alternative way to satisfy the EPP in Italian, which is unavailable in English, and have led to a view in which the presence of expletives is related directly to the pro-drop parameter:

(4) a. * *(It) rains.*

     b. *Piove.*   (Italian)
         rains

(5) a. * *(There) have arrived three girls.*

     b. *Sono arrivate tre   ragazze.*   (Italian)
         are   arrived three girls

1.2 Exceptional expletives

The predictions that follow from the characterization of expletives above are broadly speaking correct in that, typically, (i) expletives are not optional, (ii) they lack semantic content, and (iii), pro-drop languages do not display expletives as extensively as non-pro-drop languages do (Newmeyer 2005), confirming the hypothesis that their presence correlates with the negative setting of the null subject parameter.

However, additional research reveals that even in languages which allow non overt subjects there are occurrences of what seem to be expletive elements, suggesting that the correlation with a negative setting of the pro-drop parameter is not categorical. Apparent expletive elements have been attested in Finnish, Dominican Spanish and Vietnamese. The distribution and the properties of the 'expletives' in question closely resemble those of canonical subject expletives: typically, they are pronominal elements without referential value and occupying a position in the higher portion of the inflectional layer.

---

[2]There arises a conceptual tension with respect to Rizzi & Shlonsky's (2007) assumption that expletives formally satisfy the subject criterion, itself a condition implying a semantic component. We will not try to solve this issue here.

Since the customary function of expletives (namely, to satisfy a subject-related EPP requirement) can be fulfilled differently in pro-drop languages, the question is what function these elements perform in these systems. Do they also serve to satisfy some formal requirement or can they be employed for other purposes and, if the latter, do they make any semantic contribution?

In what follows we will examine such cases in more detail. We will discuss the cases of Dominican Spanish and Vietnamese, two pro-drop languages. Our analysis will reveal that the relevant expletives are fully optional devices which convey a speaker-related meaning.

In particular, we will show that in Vietnamese, the relevant expletive element appears to be allowed only in those contexts where regular, semantically vacuous expletives are required in non-pro-drop languages, like English. This suggests that even though the expletive does not fulfill the function of being a subject place holder, it maintains some connection with the subject position. We will then turn to West Flemish, a non pro-drop language, in which an expletive-like element appears in a position in the high IP-layer and conveys a speaker-oriented meaning.

The expletive-like elements which we examine seem to be distributionally alike: they all occupy a high position in the IP layer. However, we will show that, unlike Vietnamese, West Flemish expletive-like elements are not restricted only to the constructions that require expletives in non-pro-drop languages. We will suggest that this difference can be captured by the articulation of high IP-layer into specialized subject positions (Kiss 1996; Rizzi & Shlonsky 2007; Cardinaletti 2004) and optional discourse-related positions (Uriagereka 2004; Grohmann 2000).

This paper is organized as follows: §2 and §3 discuss *sitä* in Finnish and *ello* in Dominican Spanish respectively: we will see that, unlike Finnish *sitä*, the expletive *ello* conveys a speaker-related meaning. §4 illustrates the expletive-like element *nó* in Vietnamese, a radical pro-drop language. We will show that *nó* also seems to encode discourse meaning. In §5 we turn to *tet* in Flemish, a non pro-drop language. *Tet* is a pronominal element which has lost its referential value, has a discourse function and again it is located in the high IP-area.

2 Expletives in pro-drop languages: Finnish *sitä*

Holmberg & Nikanne (2002) have shown that correlating the presence of expletives with a negative setting of the pro-drop parameter is an oversimplification: Finnish, a pro-drop language, displays what look like overt expletives in a subset of cases where expletives are expected in non-pro-drop languages.

3 Expletives and speaker-related meaning

Holmberg & Nikanne (2002) show that Finnish can be classified as a pro-drop[3] language with referential null subjects (6a) and with null subjects with weather verbs (6b). However, some expletive elements can (and sometimes must) appear in pre-verbal position, precisely in those contexts typically requiring expletives in non-pro-drop languages. As is the case for the canonical expletives, Holmberg & Nikanne (2002) argue that the relevant expletives do not contribute to the interpretation of the sentence. One such expletive is the element *sitä*,[4] a partitive form of the 3rd person singular non-human pronoun. (6c) illustrates the use of *sitä* in presentational sentences:[5]

(6) (Holmberg & Nikanne 2002: 75) (Finnish)

    a. *Olen väsynyt.*
       be.1SG tired
       'I'm tired.'

    b. *Sataa (vettä).*
       Rains (water)
       'It is raining.'

    c. * *(Sitä) leikkii lapsia kadulla.*
       SITÄ play children in.street
       'There are children playing in the street.'

Sitä immediately precedes the inflected verb or auxiliary, as in (6c), and follows left-peripheral focalized constituents, as in (7). Holmberg & Nikanne (2002) argue that *sitä* does not occupy the specifier of TP, but rather the specifier of the topmost topic-related functional projection in the inflectional domain; the specifier of this projection is filled by an argument with the feature [-Foc]. When no suitable argument with the feature [-Foc] is available, *sitä* is inserted:

---

[3]Finnish is classified as a *partial null-subject language* in the typology in Holmberg & Roberts (2009). This implies that null referential subjects are restricted to 1st and 2nd person, while 3rd person subjects can only be null when bound by a higher argument (Holmberg 2005; 2010).
[4]For the sake of completeness, we add that Finnish has a second expletive, *se*, the nominative pendant of *sitä* (Holmberg & Nikanne 2002: 100, note 3), which is inserted as the subject of weather verbs and in constructions with an extraposed clause. For reasons of space, we cannot discuss this element.
[5]Holmberg & Nikanne (2002: 81–83) also discuss verb-initial sentences without expletives. We cannot go into these here for reasons of brevity.

(7) (Holmberg & Nikanne 2002: 93) (Finnish)

    a. NAMA LAPSET *sitä olisivat oppineet uimaan.*
       these children SITÄ have.COND.3PL learn to.swim
       'THESE CHILDREN would have learned to swim.'

    b. * *Sitä* NAMA LAPSET *olisivat oppineet uimaan.*
       SITÄ these children have.COND.3PL learn to.swim

On the basis of distributional facts such as those above, Holmberg & Nikanne (2002) conclude that expletive *sitä* satisfies a formal EPP-requirement, associated with a topic projection in the inflectional domain that dominates the projection encoding subject agreement; they suggest that the relevant projection might be the high functional projection 'FP' postulated by Uriagereka (2004) for Romance and that its availability is related from the general properties of Finnish as a Topic-prominent language (see Kiss 1995).

The patterns discussed by Holmberg & Nikanne (2002) provide evidence that, although it is generally true that languages that can dispense with overt subjects do not require expletives in the same way as non null-subject languages like English do, pro-drop systems may still feature expletives. The behavior of *sitä*, thus, reveals that the correlation between the distribution of expletives and the null-subject parameter is more complex than originally thought. At the same time, *sitä* appears to be employed to fulfill a function similar to that fulfilled by prototypical subject expletives, namely that of satisfying a formal EPP-requirement of some kind.

3 Expletives and Discourse Functions: *ello* in Dominican Spanish

As highlighted above, one implicit assumption in the literature is that the prototypical expletive is inserted for formal reasons and lacks interpretive effects. However, this generalization has also been challenged. For a number of Romance pro-drop languages, neuter strong pronouns and demonstratives have been reported to act as optional expletive subjects (see Bartra-Kaufmann 2011 for an overview); a number of these have been claimed to contribute to the discourse interpretation of the sentence. One such case is the expletive use of the pronoun *ello* reported for Dominican Spanish (DS).

The pronoun *ello* occurs in configurations which in the non-pro-drop languages typically require an expletive, such as impersonal and weather constructions and with unaccusative post-verbal subjects (Bullock & Toribio 2009; Martínez Sanz 2011; Muñoz Pérez 2014; Gupton & Lowman 2014):

(8) (Muñoz Pérez 2014: 156) (DS)

   a. *(Ello)* tiene que haber otro paso.
      ELLO should that to be other path
      'It should be other paths.'

   b. *(Ello)* no está lloviendo aquí pero allá sí.
      ELLO not is raining here but there yes
      'It is not raining here, but it is there.' (Bullock & Toribio 2009: 57)

   c. *(Ello)* casi no ha pasado ni u vehicolo.
      ELLO almost not has passed no a vehicle
      'Almost no vehicle has passed.'

This use of *ello* is incompatible with an overt pre-verbal subject (Martínez Sanz 2011: 65). Because of its complementary distribution with a pre-verbal DP subject, the position of *ello* has been equated with the canonical subject position, i.e. SpecTP:

(9) (Martínez Sanz 2011: 65) (DS)

   * **Ello** yo no sé por qué mi papá me puso Almeida.
     ELLO I not know why my dad me called.3SG Almeida
   'I don't know why my dad named me Almeida.'

To all intents and purposes, DS *ello* has the properties of an expletive: it is formally like a pronominal element, it lacks referential content, it occupies a high IP-position, it occurs in the contexts that display expletives in the non-pro-drop languages. Unlike regular expletives, though, *ello* is optional. In line with the generalization that pro-drop languages typically lack expletives, Muñoz Pérez (2014) points out that the pronominal system of DS is currently changing as speakers tend to produce more overt pronouns than European Spanish speakers (Otheguy et al. 2007), suggesting that in fact DS is losing its pro-drop properties. In this scenario, the occurrence of an overt expletive would no longer be unexpected and rather than complicating the picture it would indeed corroborate the hypothesis that the presence of overt expletives correlates with a negative setting of the pro-drop parameter (however formulated).

As mentioned, *ello* lacks referential content and, in this respect, appears to be like a regular expletive. However, exploring observations in Martín Zorraquino

& Portóles Lázaro (1999) and Hinzelin & Kaiser (2007) signal that, while indeed non-referential, dislocated uses of DS *ello* encode *point of view*. They identify the pronoun as a left-peripheral discourse marker conveying the speaker's commitment to the proposition:

(10)   (Hinzelin & Kaiser 2007: 173)   (DS)
       Ello... así decían.
       ELLO so say.IMP.3PL
       'Well, that's how they were saying it.'

While Hinzelin & Kaiser (2007) focus on dislocated *ello* (10), Gupton & Lowman (2014: 344–345) extend the analysis of *ello* as a *point-of-view* discourse marker to IP-internal expletives. They also argue that DS does not behave like partial null-subject languages or non-null-subject languages, but is more like archaic Romance pro-drop languages such as European Portuguese and Galician in that it has the other identifying properties such as (sporadic) finite-verb enclisis, clitic tripling, and personal infinitives.

Pursuing Uriagereka's (2004) proposal, Gupton & Lowman (2014) propose that *ello* occupies the specifier position of a projection FP dominating TP which encodes the speaker's point of view. Observe that the position assigned to *ello* by Gupton & Lowman (2014) is similar to that associated by Holmberg & Nikanne (2002) with Finnish *sitä*, but while the latter is not associated with any semantic content, DS *ello* conveys speaker-related meaning.

The conclusions in Gupton & Lowman (2014) are tentative and further work is needed to substantiate their analysis and explore its impact for other similar pronominal elements in Romance but, if their interpretation of the role of DS *ello* is correct, it supports the idea that expletives can be associated with interpretive content.

4 Vietnamese *nó*

Like many East Asian languages (e.g. Chinese, Japanese, Korean and Thai), Vietnamese is a radical pro-drop language (Huang 1984) without agreement marking on the verb and in which arguments can be freely omitted: (11a) illustrates subject omission, (11b) object omission:

(11) a. *Mary thích Tom. Và Ø cũng thích Peter.*   (Vietnamese)
          Mary like   Tom and Ø also like Peter
          'Mary$_i$ likes Tom. She$_i$ also likes Peter.'

b. *Mary thích Tom. Nhưng Peter không thích Ø.*
   Mary like Tom but   Peter NEG   like Ø
   'Mary likes Tom_i. But Peter does not like him_i.'

Surprisingly then, in spoken Vietnamese, in addition to its referential use, the pronoun *nó* optionally appears in contexts typically displaying expletive subjects in non-pro-drop languages (Nguyen & Nguyen 2011; Dao 2012). Like prototypical expletives, Vietnamese *nó* is formally related to a pronoun, it lacks referential content and it cannot be focused. In (12a), *nó* appears to be the subject of a weather predicate, in (12b) it occurs with an existential predicate, and in (12c–12e) it occurs with unaccusative predicates. In all these cases, *nó* is non-referential:

(12) a. *(Nó) mưa bây-giờ đấy.*   (Vietnamese)
        NÓ   rain now   PRT
        'It is about to rain now.'

   b. *(Nó) không có   cái bút nào.*[6]
      NÓ   NEG   exist CLF pen any
      'There are no pens.'

   c. *(Nó) ngã thằng bé.*
      NÓ   fall CLS   boy
      'A/the boy fell.'

   d. *(Nó) chết cá   tao.*
      NÓ   die fish mine
      'My fish died.'

   e. *(Nó) cháy cái nhà   kho.*
      NÓ   burnt CLF house store
      'A warehouse burned.'

4.1 The interpretation of nó

In contrast with Finnish *sitä*, but in line with some proposals concerning DS *ello*, Vietnamese *nó* does contribute to the interpretation of the clause. Specifically, inserting *nó* narrows down the contexts in which the sentence is appropriate in terms of speaker-related epistemic specificity (Greco et al. 2017).

---

[6] (12b) is ambiguous between the existential and a possessive interpretation with *nó* interpreted as a referential subject pronoun '(S)he doesn't have any pen'. We only discuss the existential reading.

We first illustrate the interpretive effect brought about *nó* in existential patterns. Existential sentences like (13) are ambiguous between being either generic statements asserting (or denying) the existence of an entity in general or being contextual statements about the existence of an entity in a specific situation: (13) either denies the existence of ghosts in general or it denies the presence of ghosts in the context of utterance (while not excluding their existence as such):

(13) a. *Không có ma.* (Vietnamese)
   NEG exist ghost
 b. Generic: 'Ghosts do not exist.'
 c. Contextual: 'There are no ghosts speaking of a certain place/time.'

Inserting *nó* restricts the domain of validity of the assertion that 'there are no ghosts' to a specific context, thus narrowing down the contextualization potential of the containing sentence.

(14) a. **Nó** *không có ma.* (Vietnamese)
   NÓ NEG exist ghost
 b. # Generic: 'Ghosts do not exist.'
 c. Contextual: 'There are no ghosts speaking of a certain place/time.'

The 'contextualizing' effect of *nó* is also found in sentences with post-verbal unaccusative subjects (12c–12e). These structures are thetic sentences whose semantic contribution is to assert the existence of an eventuality of a certain kind (Ladusaw 1994). Typically, these sentences can be uttered out of the blue and they can be used as answers to questions like '*What happened?*'. In a thetic sentence, the subject is represented as part of the predicative nucleus (e.g. as a mere participant of an event). (15) asserts the existence of an event of burning involving a warehouse as the main participant. In thetic sentences, *nó* contributes the implication that the eventuality expressed in the clause is specifically identifiable in or anchored to a given context:

(15) *(Nó) cháy cái nhà kho.* (Vietnamese)
   NÓ burnt CLF house store
   'A warehouse burned.'

This contextualization effect of *nó* appears to be speaker-related: in thetic sentences *nó* is only felicitous in contexts in which the speaker disposes of sufficient background information to report on a specific event. (16) and (17) illustrate the speaker-anchoring achieved by *nó*.

3 Expletives and speaker-related meaning

Context 1: After meeting a friend who told him that there had been a fire in New York last week and that a warehouse burned down, the speaker utters (16) as a report.

(16) (*Nó*) *cháy cái nhà kho rồi* (Vietnamese)
 NÓ burnt CLF house store already
 'A warehouse burned.'

In this context, information available to the speaker allows him to supply specific spatial and temporal coordinates for the eventuality he's referring to. In this context *nó* is appropriate, although not obligatory.

Context 2: The speaker has seen on the television that there had been a fire and that a warehouse has burned down but lacks any further information about this event such as its temporal and locative coordinates. All he knows is that an event of burning took place. In this context, the speaker may utter (16), but, crucially, inserting *nó* would be infelicitous:

(17) (#*Nó*) *cháy cái nhà kho rồi* (Vietnamese)
 NÓ burnt CLF house store already
 'A warehouse burned.'

Though space prevents a fuller discussion of this point, the crucial requirement for the insertion of the expletive nó appears to be the possibility of the speaker having a specific event in mind (see Greco et al. 2017). In this respect, the discourse-related meaning of *nó* can be conceived of as related to some form of speaker-oriented epistemic specificity (Hellan 1981; Farkas 2002).

Even when the conditions for its use are met, *nó* is never obligatory, since the contextualization effect can be conveyed implicitly in the context of utterance: inserting *nó* restricts the felicitous contexts of the utterance to a subset of the contexts available without the expletive.

4.2 The syntax of nó

The Vietnamese IP-domain displays a rigidly ordered array of functional morphemes, such as pre-verbal temporal and aspectual markers (Duffield 2013; Phan 2013), the topmost of which is the future marker *sẽ*. In what looks like its expletive use, the pronoun *nó* occupies a position dominating this element: (18) illustrates the relevant pattern with the weather verb *mưa* ('rain'), (19) illustrates the existential pattern and (20) illustrates unaccusative *ngã* ('fall'):

(18) a. *Nó sẽ mưa bây-giờ đấy.* (Vietnamese)
    NÓ FUT rain now PRT
    'It will rain now.'

  b. **Sẽ nó mưa bây-giờ đấy.*
    FUT NÓ rain now PRT
    'It will rain now.'

(19) a. *Nó sẽ không có cái bút nào.*
    NÓ FUT NEG exist CLF pen any
    'There will be no pens.'

  b. **Sẽ nó không có cái bút nào.*
    FUT NÓ NEG exist CLF pen any
    'There will be no pens.'

(20) a. *Nó sẽ ngã thằng bé.*
    NÓ FUT fall CLF little
    'A/The boy will fall.'

  b. **Sẽ nó ngã thằng bé.*
    FUT NÓ fall CLF little
    'A/The boy will fall.'

Vietnamese also displays left peripheral scope-discourse markers. For example, *thì* and *là* are associated with topicalized constituents. Following Rizzi (1997), we analyze these markers as the heads of projections whose specifiers host topicalized constituents:

(21) a. *Thằng Nam thì/là sẽ ăn cái này đấy.* (Vietnamese)
    CLF Nam TOP/TOP FUT eat CLF this PRT
    'As for Nam, he will eat this thing.'

  b. *Cái này thì/là thằng Nam sẽ ăn đấy.*
    CLF this TOP/TOP CLF Nam FUT eat PRT
    'As for this thing, Nam will eat it.'

  c. *Lúc khác thì/là thằng Nam sẽ ăn cái này đấy.*
    time other TOP/TOP CLF Nam FUT eat CLF this PRT
    'At another time, Nam will eat this thing.'

As illustrated in (22), in its expletive use, *nó* remains lower than the left-peripheral markers *thì* and *là*:

3 Expletives and speaker-related meaning

(22) a. (*nó) Trên bàn (*nó) thì/là (nó) sẽ không có cái bút nào
NÓ On table NÓ TOP/TOP NÓ FUT NEG exist clf pen any
(Vietnamese)

'On the table, there will be no pens.'

In addition, *nó* cannot occur to the left of overt pre-verbal subjects, be they referential DPs or personal pronouns:

(23) *Nó thằng Nam/tao/mày sẽ gặp Hòa ngày-mai. (Vietnamese)
NÓ CLF Nam/I/you FUT meet Hòa tomorrow

'Nam/I/you will meet Hòa tomorrow.'

From the distributional data, we conclude that *nó* occupies a position in the highest portion of the inflectional layer, immediately dominated by the left-peripheral topic projection:

(24) thì$_{[Topic]}$ > là$_{[Topic]}$ > nó > sẽ$_{[Future]}$ > đã$_{[Perfect]}$ > đang$_{[durative]}$ > VP

Assuming that *nó* occupies a high position in the inflectional domain, two avenues can be envisaged to identify the nature of its position: one explores the subject properties of *nó*, the other explores its speaker-related discourse properties. We discuss these in turn.

The specificity effect of *nó* and the fact that it anchors the proposition to the speaker's context provides additional empirical support that, while non-referential, expletives can encode speaker-oriented meaning. Pursuing this line of thinking, *nó* could be associated with a high discourse-related functional projection in the IP domain which encodes *point of view*. This conclusion would be close to that reached for DS *ello* by Gupton & Lowman (2014). It also implies that a high projection in the IP-layer may convey discourse-related functions that are otherwise instantiated in the left periphery.

However, any account of the syntactic position of *nó* has to capture the fact that, besides the semantic contribution, *nó* is in complementary distribution with pre-verbal subjects, as illustrated in (23). This suggest that *nó* retains some subject properties and could be related to the hypothesis that there is a specialized subject position in the inflectional domain with a subject of predication feature. This projection attracts referential subjects in a number of cases, yielding a structure like (25):

(25) [$_{IP}$ ... DP$_{i\,[+subject\text{-}of\text{-}predication]}$ ... [$_{vP}$ ... t$_i$ ...]]

In a number of languages, however, thetic predicative structures leave the subject in-situ, without attracting it to the high IP-field. To capture the complementary distribution of pre-verbal subjects and *nó*, one might propose that *nò* appears only in thetic structure where the referential subject is either absent or left in-situ and that in these structures *nó* occupies the pre-verbal position, namely the position occupied by the referential subject in structures like (25).

Rizzi (2006) relates the 'subject of predication' property in (25) to a specialized projection for the subject, SubjP, reinterpreting the EPP feature standardly associated with T in terms of a Subject Criterion. One might then propose that *nó* is located in SubjP and assume that in Vietnamese Subj may encode specificity (in a way that is reminiscent of Kiss 1996 and Cardinaletti 2004).

5 West Flemish *tet*

In this section we turn to another non-referential element which is formally related to a pronoun and which might at first sight be labeled as 'expletive': pleonastic particle *tet* in West Flemish (WF), which is not a pro-drop language. Like Finnish *sitä*, DS *ello* and Vietnamese *nó*, the element will be shown to occupy a high position in the inflectional domain and, like DS *ello* and Vietnamese *nó*, it will be shown to convey discourse-related meaning.

In contrast with Vietnamese *nó*, however, WF *tet* does not show a complementary distribution with any type of overt subjects: it is compatible with all finite clauses[7] and can co-occur with both lexical subjects and the existential expletive *er*. As illustrated by (26), in finite sentences with a full DP subject, *tet* can be inserted to the immediate left of the canonical subject position. In all instances, *tet* is optional. In the contemporary WF dialect described here, the form *tet* does not have any referential use.

(26) a. *Morgen   goa (tet) Valère niet kommen.*   (WF)
       Tomorrow goes TET Valere not come
       'Tomorrow Valère is not coming.'

   b. *... dat (tet) Valere nie goa kommen*
       ... that TET Valère not goes come
       '...that Valère isn't coming.'

---

[7]For detailed discussion see also Haegeman 2008. *Tet* is compatible with infinitival clauses that allow an overt nominative subject. For reasons of space we cannot discuss this here.

The nature of the form *tet* is unclear but it merits some discussion. De Vogelaer (2005: 209–210) speculates that it may derive from a strong masculine or neuter pronoun (see De Vogelaer & Devos 2008). Instead of *tet*, other Flemish dialects and the regional variety of Flemish referred to as the *tussentaal* (De Caluwe et al. 2013) deploy a strong form of the nominative masculine pronoun *hij*, a form which definitely has a clear co-existing referential use (De Vogelaer & Devos 2008; Guéron & Haegeman 2012). For reasons of space, these alternative forms are not discussed in this paper but for completeness'sake we illustrate the use of *hij* with some examples attested in the informal spoken language by a Brabant speaker (27a) and a Ghent speaker (27b):

(27) a. *We moeten wij uitprikken en dat telt hij niet mee.* (WF)
we must we logout and that counts *hij* not with.
'We have to log out and that does not count.'

b. *Dat kan hij later ook.*
that can *hij* later too
'We can do that later too.'

Our discussion focuses on the use of *tet* in the WF dialect of Lapscheure. §5.1 discusses its syntactic position. §5.2 turns to its interpretive effect. §5.3 discusses the syntax of *tet* and §5.4 briefly turns to its development.

5.1 The distribution of *tet*

West Flemish is not a pro-drop language in the standard sense[8] and the language systematically deploys expletive subjects. (28a) illustrates weather verbs, (28b) illustrates extraposed subject clauses, (28c) and (28d) illustrate existential patterns. As a generalization, indefinite subjects in WF cannot occupy the canonical subject position and expletive insertion is obligatory, including in transitive patterns (28d):

(28) a. *Vrydag goat = t regenen.* (WF)
Friday goes it rain
'It is going to rain on Friday.'

b. *T'is nie woar dat ze vrijdag moet werken.*
it is not true that she Friday must work
'It is not true that she must work on Friday.'

---

[8]If subject clitics are the spell out of agreement features on C or on V (Bennis & Haegeman 1984), one might argue that WF has a null subject.

    c. *kpeinzen dat=ter   veel   volk   goat kommen.*
       I think   that there much people will come
       'I think that many people will come.'

    d. *kpeinzen dan=   der   veel   studenten dienen boek goan kopen.*
       I think   that.PL there many students that   book will buy
       'I think that many students will buy that book.'

The element *tet* can be inserted in all finite clauses, in embedded clauses (29a,b), in non-subject-initial V2 root clauses (29c,d) and in subject-initial V2 root clauses (29d):

(29)   a. *Ik peinzen dat tet Valere vrydag moet werken.*   (WF)
         I think   that TET Valere Friday must work
         'I think that Valery must work on Friday.'

       b. *Oa tet Valere vrydag moet werken...*
         if   TET Valere Friday must work...
         'If Valery must work on Friday...'

       c. *Woar is tet menen paraplu?*
         Where is TET my   umbrella
         'Where is my umbrella?'

       d. *Vrydag moet tet Valere werken.*
         Friday must TET Valere work
         'On Friday Valery must work.'

       e. *Valère moet tet vrydag werken.*
         Valère must TET Friday work
         'Valery must work on Friday.'

The distribution of *tet* is not sensitive to the nature of the subject, in particular it can co-occur with a DP subject (29), with a clitic subject (30a), with a clitic subject doubled by a full pronominal subject (30b), in sentences with expletive subjects with weather verbs (30c), in extraposition patterns with expletive *t* (30d), as well as in existential sentences with expletive *der* (30e). In the dialect described (cf. De Vogelaer & Devos 2008), *tet* cannot itself take on the function of the expletive, omission of the expletives in (30c–e) systematically leads to ungrammaticality:

(30)   a. *Oa=ze tet vrydag moet werken ...*   (WF)
         if=she TET Friday must work

b. *Oa=ze tet zie vrydag moet werken ...*
   if=she TET she Friday must work
   'If she must work on Friday...'

c. *oat=*(t) tet vrydag regent ...*
   if=it   TET Friday rains
   'if it rains on Friday...'

d. *oat=*(t) tet woar is dat=ze vrydag moet werken ...*
   if=it   TET true is that=she Friday must work
   'If it's true that she must work on Friday...'

e. *oat=*(der) tet veel volk komt...*
   if=there TET much people comes...
   'If there are many people coming...'

The occurrence of *tet* is independent of the nature of the predicate, it is compatible with all types of predicates including, for instance, transitive patterns with subjects in the canonical subject position:

(31) *dat tet Valère dat niet gezeid eet*   (WF)
      that TET Valère that not said has

Linearly, *tet* occupies a fixed position: it follows the (agreeing) complementizer and any subject (or object) clitics that may have adjoined to that, and it immediately precedes the canonical subject position. Importantly, apart from the object clitics *t*, *ze* and *der*, *tet* is the only constituent that can separate the complementizer from the definite subject. Interjections and discourse particles or adverbial adjuncts cannot be inserted in this position:

(32) a. * *Oa toch Valere moet werken...*   (WF)
            if PART Valere must work...

     b. * *Oa vrydag Valere moet werken...*
            if Friday Valere must work...

Nor can such elements separate *tet* from the complementizer (33a,b) or from the canonical subject (33c,d):

(33) a. * *Oa toch/vrydag tet Valere moet werken...*   (WF)
            if PART/Friday TET Valere must work...

     b. * *Oa tet toch/vrydag Valere moet werken...*
            if TET PART/Friday Valere must work...

In root clauses, *tet* immediately follows the inflected verb from which it can only be separated by clitics. In non subject-initial V2 (34a) *tet* precedes the definite DP subject, to which it is adjacent. In subject-initial V2 sentences (34b) *tet* follows the finite verb (see van Craenenbroeck & Haegeman 2007 for the relevance of these data for the analysis of V2):

(34) a. *Vrydag moet (*toch) tet (*toch) Valere werken.* (WF)
 Friday must (*PART) TET (*PART) Valere work
 'Friday, Valère has to work.'

 b. *Valere moet (*toch) tet (toch) vrydag werken.*
 Valere must (*PART) TET (PART) Friday work
 'Friday, Valère has to work.'

5.2 The interpretation of *tet*

The element *tet* lacks referential content and co-occurs with any kind of subject (Haegeman 2008). Unlike Finnish *sitä*, but like DS *ello* and Vietnamese *nó*, *tet* makes an interpretive contribution to the clause by narrowing down the contextualization possibilities for the utterance. However, the semantic contribution of *tet* is not identical to that of *nó*. While the Vietnamese expletive relates to the speaker's epistemic state, *tet* introduces speaker-related emphasis and contrasts the containing utterance with the discourse. By inserting *tet*, the speaker signals that the propositional content of the utterance containing *tet* conflicts with some contextually salient assumptions. For example, the *wh*-question in (35a) asks for the identity of a person. The unmarked answer to (35a) is (35b). (35c), with *tet*, will be a felicitous answer to (35a) if, for some reason, Valère's presence is unexpected to the speaker and conflicts with his discourse background:

(35) a. *Wien is dadde?* (WF)
 who is that
 'Who's that?'

 b. *Dat is Valère.*
 that is Valère
 'That's Valère.'

 c. *Dat is tet Valère!*
 that is TET Valère
 'That's Valère!'

3 Expletives and speaker-related meaning

Recall that *tet* is never obligatory. The conflict in contextualization need not be encoded, or the speaker may achieve the effect differently, for instance by stressing *Valère* in (35b).

(29c), repeated here as (36), illustrates the same point: without *tet*, it is a neutral question about the location of the speaker's umbrella, with *tet* the question is appropriate if the umbrella is unexpectedly missing:

(36)   Woar is (tet) menen paraplu?   (WF))
       where is TET my   umbrella
       /glt 'Where is my umbrella?'

Given its discourse function, one might be inclined to assimilate *tet* to discourse-related adverbs, particles, or interjections. However, as we have discussed, such elements are distributionally different.

5.3 The syntax of *tet*

Because *tet* to some extent alternates with focal stress, one might associate it with the left peripheral FocP (Rizzi 1997). This is not plausible, though, because *tet* occurs in *wh*-questions (36). If the *wh*-constituent *woar* ('where') occupies the specifier of the root FocP, the position of *tet* must be lower than the left-peripheral FocP. *Tet* follows the complementizer and it precedes the definite subject DP. These data suggest that *tet* occupies a high IP-related functional position. If definite DP subjects occupy the canonical subject position (i.e. the specifier of TP or SubjP), the functional projection hosting *tet*, FP, must immediately dominate the projection hosting the subject. The fact that *tet* occurs to the right of clitic subjects follows if these are cliticized to the C-domain, as is commonly assumed. (37) is a schematic representation:

(37)   [$_{CP}$ [$_C$ da] [$_{FP}$ tet [$_F$] [$_{TP}$ Valere vrydag moet werken]]]

All V2 clauses are derived by finite V movement to C (van Craenenbroeck & Haegeman 2007). It follows from (37) that in V2 clauses *tet* will be adjacent to the finite verb in V2 sentences, from which it can only be separated by those clitics that can themselves right-adjoin to the finite verb in C.[9] In line with van Craenenbroeck & Haegeman (2007), van Craenenbroeck & van Koppen (2012);

---

[9] An alternative is that the relevant projection in the low left periphery, but this approach would have important ramifications. In particular, if *tet* is in a left-peripheral projection, the complementizer *dat* and the finite verb in V2 patterns must themselves occupy a higher left peripheral position, the nature of which would need to be clarified.

Guéron & Haegeman (2012) propose that FP is Uriagereka's FP, (Uriagereka 2004; Carrilho 2008), and following Grohmann (2000) they reinterpret the projection as one encoding Point of View:

(38)   CP > FinP > PovP > TP

5.4 Cross-speaker variation and the nature of *tet*

Though, informally speaking, *tet* appears to be located somewhere in a 'subject zone' of the clause, and is sandwiched between the clitic subject and the full pronominal subject (30b), *tet* cannot be assimilated to the expletives which satisfy a formal requirement because such expletives in fact co-occur with *tet*.

Note that the wide distribution of *tet* or its analogue *hij* in some varieties of Flemish, including that described here, is not shared by all speakers. Based on a native speaker questionnaire, De Vogelaer & Devos (2008: 272, 278) speculate that the current distribution of *tet/hij* is a recent extension which has taken it beyond its original doubling function. The strong pronouns originally served as 'topic markers' used to double third person clitic subjects, including expletive subjects. At this stage, the doubling pronoun matched the clitic pronoun in gender and number. The pronouns could also be used to double an expletive clitic subject. In their extended use, the elements *hij, (t)jij* or *tet* have come to be used more liberally and co-occur with all subjects, regardless of their gender and number. With the extension, the restriction by person and number features postulated for the topic marking function of the doubling pronouns has been lost. We speculate that it is at this point that the pronominal elements lost their phi features, i.e. their nominal properties. With the loss of the nominal properties, then, the element has acquired a new discourse function and a wider distribution.

6 Recycling expletives as discourse particles

In this paper we started out from the fairly standard view of expletive elements as pronominals which have lost their referential content and have become place holders for the subjects in contexts in which a formal requirement imposes the presence of a subject and in which no suitable DP subject can fulfill the requirement. The standard view on expletives leads to a set of generalizations: (i) they are generally unexpected in pro-drop languages, (ii) they are semantically vacuous, (iii) they are not optional.

In our paper, we investigate a set of pronominal forms that have lost their referential meaning and might at first sight be analyzed as expletives. The data discussed lead to a more nuanced view of the nature of expletives, in which the generalizations outlined above seem to be challenged. With respect to the correlation between the availability of expletives and the pro-drop nature of a language, there are cases, like Finnish *sitä,* where a pro-drop language may still employ expletive elements in a subset of contexts, if needed because of EPP-requirements.

In addition, the case of DS *ello* illustrates a class of expletives or expletive-like elements without referential content which, though retaining the distributional properties of expletives, seems to have acquired a discourse-related meaning. Pursuing this point, we have discussed two additional instances of pronominal forms that have lost their referential meaning and seem to have acquired a discourse function.

Vietnamese *nó* is a pronominal form without referential content that has acquired some discourse-related meaning: *nó* serves to narrow down the contextualization properties of the utterance that contains it. WF *tet* originates as a strong pronominal form, it has lost its referential value and it has the discourse function of constraining the contextualization of the containing utterance to those contexts where the utterance's propositional content conflicts with the speakers' prevalent assumptions.

Since it is in complementary distribution with lexical subjects and is restricted to certain predicate types, we proposed that Vietnamese *nó* is located in a dedicated subject projection that encodes specificity and which is otherwise occupied by lexical subjects. Differently, WF *tet,* while originating as a strong pronominal doubler of, among others, an expletive subject clitic, and while being located in what appears to be the subject portion of the clause, never takes on any subject function and never competes with a subject constituent for the same position. We propose that *tet* appears in an optional position encoding *point of view* which is not subject-related.

The data we have discussed here lead to a more complex picture of the nature of expletives and their function in the grammar. The elements we have discussed here all share the property that they are pronominal forms having lost referential value, the hallmark of the prototypical expletive, but while the prototypical expletive has a purely formal function, DS *ello,* Vietnamese *nó* and Flemish *tet* are pronominal elements which, having lost their referential meaning, seem to have acquired discourse-related functions.

Ciro Greco, Liliane Haegeman & Trang Phan

Acknowledgements

We dedicate this paper to Anders Holmberg, whose work on Finnish expletives has sparked our own. Our research was funded by FWO Belgium as part of project 2009-Odysseus-Haegeman-G091409.

Abbreviations

Abbreviations used in this article follow the Leipzig Glossing Rules' instructions for word-by-word transcription, available at: https://www.eva.mpg.de/lingua/pdf/Glossing-Rules.pdf.

The non-standard abbreviation used:

PRT Particle

References

Alexiadou, Artemis & Elena Anagnostopoulou. 1998. Parametrizing AGR: Word order, V-movement and EPP-checking. *Natural Language & Linguistic Theory* 16. 491–539.

Bartra-Kaufmann, Anna. 2011. Recycled neuter expletive pronouns and the nature of the left periphery: Ell and relatives revisited. *Catalan Journal of Linguistics* 10. 185–219.

Bennis, Hans & Liliane Haegeman. 1984. On the status of agreement: COMP and INFL in Flemish dialects. In Wim de Geest & Yvan Putseys (eds.), *Proceedings of the International Conference on Complementation*, 33–53. Dordrecht: Foris.

Bolinger, Dwight. 1977. *Meaning and form*. London: Longman.

Bullock, Barbara & Almeida Jacqueline Toribio. 2009. Reconsidering Dominican Spanish: Data from the rural Cibao. *Revista Internacional de Linguistica Iberoamericana* 14. 49–73.

Cardinaletti, Anna. 2004. Towards a cartography of subject positions. In Luigi Rizzi (ed.), *The structure of CP and IP*, 115–165. New York: Oxford University Press.

Carrilho, Ernestina. 2008. Beyond doubling: Overt expletives in European Portuguese dialects. In Sjef Barbiers, Olaf Koeneman, Marika Lekakou & Margreet van der Ham (eds.), *Microvariation in syntactic doubling*, 302–323. Leiden: Brill.

Chomsky, Noam. 1981. *Lectures on government and binding*. Dordrecht: Foris.

Chomsky, Noam. 1995. *The minimalist program.* Cambridge, MA: MIT Press.

van Craenenbroeck, Jeroen & Liliane Haegeman. 2007. The derivation of subject initial V2. *Linguistic Inquiry* 38. 167–178.

van Craenenbroeck, Jeroen & Marjo van Koppen. 2012. *How to void a phase. Anti-intervention effects with clitic doubling in Dutch dialects.* Ghent/Missouri Complementizer agreement workshop.

Dao, Huy Linh. 2012. Intransitivité scindée, passif et sujet impersonnel en vietnamien. In Jan Radimský (ed.), *Actes du 31e Colloque International sur le Lexique et la Grammaire*, 49–55. České Budějovice: Université de Bohême du Sud à České Budějovice.

De Caluwe, Johan, Steven Delarue, Anne-Sophie Ghyselen & Chloé Lybaert. 2013. *Tussentaal.* Ghent: Academia Press.

De Vogelaer, Gunther. 2005. *Subjects markering in de Nederlandse en Friese dialecten.* Ghent University dissertation.

De Vogelaer, Gunther & Magda Devos. 2008. On geographical adequacy, or: How many types of subject doubling in Dutch. In Sjef Barbiers, Olaf Koeneman, Marika Lekakou & Margreet van der Ham (eds.), *Microvariation in syntactic doubling*, 251–276. Leiden: Brill.

Duffield, Nigel. 2013. Head-First: On the head-initiality of Vietnamese clauses. In Daniel Hole & Elisabeth Löbel (eds.), *Linguistics of Vietnamese: An international survey*, 127–155. Berlin: de Gruyter Mouton.

Farkas, Donka. 2002. Specificity distinction. *Journal of Semantics* 19. 213–243.

Greco, Ciro, Liliane Haegeman & Trang Phan. 2017. On *Nó* an optional expletive in vietnamese. In Federica Cognola & Jan Casalicchio (eds.), *Understanding null subjects: A synchronic and diachronic perspective.* Oxford: OUP.

Grohmann, Kleanthes. 2000. Towards a syntactic understanding of prosodically reduced pronouns. *Theoretical Linguistics* 26. 175–210.

Guéron, Jacqueline & Liliane Haegeman. 2012. Je est un autre. Subject positions, point of view and the neuter pronoun *tet* in West Flemish. In Laura Brugé, Anna Cardinaletti, Giuliana Giusti, Nicola Munaro & Cecilia Poletto (eds.), *Functional heads*, 69–80. Oxford: Oxford University Press.

Gupton, Timothy & Sarah Lowman. 2014. An F projection in Cibeño Dominican Spanish. In Jennifer Amaro, Gillian Lord, Ana de Prada Pérez & Jessi Aaron (eds.), *Proceedings of the 16th Hispanic Linguistics Symposium*, 338–348. Somerville, MA.

Haegeman, Liliane. 2008. Pleonastic tet in West Flemish and the cartography of subject positions. In Sjef Barbiers, Olaf Koeneman, Marika Lekakou & Margreet van der Ham (eds.), *Microvariation in syntactic doubling*, 277–290. Leiden: Brill. DOI:10.1163/9781848550216_010

Hellan, Lars. 1981. On semantic scope. In Frank Heny (ed.), *Ambiguities in intensional contexts*, 47–81. Dordrecht: D. Reidel Publishing Company.

Hinzelin, Marc-Oliver & Georg Kaiser. 2007. El pronombre ello en el léxico del español dominicano. In Wiltrud Mihatsch & Monika Sokol (eds.), *Language contact and language change in the caribbean and beyond / lenguas en contacto y cambio lingüístico en el caribe y más allá*, 171–188. Frankfurt am Main: Peter Lang.

Holmberg, Anders. 2005. Is there a little pro? Evidence from Finnish. *Linguistic Inquiry* 36(4). 533–564.

Holmberg, Anders. 2010. Null subject parameters. In Theresa Biberauer, Anders Holmberg, Ian Roberts & Michelle Sheehan (eds.), *Parametric variation: Null subjects in minimalist theory*, 88–124. Cambridge: Cambridge University Press.

Holmberg, Anders & Urpo Nikanne. 2002. Expletives, subjects, and topics in Finnish. In Peter Svenonius (ed.), *Subjects, expletives, and the EPP*, 71–106. Oxford: Oxford University Press.

Holmberg, Anders & Ian Roberts. 2009. Introduction: Parameters in minimalist theory. In Theresa Biberauer, Anders Holmberg, Ian Roberts & Michelle Sheehan (eds.), *Parametric variation: Null subjects in minimalist theory*, 1–57. Cambridge: Cambridge University Press.

Huang, C. T. James. 1984. On the distribution and reference of empty pronouns. *Linguistic Inquiry* 15. 531–574.

Kiss, Katalin. 1995. Introduction. In Katalin Kiss (ed.), *Discourse configurational languages*, 3–27. New York: Oxford University Press.

Kiss, Katalin. 1996. Two subject positions in English. *The Linguistic Review* 13. 119–142.

Ladusaw, William. 1994. Thetic and categorical, stage and individual, weak and strong. In Mandy Harvey & Lynn Santelmann (eds.), *Proceedings of SALT IV*, 220–229. Ithaca, NY: Cornell University, Department of Modern Languages & Linguistics.

Martín Zorraquino, Maria Antonia & José Portóles Lázaro. 1999. Los marcadores del discurso. In Ignacio Bosque & Violeta Demonte (eds.), *Gramática descriptiva de la lengua española*, 4051–4213. Madrid: Espasa.

Martínez Sanz, Cristina. 2011. *Null and overt subjects in a variable system: The case of Dominican Spanish*. University of Ottawa dissertation.

Mohr, Sabine. 2005. *Clausal architecture and subject positions: Impersonal constructions in the Germanic languages*. Amsterdam: John Benjamins.

Muñoz Pérez, Carlos. 2014. Dominican ello as a non-deleted null expletive. *An International Journal of Hispanic Linguistics* 3. 155–161.

Newmeyer, Frederick J. 2005. *Possible and probable languages.* Oxford: Oxford University Press.

Nguyen, Van Hiep & Hoang Thuy Nguyen. 2011. *Về chủ ngữ giả trong tiếng Việt (Dummy subjects in Vietnamese).* Paper presented at International Conference on Linguistics Training and Research in Vietnam, 11th November, Hà Nội.

Otheguy, Ricardo, Ana Zentella & David Livert. 2007. Language and dialect contact in Spanish in New York: Toward the formation of a speech community. *Language* 83. 770–802.

Phan, Trang. 2013. *Syntax of Vietnamese aspect.* University of Sheffield dissertation.

Rizzi, Luigi. 1982. *Issues in Italian syntax.* Berlin: Walter de Gruyter.

Rizzi, Luigi. 1997. The fine structure of the left periphery. In Liliane Haegeman (ed.), *Elements of grammar: Handbook in generative syntax*, 281–337. Dordrecht: Kluwer.

Rizzi, Luigi. 2006. On the form of chains: Criterial positions and ECP effects. In Lisa Lai-Shen Cheng & Norbert Corver (eds.), *Wh-movement: Moving on*, 97–134. Cambridge: MIT Press.

Rizzi, Luigi & Ur Shlonsky. 2007. Strategies of subject extraction. In Uli Sauerland & Hans-Martin Gärtner (eds.), *Interfaces + recursion = language? Chomsky's Minimalism and the view from Syntax-Semantics*, 115–116. Berlin: Mouton de Gruyter.

Uriagereka, Juan. 2004. *A peripheral pleonastic in Western Iberian.* Paper presented at "Expletive Subjects in Romance and Germanic Languages". Konstanz, November 2004.

Chapter 4

Places

Tarald Taraldsen
University of Tromsø

> In Norwegian, a locative PP can occur as the subject of the copula just in case the complement of the copula is a relative construction with *sted* or *place*, both meaning 'place', as its head noun. I examine the properties of this construction and ultimately propose an analysis based on a specific view of locative PPs as well as a novel assumption about the ways A-movement and A'-movement may interact.

1 Introduction

In this article, I will look at some curious properties of Norwegian sentences like those in (1–2):[1]

(1) I Tromsø er et bra sted å bo.
 in Tromsø is a nice place to live.

(2) I Tromsø er et sted det er morsomt å arbeide.
 in Tromsø is a place it is fun to work

I will present evidence that the initial PPs in (1–2) are in the usual subject position. After rejecting an alternative analysis in §3, I will also argue that these PPs are derived subjects raised to the subject position of the copula from inside

---

[1]The meaning is not 'In Tromsø there is a nice place to live' which would be the meaning of (i):

(i) I Tromsø er det et bra sted å bo.
 in Tromsø is it a nice place to live.

the relative clause[2] and will discuss the theoretical issues that arise from this (§4).

A key fact about sentences like (1–2) is that the head noun of the relative construction must be *sted* or *plass*, which both means 'place'.[3] Correspondingly, a key element in the analysis I suggest, is the special status of these nouns in the formation of locative expressions.

2 Some basic facts

I will begin by identifying the special properties that sentences like (1–2) have.

2.1 Spatial PPs as subjects of copulative sentences

In (1–2), the locative PP *i Tromsø* 'in Tromsø' is linked by the copula to a predicate consisting of a relative clause headed by a noun:

(3) I Tromsø er et bra sted å bo.
     in Tromsø is a nice place to live

(4) I Tromsø er et sted det er morsomt å arbeide.
     in Tromsø is a place it is fun   to work

The usual tests suggest that the PP is really the subject:

(5) a. Derfor   er i Tromsø blitt   et bra sted å bo.
       therefore is in Tromsø become a nice place to live

    b. Nå   er i Tromsø blitt   et sted det er morsomt å arbeide.
       now is in Tromsø become a place it is fun   to work

---

[2]I take *et bra sted å bo* in (1) to contain an infinitival relative clause, ignoring the question how such constructions relate to Tough Movement constructions like *Dette stedet er bra å bo på* – 'This place is nice to live in'. The fact that the stranded preposition cannot be left out in the Tough Movement constructions (see the comments on example 29 in §4.1) suggests that the relation cannot be too tight.

[3]Plass can replace sted in (1–2), as in (i–ii), and all other grammatical examples in the text:

(i) I Tromsø er en bra plass å bo.
     in Tromsø is a nice place to live

(ii) I Tromsø er en plass det er morsomt å arbeide.
     in Tromsø is a place it is fun   to work

(6) a. *I Tromsø synes å være et bra sted å bo.*
   in Tromsø seems to be   a nice place to live

   b. *I Tromsø påstås   å være et sted det er morsomt å arbeide.*
   in Tromsø is.claimed to be   a place it   is fun   to work

(7) a. *I Tromsø mener vi (*at) er et bra sted å bo.*
   in Tromsø think we (*that) is a nice place to live

   b. *I Tromsø synes vi (*at) er et sted det er morsomt å arbeide.*
   in Tromsø think we (*that) is a place it is fun   to work

The examples in (5) show that the PP appears between an auxiliary in the V2-position and a participle just like ordinary subjects. Those in (6) show PPs undergoing raising-to-subject, and the examples in (7) illustrate the *that*-trace effect triggered by extraction of PPs like those in (1–2).[4]

2.2 The importance of the relative clause

The relative clause is essential:

(8) **I Tromsø er et bra sted nord for Polarsirkelen.*
   in Tromsø is a nice place north of the Arctic Circle

(8) contrasts with (9), where the subject is not a PP:

(9) *Tromsø er et bra sted nord for Polarsirkelen.*
   Tromsø is a nice place north of the Arctic Circle

2.3 The importance of the head noun

It is also essential that the head noun of the relative clause be *sted* or *plass* (both 'place'):

(10) a. **I Tromsø er en bra by å bo.*
   in Tromsø is a nice city to live

   b. **I Tromsø er en by det er morsomt å arbeide.*
   in Tromsø is a city it is fun   to work

---

[4]Norwegian speakers show variation with respect to *that*-t effect. Speakers who tolerate at 'that' in *Hvem tror du at har vunnet?* 'who think you that has won etc., should also allow it in (7).

This is presumably related to the fact that *sted* and *plass* are the only nouns that can form a locative adjunct without a (overt) preposition:

(11) a. *Vi arbeidet (på) det samme stedet/den samme plassen i tre år.*
we worked (at) the same place for three years

b. *Vi har nettopp besøkt et sted/en plass vi bodde (på) i 1981.*
we have just visited a place we lived (at) in 1981

(12) a. *Vi arbeidet *(i) den samme byen i tre år.*
we worked *(in) the same city for three years

b. *Vi har nettopp besøkt en by vi bodde *(i) for ti år siden.*
we have just visited a city we lived *(in) ten years ago

2.4 No stranded preposition in the relative clause

If a stranded preposition is inserted into the relative clause in (10), just as in (12b), the outcome is still ungrammatical, in contrast with (14):

(13) a. **I Tromsø er en bra by å bo i.*
in Tromsø is a nice city to live in.

b. **I Tromsø er en by det er morsomt å arbeide i.*
in Tromsø is a city it is fun to work in.

(14) a. *Tromsø er en bra by å bo i.*
Tromsø is a nice city to live in.

b. *Tromsø er en by det er morsomt å arbeide i.*
Tromsø is a city it is fun to work in.

Likewise, the stranded preposition, which is optional in (11b), makes (1–2) ungrammatical:

(15) a. **I Tromsø er et bra sted å bo på.*
in Tromsø is a nice place to live at

b. **I Tromsø er et sted det er morsomt å arbeide på.*
in Tromsø is a place it is fun to work in

In this case, the subject must lose its preposition exactly as in (14) and (9):[5]

---

[5]These sentences are also fine without a stranded preposition in the relative clause, just like (1–2):

(16) a. *Tromsø er et bra sted å bo på.*
     Tromsø is a nice place to live at
   b. *Tromsø er et sted det er morsomt å arbeide på.*
     Tromsø is a place it is fun to work at

2.5 Summary

The data I have reviewed, gives rise to the following questions:

(17) a. Why must the predicative noun be *sted* or *plass* when the subject of the copula is a PP?
   b. Why must there be a relative clause modifying the predicative noun?
   c. Why can't there be a stranded preposition in the relative clause?

In the next section, I will sketch two ways of providing answers to these questions. Both ultimately turn on where PPs can be introduced by external merge, but make different assumptions as to where exactly that is.

3 Two analytical options

The first analysis suggested below answers question (17a) by saying that when the subject of the copula is a PP, the complement of the copula must be a PP as well. Then, the contrast between (1–2) and sentences like (10) follows, if *sted* and *plass* license a silent locative P, but no other noun does, as suggested by the contrast between (11) and (12). However, this account requires untenable auxiliary assumptions to provide answers to (17b–17c). The second analysis answers questions (17b–17c) directly by claiming that a PP subject must be a derived subject, but an answer to 17a will only be forthcoming in §4.

3.1 Categorial matching

Suppose we take the grammaticality of (18) without *på* to mean that *sted* and *plass* allow a locative preposition to be silent:

(i) a. *Tromsø er et bra sted å bo.*
     Tromsø is a nice place to live
   b. *Tromsø er et sted det er morsomt å arbeide.*
     Tromsø is a place it is fun to work

(18) a. *Vi arbeidet (på) det samme stedet/den samme plassen i tre år.*
we worked (at) the same place for three years

b. *Vi har nettopp besøkt et sted/en plass vi bodde (på) i 1981.*
we have just visited a place we lived (at) in 1981

In (19), P represents the silent locative preposition:

(19) a. *Vi arbeidet P det samme stedet/den samme plassen i tre år.*
we worked the same place for three years

b. *Vi har nettopp besøkt et sted/en plass vi bodde P i 1981.*
we have just visited a place we lived in 1981

Then, the obligatoriness of the overt preposition in (12) may be taken to show that only *sted* and *plass* license a silent P:

(12) a. *Vi arbeidet *(i) den samme byen i tre år.*
we worked *(in) the same city for three years

b. *Vi har nettopp besøkt en by vi bodde *(i) for ti år siden.*
we have just visited a city we lived *(in) ten years ago

Correspondingly, (1–2) might be taken to contain silent prepositions too, as in (20):

(20) a. *I Tromsø er [$_{PP}$ P et bra sted å bo.]*
in Tromsø is a nice place to live

b. *I Tromsø er [$_{PP}$ P et sted det er morsomt å arbeide.]*
in Tromsø is a place it is fun to work

But (10) may not:

(10) a. ** I Tromsø er en bra by å bo.*
in Tromsø is a nice city to live

b. ** I Tromsø er en by det er morsomt å arbeide.*
in Tromsø is a city it is fun to work

(21) a. ** I Tromsø er [$_{PP}$ P en bra by å bo].*
in Tromsø is a nice city to live

b. ** I Tromsø er [$_{PP}$ P en by det er morsomt å arbeide].*
in Tromsø is a city it is fun to work

4 Places

Then, the ungrammaticality of (10) might be due to a mismatch between the category of the subject and the category of the complement of the copula:

(22) a. [$_{PP}$ I Tromsø] er [$_{DP}$ en bra by å bo].
      in Tromsø is   a nice city to live

b. [$_{PP}$ I Tromsø] er [$_{DP}$ en by det er morsomt å arbeide].
   in Tromsø is   a city it is fun   to work

It should be clear that this approach does not presuppose that *er* 'is' has the semantics of an "identificational copula". In fact, *er* is to be regarded as an identity function passing on the denotation of its complement. The complement of *er*, then, is the predicate that would have to be applicable to the subject, but the type of things the predicate applies to may be determined by its syntactic category. Thus, the analysis we are examining is ultimately based on the assumption that the syntactic categories DP and PP correspond to different semantic types.[6]

But to answer question (17b), we must also assume that a preposition cannot be merged to the complement of the copula so that (8) cannot be analyzed as in (22):

(8) *I Tromsø er et bra sted nord for Polarsirkelen.
    in Tromsø is a nice place north of the Arctic Circle

(23) [$_{PP}$ I Tromsø] er [$_{PP}$ P et bra sted nord for Polarsirkelen].
     in Tromsø is   a nice place north of the Arctic Circle

Then, (1-2) must be derived as indicated in (24):

(24) a. [$_{PP}$ I Tromsø] er [$_{CP}$[$_{PP}$ P et bra sted] å bo P̶P̶].
      in Tromsø is   a nice place to live

b. [$_{PP}$ I Tromsø] er [$_{CP}$[$_{PP}$ P et sted] det er morsomt å arbeide P̶P̶].
   in Tromsø is   a place it is fun   to work

If so, we also have answer to question (17c). Given the stranded preposition, the sentences in (15) must parsed as in (25):

(15) a. *I Tromsø er et bra sted å bo på.
        in Tromsø is a nice place to live at

---

[6]Sentences like *Tromsø er i Nord Norge* - Tromsø is in Northern Norway - are fine. In these, *er* can be replaced with *ligger* 'lies' or 'is situated', an option not available when the subject is a PP as in (1-2) or when *er* has an adjectival complement. That is, *er* 'is' can also be assigned a meaning such that its complement is not predicated of the subject the way it is in (1-2).

b. * I Tromsø er et sted   det er morsomt å arbeide på.
   in Tromsø is a place   it is fun   to work   in

(25) a. [_PP_ I Tromsø] er [_CP_[_DP_ et bra sted] å bo [_PP_ på ~~DP~~]].
        in Tromsø is   a nice place to live   at

   b. [_PP_ I Tromsø] er [_CP_[_DP_ et sted] det er morsomt å arbeide [_PP_ på ~~DP~~]].
      in Tromsø is   a place it is fun   to work   at

But the derivation indicated in (24) would be a "head raising" derivation of the relative constructions where the raised constituent is a PP, and although the head raising analysis may be justified when the head is a NP or DP (see §4.3 below), extending it to PPs raises a number of problems. In particular, it begs the question why the silent P in (24) cannot be replaced with an overt preposition:

(26) a. * I Tromsø er på et bra sted å bo.
        in Tromsø is at a nice place to live

   b. * I Tromsø er på et sted det er morsomt å arbeide.
      in Tromsø is at a place it is fun to work

In fact, head-raising must be allowed to pied-pipe a preposition only when the complement of the preposition is a wh-phrase. Thus, (27a) is acceptable (in a formal register), but (27b) is not:

(27) a. Vi fant   et sted   på hvilket det er morsomt å arbeide.
         we found a place at which   it is fun   to work

   b. * Vi fant på et sted det er morsomt å arbeide.
         we found at a place it is fun   to work

Hence, the matching account seems to rest on untenable assumptions.

3.2 The subject PP comes from the relative clause

The second line of analysis I will look at, is based on the assumption that a PP may not appear in the subject position of the copula by external merge. This may follow from proposals like those in Kayne (2000: 282–313), which, among other things, are designed to account for subject/object asymmetries with respect to prepositional complementizers.

If so, we are led to conclude that a subject PP is always a derived subject, a PP formed below the subject position and subsequently raised, as in sentences with "locative inversion". But then the PP subject in (1–2) must be a derived subject too.

When we ask where the subject PP in (1–2) comes from, the only possible answer seems to be that it actually has been extracted from the relative clause:

(28) [_PP_ i Tromsø] er [et bra sted å bo ~~PP~~].   =(1)
          in Tromsø is   a nice place to live

This analysis provides a straightforward explanation why (8) and (15) are ungrammatical:

(8)   a. *I Tromsø er et bra sted   nord for Polarsirkelen.
             in Tromsø is a nice place north of the Arctic Circle

(15) a. *I Tromsø er et bra sted å bo på.
             in Tromsø is a nice place to live at.

      b. *I Tromsø er et sted det er morsomt å arbeide på.
             in Tromsø is a place it is fun   to work   in

In (8), there is no position the subject PP could have moved from, since there is no constituent modifiable by a PP. In (15), there is a position modifiable by a PP (the VP headed by *bo* 'live'), but the subject PP cannot have moved from that position, since there is a stranded P. Thus, we have answers to the questions (17b–17c).

On the other hand, the new analysis does not yet provide an answer to question (17a), i.e. it doesn't explain why no other noun can replace *sted* or *plass* in (1–2). It also raises the question how a locative PP manages to raise to the subject position of the copula from inside a relative construction. In the next section, however, I will suggest an answer to this question which also leads to an answer to question (17a).

3.3 Summary

I began this section by sketching an apparently simple account of (1–2) based on categorial matching, This account would provide an answer to question (17b), but cannot answer questions (17a) and (17c) without adding assumptions that were seen to be untenable. Thus, I suggested a different analytical option based on the assumption that the PP subject in (1–2) must be a derived subject moved out of the relative clause. This analysis will be more fully developed in the next section.

Tarald Taraldsen

4 The proposal

To develop the analysis sketched in §3.2, I will first attempt to capture what is special about *sted* and *plass*. This will provide a way of understanding how a locative PP can move out of the relative clause in the derivation of (1–2) just in case the head of the relative construction is *sted* or *plass*.

4.1 What's special about *sted*?

Saying that *sted* and *plass* can be locatives without an overt preposition because they have the unique property of licensing a silent locative preposition, seems to beg the question why exactly only *sted* and *plass* should have this property. There is also an empirical issue. Consider first (29), where the stranded preposition cannot be omitted:

(29) *Dette stedet er bra å bo *(på).*
 this place is nice to live at

(29) with the stranded preposition is simply a Tough Movement construction with a stranded preposition analogous to *This problem is hard to talk about*. But why couldn't (29) without *på* 'at' simply have a stranded silent P instead of *på*?

The answer to that might be that the P cannot remain silent when stranded. But then we have a problem with the following:

(30) a. *Vi besøkte et sted vi hadde bodd i fem år*
 we visited a place we had lived for five years
 b. *Tromsø er et bra sted å bo.*
 Tromsø is a nice place to live.

In these, *sted* originates as (part of) a locative modifier in the relative clause. If *sted* can only be a locative modifier when accompanied by a silent or overt preposition, there must be a silent P in (30) which is either stranded or has been carried along under relativization (assuming for the sake of the argument that the head-raising analysis can be extended to PPs in spite of the problem noted in §3.1). If we conclude from (29) that a stranded preposition cannot be silent, we must also say that the P associated with *sted* actually has been pied-piped in (30). But this runs up against the problem that overt prepositions cannot be pied-piped in this way in sentences otherwise similar to (30):

(31) a. *Vi besøkte en by vi hadde bodd i i fem år.*
 we visited a city we had lived in for five years

b. *Vi besøkte i en by vi hadde bodd i fem år.
   we visited in a city we had lived for five years

This may be due either to the way movement works in the derivation of relatives (that is, a P can be pied-piped only when its complement is a wh-phrase) or to the fact that *besøke* 'visit' selects a DP complement, while relativizing a PP as in (31b) makes it impossible to analyze the relative construction as a DP. Either way, we are now led to conclude that a silent P associated with *sted* in (30) can be neither stranded nor pied-piped. In other words, there cannot be a silent P associated with *sted* in (30).

This leads me to abandon the idea that *sted* and *plass* functioning as locative modifiers must come with a silent P. Instead, I submit that these nouns are able to be locative modifiers without a preposition (silent or otherwise) because they are inherently locative, i.e. because they mean 'place'.

Putting this in slightly more precise terms, I propose that a noun whose meaning is just 'place' can be used as a locative modifier providing a spatial coordinate for an eventuality without needing a preposition to create this relation. This is in fact what we see in (30).

From this point of view, what sets *sted* and *plass* apart from *by* 'city' and other nouns, is that only the former can be pure expressions of location.

4.2 Places and things

Given the preceding, one may well wonder why *sted* ever co-occurs with a locative preposition, as it optionally does:

(32) Vi bodde (på) et sted i Nord-Norge.
      we lived (at) a place in Northern Norway

To approach this question, we should first ask the question what the preposition is actually doing in sentences like (33):

(33) Vi bodde *(i) en by i Nord-Norge.
      we lived *(in) a city in Northern Norway

I have already suggested that a locative preposition is not always needed to license a locative modifier. I will now propose that locative prepositions create a relation between a purely place-denoting noun and another noun. In (30), the other noun is *by*, and I suggest that the structure of *i en by* 'in a city' is roughly as in (34):

Tarald Taraldsen

(34) [STED [i [en by]]]
      place in a city

That is, *i* 'in' assigns a space denoted by silent *sted* in its Spec as the location of the city picked as the denotation of *en by* 'a city'. The difference between *i* 'in' and *på* 'on, at' is that *i* associates this space with the interior of an object denoted by its complement, while *på* associates it with the surface of that object.[7] But the preposition is not otherwise instrumental in creating a locative modifier. Only *sted* is.

Thus, *sted* as a locative modifier does not need a preposition when its denotation is not to be associated with the denotation of another noun phrase. Therefore, (32) without *på* 'at' can be analyzed as in (35), without a silent P:[8]

(35) Vi [vp bodde   [NP et sted i Nord-Norge]].
      we   lived (at)   a place in Northern Norway

The fact that the preposition *på* may nevertheless occur in (32), can then be accounted for by attributing two distinct interpretations to *sted*: It can denote a space, as in (35), but it can also denote a "thing" (located in some space), just like *by* 'city' On the second interpretation, it can only be a locative modifier by having the preposition *på* associating it with a space-denoting STED just as in (34):

(36) Vi [vp bodde [STED [på [NP et sted i Nord-Norge]]].
      we   lived   (at)   a place in Northern Norway

Returning now to the fact that the stranded preposition cannot be omitted in (29), I tentatively suggest that the subject of a Tough Movement construction may denote "things", but not spaces:

(29) Dette stedet er bra å bo *(på).
      this place is nice to live at

Then, *på* is obligatory in (29) for the same reason as in (33).

---

[7] The distribution of *på* 'on, at' vs. *i* 'in' raises additional issues that will be ignored here. For example, place names denoting cities in the inland or islands admit *på*, e.g. *på Hamar, på Island* 'on Iceland', while names of coastal cities require *i*, e.g. *i Oslo, i Tromsø*.

[8] I abstract away from V2 movement and the question whether *et* 'a' is a D or part of NP, which seems immaterial at this point.

4.3 The head-raising analysis of relative constructions

To complete the analysis of sentences like (30) and explain the contrast between (30) and (37), we need to adopt the head-raising analysis of relatives advocated by Vergnaud (1974) and Kayne (1994) among others.

(30) a. *Vi besøkte et sted vi hadde bodd i fem år.*
 we visited a place we had lived for five years

 b. *Tromsø er et bra sted å bo.*
 Tromsø is a nice place to live

(37) a. *Vi besøkte en by vi hadde bodd *(i) i fem år.*
 we visited a place we had lived in for five years

 b. *Tromsø er et bra sted å bo *(i).*
 Tromsø is a nice place to live in

The contrast between (30) and (37) follows immediately on the head-raising analysis:

(38)

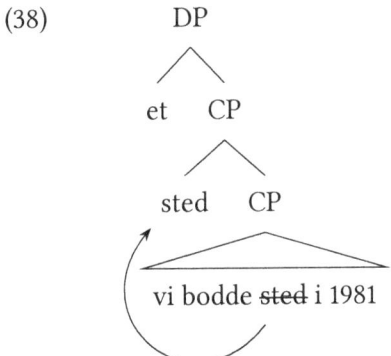

(39)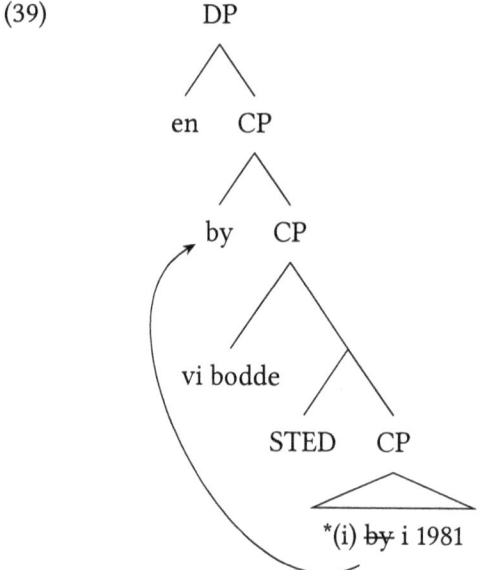

But on a derivation involving operator-movement, the difference between *by* and location-denoting *sted* is neutralized at the point of the derivation where the decision to merge a preposition must be made:

(40)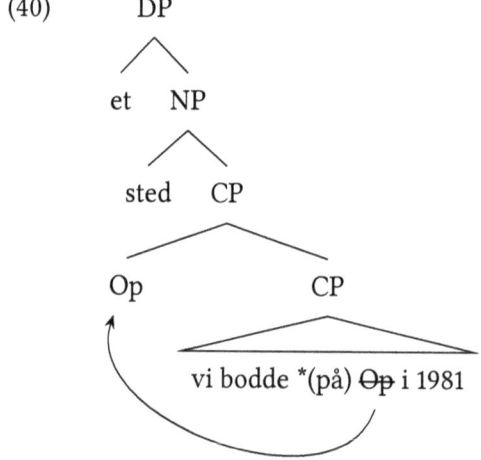

(41)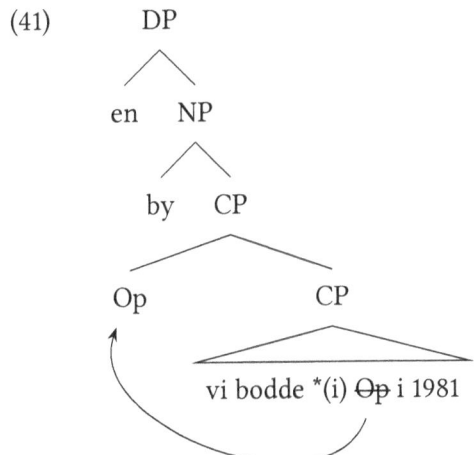

The head-raising analysis of relatives will be crucial in what follows.

4.4 Where does *sted* come from in (1–2)?

On the head-raising account of relative constructions, the analysis sketched in §3.2 seems to run up against a serious problem: Where does *sted* 'place', the head of the relative clause in (1–2), come from, if the subject PP originates as a locative modifier inside the relative clause?:

(1) I Tromsø er et bra sted å bo.
    in Tromsø is a nice place to live

(2) I Tromsø er et sted det er morsomt å arbeide.
    in Tromsø is a place it is fun to work

In particular, it would seem as if *sted* and *i Tromsø* cannot both start out as locative modifiers in the relative clause.

But in §4.2, I proposed that a silent STED occurs inside locative PPs as in (42):

(42) [STED [i [Tromsø]]]
     place in Tromsø

Taking STED to be a regular syntactic object in (42), in fact a noun phrase, we can now entertain the possibility that movement can apply to it. If so, the structure of (1–2) at a point of the derivation where the PP has not yet raised to the subject position, may be as in (43), still assuming the head-raising analysis of relatives:[9]

(43) a. *er [$_{DP}$ et bra [$_{CP}$ **sted** [å bo [~~sted~~ [i [Tromsø]]]]]*
      is   a nice   place   to live   in Tromsø

b. *er [$_{DP}$ et [$_{CP}$ **sted** [det er morsomt å arbeide [~~sted~~ [i [Tromsø]]]]]*
    is   a   place   it is fun   to work   in Tromsø

(I'm assuming that *sted* can only be silent when it remains in the Spec of a preposition.)

Then, either the remnant [~~sted~~ [i [Tromsø]]] or just [i [Tromsø]] raises to the subject position. Assuming that the remnant raises, (1–2) are parsed as in (44):

(44) a. *[~~sted~~ [i [**Tromsø**]]] er [$_{DP}$ et bra [$_{CP}$ sted [å bo ~~[sted [~~ i [*
           in Tromsø   is   a nice   place   to live   in
Tromsø]]]]]
Tromsø

b. *[~~sted~~ [i [**Tromsø**]]] er [$_{DP}$ et [$_{CP}$ sted [det er morsomt å arbeide*
           in Tromsø   is   a   place   it is fun   to work
~~[sted [i [Tromsø]]~~]]]
in Tromsø

Notice that a parallel derivation is not available to (45): On the assumptions made in §4.2, no noun other than *plass* 'place' can replace *STED* in (42):

---

[9] In 43–44, the indefinite article *et* and the adjective *bra* are taken to be merged onto the relative CP, like the definite article *the* in Kayne's (1994) analysis of relatives, but it may also be possible to replace (43) with (i) or (ii):

(i) *er [$_{CP}$ [$_{NP}$ et bra **sted**] [å bo [[~~$_{NP}$ et bra sted~~] [i [Tromsø]]]]]*
    is   a nice place   to live   in Tromsø

(ii) *er [$_{DP}$ et [$_{CP}$[$_{NP}$ bra **sted**] [å bo [[~~$_{NP}$ bra sted~~] [i [Tromsø]]]]]*
     is   a   nice place   to live   in Tromsø

Deciding between the options will in part turn on determining the structure of *et bra sted i Tromsø* 'a nice place in Tromsø' in sentences in like (iii):

(iii) *Vi fant et bra sted i Troms.ø*
      we found a nice place in Tromsø

(45) a. *I Tromsø er en bra by å bo.
 in Tromsø is a nice city to live

 b. *I Tromsø er en by det er morsomt å arbeide.
 in Tromsø is a city it is fun to work

Thus, (45) is excluded because *by* 'city' has no position in the relative clause to originate from.

Notice also that on the analysis in §4.2, this still correlates with the fact that *by* cannot be a prepositionless locative, unlike *sted*:

(46) a. Vi arbeidet (på) det samme stedet/den samme plassen i tre år.
 we worked (at) the same place for three years

 b. Vi har nettopp besøkt et sted/en plass vi bodde (på) i 1981.
 we have just visited a place we lived (at) in 1981

(47) a. Vi arbeidet *(i) den samme byen i tre år.
 we worked *(in) the same city for three years

 b. Vi har nettopp besøkt en by vi bodde *(i) for ti år siden.
 we have just visited a city we lived *(in) ten years ago

Thus, our current set of hypotheses also provides a satisfactory answer to question (17a).

4.5 Locality and minimality

We are still left with the problem that the analysis in §3.2 must allow the PP to undergo A-movement out of relative clause.

In the derivation leading to (1–2) via the structures in (44), the PP moves to an A-position from a position inside the relative clause. This is of course at odds with standard assumptions. Relative constructions are generally assumed to be islands for any kind of movement. In addition, A-movement is not expected to cross intervening A-positions such as the covert subject of the infinitive in (44a) (not shown in the representations) and the expletive subject *det* 'it' in (44b). This is in fact what Relativized Minimality is designed to exclude.

The proposal in §4.4 suggests a solution. The basic intuition is that the A-movement of the PP leading to (44) is in a sense parasitic on the A'-movement of *sted* 'place'.

Taking island conditions and minimality as constraints on derivations, I want to suggest that since A'-moved *sted* is subextracted from [*sted* [*i* [*Tromsø*]]], the remnant [~~sted~~ [*i* [*Tromsø*]]] can be accessed by movement as if it were sitting in the same position as the previously moved *sted*.

An immediate objection to this might be that *sted* is moved to an A'-position (Spec-CP, on our analysis inherited from Kayne 1994) so that moving the remnant as if it were sitting in that position would make the movement of the remnant to the subject position similar to improper movement. However, if "relative clause extraposition" is analyzed as the outcome of movement of the "head" of a relative construction (stranding the rest of the relative clause) as proposed by Kayne (1994), the grammaticality of sentences like (48) shows that the head noun can undergo A-movement:

(48) A man appeared who we had never seen before

That is, although the head noun has raised to Spec-CP by A'-movement (on the head-raising analysis), it can still go on to raise to a subject position. Correspondingly, saying that the remnant containing the PP can raise to the subject position as in (42) because it can move as if it were in the position held by *sted*, the head noun of the relative construction, would appear less obviously incorrect.

Crucially, this derivation only gives rise to sentences where the location associated with the subject PP is co-extensive with the space denoted by *sted* 'place', as in (1–2). With the verb *ligge* 'lie, be located within', a subject must be associated with a proper subspace of the location denoted by the locative complement:

(49) a. *Tromsø ligger (på) et bra sted å bo.*
           Tromsø lies   (on) a nice place to live
      b. *Tromsø ligger (på) et sted det er bra å bo.*
           Tromsø lies   (on) a place it is nice to live

These are similar to:

(50) *Tromsø ligger i Nord-Norge.*
       Tromsø lies   in Northern   Norway

Correspondingly, we correctly predict the impossibility of substituting *ligger* 'lies' for *er* in sentences like (1–2) (see footnote 6):[10]

(51) a. *I Tromsø ligger et bra sted å bo.
          in Tromsø lies   a nice place to live

      b. *I Tromsø ligger et sted det er morsomt å arbeide.
          in Tromsø lies   a place it is fun   to work

5 Conclusion

In this article, I have primarily endeavored to characterize the puzzles surrounding the existence of Norwegian sentences like (1–2). I have also suggested a line of analysis that seems plausible to me, but clearly stands in need of much elaboration in order to fit into current syntactic theories.

References

Kayne, Richard S. 1994. *The antisymmetry of syntax.* Cambridge, MA: MIT Press.
Kayne, Richard S. 2000. *Parameters and universals.* New York: Oxford University Press.
Vergnaud, Jean-Roger. 1974. *French relative clauses.* Cambridge, Mass. Doctoral dissertation.

---

[10]The sentences in (51) are fine with the initial PP as a fronted adverbial of the sort seen in *I Tromsø ligger Ishavskatedralen* – In Tromsø lies The Arctic Cathedral. The following are ungrammatical:

(i) *Nå ligger i Tromsø et bra sted å bo.
     now lies in Tromsø a nice place to live

(ii) *I Tromsø synes å ligge et bra sted å bo.
     in Tromsø seems to lie   a nice place to live

Chapter 5

Flexibility in symmetry: An implicational relation in Bantu double object constructions

Jenneke van der Wal

Harvard University

> This paper presents new data from Bantu languages, from which a hitherto unnoticed typological pattern emerges: A) language-internally, causative, applicative and lexical ('give') ditransitives can differ with respect to symmetry; B) crosslinguistically, they are in an implicational relationship: if a language is symmetrical for one type of predicate, it is symmetrical for the predicate types to its right as well:
>
> causative > applicative > lexical ditransitive
>
> This can be accounted for if symmetry is due to low functional heads being flexible to license an argument in either their complement or their specifier (Haddican & Holmberg 2012; 2015). This flexibility is argued to be a sensitivity to topicality. The implicational relation can then be seen as a requirement for lower functional heads to have the same sensitivity: if Caus can license its specifier, then HAppl and LAppl should also be able to do so.

1 Introduction

Baker et al. (2012: 54) note that "for more than thirty years, symmetrical and asymmetrical object constructions have been a classic topic in the syntax of Bantu languages and beyond". Bresnan & Moshi (1990) divided Bantu languages into two classes -symmetrical and asymmetrical- based on the behaviour of objects in ditransitives: languages are taken to be symmetrical if both objects of a ditransitive verb behave alike with respect to passivisation and pronominalisation (see Ngonyani 1996; Buell 2005 for further tests). In Zulu, for example, either

object can be object-marked on the verb (1), and either object can be the subject of a passive verb (2).

Zulu (Adams 2010: 11)

(1) a. *U-mama u-nik-e   aba-ntwana in-cwadi.*
       1a-mama 1SM-give-PFV 2-children 9-book
       'Mama gave the children a book.'

   b. *U-mama u-**ba**-nik-e   in-cwadi (aba-ntwana).*
       1a-mama 1SM-2OM-give-PFV 9-book 2-children
       'Mama gave them a book (the children).'

   c. *U-mama u-**yi**-nik-e   aba-ntwana (in-cwadi).*
       1a-mama 1SM-9OM-give-PFV 2-children 9-book
       'Mama gave the children it (a book).'

(2) a. *In-cwadi y-a-fund-el-w-a   aba-ntwana.*
       9-book 9SM-REM.PST-read-APPL-PASS-FV 2-children
       'The book was read (for) the children.'

   b. *Aba-ntwana b-a-fund-el-w-a   in-cwadi.*
       2-children 2SM-REM.PST-read-APPL-PASS-FV 9-book
       'The children were read a book.'

However, it has become clear that the situation is not that black-and-white, with 'symmetrical languages' showing asymmetry in some part of the language (Schadeberg 1995, cf. Rugemalira 1991; Thwala 2006). It is already known that this asymmetry can be found in a number of ways. First, languages can be symmetrical only for a subpart of the tests (e.g. for object marking but not word order; Ngonyani 1996; Moshi 1998; Riedel 2009). Second, languages can vary in symmetry for different combinations of thematic roles (e.g. instruments versus benefactives; Baker 1988; Marantz 1993; Alsina & Mchombo 1993; Simango 1995; Ngonyani 1996; 1998; Zeller & Ngoboka 2006; Jerro 2015 and many others). Third, we are starting to see that combinations of syntactic operations (e.g. relativisation, passivisation, object marking) may also show asymmetry in otherwise symmetrical languages (Adams 2010; Zeller 2014; Holmberg et al. 2015), see also §4.2.

This paper presents new data from Bantu languages, exhibiting a fourth way in which symmetrical languages can show asymmetry. From this, a hitherto unnoticed typological pattern emerges: A) language-internally, causative, applicative and lexical ('give') ditransitives can differ with respect to symmetry; B) crosslinguistically, they are in an implicational relationship: if a language is symmetrical for one type of predicate, it is symmetrical for the predicate types to its right in (3) as well.

(3) causative > applicative > lexical ditransitive > (more restricted)
   type 1   type 2   type 3   type 4

Having discovered this pattern, we want to understand and explain it, which is where Haddican & Holmberg's (2012; 2015) analysis of symmetry proves useful. In §2, I first show and illustrate the discovered pattern in different languages. In §3 I propose a theoretical analysis for asymmetry and the implicational relation of symmetry, while §4 presents potential trouble. Note that in the current paper I restrict myself to the thematic roles of Causee, Benefactive, Recipient and Theme; see the conclusion in §5 for some discussion on other roles.

2 Not all ditransitives are equal

Apart from lexical ditransitive predicates such as 'give' or 'teach', Bantu languages can productively create ditransitive predicates by increasing the valency of verbs with applicative and causative derivations (marked morphologically on the verb), as shown in (4) and (5), respectively.

Makhuwa (van der Wal 2009: 71 and database)

(4) a. *Amíná o-n-rúwá eshimá.*
       1.Amina 1SM-PRES.CJ-stir 9.shima
       'Amina prepares shima.'

   b. *Amíná o-n-aá-rúw-él' éshimá anámwáne.*
       1.Amina 1SM-PRES.CJ-2OM-stir-APPL.FV 9.shima 2.children
       'Amina prepares shima for the children.'

(5) a. *Ál' átthw' áálá aa-wárá eshaphéyu.*
       2.DEM 2.people 2.DEM 2SM.PERF.DJ-wear 10.hats
       'These people wear hats.'

   b. *O-ḿ-wár-íh-á mwalápw' ááwé ekúwó.*
       1SM.PERF.DJ-1OM-wear-CAUS-FV 1.dog 1.POSS.1 9.cloth
       'She dressed her dog in a cloth.'

117

Although the Benefactive (children) and the Causee (dog) fully belong to the argument structure of the verb, just like the Recipient and Theme in a lexical ditransitive such as 'give', not all languages treat the two objects in these three types of ditransitives in the same symmetrical or asymmetrical way. As mentioned, an implicational relationship appears between the symmetrical behaviour of double objects in causatives, applicatives and lexical ditransitives, as in (3) above. The types of symmetry patterns are illustrated for object marking in various languages below; passivisation is in the various languages confirmed or expected to follow the same pattern, but only object marking will be discussed in this paper.

2.1 Type 1: fully symmetrical

On one end of the continuum are languages that behave symmetrically for all three types of ditransitive constructions. Zulu is one such language: both objects behave symmetrically, whether they belong to a lexical ditransitive verb or a derived applicative or causative. This is illustrated for object marking in (6–8) and yields the same results for passivisation. Zulu is thus a language of type 1: symmetrical for all types of verbs.

Zulu (Zeller 2011, see also Zeller 2012)

(6) lexical ditransitive

a. *UJohn u-nik-a abantwana imali.*
   1a.John 1SM-give-FV 2.children 9.money
   'John is giving the children money.'

b. *UJohn u-ba-nik-a imali (abantwana).*
   1a.John 1SM-2OM-give-FV 9.money 2.children
   'John is giving them money (the children).'

c. *UJohn u-yi-nik-a abantwana (imali).*
   1a.John 1SM-9OM-give-FV 2.children 9.money
   'John is giving it to the children (the money).'

(7) applicative
   a. *ULanga u-phek-el-a   umama   inyama.*
      1a.Langa 1SM-cook-APPL-FV 1a.mother 9.meat
      'Langa is cooking meat for mother.'
   b. *ULanga u-**m**-phek-el-a   inyama (umama).*
      1a.Langa 1SM-1OM-cook-APPL-FV 9.meat 1a.mother
      'Langa is cooking meat for her (mother).'
   c. *ULanga u-**yi**-phek-el-a   umama   (inyama).*
      1a.Langa 1SM-9OM-cook-APPL-FV 1.mother 9.meat
      'Langa is cooking it for mother (the meat).'

(8) causative
   a. *ULanga u-phek-is-a   umama   ukudla.*
      1a.Langa 1SM-cook-CAUS-FV 1a.mother 15.food
      'Langa helps/makes mother cook food.'
   b. *ULanga u-**m**-phek-is-a   ukudla (umama).*
      1a.Langa 1SM-1OM-cook-CAUS-FV 15.food 1a.mother
      'Langa helps/makes her cook food (mother).'
   c. *ULanga u-**ku**-phek-is-a   umama   (ukudla).*
      1a.Langa 1SM-15OM-cook-CAUS-FV 1a.mother 15.food
      'Langa makes mother cook it (the food).'

The same full symmetry has been observed in Kimeru (Hodges 1977), Shona (Mugari 2013; Mathangwane & Osam 2006), Lubukusu (Baker et al. 2012), Kinyarwanda (Zeller & Ngoboka 2014; Ngoboka 2005), Kîîtharaka (Muriungi 2008), and Kikuyu (Peter Githinji, personal communication).

2.2 Type 2: only lexical and applicative symmetrical

One step further down the cline are languages of type 2, where objects of applicatives and lexical ditransitives behave symmetrically, but objects of causatives do not. In Southern Sotho, either object of lexical ditransitives and applicatives can be object-marked, as in (9) and (10),[1] whereas with a causative only the Causee can be marked, not the Theme (11).

---

[1] But see the influence of animacy as pointed out for Sesotho by Morolong & Hyman (1977) and comparatively discussed in Hyman & Duranti (1982).

Southern Sotho

(9) lexical ditransitive (Thabo Ditsele, personal communication)

    a. *Ntate o fa bana lijo.*
       1.father 1SM give 2.children 5.food
       'Father gives the children food.'

    b. *Ntate o **ba** fa lijo.*
       1.father 1SM 2OM give 5.food
       'Father gives them food.'

    c. *Ntate o **li** fa bana.*
       1.father 1SM 5OM give 2.children
       'Father gives it to the children.'

(10) applicative (Machobane 1989: 24)

    a. *Banana ba-pheh-el-a 'me nama.*
       2.girls 2SM-cook-APPL-FV 1.mother 9.meat
       'The girls are cooking meat for my mother.'

    b. *Banana ba-**mo**-pheh-el-a nama.*
       2.girls 2SM-cook-APPL-FV 9.meat
       'The girls are cooking meat for her.'

    c. *Banana ba-**e**-pheh-el-a 'me.*
       2.girls 2SM-9OM-cook-APPL-FV 1.mother
       'The girls are cooking it for my mother.'

(11) causative (Machobane 1989: 31)

    a. *Ntate o-bal-is-a bana buka.*
       1.father 1SM-read-CAUS-FV 2.children 9.book
       'My father makes the children read the book.'

    b. *Ntate o-**ba**-bal-is-a buka.*
       1.father 1SM-2OM-read-CAUS-FV 9.book
       'My father makes them read the book.'

    c. * *Ntate o-**e**-bal-is-a bana.*
       1.father 1SM-9OM-read-CAUS-FV 2.children
       int. 'My father makes the children read it.'

5 Flexibility in symmetry

The same pattern is found in Otjiherero, as shown in (12–14):
Otjiherero

(12) lexical ditransitive (Jekura Kavari, personal communication)
   a. *Omukazendu ma pe ovazandu ovikurya.*
      1.woman PRES 1SM.give 2.boys 8.food
      'The woman gives the boys food.'
   b. *Omukazendu me **ve** pe ovikurya.*
      1.woman PRES.1SM 2OM give 8.food
      'The woman gives them food.'
   c. *Omukazendu me **vi** pe ovazandu.*
      1.woman PRES.1SM 8OM give 2.boys
      'The woman gives it to the children.'

(13) applicative (Marten & Kula 2012: 247)
   a. *Má-vé **vè** tjáng-ér-é òm-bàpírà.*
      PRES-2SM 2OM write-APPL-FV 9-letter
      'They are writing them a letter.'
   b. *Má-vá **i** tjáng-ér-é òvà-nâtjé.*
      pres-2SM 9OM write-APPL-FV 2-children
      'They are writing the children it.'

(14) causative (Jekura Kavari, personal communication)
   a. *Ma-ve **ve** tjang-is-a om-bapira.*
      PRES-2SM 2OM write-CAUS-FV 9-letter
      'They make them write a letter.'
   b. ** Ma-ve **i** tjang-is-a ova-natje.*
      PRES-2SM 9OM write-CAUS-FV 2-children
      'They make the children write it.'

2.3 Type 3: only lexical symmetrical

Type 3 is yet another step down the hierarchy in (3). In KiLuguru, double objects behave symmetrically only for lexical ditransitives (15), but show asymmetries with both applicative and causative predicates (16–17).

KiLuguru (Marten & Ramadhani 2001: 266, 269)

(15) lexical ditransitive

    a. *Chibua ko-**w**-eng'-a iwana ipfitabu.*
       1.Chibua 1SM-2OM-give-FV 2.children 8.books

    b. *Chibua ko-**pf**-eng'-a iwana ipfitabu.*
       1.Chibua 1SM-8OM-give-FV 2.children 8.books
       'Chibua is giving children books.'

(16) applicative[2]

    a. *Mayi ko-**w**-ambik-il-a iwana ipfidyo.*
       1.mother 1SM-2OM-cook-APPL-FV 2.children 7.food
       'Mother is cooking food for the children.'

    b. * *Mayi ko-**pf**-ambik-il-a ipfidyo iwana.*
       1.mother 1SM-7OM-cook-APPL-FV 7.food 2.children
       int. 'Mother is cooking food for the children.'

(17) a. causative
       *Wanzehe wa-**mw**-ambik-its-a Chuma ipfidyo.*
       2.elders 2SM-1OM-cook-CAUS-FV 1.Chuma 8.food
       'The elders made Chuma cook food.'

    b. * *Wanzehe wa-**pf**-ambik-its-a ipfidyo Chuma.*
       2.elders 2SM-8OM-cook-CAUS-FV 8.food 1.Chuma
       'The elders made Chuma cook food.'

2.4 Type 4: fully asymmetrical

Finally, type 4 languages do not show any symmetrical properties in double object constructions – these have always been known as asymmetrical languages. In ditransitives, applicatives and causatives, only the Recipient/applied/Causee object can be object-marked, as shown in (18–20).

---

[2] Marten & Ramadhani (2001: 266) note that "both orders of objects are fine, but only the benefactive object may be object marked (in general, the object marked object precedes the unmarked object, and it is the first object which is emphasized. In addition, applicatives without valency change can be used for predicate emphasis".

Swahili

(18) lexical ditransitive

    a. *A-li-**m**-pa   kitabu.*
       1SM-PAST-1OM-give 7.book
       'She gave him a book.'

    b. * *A-li-**ki**-pa   Juma.*
       1SM-PAST-7OM-give 1.Juma
       'She gave it to Juma.'

(19) applicative

    a. *A-li-**m**-nunul-i-a   kitabu.*
       1SM-PAST-1OM-buy-APPL-FV 7.book
       'She bought him a book.'

    b. * *A-li-**ki**-nunul-i-a   Juma.*
       1SM-PAST-7OM-buy-APPL-FV 1.Juma
       'She bought it for Juma.'

(20) causative

    a. *A-li-**m**-kat-ish-a   kamba.*
       1SM-PAST-1OM-cut-CAUS-FV 9.rope
       'She made him cut the rope.'

    b. * *A-li-**i**-kat-isha   Juma.*
       1SM-PAST-9OM-cut-CAUS-FV 1.Juma
       'She made Juma cut it.'

2.5 Summary of (a)symmetrical patterns

The languages studied thus illustrate that 'symmetry' is not necessarily a property of a whole language, and they also show that (some of) the variation in symmetrical object marking is structured, as summarised in Table 1.

Table 1: Symmetrical properties of double object constructions cross-Bantu

	CAUS	APPL	DITRANS	languages
type 1	✓	✓	✓	Zulu, Shona, Lubukusu, Kîîtharaka, Kimeru
type 2		✓	✓	Otjiherero, Southern Sotho
type 3			✓	Luguru
type 4				Swahili etc. (asymmetrical)

3 Implications of the implicational hierarchy

This implicational relation poses an empirical as well as a theoretical question. The empirical question is the following: If the implicational hierarchy in (3) holds crosslinguistically, are there indeed no languages with symmetrical double objects for applicatives and/or causatives but not ditransitives, and similarly are there no languages with symmetrical causatives but no symmetrical applicatives? This is a very clear empirical prediction that should be tested as more data become available for more languages.

Assuming that the pattern in Table 1 is not accidental, the theoretical question is how this implicational relation can be accounted for in a model of syntax. In order to answer that question, we need to establish how symmetry is derived, which in turn requires a theory of the functional structure of the lower part of the clause and of object marking. I first present the structure of ditransitives in §3.1 and the mechanics of object marking in §3.2, then I introduce Haddican and Holmberg's (2012; 2015) analysis of symmetry in §3.3, and I add a motivation for it in §3.4. With all these ingredients in place (summary in §3.5), I return to the implicational relationship in §3.6.

3.1 The structure of ditransitives

Following Pylkkänen (2008), and considering the overt applicative and causative morphology in Bantu, I take the Recipient in a lexical ditransitive to be introduced by a low applicative head (LApplP), under V (21a). The Benefactive for an applied verb is introduced by a high applicative head (HApplP), between V and v (21b). For causatives, I assume that the Causee is introduced by a causative head (CausP) between V and v (21c), although one could equally well assume a double little v with Caus in between, forming a bi-eventive structure (see further Pylkkänen 2008 on different heights of causatives).

(21)

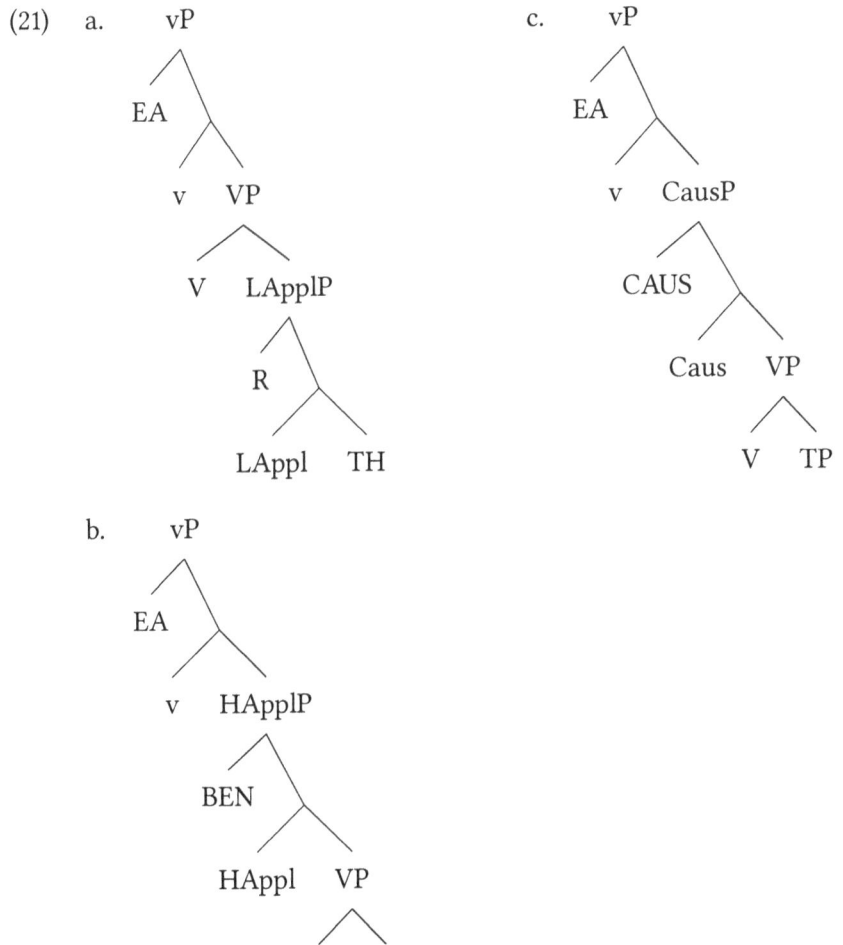

If these structures underlie the double object constructions discussed, then they (and indeed the underlying conceptual considerations of generative grammar) suggest that asymmetry is basic, and symmetry is derived.[3] This appears

---

[3]This may be different for locative or instrumental applicatives – tests involving animacy could help to assess whether there is a 'dative alternation' as in English or a true double object construction, see Oehrle (1976), among others.

to be correct, since asymmetries keep cropping up in otherwise symmetrical languages but never the other way around, suggesting that asymmetry is always available and hence more basic. Furthermore, the asymmetry is always the same across Bantu: the Benefactive, Causee, or applied (i.e. higher) argument displays object properties, where the Theme argument lacks them. This supports an analysis of symmetry in terms of a derived accessibility of the Theme, i.e. the Theme starts out low and becomes available for syntactic operations (by movement, different featural probing or annihilating the intervening argument). This is further discussed in §3.3.

3.2 Object marking in ditransitives

I assume that Bantu object marking in ditransitives is the result of an Agree relation between little v and one of the objects. Within the Probe-Goal system of Agree (Chomsky 2001), I assume that object markers are the spell-out of little v's uninterpretable φ features agreeing with the interpretable φ features of an object Goal (Roberts 2010).[4] I further assume that lower arguments need Case licensing,[5] and that Case licensing can be independent of φ agreement, in the sense that a lower functional head can be Case-licensing but not carry uφ features (Baker 2012; Preminger 2014; Bárány 2015). Lower functional heads can thus have a [uφ] and/or a [Case] feature.

In a monotransitive structure, the uninterpretable features on v simply probe, find the first and only object (the Theme) and agree with it. In a double object construction, however, the Theme argument is always lower than the Recipient/Benefactive/Causee argument. Assuming that locality conditions hold (Minimal Link Condition),[6] the Theme is not available for agreement with the v or T head for object marking and passivisation, respectively. This is due to one of two reasons: either the higher argument will intervene between the Probe on v/T and the Theme, or the Appl/Caus head will already have licensed the Theme, making

---

[4]Under Roberts' (2010) approach, object marking is the spell-out of an Agree relation with a defective Goal: if the features of the Goal are a subset of the features of the Probe, the Agree relation is indistinguishable from a copy/movement chain, where normally only the highest copy is spelled out. The lower copy is not spelled out, due to chain-reduction (Nunes 2004). This gives rise to incorporation of the Goal, being spelled out on the Probe. Whether the Agree relation is spelled out morphologically is thus dependent on the structure of the Goal. See Iorio (2014) for details on the approach as applied to the Bantu language Bembe, and van der Wal (2015a) for a comparative approach to Bantu object marking.

[5]This is debatable for the Bantu languages; see Diercks (2012); van der Wal (2015b) and Sheehan & van der Wal (2016). However, the debatable status mostly concerns nominative Case.

[6]But see Baker & Collins (2006) who propose parameterisation of the Minimal Link Condition.

it inactive for further Agree relations. This is what results in asymmetry: the LAppl/HAppl/Caus head always licenses the Theme in its c-command domain, and v can only license the highest argument. Since only v has φ features, it follows that only the highest object can be spelled out as object marking (if the Goal is defective). This is represented in (22).

(22) v agrees with BEN (and can spell out as object-marker)

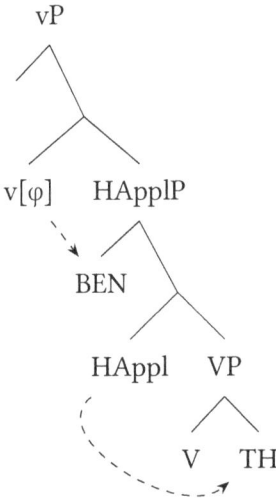

3.3 Symmetry

In "symmetrical languages" the Theme can also be object marked. The [uφ] features of v must thus have established an Agree relation with the lower Theme, despite an intervening Benefactive.[7] Assuming locality conditions, if the Theme is agreed with, it must either have been higher than the Benefactive at the time of agreement (the locality approach), or the Benefactive must have somehow been invisible for v's Probe (the Case approach).

The locality analysis is proposed by McGinnis (1998a; 2001); Anagnostopoulou (2003); Doggett (2004); Pylkkänen (2008); Jeong (2007). They propose that a high applicative between V and v supplies a landing place for the Theme object in a second specifier (23), whether attracted by Appl itself or moving to a phase edge (Appl being argued to be a phase head). This results in the Theme being closer to v than the applied argument.

---

[7] I will illustrate the analysis with a high applicative, but the same holds for the low applicative and the causative.

(23)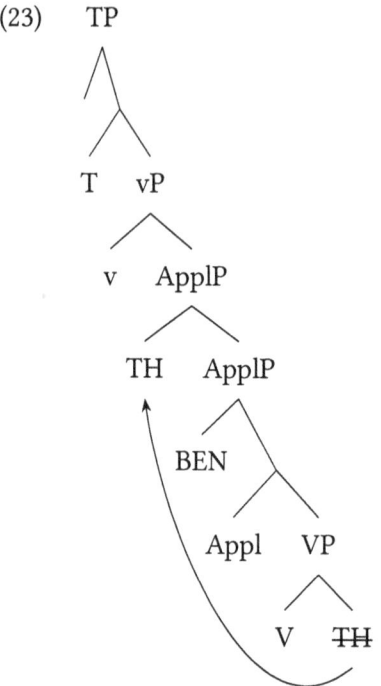

Ura (1996) and Anagnostopoulou (2003) explicitly link this movement to object shift (cf. Kramer 2014; Harizanov 2014; Baker & Kramer 2015). However, there is not always evidence for such movement, for example when a language is by and large symmetrical but has a very strict word order, as in Luganda. Luganda double objects display symmetrical behaviour for the two tests of pronominalisation (24) and passivisation (25).

Luganda (Ssekiryango 2006: 67, 72)

(24) a. *Maama a-wa-dde taata ssente.*
1.mother 1SM-give-PFV 1.father 10.money
'Mother has given father money.'

b. *Maama a-mu-wa-dde ssente.*
1.mother 1SM-1OM-give-PFV 10.money.
'Mother has given him money.'

c. *Maama   a-zi-wa-dde   taata.*
      1.mother 1SM-10OM-give-PFV   1.father
      'Mother has given it father.'

(25) a. *Maama   a-were-ddw-a   ssente.*
        1.mother 1SM-give-PASS-FV money
        'Mother has been given money.'

   b. *Ssente   zi-were-ddw-a   maama.*
      10.money 10SM-give-PASS-FV   1.mother
      'The money has been given to mother.'

Nevertheless, Luganda shows a strict order Recipient > Theme, as is clear from (26) as compared to (24a).

(26) Luganda (Ssekiryango 2006: 69)
   * *Maama   a-wa-dde   ssente   taata.*
      1.mother 1SM-give-PFV   10.money   1.father
      int. 'Mother gave father money.'

Furthermore, Haddican & Holmberg (2012; 2015) show that the correlation between object shift and symmetry is not corroborated by their research on Norwegian and Swedish, and they find that it is insufficient to rely on *just* locality to account for all the patterns found in Germanic languages.

Another problematic aspect of the locality-based approach, at least for McGinnis (2001), is that it predicts low applicatives to never be symmetrical. McGinnis proposes that lower arguments can only move to the second specifier of a phase head, that is, it 'leapfrogs' to the escape hatch. This functions well with high applicatives but does not work for low applicatives because, under McGinnis' analysis, this HAppl is a phase whereas LAppl is not. However, even if LAppl could be a phase, then it would still not allow the Theme to be moved to its specifier, since this would involve moving too locally, the same argument merging again with the same head. Abels (2003) observes that because of antilocality, direct complements of phase heads are frozen: they cannot escape by moving to the specifier of the phase head. For double object constructions, this means that the Theme in a low applicative can never move higher than the Recipient (unless there is a higher phase head it can move to), and therefore it will never be the first argument found by v. However, if lexical ditransitives involve a low applicative (as suggested by their semantics), such symmetrical low applicative structures do exist – they are even the most frequent in comparison with other ditransitive predicates, as the data in §2 show.

Haddican & Holmberg (2012; 2015) propose a different approach to symmetry in double object constructions: symmetry can derive from locality, but can also derive from variation in whether the extra Case associated with an applicative construction is assigned to the Theme or the Benefactive. This can be rephrased as variation in the ability of a functional head (applicative, causative) to assign Case to either the Theme object in its complement or to the Benefactive object in its specifier, as represented in (27). This means that v agrees with the remaining object, which can be either the Benefactive or the Theme, thereby deriving symmetry.

(27)

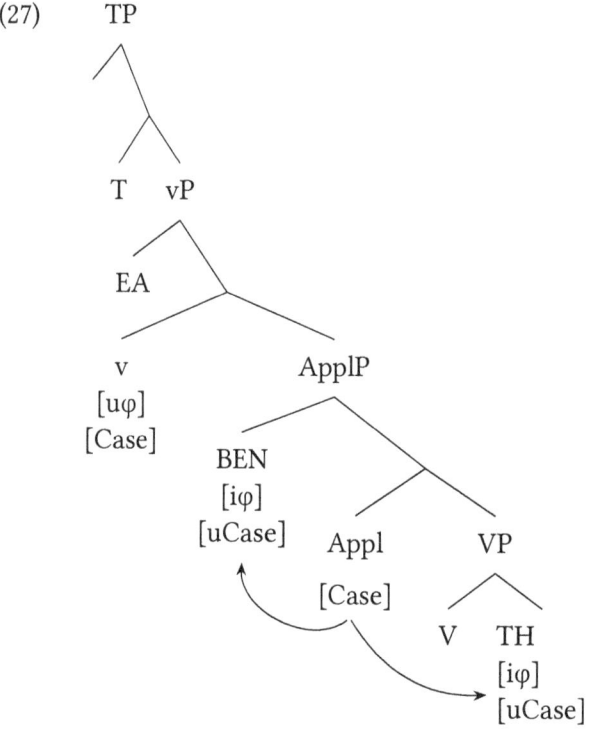

There are thus two possible derivations. If the applicative head agrees with the Theme, then v agrees with the highest argument (Benefactive); this is the same as in asymmetrical languages, see (22).[8] If in a symmetrical language the applicative

---

[8] Beyond Bantu there is another type of asymmetrical language with a so-called "indirective alignment" of double objects, where the lower functional head always licenses its specifier (e.g. Italian). This is an independent parameter (see §3.6).

head assigns Case to its specifier, i.e. to the Benefactive that it introduces, then this argument becomes invisible to v (cf. McGinnis 1998b).[9] The Theme object can thus be probed by v, which agrees with it in both Case and φ, and potentially spell out as an object marker, as represented in (28).

(28) v agrees with TH (and can object-mark it)

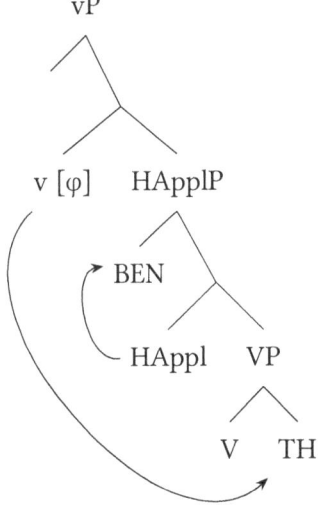

Note that the applicative head here only has a [Case] feature and no [uφ] features. The presence of the Case feature ensures that the second object is licensed (and invisible for v), whereas the absence of [uφ] features on Appl means that the argument agreeing with Appl cannot be object-marked: only the argument agreeing with v can spell out as an object marker. The presence of [uφ] just on v also accounts for the fact that there is only one object marker.

In languages with multiple object markers, such as Kinyarwanda (29), I speculate that lower functional heads introducing an argument also carry φ features and can therefore spell out additional object markers.

(29) Kinyarwanda (JD61, Beaudoin-Lietz et al. 2004: 183)
 Umugoré a- ra- na- ha- ki- zi- ba- ku- n-
 1woman SM1- DJ- ALSO- OM16- OM7- OM10- OM2- OM2SG- OM1SG-

---

[9] Assuming no defective intervention clause-internally, which has been argued for by Anagnostopoulou (2003) and Bobaljik (2008). See also Bruening (2014) for an argument against defective intervention per se.

someesheeshererereza.
read.CAUS.CAUS.APPL.APPL

'The woman is also making us read it (book) with them (glasses) to you for me there (in the house).'

The derivation of multiple object markers would be as follows. Following Julien (2002) I take it that the Bantu verb head moves in the lower part of the clause, picking up derivational suffixal morphology. The verb also gathers the φ features on the different functional heads that are spelled out as prefixes at the completion of the phase. Further prefixes such as negation, the subject marker and TAM morphology are heads that are spelled out in their individual positions and phonologically merged to the stem. The different derivations for object marking prefixes and other prefixes are reflected in the status of the stem plus the object marker(s) as a separate domain for tone rules, known as the "macrostem".

This analysis predicts that agreement with the Theme is always possible in these languages, i.e. that languages with multiple object markers are always symmetrical. This is indeed borne out for Tswana, Kinyarwanda, Kirundi, Ha, Haya, Luganda, Tshiluba, Totela and Chaga, the *only* exception so far being Sambaa. Riedel (2009) shows that Sambaa only allows object marking of the Theme if the Benefactive is also object marked, hence an asymmetrical pattern. This suggests that the additional probe responsible for multiple object marking in Sambaa is located not on lower functional heads, but on a higher functional head; see van der Wal (submitted). For the current paper I focus on languages with only one object marker.

3.4 Flexibility vs. optionality

A question for this approach to flexibility, which Haddican & Holmberg (2012; 2015) do not address, is what determines whether a low functional head licenses an argument in its specifier or its complement. In an explanatory analysis this should not be completely optional. The hypothesis I want to put forward is that the 'direction' of licensing by a flexible head is determined by relative topicality of the two arguments.

Concretely, the applicative head will Case-license the less topical of the two objects (Theme and Benefactive). The applicative head can do so because it introduces one of the arguments while also being merged with a structure that contains an unlicensed argument, thus 'seeing' both arguments. This analysis has obvious parallels with Adger & Harbour's (2007) proposal to account for restrictions in the cooccurrence of speech act participants (PCC effects), where the applicative head can also see both arguments. A difference is that in their analysis the applicative head can only license the Person values on the Theme that the Recipient does *not* have, whereas in my analysis it can only value a subset of what it *does* have. Where the current account can still be extended along the lines of Adger & Harbour (2007) is the sensitivity of Appl to Person as well, not only to account for PCC effects but also for animacy effects as observed for Sotho (Morolong & Hyman 1977) and Zulu (Zeller 2011). Preliminary results show that sensitivity to Person indeed accounts for the attested animacy patterns (van der Wal 2016).

More technically, I propose that the applicative head has a [uTopic] probe which is restricted by the value of the Benefactive argument in its specifier: the head can only license arguments that are equal or lower in topicality than the argument it introduces. If the probed Theme is equal or lower in topicality than the Benefactive, then default Agree/Case-licensing downwards takes place. If the probed Theme is higher in topicality, the head instead licenses the Benefactive in the specifier. This can also be captured in binary terms, where objects have a topic feature with a + value or an absence of value.

When the Benefactive is specified as [topic: +], the applicative head licenses any Theme, whether [topic: +] or [topic: _], as represented in (30).

(30)

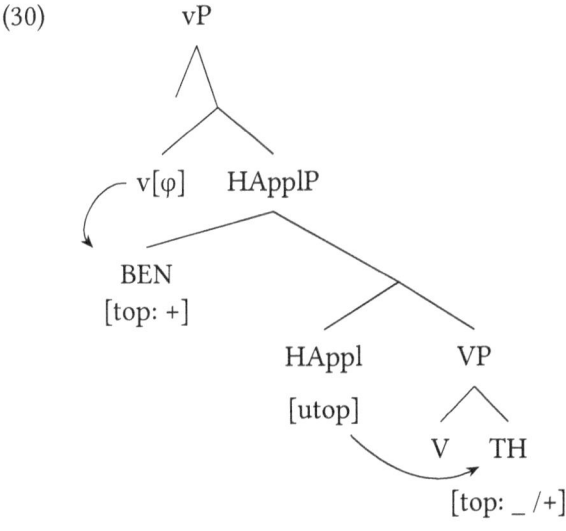

The Theme's absence of a value for topicality ([topic: _]) is compatible with the positive value for topicality on the Benefactive and hence the applicative head licenses the Theme. This entails that little v will in this situation always agree with the more topical Benefactive.

When the Theme is specified [topic: +], the values of head and Theme are compatible as well, and Appl will by default license the Theme, leaving the Benefactive again to be Case-licensed (and agreed with) by v. In other words, when both objects are topical, only the higher will be object-marked. This is in fact borne out in Zulu: when both DP objects are dislocated, only the higher can be object-marked. In (31) we know that both objects are dislocated because of the disjoint form of the verb and the accompanying prosodic phrases (not indicated here), see further Zeller (2015).

(31) Zulu (Adams 2010 via Zeller 2012: 224, 225)

a. *Ngi-ya-m-theng-el-a   u-Sipho   u-bisi.*
   1SG.SM-PRES.DJ-1OM-buy-APPL-FV 1a-Sipho 11-milk

b. *Ngi-ya-m-theng-el-a   u-bisi   u-Sipho.*
   1SG.SM-PRES.DJ-1OM-buy-APPL-FV 11-milk 1a-Sipho
   'I am buying milk for Sipho.'

c. * *Ngi-ya-lu-theng-el-a   u-Sipho   u-bisi.*
   1SG.SM-PRES.DJ-11OM-buy-APPL-FV 1a-Sipho 11-milk

d. * *Ngi-ya-lu-theng-el-a   u-bisi   u-Sipho.*
   1SG.SM-PRES.DJ-11OM-buy-APPL-FV 11-milk 1a-Sipho
   int. 'I am buying milk for Sipho.'

When the Benefactive is [topic: _], this is also the restriction on the probing applicative head. Hence, if the Theme is [topic: _], this is perfectly compatible with the Benefactive (and hence the applicative head), and Case-licensing from the applicative head is by default downwards, leaving v to agree with and Case-license the Benefactive.[10] However, if the Theme is [topic: +], this is not compatible with the absence of a topic value, and hence the applicative head will Case-license the Benefactive in its specifier, leaving the topical Theme to be agreed with and Case-licensed by v, as sketched in (32).

---

[10]It is in fact not possible to ascertain that v agrees with the Benefactive when both are non-topical since the object marker will in such cases not be spelled out anyway (under the view that the object marker spells out the features of a defective goal, i.e. φP, as in Roberts 2010). The correct V DP DP order comes out whether Appl licenses Theme or Benefactive, so at present this is irrelevant to the discussion.

(32)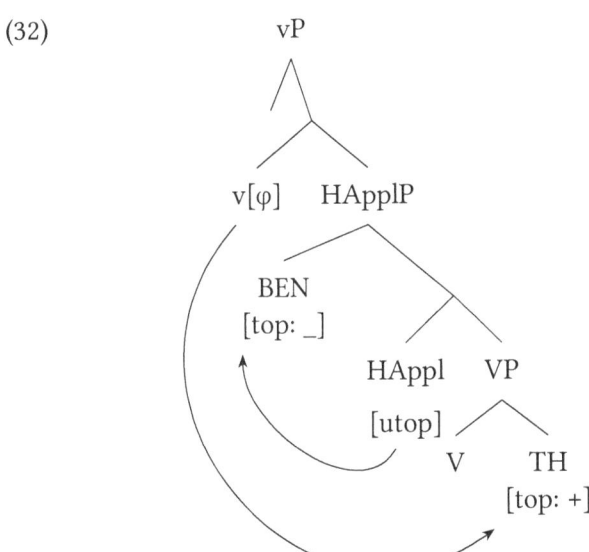

A consequence of this analysis is that it is the more topical of the two arguments that will be left available for agreement with v. Indeed, object marking (= agreement with v) is crosslinguistically typically with the more topical or given object, in differential object marking as well as pronominalisation (see e.g. Adams 2010; Zeller 2014; 2015 for Zulu, Bax & Diercks 2012 for Manyika). Moreover, in a passive clause where v does not have either Case or φ features, T agrees with the more topical argument. This is expected, since it is known that a functional motivation behind a passive is the promotion of an erstwhile object not only to the syntactic function of subject, but also to the discourse function of topic (Givón 1994: 9). This is especially true for the Bantu languages where the preverbal domain favours or is restricted to topical elements (e.g. Morimoto 2006; Henderson 2006; Zeller 2008; Zerbian 2006; van der Wal 2009; Yoneda 2011).

The sensitivity of low functional heads to information structure is not a new proposal: Creissels (2004); Marten (2003); Cann & Mabugu (2007) and de Kind & Bostoen (2012) also show that applicatives are more than simple argument-introducing heads; in various Bantu languages they can be used with a non-canonical, information-structural, interpretation. To give just one example, Creissels (2004) first shows the familiar function of introducing a Benefactive argument in Tswana (33a), and the function of making a peripheral argument (the locative 'in the pot' in 33b) into a proper argument of the predicate.

(33) Tswana (S31, Creissels 2004: 13, adapted)
    a. *Lorato o tlaa ape-el-a bana motogo.*
       1.Lorato 1SM FUT cook-APPL-FV 2.children 3.porridge
       'Lorato will cook the porridge for the children.'
    b. *Lorato o tlaa ape-el-a motogo mo pitse-ng.*
       1.Lorato 1SM FUT cook-APPL-FV 3.porridge PREP 9.pot-LOC
       'Lorato will cook the porridge in the pot.'

Interestingly, Creissels then shows that applicatives in Tswana can also have a non-canonical function as triggering a focus reading of the locative (34).

(34) Tswana (S31, Creissels 2004: 15)
    Lorato o ape-el-a mo jarate-ng.
    1.Lorato 1SM cook-APPL-FV PREP 9.yard-LOC
    'Lorato does the cooking *in the yard*.'

This can be taken as independent evidence for the sensitivity of the applicative head, and potentially other low functional heads, to discourse-related properties.

3.5 Interim summary

To summarise, assuming that double object constructions always involve an additional low functional head such as a causative, or a low or high applicative, the default structure is asymmetrical with the Theme lower than the Recipient/Benefactive/Causee argument. We can account for symmetrical behaviour of objects by appealing to flexibility of such a functional head to Case-license either the Theme in its complement or the argument in its specifier. I suggest that this is determined by the relative topicality of the two arguments. With this analysis of symmetry in place, we can return to the question of how we can understand the implicational relation between causative, applicative and lexical ditransitive predicates and symmetry.

3.6 Capturing the implicational relationship

The partial symmetry discovered for different predicate types can now be understood as subsets of low functional heads being flexible in licensing their complement or specifier. Languages vary, then, in which heads have this flexibility, i.e. flexible licensing must be parameterised. The implicational relation between different predicates can thus be captured in the following parameter hierarchy (35).

(35) Parameter hierarchy for the degree of symmetry
Can low functional heads license their specifier?

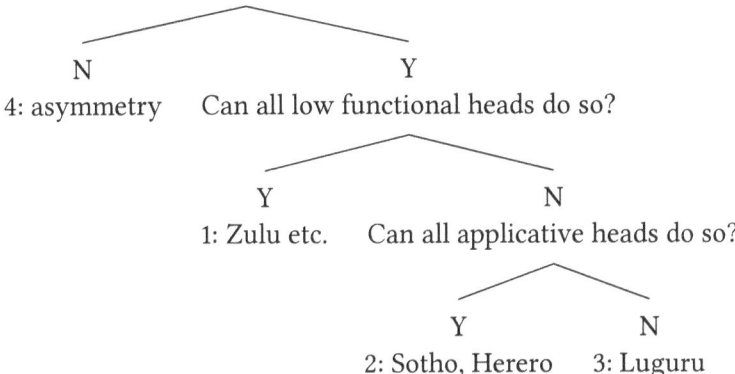

Apart from capturing the implicational relation between the different types of ditransitives, this parameter hierarchy is motivated by conceptual reasons too. First, organising parameters in a dependency relation rather than postulating independent parameters drastically reduces the number of possible combinations of parameter settings, i.e. the number of possible grammars, as shown by Roberts & Holmberg (2010), and Sheehan (2014).

Second, the parameter hierarchy can serve to model a path of acquisition that is shaped by general learning biases (the 'third factor' in language design, Chomsky 2005). Biberauer & Roberts (2015) suggest that two general learning biases combine to form a 'minimax search algorithm':

(36) Feature Economy (FE): postulate as few features as possible to account for the input [generalised from Roberts & Roussou 2003]

(37) Input Generalisation (IG): maximise available features [generalised from Roberts 2007]

If both FE and IG are observed with respect to applicative and causative heads, no features will be postulated on these heads, which for the current analysis of double objects results in default downward licensing and hence an asymmetrical system. When the language gives evidence that the higher object is sometimes licensed by a lower functional head, then an upwards licensing property must be postulated for such heads. This violates FE, but by IG the property is now taken to be present on all heads, leading to a system that is completely symmetrical (type 1). If the language then gives evidence that *some* heads are asymmetrical, the parameter question is which subset of heads has the property, e.g. applicatives versus causatives.[11] We thus derive a 'none-all-some' order of implicational parameters and of parameter acquisition.

If topicality is indeed the motivation for flexible licensing, then the parameter can be rephrased as 'Which heads are sensitive to topicality?'. In fact, this fits into a more general hierarchy of ditransitive alignment patterns (Sheehan 2013), which captures two types of asymmetry. The first is secundative alignment, where the Recipient object behaves like the monotransitive object, i.e. 'I gave him the cake' but not *'I gave my friend it' (as in English). The second is indirective alignment, where the Theme behaves like the monotransitive object, i.e. 'I gave my friend it' but not *'I gave him the cake' (as in Italian). See further the typological overviews in Malchukov (2010; 2013).

(38) Parameter hierarchy for (a)symmetry in ditransitive alignment

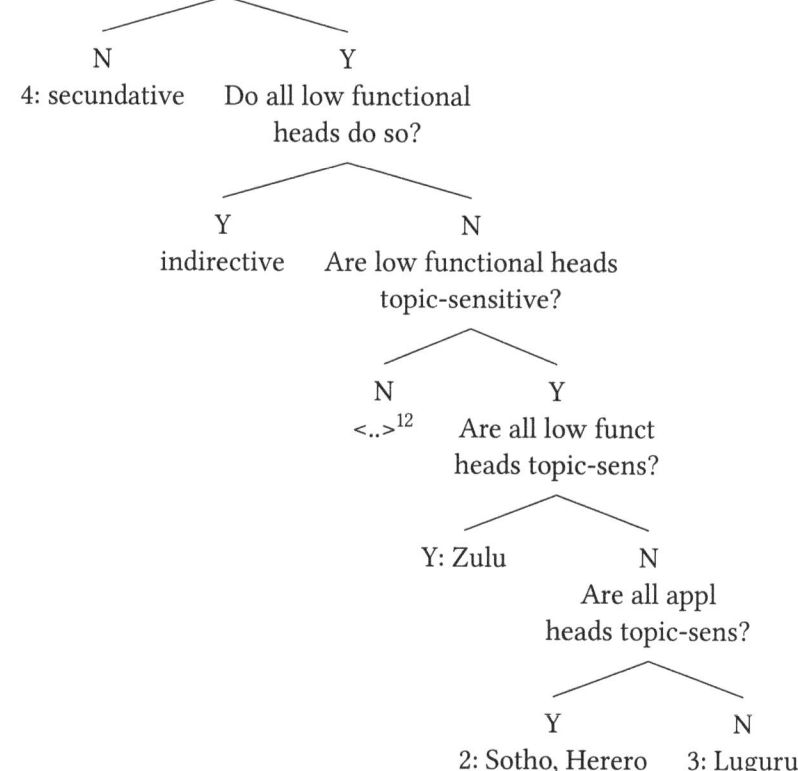

---

[11]It remains to be seen what precise feature specification singles out the set of applicative heads.

4 Potential trouble

Even within the type 1 languages, which are fully symmetrical, patches of asymmetry emerge, particularly in combinations of derivations (passive, applicative, causative). I discuss two here.

4.1 Combinations of extensions

In Zulu, objects of doubly derived verbs with both a causative and an applicative still behave symmetrically. That is, the Causee (39b), the Benefactive (39a) or the Theme (39c) can be object marked.

(39) Zulu (Zeller 2011)
applicative + causative

a. *Usipho u-**m**-fund-is-el-a abafundi Zulu (uLanga).*
1aSipho 1SM-1OM-learn-CAUS-APPL-FV 2.student 7.Zulu 1a.Langa
'Sipho is teaching the students Zulu for him (Langa).'

b. *Usipho u-**ba**-fund-is-el-a uLanga Zulu (abafundi).*
1aSipho 1SM-2OM-learn-CAUS-APPL-FV 1a.Langa 7.Zulu 2.student
'Sipho is teaching them Zulu for Langa (the students).'

c. *Usipho u-**si**-fund-is-el-a uLanga abafundi (Zulu).*
1aSipho 1SM-7OM-learn-CAUS-APPL-FV 1a.Langa 2.student 7.Zulu
'Sipho is teaching it to the students for Langa (Zulu).'

This forms an interesting contrast with Kîîtharaka. Kîîtharaka is also a type 1 symmetrical language, like Zulu: either object can be object-marked in applicatives (40) as well as causatives (41).
Kîîtharaka (Muriungi 2008: 83, 84)

(40) applicative

a. *Maria a-kû-**mî**-tûm-îr-a John.*
1.Maria 1SM-T-9OM-send-APPL-FV 1.John
'Maria has sent it to John.' (a letter)

---

[12]This is a theoretical possibility that I have not encountered in the data, representing flexible licensing that is sensitive to other factors.

b. *Maria a-kû-**mû**-tûm-îr-a barûa.*
   1.Maria 1SM-T-1OM-send-APPL-FV 9.letter
   'Maria has sent him/her a letter.'

(41) causative

   a. *Mu-borisi a-kû-**mî**-nyu-ithi-a mû-ûragani.*
      1-police 1SM-T-9OM-drink-CRC-FV 1-murderer
      'The policeman has coerced the murderer to drink it.' (the poison)

   b. *Mu-borisi a-kû-**mû**-nyu-ithi-a cûmû.*
      1.-police 1SM-T-1OM-drink-CRC-FV 9-poison
      'The policeman has coerced him/her to take the poison.'

However, when a predicate has both a causative and an applicative derivation, the objects in Kîîtharaka are no longer symmetrical: only the applied object can be object-marked (42a), and object-marking the Causee or the Theme results in ungrammaticality (42b, c).

(42) applicative + causative (Muriungi 2008: 83)

   a. *I-ba-ra-**ka**-thamb-ith-î-îr-i-e Maria nyomba.*
      FOC-2SM-PSTY-12OM-wash-CRC-APPL-PFV-IC-FV 1.Maria 9.house
      'They coerced Maria to wash the house for it (e.g the cat).'

   b. ** N-a-ra-**ba**-thamb-ith-î-îr-i-e ka-baka nyomba.*
      FOC-1SM-PSTY-2OM-wash-CRC-APPL-PFV-IC-FV 12-cat 9.house
      'He/she coerced them to wash the house for the cat.'

   c. ** I-ba-ra-**mî**-thamb-ith-î-îr-i-e Maria ka-baka.*
      F-2SM-PSTY-9OM-wash-CRC-APPL-PFV-IC-FV 1.Maria 12-cat
      'They coerced Maria to wash it for the cat.'

My hypothesis is that this sudden asymmetry is due to Kîîtharaka having a combination of the short and long causative (Bastin 1986), glossed by Muriungi as 'CRC' (coerce causative) and 'IC' (inner causative), which occur on either side of the applicative. It may thus be that the coerce causative is flexible, but the structurally higher inner causative is not. If this is true, the hierarchy in (38) should involve an extra layer asking about different types of causatives.[13]

---

[13]See also Ngonyani & Githinji's (2006) multiple applicatives in Kikuyu, which appear to behave asymmetrically despite the language's otherwise fully symmetrical properties. It remains to be seen how animacy plays a role in these counterexamples, and also at which height the higher applicative is merged.

4.2 Symmetry in passives

In Zulu, Lubukusu, Kinyarwanda and Luganda both object marking and passivisation are symmetrical: either object can be object-marked and either object can become the subject of a passive. However, the languages differ in the combination of these operations.

In Kinyarwanda and Luganda, either object can be object-marked in the active as well as the passive. That is, the Theme can be object-marked in a Benefactive passive (43b, 44a), and the Benefactive can be object-marked in a Theme passive (43c, 44b).

(43) Kinyarwanda (Ngoboka 2005: 88, glosses adapted)
symmetrical passive OM

    a. *Umusore y-a-hiing-i-ye umugore umurima.*
       1.young.man 1SM-PST-plough-APPL-ASP 1.woman 3.field
       'The young man ploughed the field for the woman.'

    b. *Umugore y-a-**wu**-hiing-i-w-e n' umusore.*
       1.woman 1SM-PST-3OM-plough-APPL-PASS-ASP by 1.young.man
       lit. 'The woman was it ploughed for by the young man.'

    c. *Umurima w-a-**mu**-hiing-i-w-e n' umusore.*
       3.field 3SM-PST-1OM-plough-APPL-PASS-ASP by 1.young.man
       'The field was ploughed (for) her by the young man.'

(44) Luganda (Ranero 2015)

    a. *O-mw-ana y-a-zi-w-ew-a luli e-ssente.*
       AUG-1-child 1SM-PST-9aOM-give-PASS the.other.day AUG-9a.money
       'The child was given it the other day, the money.'

    b. *E-ssente za-a-mu-w-ew-a luli o-mw-ana.*
       AUG-9a.money 9aSM-PST-1OM-give-PASS the.other.day AUG-1-child
       'The money was given to him/her the other day, the child.'

In Zulu and Lubukusu, on the other hand, the Benefactive/Recipient cannot be object-marked in a (otherwise perfectly acceptable) Theme passive, as in (45b) and (46b), whereas the opposite is still possible, as shown in (45a) and (46a).

(45) Lubukusu (Justine Sikuku p.c. July 2015)

    a. Recipient-passive with Theme-OM
        *Baa-sooreri ba-a-**chi**-eeb-w-a*   *(chi-khaafu).*
        2.boys   2SM-PAST-10OM-give-PASS-FV 10-COWS
        'The boys were given them (cows).'

    b. ?? Theme-passive with Recipient-OM
        *Chi-kaafu cha-a-**ba**-eeb-w-a*   *(baa-sooreri).*
        10-COWS   10SM-PST-2OM-give-PASS-FV 2-boys
        'Cows were given to them (the boys).'

(46) Zulu (Adams 2010: 26)

    a. Recipient-passive with Theme-OM
        *Aba-ntwana ba-ya-**yi**-fund-el-w-a*   *(in-cwadi).*
        2-child   2SM-PRES.DJ-9OM-read-APPL-PASS-FV 9-book
        'The children are being read it (the book).'

    b. * Theme-passive with Recipient-OM
        *In-cwadi i-ya-**ba**-fund-el-w-a*   *(aba-ntwana).*
        9-book   9SM-PRES.DJ-2OM-read-APPL-PASS-FV 2-children
        int. 'The book is being read to them (the children).'

The generalisation is thus that the Theme can be object-marked in a Benefactive passive, but the Benefactive cannot be object-marked in a Theme passive. The same asymmetry holds for extraction: the Theme can be extracted from a Benefactive passive, but the Benefactive cannot be extracted from a Theme passive. Interestingly, Norwegian and North-Western English, which are otherwise symmetrical too, show the same restriction as Zulu and Lubukusu. Crucially, there are no languages in which the asymmetry is the other way around (i.e. banning Theme extraction in a Benefactive passive).

A promising analysis of this asymmetry in passives takes v to be a phase in the active, but *not* to be a phase in the passive (Chomsky 2008; Legate 2012). Instead, in the passive, Appl (or Caus) is a phase and bears φ features, since Appl is now the highest head with full argument structure (see Chomsky's (2008) definition of the lower phase). If object marking is indeed the spell-out of a (downward) Agree relation, the exceptional presence of φ features on Appl in Zulu and Lubukusu passives implies that only the Theme can be object-marked, since the Benefactive is higher than Appl and upwards agreement cannot be spelled out as an object marker (under Roberts' 2010 approach to clitics). Either object is thus still available for passivisation, but only the Theme can be object-marked in the passive. For Kinyarwanda, I proposed at the end of §3.3 that Appl is endowed with φ features in the active too (accounting for the occurrence of multiple object markers) – the presence of φ features is thus independent of phasehood in this language, which could explain the consistent symmetry throughout the passive in this language. The same goes for Luganda, which also allows multiple object markers.

This analysis for the combination of passive and extraction is further pursued in joint work with Anders Holmberg and Michelle Sheehan, suggesting that movement of the Theme to the outer specifier of the Appl phase head traps the Benefactive object for A-bar movement to specCP (under PIC2).

5 Summary and conclusion

Upon closer examination, Bantu languages that display symmetrical double object constructions all show some asymmetry. A novel type of partial asymmetry presented in this paper is the variation between different types of ditransitive predicates, which appears to have an implicational pattern: if a language is symmetrical for causatives, it is also symmetrical for applicatives, and if it is symmetrical for applicatives, it is also symmetrical for lexical ditransitive predicates. Assuming that object marking spells out agreement on little v, and assuming that second objects are introduced by separate lower functional heads (Caus, HAppl and LAppl), symmetrical behaviour of multiple objects can be understood as the ability of such heads to Case-license either the argument they introduce in their specifier or the lower argument in their complement. Which argument it licenses depends on their relative topicality, with the low functional head licensing the least topical of the two. The remaining argument will be Case-licensed and agreed with by little v (active) or T (passive), which thus explains object marking and passivisation of the most topical argument. The implicational relationship between the types of predicates can be captured in a parameter hierarchy, motivated by third-factor principles.

Further research should clearly take into account more Bantu languages to test whether the appearing implicational pattern indeed holds true (especially since type 3 is now only confirmed for one language, Luguru). A particularly interesting language to look at here is Kinande, which shows a linker between two objects. Baker & Collins (2006) propose an account in terms of Case-licensing, which however Schneider-Zioga (2014) shows to not account for constructions in which the linker appears between an argument and an adjunct.

Jenneke van der Wal

The current paper only concerns double object constructions with two DP arguments that have thematic roles as Causee, Benefactive, Recipient and Theme. Taking into account predicates with a DP and a PP argument (cf. Bruening 2010; Jeong 2007; Baker & Kramer 2015) and other grammatical roles such as Locatives and Instrumentals is likely to change the picture (see e.g. Baker 1988; Gerdts & Whaley 1991; 1993; Marantz 1993; Alsina & Mchombo 1993; Ngonyani 1996; 1998; Simango 1995; Nakamura 1997; Ngoboka 2005; 2016; Zeller & Ngoboka 2006; Jerro 2015), as well as possessor raising constructions that take a similar shape (Simango 2007; Morolong & Hyman 1977). However, it should be established beforehand whether the base-generated structure of these (locative, instrumental) constructions are the same as for the double object construction, considering that the so-called dative alternation is argued to actually be based on different underlying structures (Pesetsky 1995; Harley 2002; Bruening 2010; see also footnote 3).

A final point is that the current paper considers primarily object marking, with an extension to A-movement in the passive, but not much is known about the symmetrical or asymmetrical behaviour of different (causative, applicate) predicates for A-bar operations such as relativisation (Nakamura 1997), which the proposed analysis does not make any independent predictions for.

Abbreviations and symbols

Numbers refer to noun classes, or to persons when followed by SG or PL.

APPL	applicative	OM	object marker
ASP	aspect	OPT	optative
BEN	Benefactive	PASS	passive
CJ	conjoint verb form	POSS	possessive
CAUS	causative	PAST	past tense
CRC	coerce	PROG	progressive
DEM	demonstrative	R	Recipient
DJ	disjoint verb form	RECPAST	recent past
DOC	double object construction	SM	subject marker
FV	final vowel	T	tense
IC	inner causative	TH	theme
int	intended meaning		

Acknowledgements

This research is funded by the European Research Council Advanced Grant No. 269752 *Rethinking Comparative Syntax*. I want to express my thanks to Michael Marlo, Michael Diercks, Rodrigo Ranero, Nancy Kula, Jochen Zeller, Jean Paul Ngoboka, Leston Buell, David Iorio, Jekura U. Kavari, Thabo Ditsele, Hannah Gibson, Lutz Marten, Justine Sikuku, Andrej Malchukov, Carolyn Harford, Claire Halpert, Nikki Adams, Patricia Schneider-Zioga, Peter Githinji, Chege Githiora, Paul Murrell, Joyce Mbepera, Judith Nakayiza, Saudah Namyalo and the ReCoS team (Ian Roberts, Michelle Sheehan, Timothy Bazalgette, Alison Biggs, Georg Höhn, Theresa Biberauer, Anders Holmberg, Sam Wolfe and András Bárány), for sharing and discussing thoughts and data with me. Thanks also to the audiences at CALL 2015 and LAGB 2015, and to two anonymous reviewers. Any errors and misrepresentations are mine only.

References

Abels, Klaus. 2003. *Successive cyclicity, anti-locality and adposition stranding*. University of Connecticut (Storrs) dissertation.

Adams, Nikki B. 2010. *The Zulu ditransitive verb phrase*. University of Chicago dissertation.

Adger, David & Daniel Harbour. 2007. Syntax and synchretisms of the person case constraint. *Syntax* 10(1). 2–37.

Alsina, Alex & Sam Mchombo. 1993. Object asymmetries and the Chichewa applicative construction. In Sam Mchombo (ed.), *Theoretical aspects of Bantu grammar*, 17–45. Stanford: CSLI.

Anagnostopoulou, Elena. 2003. *The syntax of ditransitives*. Berlin: Mouton de Gruyter.

Baker, Mark. 1988. Theta theory and the syntax of applicatives in Chichewa. *Natural Language & Linguistic Theory* 6. 353–389.

Baker, Mark. 2012. On the relationship of object agreement and accusative case: Evidence from Amharic. *Linguistic Inquiry* 43(2). 255–274.

Baker, Mark & Chris Collins. 2006. Linkers and the internal structure of vP. *Natural Language & Linguistic Theory* 24. 307–354.

Baker, Mark & Ruth Kramer. 2015. Doubling Clitics are Pronouns: Agree, Move, Reduce, & Interpret. Ms. Rutgers University and Georgetown University.

Baker, Mark, Ken Safir & Justine Sikuku. 2012. Sources of (a)symmetry in Bantu double object constructions. In Nathan Arnett & Ryan Bennett (eds.), *Proceedings of the 30th West Coast Conference on Formal Linguistics*, 54–64. Cascadilla Proceedings Project.

Bárány, András. 2015. *Differential object marking in Hungarian and the morphosyntax of case and agreement*. University of Cambridge dissertation.

Bastin, Yvonne. 1986. Les suffixes causatifs dans les langues bantoues. *Africana Linguistica* 10. 55–145.

Bax, Anna & Michael Diercks. 2012. Information structure constraints on object marking in Manyika. *Southern African Linguistics and Applied Language Studies* 30(2). 185–202.

Beaudoin-Lietz, Christa, Derek Nurse & Sarah Rose. 2004. Pronominal object marking in Bantu. In Akinbiyi Akinlabi & Oluseye Adesola (eds.), *Proceedings of the 4th World Congress of African Linguistics, New Brunswick (2003)*, 175–188. Cologne: Rüdiger Köpper.

Biberauer, Theresa & Ian Roberts. 2015. Rethinking formal hierarchies: A proposed unification. *Cambridge Occasional Papers in Linguistics* 7. 1–31.

Bobaljik, Jonathan D. 2008. Where's φ? Agreement as a post-syntactic operation. In Daniel Harbour, David Adger & Susana Béjar (eds.), *Phi-Theory: Phi features across interfaces and modules*, 295–328. Oxford: Oxford University Press.

Bresnan, Joan & Lioba Moshi. 1990. Object asymmetries in comparative Bantu syntax. *Linguistic Inquiry* 21(2). 147–185.

Bruening, Benjamin. 2010. Double object constructions disguised as prepositional datives. *Linguistic Inquiry* 41(2). 287–305.

Bruening, Benjamin. 2014. Defects of defective intervention. *Linguistic Inquiry* 45(4). 707–719.

Buell, Leston C. 2005. *Issues in Zulu morphosyntax*. Los Angeles: University of California dissertation.

Cann, Ronnie & Patricia Mabugu. 2007. Constructional polysemy: The applicative construction in ChiShona. In Marina Rakova, Gergely Pethö & Csilla Rákosi (eds.), *The cognitive basis of polysemy*, 221–245. Frankfurt: Peter Lang Publishing Group.

Chomsky, Noam. 2001. Derivation by phase. In Michael Kenstowicz (ed.), *Ken Hale: A life in language*, 1–52. Cambridge, MA: The MIT Press.

Chomsky, Noam. 2005. Three factors in language design. *Linguistic Inquiry* 36(1). 1–22.

Chomsky, Noam. 2008. On phases. In Roberto Freidin, Carlos P. Otero & Maria L. Zubizarreta (eds.), *Foundational issues in linguistic theory: Essays in honor of Jean-Roger Vergnaud*, 133–166. Cambridge, MA: MIT Press.

Creissels, Denis. 2004. *Non-canonical applicatives and focalization in Tswana*. Paper presented at Syntax of the World's Languages, Leipzig.

de Kind, Jasper & Koen Bostoen. 2012. The applicative in CiLubà grammar and discourse: A semantic goal analysis. *Southern African Linguistics and Applied Language Studies* 30(1). 101–124.

Diercks, Michael. 2012. Parameterizing case: Evidence from Bantu. *Syntax* 15(3). 253–286.

Doggett, Teal Bissell. 2004. *All things being unequal: Locality in movement*. MIT dissertation.

Gerdts, Donna B. & Lindsay Whaley. 1991. Locatives vs. instrumentals in Kinyarwanda. In K. Hubbard (ed.), *Proceedings of the Seventeenth Annual Meeting of the Berkeley Linguistics Society: Special session on African language structures*. 87–97. University of California, Berkeley, California.

Gerdts, Donna B. & Lindsay Whaley. 1993. Kinyarwanda applicatives and some universal laws. In T. Heift & P. McFetridge (eds.), *Working papers in linguistics, Vol. 2*, 59–88. Simon Fraser University.

Givón, Talmy (ed.). 1994. *Voice and inversion: Typological studies in language*. Amsterdam: John Benjamins.

Haddican, William & Anders Holmberg. 2012. Object movement symmetries in British English dialects: Experimental evidence for a mixed case/locality approach. *Journal of Comparative Germanic Linguistics* 15. 189–212.

Haddican, William & Anders Holmberg. 2015. Four kinds of object asymmetry. In Ludmila Veselovská & Markéta Janebová (eds.), *Complex visibles out there. Proceedings of the Olomouc Linguistics Colloquium (2014): Language use and linguistic structure* (Olomouc Modern Language Series 4), 145–162. Olomouc: Palacky University.

Harizanov, Boris. 2014. Clitic doubling at the syntax-morphophonology interface: A-movement and morphological merger in Bulgarian. *Natural Language & Linguistic Theory* 32. 1033–1088.

Harley, Heidi. 2002. Possession and the double object construction. *Linguistic Variation Yearbook* 2. 29–68.

Henderson, Brent. 2006. *The syntax and typology of Bantu relative clauses*. University of Illinois at Urbana-Champaign dissertation.

Hodges, Kathryn S. 1977. Causatives, transitivity and objecthood in Kimeru. In Martin Mould & Thomas J. Hinnebusch (eds.), *Papers from the eighth conference on African linguistics*, 113–125. Los Angeles: University of California.

Holmberg, Anders, Michelle Sheehan & Jenneke van der Wal. 2015. *Movement from the double object construction is never fully symmetrical*. Paper presented at Meeting of the LAGB, UCL, London.

Hyman, Larry M. & Alessandro Duranti. 1982. On the object relation in Bantu. In Paul J. Hopper & Sandra A. Thompson (eds.), *Syntax and Semantics: Studies in transitivity*, 217–239. New York: Academic Press.

Iorio, David. 2014. *Subject and object marking in Bembe*. Newcastle University dissertation.

Jeong, Youngmi. 2007. *Applicatives. Structure and interpretation from a minimalist perspective*. Amsterdam: John Benjamins.

Jerro, Kyle. 2015. Revisiting object symmetry in Bantu. In Ruth Kramer, Elizabeth C. Zsiga & One Tlale Boyer (eds.), *Selected Proceedings of the 44th Annual Conference on African Linguistics*, 130–145. Somerville, MA: Cascadilla Proceedings Project.

Julien, Marit. 2002. *Syntactic heads and word formation*. Oxford: Oxford University Press.

Kramer, Ruth. 2014. Clitic doubling or object agreement: The view from Amharic. *Natural Language & Linguistic Theory* 32(2). 593–634.

Legate, Julie Anne. 2012. The size of phases. In Ángel J. Gallego (ed.), *Phases*, 233–250. Berlin: De Gruyter.

Machobane, 'Malillo. 1989. *Some restrictions of the Sesotho transitivizing morpheme*. Montreal: McGill University dissertation.

Malchukov, Andrej L. 2010. Ditransitive constructions: A typological overview. In Andrej L. Malchukov, Martin Haspelmath & Bernard Comrie (eds.), *Studies in ditransitive constructions: A comparative handbook*, 1–64. Berlin: De Gruyter Mouton.

Malchukov, Andrej L. 2013. Alignment preferences in basic and derived ditransitives. In Dik Bakker & Martin Haspelmath (eds.), *Language across boundaries. Studies in memory of Anna Siewierska*, 263–291. Berlin: Mouton de Gruyter.

Marantz, Alec. 1993. Implications of asymmetries in double object constructions. In Sam Mchombo (ed.), *Theoretical aspects of Bantu grammar*, 113–150. Stanford, CA: CSLI.

Marten, Lutz. 2003. The dynamics of Bantu applied verbs: An analysis at the syntax-pragmatics interface. In Kézié K. Lébikaza (ed.), *Actes du 3e Congrès*

Mondial de Linguistique Africaine Lomé (2000), 207–221. Cologne: Rüdiger Köppe Verlag.

Marten, Lutz & Nancy C. Kula. 2012. Object marking and morphosyntactic variation in Bantu. *South African Journal of African Languages* 30(2). 237–253.

Marten, Lutz & Deograsia Ramadhani. 2001. An overview of object marking in Kiluguru. *SOAS Working Papers in Linguistics* 11. 259–275.

Mathangwane, Joyce T. & E. Kweku Osam. 2006. Grammatical relations in Ikalanga. *Studies in African Linguistics* 35(2). 189–208.

McGinnis, Martha. 1998a. Locality and inert case. In Pius N. Tamanji & Kiyomi Musumoto (eds.), *Proceedings of NELS 28*, 267–281. Amherst, MA: GLSA Publications, University of Massachusetts.

McGinnis, Martha. 1998b. *Locality in A-movement*. University of Toronto dissertation.

McGinnis, Martha. 2001. Variation in the syntax of applicatives. *Linguistics Variation Yearbook* 1. 105–146.

Morimoto, Yukiko. 2006. Agreement properties and word order in comparative Bantu. *ZAS Papers in Linguistics* 43. 161–188.

Morolong, 'Malillo & Larry M. Hyman. 1977. Animacy, objects and clitics in Sesotho. *Studies in African Linguistics* 8. 199–218.

Moshi, Lioba. 1998. Word order in multiple object constructions in KiVunjo-Chaga. *Journal of African Languages and Linguistics* 19. 137–152.

Mugari, Victor. 2013. Object marking restrictions on Shona causative and applicative constructions. *Southern African Linguistics and Applied Language Studies* 31(2). 151–160.

Muriungi, Peter. 2008. *Phrasal movement inside Bantu verbs: Deriving affix scope and order in Kîîtharaka*. University of Tromsø dissertation.

Nakamura, Masanori. 1997. Object extraction in Bantu applicatives: Some implications for minimalism. *Linguistic Inquiry* 28(2). 252–280.

Ngoboka, Jean Paul. 2005. *A syntactic analysis of Kinyarwanda applicatives*. Durban: University of KwaZulu-Natal MA thesis.

Ngoboka, Jean Paul. 2016. *Locatives in Kinyarwanda*. Durban: University of KwaZulu-Natal dissertation.

Ngonyani, Deo. 1996. *The morphosyntax of applicatives*. University of California, Los Angeles dissertation.

Ngonyani, Deo. 1998. Properties of applied objects in Kiswahili and Kindendeule. *Studies in African Linguistics* 27. 67–95.

Ngonyani, Deo & Peter Githinji. 2006. The asymmetric nature of Bantu applicative constructions. *Lingua* 116. 31–63.

Nunes, Jairo. 2004. *Linearization of chains and sideward movement.* Cambridge, MA: MIT Press.
Oehrle, Richard. T. 1976. *The grammatical status of the English dative alternation.* Cambridge, MA: MIT dissertation.
Pesetsky, David. 1995. *Zero syntax: Experiencers and cascades.* Cambridge, MA: The MIT Press.
Preminger, Omer. 2014. *Agreement and its failures.* Cambridge, MA: The MIT Press.
Pylkkänen, Liina. 2008. *Introducing arguments.* Cambridge, MA: MIT Press.
Ranero, Rodrigo. 2015. *The syntax of dislocated objects in Luganda.* Cambridge: University of Cambridge MPhil dissertation.
Riedel, Kristina. 2009. *The syntax of object marking in Sambaa: A comparative perspective.* Utrecht: LOT.
Roberts, Ian. 2007. *Diachronic syntax.* Oxford: Oxford University Press.
Roberts, Ian. 2010. *Agreement and head movement: Clitics, incorporation, and defective goals.* Cambridge, MA: The MIT Press.
Roberts, Ian & Anders Holmberg. 2010. Introduction: Parameters in minimalist theory. In Theresa Biberauer, Anders Holmberg, Ian Roberts & Michelle Sheehan (eds.), *Parametric variation. Null subjects in minimalist theory*, 1–57. Cambridge: Cambridge University Press.
Roberts, Ian & Anna Roussou. 2003. *Syntactic change: A minimalist approach to grammaticalization.* Cambridge: Cambridge University Press.
Rugemalira, Josephat M. 1991. What is a symmetrical language? Multiple object constructions in Bantu. In Kathleen Hubbard (ed.), *17th annual meeting of the Berkeley Linguistics Society: Papers from the special session*, 200–209. Berkeley: Berkeley Linguistics Society.
Schadeberg, Thilo C. 1995. Object diagnostics in Bantu. In E. 'Nolue Emenanjo & Ozo-mekuri Ndimele (eds.), *Issues in African languages and linguistics*, 173–180. Aba: National Institute for Nigerian Languages.
Schneider-Zioga, Patricia. 2014. The linker in Kinande re-examined. In Ruth Kramer, Elizabeth C. Zsiga & One Tiale Boyer (eds.), *Selected Proceedings of the 44th Annual Conference on African Linguistics*, 254–263. Somerville, MA: Cascadilla Proceedings Project.
Sheehan, Michelle. 2013. *Parameter hierarchies: The case of Case.* Handouts of lecture series given at Unicamp, Campinas.
Sheehan, Michelle. 2014. Towards a parameter hierarchy for alignment. In Robert E. Santana-LaBarge (ed.), *Proceedings of WCCFL 31*, 399–408. Somerville, MA: Cascadilla Press.

Sheehan, Michelle & Jenneke van der Wal. 2016. Do we need abstract Case? In Kyeong-min Kim, Pocholo Umbal, Trevor Block, Queenie Chan, Tanie Cheng, Kelli Finney, Mara Katz, Sophie Nickel-Thompson & Lisa Shorten (eds.), *Proceedings of the 33rd WCCFL*, 351–360. Somerville, MA: Cascadilla Proceedings Project.

Simango, Silvester Ron. 1995. *The syntax of Bantu double object constructions.* University of South Carolina dissertation.

Simango, Silvester Ron. 2007. Enlarged arguments in Bantu: Evidence from Chichewa. *Lingua* 117(6). 928–949.

Ssekiryango, Jackson. 2006. Observations on double object construction in Luganda. In Olaoba F. Arasanyin & Michael A. Pemberton (eds.), *Selected Proceedings of the 36th Annual Conference on African Linguistics.* Somerville, MA: Cascadilla Proceedings Project.

Thwala, Nhlanhla. 2006. Parameters of variation and complement licensing in Bantu. *ZAS Papers in Linguistics* 43. 209–232.

Ura, Hiroyuki. 1996. *Multiple feature-checking: A theory of grammatical function splitting.* MIT dissertation.

van der Wal, Jenneke. 2009. *Word order and information structure in Makhuwa-Enahara.* Utrecht: LOT.

van der Wal, Jenneke. 2015a. Bantu object clitics as defective goals. *Revue Roumaine de Linguistique* LX(2–3). 277–296.

van der Wal, Jenneke. 2015b. Evidence for abstract Case in Bantu. *Lingua* 165. 109–132.

van der Wal, Jenneke. 2016. *Obligatory marking of prominence: Parameters of Bantu object marking.* Paper presented at Cambridge Comparative Syntax 5, Cambridge, UK.

van der Wal, Jenneke. Submitted. The AWSOM correlation in comparative Bantu object marking. In Katharina Hartmann, Johannes Mursell & Peter Smith (eds.), *Agree to agree: Agreement in the Minimalist Program.* Berlin: Language Science Press.

Yoneda, Nobuko. 2011. Word order in Matengo (N13): Topicality and informational roles. *Lingua* 121(5). 754–771.

Zeller, Jochen. 2008. The subject marker in Bantu as an antifocus marker. *Stellenbosch Papers in Linguistics* 38. 221–254.

Zeller, Jochen. 2011. *Aspects of object marking in Zulu.* Paper presented at LSSA conference, Rhodes University, Grahamstown.

Zeller, Jochen. 2012. Object marking in isiZulu. *Southern African Linguistics and Applied Language Studies* 30(2). 219–235.

Zeller, Jochen. 2014. Three types of object marking in Bantu. *Linguistische Berichte* 239. 347–367.

Zeller, Jochen. 2015. Argument prominence and agreement: Explaining an unexpected object asymmetry in Zulu. *Lingua* 156. 17–39.

Zeller, Jochen & Jean Paul Ngoboka. 2006. Kinyarwanda locative applicatives and the minimal link condition. *South African Journal of African Languages* 24. 101–124.

Zeller, Jochen & Jean Paul Ngoboka. 2014. On parametric variation in Bantu, with particular reference to Kinyarwanda. *Transactions of the Philological Society* 113(2). 1–26.

Zerbian, Sabine. 2006. *Expression of information structure in Northern Sotho.* Berlin: Humboldt University dissertation.

Chapter 6

Defective intervention effects in two Greek varieties and their implications for φ-incorporation as Agree

Elena Anagnostopoulou
University of Crete

> In this paper, I argue that pro-drop configurations cannot be analyzed as formally identical to downward Agree configurations. I take as a starting point the observation that in monoclausal constructions clearly involving downward Agree, as in Icelandic and Dutch, the presence of a dative intervener does not block Agree between T and a lower nominative argument. I then investigate two types of intervention effects in Standard and Northern Greek and argue that intervention effects in the presence of an indirect object arise always, regardless of whether the nominative subject is overt or covert and regardless of whether a subject DP remains in its base position or moves overtly. This leads me to conclude that the relevant constructions always display movement.

1 Introduction

In his seminal paper on Null Subject Parameters, Holmberg (2010) argues that pro-drop configurations in consistent and partial Null Subject Languages always involve incorporation of a φP to T.[1] This type of incorporation, however, is claimed not to be movement. Adopting the theory of Roberts (2010), Holmberg

---

[1] Holmberg argues that the two language types differ in whether T contains a D feature or not. In consistent Null Subject Languages, T contains D and therefore null subjects can be definite. In partial Null Subject Languages, on the other hand, T lacks D and therefore null subjects are either arbitrary/indefinite or expletive but never definite.

proposes that incorporation of a φP in T is the direct effect of Agree (Chomsky 2001) and works as follows. Finite T has a set of unvalued φ-features and probes for a category with matching valued features (step 1 in 1). The defective subject pronoun in vP has the required valued φ-features which are copied by T and thus value T's uφ-features. At the same time, T values the subject's unvalued case feature (step 2 in 1). As a result, T shares all of φ's feature values. The result is the same as if φ had moved, by head movement, incorporating into T, but without actual movement taking place. According to Holmberg, the advantage of headmove as Agree is that it avoids the problem posed by head movement, namely the lack of c-command between the links of a head chain (but see Lechner 2006; 2007). Following Roberts (2010), Holmberg (2010) furthermore proposes that the probe and the goal form a chain, which is subject to chain reduction falling under the rules in (2). The subject φP is therefore not pronounced (by 2a; indicated under step 3 in 1), and the chain is pronounced in the form of an affix on the finite verb or auxiliary, following incorporation of V+v into T.

(1) 1. [T, D, uφ, NOM] [$_{vP}$ [3SG, uCase] v....] →
     2. [T, D, 3SG, NOM] [$_{vP}$ [3SG, NOM] v...] →
     3. [T, D, 3SG, NOM] [$_{vP}$ ~~[3SG, NOM]~~ v..]

(2) a. Pronounce the highest chain copy.
     b. Pronounce only one chain copy.

In this paper, I present an argument based on intervention effects that φ-incorporation in the sense of Holmberg (2010) and Roberts (2010) cannot be reduced to downward Agree. Specifically, I discuss monoclausal configurations displaying agreement between the verb and a subject DP in Icelandic and Dutch and show that when agreement is the result of downward Agree, an intervener does not block Agree between T/v and the subject. By contrast, constructions in which the subject moves to spec,TP are subject to intervention effects in both languages. I then discuss comparable intervention effects in two varieties of Greek, Standard and Northern Greek, which are both consistent Null Subject Languages. Crucially, intervention effects arise always, regardless of whether the subject is overt or covert, and regardless of the preverbal vs. postverbal position of the subject when this is overt. In view of the Agree vs. Move asymmetry regarding monoclausal intervention in non-Null Subject Languages, the presence of

6 Defective intervention effects in two Greek varieties

intervention effects in Null Subject Languages leads to the conclusion that what Holmberg and Roberts call "φ-incorporation" involves actual movement.[2]

2 No intervention on local Agree, intervention on local Move: Icelandic and Dutch

As is widely discussed in recent years (Holmberg & Hróarsdóttir 2003 and many others), "defective intervention effects" (Chomsky 2000) on downward Agree arise in biclausal constructions. In Icelandic, a matrix raising predicate cannot enter Agree with an embedded nominative argument in number across an intervening dative experiencer subject, as in (3a), while agreement is possible if the intervener moves to the higher clause, as in (3b) (Watanabe 1993; Schütze 1997):

---

[2]An anonymous reviewer strongly objects to the idea of abandoning Holmberg's non-move incorporation and suggests that the asymmetry discussed in the paper is not necessarily an argument against it. I am quoting from the reviewer: "The paper relies crucially on this derivational analysis (or "hierarchical-structural") of IE (intervention effect). It does not attempt to explore (not even refer) to potential alternatives, which could ultimately "save" Holmberg's Agree analysis. Suppose that IE are not so construed, being rather "informational" (prosodic), read off linear strings (and probably subject to variable interpretive judgments). Then the constraints on their presence (or absence) do not depend on Agree/Move choices, but crucially on the information structure of the intervener (see e.g. Tomioka 2007 or Eilam 2009, among others). This potential analysis of IE is compatible with the general absence of IE in Amharic, and extendable to alternative questions in which an intervener preceding a disjunctive phrase removes the alternative question reading, leaving the yes/no reading. Other "semantic" accounts of IE have been brought up by Beck (2006) and others, which may or may not be adequate. The point is not whether or not the Move account of the IE asymmetry is or is not correct; the paper does not show that it is unavoidable, and it does not attempt to look at alternatives that preserve Agree incorporation as generally relevant for both IE and non-IE contexts." The reviewer is certainly correct that the argument made in the paper crucially relies on a derivational analysis of strong and weak intervention effects (IEs), and might also turn out to be correct that an informational account of IEs could rescue Holmberg's non-move incorporation. However, semantic/pragmatic accounts of IEs along the lines of Beck (2006); Tomioka (2007) and Eilam (2009) have been discussed in the context of wh-movement, and it is not obvious whether and how they can be extended to capture intervention effects in Move and Agree in passives, unaccusatives, raising and expletive-associate constructions of the type discussed here. In the absence of such an account for A movement, I do not see why one should not construct an argument based on the standard view of IEs. Exploring alternatives in order to preserve Agree Incorporation is the aim of a different paper. Note that, as mentioned in the main text, the main advantage of Agree incorporation according to Holmberg is that it avoids head movement. In agreement with Lechner (2006; 2007; 2009); Baker (2009) and others I do not share the view that head movement should be dispensed with.

(3) Icelandic

    a. *Mér   ?*virðast/virðist [Jóni   vera taldir   t líka hestarnir].*
       Me.DAT seemed.PL/SG   Jon.DAT be believed.PL t like horses.NOM
       'I perceive John to be believed to like horses.'

    b. *Jóni   virðast/?*virðist [t vera taldir   t líka hestarnir].*
       Jon.DAT seemed.PL/SG   t be   believed.PL t like horses.NOM
       'John seems to be believed to like horses.'

But in monoclausal constructions things are different, as stressed by Bobaljik (2008). In Icelandic monoclausal configurations featuring an expletive or a PP in the preverbal position, number agreement between the inflected verb and a lower nominative argument across an intervening dative is always possible, and generally obligatory, as shown by the data in (4) (from Jónsson 1996 and Zaenen et al. 1985; Bobaljik 2008: 298, 321):

(4) Icelandic

    a. *Það líkuðu einhverjum   þessir sokkar.*
       expl liked.PL someone.DAT these socks.NOM
       'Someone liked these socks.'

    b. *Um   veturinn voru   konunginum gefnar ambáttir.*
       In the winter were.PL the king.DAT given slaves.NOM
       'In the winter the king was given (female) slaves.'

    c. *Það voru   konungi gefnar ambáttir   í   vettur.*
       EXPL were.PL king.DAT given slaves.NOM in winter
       'There was a king given maidservants this winter.'

    d. *Það voru   einhverjum   gefnir þessir sokkar.*
       EXPL were.PL someone.DAT given these socks.NOM
       'Someone was given these socks.'

Bobaljik concludes that defective intervention on downward Agree does not arise in monoclausal configurations. He furthermore proposes to view the contrast between biclausal and monoclausal constructions as an argument for a domain-based characterization of intervention effects according to which, the position of the dative is indicative of the presence of a domain boundary in (3a) but not in (3b); cf. Nomura (2005).

The conclusion that downward Agree in monoclausal constructions is not subject to defective intervention is reinforced by evidence from Dutch discussed

6 Defective intervention effects in two Greek varieties

in Anagnostopoulou (2003). Dutch passives and unaccusatives with an *in situ* nominative subject following a dative DP are grammatical, as shown in (5) (Den Dikken 1995: 208, fn 26). Notice that both the dative and the nominative argument are vP internal, since they follow the adverb *waarschijnlijk* which is taken to mark the left edge of the vP:

(5) Dutch

    a. *dat waarschijnlijk [$_{vP}$ Marie   het boek   gegeven] wordt*
        That probably   Mary.DAT the book.NOM given   is

    b. *dat waarschijnlijk [$_{vP}$ Marie   het boek   bevallen] zal*
        that probably   Mary.DAT the book.NOM please   will

    c. *dat waarschijnlijk [$_{vP}$ de jongen   de teugels   ontglipten]*
        that probably   the boys.DAT the reins.NOM slipped

The facts in (5) provide evidence that T, which I take to be situated to the right of the vP where the auxiliaries reside in (5a) and (5b), can enter downward Agree with an in situ nominative across a higher dative, i.e. the dative does not cause an intervention effect for Agree between T and the nominative argument vP-internally.

Crucially, an intervention effect does arise when the nominative argument undergoes overt NP-movement to spec,TP across the vP internal dative. Consider the following contrast observed by Den Dikken (1995: 207–208):

(6) Dutch

    a. ?* *dat [$_{TP}$ het boek   waarschijnlijk [$_{vP}$ Marie   ~~het book~~*
          that   the book.NOM probably   Mary.DAT
        gegeven] wordt]
        given   is

    b. *dat [$_{TP}$ het boek   Marie   waarschijnlijk [$_{vP}$ ~~Marie het book~~*
        that   the book.NOM Mary.DAT probably
        gegeven] wordt]
        given   is
        'that the book is probably given to Mary'

In (6), movement of the nominative theme leads to a relatively mild deviance if the DP goal occurs to the right of the adverb *waarschijnlijk*, as in (6a), and results in a fully well-formed output when it occurs to its left, as in (6b). If argument placement to the left of VP-external adverbs signifies scrambling, then these facts suggest that passivization across an intervening DP goal is subject to an intervention effect in Dutch, unless the goal undergoes scrambling. Anagnostopoulou (2003) argues that DP scrambling of the intervener, just like cliticization of genitive IO interveners in Greek (see §4 below for cliticization), is a strategy to obviate intervention effects. The same contrast is found in (non-alternating) unaccusatives, as shown in (7) and (8):

(7) Dutch
    a. ?* *dat het boek   waarschijnlijk Marie   bevallen zal*
        that the book.NOM probably   Mary.DAT please   will
    b. *dat het boek   Marie   waarschijnlijk bevallen zal*
        that the book.NOM Mary.DAT probably   please   will
        'that the book will probably appeal to Mary'

(8) Dutch
    a. ?? *dat de teugels   waarschijnlijk de jongen   ontglipten*
        that the reins.NOM probably   the boys.DAT slipped
    b. *dat de teugels   de jongen   waarschijnlijk ontglipten*
        that the reins.NOM the boys.DAT probably   slipped
        'that the reins probably slipped out of the boys' hands'

While it blocks Move, the vP internal dative does not block Agree between the nominative and T, as was shown in (5). In order to account for this difference between Move and Agree with respect to intervention, Anagnostopoulou (2003: 222) proposed that the features turning Dutch datives into interveners are their D/EPP-features, and not their Case/φ-features. Icelandic shows that the Agree-Move asymmetry with respect to intervention is more general. As is well-known and widely discussed in the literature, in the counterparts of (4) lacking an expletive or a PP in the preverbal position, it is the higher quirky dative and not the lower nominative DP that is allowed to move to Spec,TP. I conclude that defective interveners block Move and not Agree because their D features make them interveners, and D features are relevant for Move/EPP processes, not for Agree/φ-feature valuation processes.

3 Pro-drop and case distribution in two varieties of Greek

As is well known, Greek is a language showing all the properties associated with consistent Null Subject Languages. It has definite subject omission (9), lack of expletives with impersonal and weather verbs (10), absence of that-trace effects (11), availability of VS, VSO and VOS orders (12):

(9) Definite subject omission
graf-o,   graf-is,   graf-i,   graf-ume, graf-ete, graf--un
write.1SG, write.2SG, write.3SG, write.1PL, write.2PL, write.3PL
'I write, you write, he/she/it writes, we, you, they write'

(10) No expletives with impersonal and weather verbs
Fenet-e   oti tha vreks-i.
Seem.3SG that FUT rain.3SG
'It seems that it will rain.'

(11) No that-trace effects
Pjos ipes   oti efige?
Who said.2SG that left
'*Who did you say that left?'

(12) VS, VSO, VOS orders

a. *Efige   o   Janis.*
left.3SG the Janis.NOM
'John left.'

b. *Egrapse   o   Janis   to vivlio.*
wrote.3SG the Janis.NOM the book.ACC

c. *Egrapse   to vivlio   o   Janis.*
wrote.3SG the book.ACC the Janis.NOM
'John wrote the book.'

In addition, Greek lacks the null indefinite/ arbitrary subject typically found in partial Null Subject Languages (Holmberg 2010). It has (i) null exclusive 3rd person plural indefinite subjects (Belletti & Rizzi 1988; Pesetsky 1995; Condoravdi 1989), (ii) null inclusive 2nd person singular subjects with arbitrary reference or (iii) overt expressions with arbitrary reference corresponding to English 'one':

(13) Greek: Indefinite Subjects

a. *Su   tilefonisan. Prepi na   itan   o   Janis.*
Cl.2GEN called.3PL. Must SUBJ was.3SG the Janis.NOM
'Someone called you. It must have been John.'

b. *Dulevis sklira stin Ellada ke xoris na plironese.*
Work.2SG hard in-the Greece and without SUBJ pay.NACT.2SG
'One works hard in Greek and without getting paid.'

c. *Dulevi kanis sklira stin Ellada ke xoris na plironete.*
Work.3SG one hard in-the Greece and without SUBJ pay.NACT.3SG
'One works hard in Greek and without getting paid.'

Greek has morphological nominative (NOM), accusative (ACC) and genitive (GEN) case. Nominative occurs on subjects, accusative on direct objects (DOs) and most prepositional complements and genitive is the case assigned DP internally. Moreover, Ancient Greek datives (DATs) were lost in Medieval Greek and have been replaced in ditransitives and two-place unaccusatives by either GENs or ACCs, depending on the dialect (see Anagnostopoulou & Sevdali 2015 for discussion and references). Standard Modern Greek and many southern dialects have GEN-ACC/NOM constructions, while Northern Greek dialects have ACC-ACC/NOM constructions (Dimitriadis 1999 and references cited there). The IO is not allowed to alternate with NOM in passives, regardless of whether it bears GEN (in Standard Greek) or ACC (in Northern Greek) in actives:

(14) Standard Greek: No GEN – NOM alternations in passives

　a. *Edosa tu Petru ena pagoto.*
　　Gave.1SG the Peter.GEN an icecream.ACC
　　'I gave Peter an ice-cream.'

　b. ** O Petros dothike ena pagoto.*
　　The Peter.NOM gave.NACT an ice-cream.ACC
　　'Peter was given an ice-cream.'

(15) Northern Greek: No ACC – NOM alternations in passives

　a. *Edosa ton Petro ena pagoto.*
　　Gave.1SG the Peter.ACC an ice-cream.ACC
　　'I gave Peter an ice-cream.'

　b. ** O Petros dothike ena pagoto.*
　　The Peter.NOM gave.NACT an ice-cream.ACC
　　'Peter was given an ice-cream.'

In both varieties, only the DO bearing accusative is allowed to alternate with NOM. Finally, both varieties qualify as consistent Null Subject Languages.

4 Weak and Strong Intervention in Standard and Northern Greek

Both Standard and Northern Greek have defective intervention effects in monoclausal passive and unaccusative constructions displaying NP-movement of the DO across the IO. However, the two types of intervention have very different properties. Here I will only discuss passivized ditransitives in the two dialects.[3]

Standard Greek has a defective intervention effect caused by the GEN IO when the NOM DO undergoes NP-movement across it, as in (16a) (Anagnostopoulou 2003). The effect is weak, i.e. the resulting sentence is deviant and not strongly unagrammatical, as is the case with Dutch (6a), and can be rescued if the intervener surfaces as a clitic or is clitic doubled, as in (16b), similarly to the Dutch scrambling strategy we saw in (6b):

(16) Standard Greek: Weak Intervention Effect
    a. ?* *To pagoto   dothike   tu Petru   apo tin Maria.*
       The ice-cream.NOM gave.NACT the Peter.GEN by the Mary
       'The ice-cream was given Peter by Mary.'
    b. *To pagoto   tu   dothike   (tu Petru)   apo tin Maria.*
       The ice-cream.NOM cl.GEN gave.NACT the Peter.GEN by the Mary
       'The ice-cream was given Peter by Mary.'

I will call this 'a weak defective intervention effect'. Experimental evidence in Georgala (2012) supports the view that, even though the deviance of (16a) is mild, an intervention effect is indeed present and is obviated in (16b). Specifically, Georgala applies the magnitude estimation experimental method (Gurman et al. 1996; Cowart 1997; Keller 2000) to such sentences and finds out that sentences like (16a) are consistently and systematically scored much lower than their counterparts in (16b) by native speakers of Standard Greek.

Northern Greek also has a defective intervention effect caused by accusative IOs in passives. The NOM theme is not allowed to move to the subject position across an intervening ACC goal, i.e. the following is ungrammatical:

(17) Northern Greek: Strong Intervention Effect
    * *To pagoto   dothike   ton Petro.*
      The ice-cream.NOM gave.NACT the Peter.ACC
    'The ice-cream was given Peter.'

---
[3] I thank Sabine Iatridou, Despina Oikonomou and Giorgos Spathas for their judgments on Northern Greek. I thank Mark Baker and Ruth Kramer for a discussion that led me to discover the Northern Greek intervention pattern.

My consultants (mentioned in footnote 3) are unanimous in judging (17) as strongly ungrammatical, and the sentence cannot be rescued by cliticization or doubling. The following is equally ungrammatical:

(18) Northern Greek: no escape strategy with clitics
 *To pagoto   ton   dothike   (ton Petro).
 The ice-cream.NOM CL.ACC gave.NACT the Peter.ACC
 'The ice-cream was given him (Peter).'

I will call this 'a strong defective intervention effect'. What seems to be crucial for the emergence of weak vs. strong defective intervention in Greek is the morphological case of the IO. In both Standard and Northern Greek the lower theme cannot undergo movement to spec,TP across a higher goal, but the effect is much stronger when the intervener is an ACC argument, as schematized in (19b), than when it is a GEN argument, as in (19a):

(19) a. [$_{TP}$ NOM T[$_{vP}$ [$_{ApplP}$ GEN ~~NOM~~]]] GEN=weak intervener
 b. [$_{TP}$ NOM T [$_{vP}$ [$_{ApplP}$ ACC ~~NOM~~]]] ACC=strong intervener

It is unclear at this point why exactly morphological case matters, since neither the GEN IO nor the ACC IO alternate with NOM in passives, as was seen in (14) and (15), i.e. both are defective interveners, in the sense of Chomsky (2000).

Moreover, we saw that GEN intervention is obviated by cliticization/clitic doubling of the intervener. The by now standard account for this fact (see e.g. Anagnostopoulou 2003; Preminger 2009 and others) is that the features blocking NP-movement of NOM to T in (19a) no longer intervene between NOM and T when cliticization takes place, because cliticization is movement targeting T, the same position targeted by NP movement, and neither the trace of clitics in (20a) nor their DP doubling associate in (20b) count anymore as interveners.

(20) a. [TP NOM cl-T [vP [$_{ApplP}$ ~~GEN NOM~~]]]
 b. [TP NOM cl-T [vP [$_{ApplP}$ GEN ~~NOM~~]]]

The question is why the same strategy cannot be employed in configurations of strong intervention, as in Northern Greek (19b). Speakers agree that the sentences substantially improve if the ACC intervener is a 1st or 2nd person clitic, as in (21), a fact suggesting that there is a problem caused by a 3rd person ACC clitic in sentences like (18) (reminiscent of the conditions triggering the spurious *se* rule in Spanish, Bonet 1991).

6 Defective intervention effects in two Greek varieties

(21) Northern Greek: improvement with 1ˢᵗ/ 2ⁿᵈ person intervener
? To   pagoto   me/se   dothike.
The ice-cream.NOM cl.ACC.1SG/2SG gave.NACT
'The ice-cream was given me/you.'

When the intervener is 3rd person, speakers resort to a GEN strategy in order to rescue sentences like (17) and (18). Standard Greek (16a) and (16b) are acceptable for Northern Greek speakers, and GEN IOs are judged not to be interveners, regardless of whether they are full DPs (though I am skeptical about this; see footnotes 4 and 6 below), clitics or clitic doubled DPs.[4] Importantly, a very similar pattern of intervention is found with objects in Northern Greek, unlike Standard Greek. In a nutshell, ACC DO 3rd person clitics cannot co-occur with ACC IO DPs (22a), two 3rd person clitics are not allowed to form ACC-ACC clusters (22b) and speakers have to resort to Standard Greek GEN-ACC clusters (22c) instead, while 1st and 2nd person ACC IOs can form clusters with 3rd person ACC DOs (22d):

(22) Northern Greek: intervention effects with objects

   a. * To   edosa   ton Petro   (to pagoto).
       Cl.ACC gave.ACT.1SG the Peter.ACC the icecream.ACC
       'I gave Peter the ice-cream.'

   b. * Ton   to   edosa   (ton Petro)   (to pagoto).
       Cl.ACC cl.ACC gave.ACT.1SG the Peter.ACC the icecream.ACC
       'I gave Peter the ice-cream.'

   c.   Tu   to   edosa   (tu Petru)   (to pagoto).
       Cl.GEN cl.ACC gave.ACT.1SG the Peter.GEN the icecream.ACC
       'I gave Peter the ice-cream.'

   d.   Me/se   to   edose   (to pagoto).
       Cl.1/2.ACC cl.3.ACC gave.ACT.3SG the icecream.ACC
       'He/she gave me/you the ice-cream.'

---

[4]There is more to be said here. It could be that my consultants, which are also speakers of Standard Greek, resort to their Standard Greek grammar and, at the same time, they belong to those speakers of Standard Greek that do not have weak defective intervention at all. Alternatively, the contrast between the sharply ungrammatical Northern Greek and the mildly ungrammatical Standard Greek version of the sentence is so strong that they judge the NOM-GEN construction as grammatical, while the magnitude estimation experimental method might show that there is still a contrast between a GEN DP and a GEN clitic.

These facts suggest that there is a problem when two 3rd person arguments bearing ACC and/or NOM enter Agree with the same head, whether this is T or v, in Northern Greek. Here I will not attempt to provide a solution to these puzzles. What matters for present purposes is the very existence of weak and strong defective intervention in Standard and Northern Greek, respectively.

5 Defective intervention under pro-drop and its implications

Neither weak defective intervention nor strong defective intervention in passives cease to occur under pro-drop of the NOM argument. Consider first the Standard Greek pattern:

(23) Standard Greek: Weak intervention under pro drop:
Apo pjon   dothike   to vivlio   ston Petro?
By whom gave.3NACT the book.NOM to-the Peter
'By whom was the book given to Peter?'
?? Dothike   tu Petru   apo ton kathigiti.
   Gave.NACT.3SG the Peter.GEN by the professor
Tu   dothike   apo ton kathigiti.
Cl.GEN gave.NACT.3SG by the professor
Tu   dothike   tu Petru   apo ton kathigiti.
Cl.GEN gave.NACT.3SG the Peter.GEN by the professor
'It was given to Peter by the professor.'

(24) Standard Greek: Weak intervention under pro drop:
Apo pjon   apagoreftike I isodos   ston Petro?
By whom forbid.3NACT the entrance.NOM to Peter
'By whom was Peter forbidden the entrance?'
? Apagoreftike   tu Petru   apo tin astinomia.*
   Forbid.NACT.3SG the Peter.GEN by the police
Tu   apagoreftike   apo tin astinomia.
Cl.GEN forbid.NACT.3SG by the police.
Tu   apagoreftike   tu Petru   apo tin astinomia.
Cl.GEN forbid.NACT.3SG the Peter.GEN by the police
'Peter was forbidden the entrance by the police.'

6 Defective intervention effects in two Greek varieties

As shown in (23) and (24), a weak intervention effect is caused by undoubled GEN DPs when the subject is null, just as with overt NOM subjects.

The same is shown in Northern Greek with strong intervention. The sharp ungrammaticality of an overt ACC IO DP or clitic, persists when the subject is covert, as shown in (25) and (26):[5]

(25) Northern Greek: Strong intervention under pro-drop

    a. Question.
        Pu   ine to vivlio   mu?
        Where is the book.NOM my.GEN
        'Where is my book'?

    b. Answer.
        * Dothike   ton Petro
          Gave.NACT.3SG the Peter.ACC.
        'It was given to Peter.'

(26) Northern Greek: Strong intervention under pro-drop

    a. Question.
        Dosane   to vivlio   ston   Petro?
        Gave.ACT.3PL the book.ACC to-the Peter
        'Did they give the book to Peter?'

    b. Answer.
        * Ne, ton   dothike   xtes.
          Yes, cl.ACC gave.NACT.3SG yesterday
        'Yes, it was given to him yesterday.'

And just as with overt NOM subjects, the relevant null subject constructions improve when the IO surfaces as a GEN DP[6] or clitic:

---

[5] I thank Despina Oikonomou (personal communication) for also providing contexts for all Northern Greek sentences below.

[6] Note that the question context provided for an undoubled GEN DP in (27a) requires emphasis on the GEN DP since it is construed as an answer to a wh-question. In this context, I would also use an undoubled genitive DP, since doubling is incompatible with focus/emphasis. I assume that the undoubled GEN undergoes covert focus movement in (27a), which is another strategy for obviating weak defective intervention. It is therefore more appropriate to check the status of sentences with an undoubled GEN DP in contexts without emphasis, like the ones in (23) and (24) above. And indeed, Despina Oikonomou (personal communication) confirms that she has a weak intervention effect with an undoubled GEN in contexts like (23) and (24) and a very strong intervention effect with an ACC IO in the same contexts, regardless of whether the ACC is a DP, a clitic or a clitic doubled DP and regardless of emphasis.

(27) Northern Greek: Improvement when IO is GEN (Standard Greek pattern)

    a. Question.
       Pu   ine to   vivlio   mu?
       Where is   the book.NOM my.GEN
       'Where is my book'?

    b. Answer.
       Dothike   tu Petru.
       Gave.NACT.3SG the Peter.GEN
       'It was given to Peter.'

(28) Northern Greek: Improvement when IO is GEN (Standard Greek pattern)

    a. Question.
       Dosane to   vivlio ston   Petro?
       Gave. NACT.3PL the   book.ACC to-the Peter
       'Did they give the book to Peter?'

    b. Answer.
       Ne, tu   dothike   xtes.
       Yes, CL.GEN gave.NACT.3SG yesterday
       'Yes, it was given to him yesterday.'

Recall that it was concluded in section 2 on the basis of evidence from Icelandic and Dutch that defective interveners block Move and not Agree because their D features make them interveners, and D features are relevant for Move/EPP processes, not for Agree/φ-feature valuation processes. If this conclusion is correct, then the presence of weak intervention in Standard Greek and strong intervention in Northern Greek under pro-drop indicates that Null Subject constructions involve not just downward Agree between T and the null subject but movement of the zero subject to T. In turn, this casts doubt on Holmberg's (2010) and Roberts's (2010) proposal that φ-incorporation of null subjects is formally indistinguishable from long distance Agree configurations. On Holmberg's account outlined in the introduction, the only difference between the Agree derivation in (29) for null nominatives in Greek and the Agree Derivation in (30) for overt nominatives in Icelandic (4) and Dutch (5) is that the probe and the goal do not form a chain and hence are not subject to chain reduction. And yet, GEN and ACC IOs are interveners in (29) while DAT IOs are not interveners in (30):

(29) 1. [T, D, uφ, NOM] [vP v [ApplP ?*⌐GEN¬/*⌐ACC¬ Appl [3SG, uCase]...] →
      2. [T, D, 3SG, NOM] [vP v [ApplP ?*⌐GEN¬/*⌐ACC¬ Appl [3SG, NOM] →
      3. [T, D, 3SG, NOM] [vP v [ApplP ?*⌐GEN¬/*⌐ACC¬ Appl [3SG, NOM]]

(30) 1. [T, D, uφ, NOM] [vP v [ApplP ⌐DAT¬ Appl [DP D [3SG, uCase] [NP N..]] →
      2. [T, D, 3SG, NOM] [vP v [ApplP ⌐DAT¬ Appl [DP D [3SG, NOM] [NP N..]] →
      3. [T, D, 3SG, NOM] [vP v [ApplP ⌐DAT¬ Appl [DP D [3SG, NOM] [NP N..]]

I therefore propose that the two derivations are not identical. In pro-drop configurations, there is movement of the subject from vP to TP, while monoclausal agreement in Icelandic and Dutch with a vP internal NOM involves downward Agree between T and NOM.[7]

What kind of movement is involved in pro-drop sentences? Perhaps the simplest analysis would be to follow Holmberg (2010) and, more generally, those who assume that pro is syntactically present but not realized at PF (Rizzi 1986; Cardinaletti & Starke 1999; Roberts 2010 and others) and to analyze pro/φ-incorporation as actual movement of pro/φ to T. Under the assumption that intervention effects of the type described above are triggered by intervening D-features, it must also be assumed that pro in consistent Null Subject Languages contains a D-layer and not just φ-features. Building on Tomioka (2003); Barbosa (2013) argues that this is correct. The different properties of consistent vs. partial Null Subject Languages w.r.t. the definiteness of pro discussed in Holmberg (2010) as well as the properties of empty arguments in radical topic drop-languages (e.g. Japanese) systematically correlate with differences in the internal make-up of

---

[7]Mark Baker (personal communication) suggests that one could appeal to the fact that agreement with a nominative argument over a dative inside the same clause is weakened, at least in Icelandic, so that there is agreement in number but not in person (Taraldsen 1995; Sigurðsson 1996 and many others) in order to explain why pro-drop languages always show defective intervention within Holmberg's Agree approach. Specifically, Mark Baker suggests that person agreement is blocked in this configuration, and if there is not a person feature on T, then T and the subject do not share all their features, so that it doesn't count anymore as a movement chain, and the lower instance does not delete. In such an approach, it is the weakening of agreement that prevents pro-drop from occurring in the relevant sentences and not locality of movement *per se*. In order for this account to work, one would have to say that person plays a role in pro-drop even of third person nominals, despite the fact that they do not have marked person features. Even though an approach along these lines is appealing, I do not think that it will work for pro-drop languages which crucially differ from Icelandic in never showing a person restriction on nominatives in configurations of downward Agree. The constructions showing such an effect in languages like Greek are clitic constructions, and the weakening effect only arises with accusative clitics (the well-known PCC effect), not with nominatives.

DPs and the availability of overt vs. covert definite object pronouns under ellipsis in the languages in question. This correlation can be explained if overt and covert arguments in consistent Null Subject Languages have a D layer missing from overt and covert arguments in partial and radical pro-drop languages.

An alternative I would like to explore, though, is to adopt Alexiadou & Anagnostopoulou' proposal (A& A 1998) that this movement has the form of [v-V]-to-T raising, thus linking the movement nature of pro-drop configurations to verb-movement as a way of satisfying the EPP. Working in the lexicalist framework of Chomsky (1995), A& A proposed that verbal agreement morphology in consistent Null Subject Languages is pronominal, i.e. it bears D features. As a result, the EPP in these languages is always satisfied via V-to-T raising. For this reason, overt preverbal subjects are Clitic Left Dislocated and never the result of A-movement to Spec,TP. On this view, the NP-movement configurations discussed in §4 for Greek do not involve NP-movement of the DP but NP-movement of the zero resumptive subject pro corresponding to overt object clitics in object CLLD constructions. This analysis has sometimes been criticized (see e.g Spyropoulos & Revithiadou 2009 for Greek), but Barbosa (2009) offers many interesting novel arguments from European vs. Brazilian Portuguese in favor of the CLLD analysis of preverbal subjects in consistent Null Subject Languages. One such argument that carries over to Greek comes from the observation that preverbal subjects in consistent Null Subject Languages are ungrammatical in contexts where CLLD is excluded for independent reasons, while they are grammatical in non-pro drop languages. Absolute constructions are the case in point. The subject must precede the Aux-V complex in these environments in English and French (from Barbosa 2009, ex. 80 and 81, while it follows Aux or the Aux-V complex in Spanish, Italian and European Portuguese (Barbosa's 82–84)):

(31) English: S-Aux/V
Your brother having called, we left.

(32) French: S-Aux/V
Ton frère ayant téléphoné, je suis parti.

(33) Spanish: V-S
Habiendo (el juez) resuelto (el juez) absolver al acusado el juicio
having (the judge) decided (the judge) to acquit the accused the trial
concluyó sin incidentes.
concluded without incidents
'The judge having decided to acquit the accused, the trial came to an end without further incidents.'

(34) Italian: Aux/V-S
 Avendo (tuo fratello) telefonato (tuo fratello) (,io sono rimasto a casa).
 having your brother called   I   am   stayed at home
 'Your brother having called, I stayed at home.'

(35) European Portuguese: V - S
 Aparecendo a Maria, vamos embora.
 Showing   up the Maria, we-leave.
 'As soon as Maria shows up, we leave.'

The same holds in Greek, where the preverbal subject is strongly deviant, as shown in (36b):

(36) Greek V-S

 a. *Emfanizomeni i Maria, tha figume.*
    Showing up   the Mary, FUT go.1PL
    'As soon as Maria shows up, we will leave.'

 b. ?* *I Maria emfanizomeni, tha figume.*
    The Mary showing up,   FUT go.1PL
    'As soon as Maria shows up, we will leave.'

Updating Alexiadou & Anagnostopoulou (1998) in a non-lexicalist model of grammar, I propose that in consistent Null Subject Languages the null subject undergoes merger with the verbal complex and is spelled out in the form of a [+ pronominal] affix on the main verb or auxiliary.[8] Subsequent raising of the

---

[8] Following Alexiadou et al. (2006; 2015) I assume that the verbal complex consists of the root, a verbalizing head introducing an event and Voice introducing an external argument. There is evidence that the external argument is introduced below the auxiliary head in the Greek perfect, because the participle is either active or passive, i.e. it contains Voice:

(i) a. *O Janis   exi   lisi   tis askisis.*
       The Janis.NOM has.3SG solved.ACT the exercises.ACC
       'John has solved the .

    b. *I   askisis   exoun   lithi   apo ton Jani.*
       The excercises.NOM have.3PL solved.NACT by the John
       'The exercises have been solved by John.'

Since the auxiliary shows subject agreement, we must assume that in these constructions the null subject raises to Aux and then merges with it. The reason why the subject must merge with the auxiliary and is not allowed to merge with the participle has to do with the fact that the auxiliary and not the participle is allowed to satisfy the EPP property of T since it is closer to T than the participle.

v+V+[pron] affix to T satisfies the EPP property of T in the manner suggested by Alexiadou & Anagnostopoulou (1998). I propose that the mode by which the zero subject combines with the verb is identical to the process by which object clitics combine with the finite verb in cliticization structures, essentially treating null subjects as clitics (see Sportiche 1996; Alexiadou & Anagnostopoulou 1998; 2001 and others). Following Nevins (2011) I assume that clitics undergo syntactic rebracketing, the Merger operation of Matushansky (2006) which rebrackets two heads that are in a specifier head configuration as a complex head:

(37) Rebracketing Merger:

Subject pro is a D head bearing φ-features, just like a clitic, and undergoes rebracketing merger from its base position in spec,VoiceP (see footnote 8) in transitives and unergatives with the complex Root-v-Voice head created by head movement of the Root to v and Voice:[9]

---

[9] In passives and unaccusatives the base position of pro is the position occupied by themes, which is probably outside the projection of the stative Root, i.e. in spec,vP, in alternating change of state unaccusatives, and a Root-complement in non-alternating unaccusatives, verbs of creation and destruction. This raises non-trivial questions concerning the point at which D[iφ] undergoes Merger with the verbal complex and whether an IO, if present, is expected to cause an intervention effect or not on Merger, if Merger happens after the verbal complex is formed (which would seem to entail that D[iφ] first moves to the edge of the position hosting the verbal complex and then rebracketing happens). These questions are left open here because they require working out where themes reside in all relevant structures, whether D[iφ] and nominative arguments more generally move to the edge of v/Voice or directly to T in passives and unaccusatives and, if the former, how exactly intervention works when Voice/v is targeted. The two Greek varieties sharply differ with respect to the latter issue. In Standard Greek, GEN IOs do not block cliticization of an ACC DO across them while 3rd person ACC IOs cause a strong intervention effect on cliticization of an ACC DO.

6 *Defective intervention effects in two Greek varieties*

(38) a.

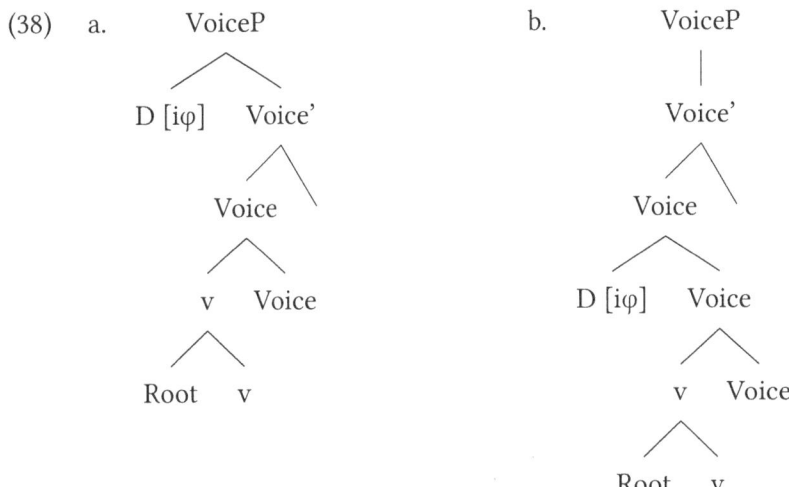

If we take suffixal agreement morphology to spell out D[iφ], then D[iφ] in (38b) is right linearized with respect to the verbal complex, while object clitics are left linearized with respect to the verbal complex. Further verb movement to T brings along the rebracketed subject which satisfies the EPP requirement of T.

6 Defective intervention and NOM *in situ* in Greek

As a final point, I will briefly discuss intervention effects in sentences where the DP argument bearing nominative Case remains *in situ* in Greek, and their implications. As already observed in Anagnostopoulou (2003: 85), Standard Greek differs from Dutch (and Icelandic) in having weak intervention effects in apparent downward Agree configurations in monoclausal constructions. Examples with *in situ* subjects still require clitic doubling or cliticization in Greek passives and unaccusatives:

(39) Standard Greek : weak intervention with in situ subjects

    a. ?* *(tu) dhothike tu Petru to vivlio.*
        Cl.GEN gave.NACT.3SG the Petros.GEN the book.NOM
        'The book was given to Peter.'

171

b. ?* *(tis)   irthe   tis Marias   to grama.*
   Cl.GEN came the Maria.GEN the letter.NOM
   'The letter came to Mary.'

c. ?* *(tu)   aresun   tu Petru   ta vivlia.*
   Cl.GEN please-3PL the Petros.GEN the books. NOM
   'Peter likes books.'

The same holds for strong intervention in Northern Greek, where a NOM theme is not allowed to co-occur with a 3rd person ACC DP or clitic or clitic doubled IO, as shown in (40):

(40) Northern Greek: strong intervention with in situ subjects

a. **Xthes   dothike   ton Petro   to pagoto.*
   Yesterday gave.NACT the Peter.ACC the ice-cream.NOM

b. **Xthes   ton   dothike   to pagoto.*
   Yesterday cl.ACC gave.NACT the ice-cream.NOM

c. **Xthes   ton   dothike   ton Petro   to pagoto.*
   Yesterday cl.ACC gave.NACT the Peter.ACC the icecream.NOM

   'The ice-cream was given to Peter yesterday.'

In order to account for this difference between Greek and Dutch/Icelandic, in Anagnostopoulou (2003) I appealed to the consistent pro-drop and clitic doubling[10] nature of Greek, as opposed to Dutch and Icelandic, and I proposed that the relation between subject agreement on V and the overt DP subject in Greek

---

[10] Note that not all Null Subject Languages are also clitic doubling languages, for example Italian and Catalan are not, at least as far as DO clitic doubling is concerned. Alexiadou & Anagnostopoulou (2001) argue that only in clitic doubling languages verbal agreement enters a doubling configuration with a full DP. As a result, Greek, Romanian and Spanish permit VSO orders with both S and O vP-internal in violation of the *Subject-in-situ Generalization*. In Italian and Catalan clitic doubling is not possible, and therefore these languages only allow VOS orders and not VSO orders. But, crucially, in VOS orders the object has moved to the edge of the vP conforming with the *Subject in situ Generalization*. This makes the prediction that if these languages have intervention effects of the type described above for Greek, these would be obviated if the nominative remained in its vP internal position, i.e. that Italian and Catalan would behave like Dutch and Icelandic and not like Greek w.r.t. intervention effects with *in situ* nominatives. I do not know whether this prediction can be tested since in these languages 'a-datives' are not interveners to begin with (presumably because they are ambiguous between a prepositional dative and an applicative dative).

is an instance of clitic doubling.[11] It is generally agreed upon that clitic doubling is a movement dependency, which means that some part of the nominative moves to T even when it is pronounced *in situ* (Alexiadou & Anagnostopoulou 2001: 224–226). Since movement is sensitive to intervention effects, the pattern in (39) follows. There are several ways to represent this clitic doubling / movement dependency (see Anagnostopoulou, to appear, for summarizing the relevant literature on clitic doubling and different proposals). Which one to choose depends on how we want to analyze null subject constructions to begin with.[12] For example, if we basically follow Holmberg's (2010) analysis with the modifications introduced above (true φ-incorporation combined with the hypothesis that null subjects also contain D), then the most adequate analysis for clitic doubling would be that the clitic is a copy of a DP moving to the host, which spelled out as a pronoun (the reverse of a resumptive pronoun chain), a possibility explored by Harizanov (2014) and Kramer (2014). On this analysis, the copy of a moved subject would be the suffixal verbal agreement. On the alternative analysis that verbal subject agreement results from merger of a subject clitic with the verbal complex, the most compatible analysis of clitic doubling would either be that doubling clitics spell out D/φ-features of the DP moving to the host (Anagnos-

---

[11] Note that analyzing agreement with subjects as an instance of clitic doubling raises the question of why object doubling imposes referentiality conditions on the doubled DP while subject doubling doesn't. This is a more general question concerning doubling analyses of agreement phenomena, as argued for by e.g. Preminger (2009) and Nevins (2011). I believe that the difference between doubling/agreement without interpretational effects vs. doubling/agreement displaying such effects should be linked to the obligatoriness of the former vs. optionality of the latter. See Baker & Kramer (2015) for an alternative view that referentiality conditions constitute the only reliable diagnostic for classifying a dependency as a doubling one.

[12] An anonymous reviewer points out that it is unsatisfying not to take a firm position regarding which analysis of pro-drop I take to be correct. In view of the complexities and debates on the Null-Subject Parameter, however, (see e.g. D'Alessandro 2015 for an overview of the relevant issues), it is beyond the scope of the present paper to address the syntax and parametrization of null subject phenomena in detail. The intervention data I discuss show that movement is a crucial component in pro-drop structures; in addition, they provide evidence that covert subjects in Greek-type languages have a D-layer and move overtly. In principle, these crucial properties can be expressed both in an A& A (1998) style-analysis and in terms of a more conventional analysis, with a null D-pronominal moving to T. In my view, the A& A analysis has the advantage that it automatically derives both movement and the presence of a D layer by linking them to the EPP-driven movement of the agreeing verb. A definitive choice between the two main analytic options, however, would require an in depth investigation of the properties of different Null Subject Languages, the nature of micro- and macro-variation in different types of null subject constructions, an analysis of partial pro drop languages, an understanding of the relationship between SVO, VSO and VOS orders in different Null Subject Languages, among other issues.

topoulou 2003) or a version of the "big DP hypothesis" according to which clitics are determiner heads, as in (41) (Torrego 1988; Uriagereka 1995 and the literature building on them), with Ds moving to the host:

(41)

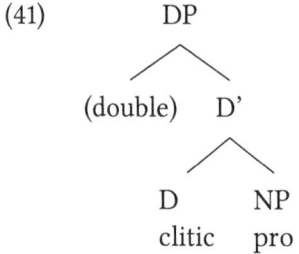

A variant of this proposal is that D is adjoined to the DP/KP (similarly to floated quantifiers) and moves to the host stranding the DP/KP (Nevins 2011). On both proposals, the subject doubling clitic would merge with the verbal complex in the way described above for non-doubling subject clitics.[13]

7 Summary

In this paper I employed intervention effects in monoclausal constructions as a way of diagnosing whether an agreement construction should be analyzed as φ-feature valuation under Agree or as the result of movement. I took as a starting point the observation that in monoclausal constructions clearly involving downward Agree, as in Icelandic and Dutch, the presence of a dative intervener does not block Agree between T and a lower nominative argument. By contrast, dative arguments in these languages do cause intervention effects blocking movement of the nominative argument to T. I then identified two types of intervention effects in two different varieties of Greek, namely weak defective intervention attested in Standard Greek and strong defective intervention found in Northern Greek. Both are consistent Null Subject Languages. I presented evidence that weak and strong intervention effects in these dialects arise always, regardless of whether the nominative subject is overt or covert and regardless of whether a

---

[13]There are other options not presented here for both null subject constructions and clitic doubling constructions. For example, one could adopt a version of Sportiche's (1996) proposal and analyze verbal subject agreement as T's φ-features which are interpretable in pro-drop languages. They combine with a zero pro or an overt subject which moves to T covertly. The difference between subject doubling constructions and object doubling constructions would be that the presence of φ-features in T are obligatory, while φ-features on v (object doubling) are optional and associated with interpretive effects.

subject DP remains in its base position or moves overtly. This led me to conclude that the relevant constructions always display movement. I explored some ways in which this movement can be represented. Choosing among the alternatives for null subject constructions also has implications for constructions with overt *in situ* nominatives, which necessitate a doubling/movement analysis in Greek, in order for intervention effects to be accounted for.

Acknowledgments

Some of the new observations presented here concerning Northern Greek intervention effects have been triggered by an e-mail conversation with Mark Baker and Ruth Kramer (Fall 2015). I thank Sabine Iatridou, Giorgos Spathas and Despina Oikonomou for their judgments on Northern (Thessaloniki) Greek, Despina Oikonomou for her feed-back on the data, Mark Baker and two anonymous reviewers for their comments. I thank Anders Holmberg for his many important contributions to syntax, his insights, and the generosity he showed towards what later became Alexiadou & Anagnostopoulou (1998) which helped tremendously an early career. If Wim Wenders had known Anders, he would have included him in the group of angels in *Der Himmel über Berlin*. This research has been supported by an Alexander von Humboldt Friedrich Wilhelm Bessel Research award which is gratefully acknowledged.

References

Alexiadou, Artemis & Elena Anagnostopoulou. 1998. Parametrizing AGR: Word order, V-movement and EPP-checking. *Natural Language & Linguistic Theory* 16. 491–539.

Alexiadou, Artemis & Elena Anagnostopoulou. 2001. The subject In-Situ generalization, and the role of Case in driving computations. *Linguistic Inquiry* 32. 193–231.

Alexiadou, Artemis, Elena Anagnostopoulou & Florian Schäfer. 2006. The properties of anticausatives crosslinguistically. In Mara Frascarelli (ed.), *Phases of Interpretation*, 187–211. Berlin/ New York: Mouton de Gruyter.

Alexiadou, Artemis, Elena Anagnostopoulou & Florian Schäfer. 2015. *External arguments in transitivity alternations. A layering approach*. Oxford: Oxford University Press.

Anagnostopoulou, Elena. 2003. *The syntax of ditransitives*. Berlin: Mouton de Gruyter.

Anagnostopoulou, Elena & Christina Sevdali. 2015. Case alternations in ancient Greek passives and the typology of case. *Language* 91. 442–481.

Baker, Mark. 2009. Is head movement still needed for Noun incorporation? The case of Mapudungun. *Lingua* 119. 148–165.

Baker, Mark & Ruth Kramer. 2015. Doubling Clitics are Pronouns: Agree, Move, Reduce, & Interpret. Ms. Rutgers University and Georgetown University.

Barbosa, Pilar. 2009. Two kinds of subject pro. *Studia Linguistica* 63. 2–58.

Barbosa, Pilar. 2013. *Pro as a minimal pronoun: Towards a unified approach to pro-drop*. Ms. University of Minho.

Beck, Sigrid. 2006. Intervention effects follow from focus interpretation. *Natural Language Semantics* 14. 1–56.

Belletti, Adriana & Luigi Rizzi. 1988. Psych verbs and θ-theory. *Natural Language and Linguistic Theory* 6(3). 291–352.

Bobaljik, Jonathan D. 2008. Where's φ? Agreement as a post-syntactic operation. In Daniel Harbour, David Adger & Susana Béjar (eds.), *Phi-Theory: Phi features across interfaces and modules*, 295–328. Oxford: Oxford University Press.

Bonet, Eulalia. 1991. *Morphology after syntax: Pronominal clitics in Romance languages*. Cambridge MA: MIT dissertation.

Cardinaletti, Anna & Michal Starke. 1999. The typology of structural deficiency: A case study of three classes of pronouns. In Henk van Riemsdijk (ed.), *Clitics in the languages of Europe*, 145–233. Berlin/New York: Mouton de Gruyter.

Chomsky, Noam. 1995. *The minimalist program*. Cambridge, MA: MIT Press.

Chomsky, Noam. 2000. Minimalist inquiries: The framework. In David Michaels Roger Martin & Juan Uriagereka (eds.), *Step by step: Essays on minimalist syntax in honor of Howard Lasnik*, 89–155. Cambridge MA: MIT Press.

Chomsky, Noam. 2001. Derivation by phase. In Michael Kenstowicz (ed.), *Ken Hale: A life in language*, 1–52. Cambridge, MA: The MIT Press.

Condoravdi, Cleo. 1989. Indefinite and generic pronouns. In *Proceedings of the West Coast Conference on Formal Linguistics*, vol. 9, 71–84. Stanford: CSLI Publications.

Cowart, Wayne. 1997. *Experimental Syntax: Applying Objective Methods to Sentence Judgements*. Thousand Oaks, Ca: Sage.

D'Alessandro, Roberta. 2015. Null subjects. In Antonio Fábregas, Jaume Mateu & Mike T. Putnam (eds.), *Contemporary linguistic parameters*, 201–226. London: Bloomsbury.

Den Dikken, Marcel. 1995. *Particles: On the syntax of verb-particle, triadic, and causative constructions*. Oxford: Oxford University Press.

Dimitriadis, Alexis. 1999. On clitics, prepositions and case licensing in standard and Macedonian Greek. In Geoffrey Horrocks Artemis Alexiadou & Melita Stavrou (eds.), *Studies in Greek syntax*, 95–113. Dordrecht: Kluwer Academic Publishers.

Eilam, Aviad. 2009. The absence of intervention Effects in Amharic: Evidence for a Non-Structural approach. *Brill's Annual of Afroasiatic Languages and Linguistics* 1. 204–254.

Georgala, Effi. 2012. *Applicatives in their structural and thematic function. A minimalist account of multitransitivity*. Ithaca NY: Cornell University dissertation.

Gurman, Bard Ellen, Dan Robertson & Antonella Sorace. 1996. Magnitude estimation of linguistic acceptability. *Language* 72. 32–68.

Harizanov, Boris. 2014. Clitic doubling at the syntax-morphophonology interface: A-movement and morphological merger in Bulgarian. *Natural Language & Linguistic Theory* 32. 1033–1088.

Holmberg, Anders. 2010. Null subject parameters. In Theresa Biberauer, Anders Holmberg, Ian Roberts & Michelle Sheehan (eds.), *Parametric variation: Null subjects in minimalist theory*, 88–124. Cambridge: Cambridge University Press.

Holmberg, Anders & Thorbjörg Hróarsdóttir. 2003. Agreement and movement in Icelandic raising constructions. *Lingua* 113. 997–1019.

Jónsson, Jóhannes Gísli. 1996. *Clausal architecture and case in Icelandic*. Amherst MA: University of Massachusetts Amherst dissertation.

Keller, Frank. 2000. *Gradience in grammar: experimental and computational aspects of degrees of grammaticality*. University of Edinburgh dissertation dissertation.

Kramer, Ruth. 2014. Clitic doubling or object agreement: The view from Amharic. *Natural Language & Linguistic Theory* 32(2). 593–634.

Lechner, Winfried. 2006. An interpretive effect of head movement. In Mara Frascarelli (ed.), *Phases of interpretation*, 45–69. Berlin/New York: Mouton de Gruyter.

Lechner, Winfried. 2007. *Interpretive effects of Head Movement*. http://ling.auf.net/lingbuzz/000178, accessed 2007-3-1.

Lechner, Winfried. 2009. A puzzle for remnant movement analyses of v2. *Linguistic Inquiry* 40. 346–356.

Matushansky, Ora. 2006. Head movement in linguistic theory. *Linguistic Inquiry* 37. 69–109.

Nevins, Andrew. 2011. Multiple agree with clitics: Person complementarity vs. Omnivorous number. *Natural Language and Linguistic Theory* 29. 939–971.

Nomura, Masashi. 2005. *Nominative case and AGREE(ment)*. Storrs: University of Connecticut dissertation.

Pesetsky, David. 1995. *Zero syntax: Experiencers and cascades*. Cambridge, MA: The MIT Press.

Preminger, Omer. 2009. Breaking agreements: Distinguishing agreement and Clitic-Doubling by their failures. *Linguistic Inquiry* 40. 619–666.

Rizzi, Luigi. 1986. Null objects in Italian and the theory of pro. *Linguistic Inquiry* 17. 501–557.

Roberts, Ian. 2010. *Agreement and head movement: Clitics, incorporation, and defective goals*. Cambridge, MA: The MIT Press.

Schütze, Carson. 1997. *Infl in child and adult language: Agreement, case and licensing*. Cambridge MA: MIT dissertation.

Sigurðsson, Halldór Ármann. 1996. Icelandic finite verb agreement. *Working Papers in Scandinavian Syntax* 57. 1–46.

Sportiche, Dominique. 1996. Clitic constructions. In Johan Rooryck & Laurie Zaring (eds.), *Phrase structure and the lexicon*, 213–277. Dordrecht: Kluwer.

Spyropoulos, Vassilios & Anthi Revithiadou. 2009. Subject chains in Greek and PF processing. In C. Halpert, J. Hartman & D. Hill (eds.), *Proceedings of the 2007 Workshop in Greek Syntax and Semantics at MIT, MTWPL*. 293–309. Cambridge, MA.

Taraldsen, Tarald Knut. 1995. On agreement and nominative objects in Icelandic. In Hubert Haider, Susan Olsen & Sten Vikner (eds.), *Studies in comparative Germanic syntax*, 307–327. Dordrecht: Kluwer Academic Publishers.

Tomioka, Satoshi. 2003. The semantics of Japanese null pronouns and its cross-linguistic implications. In Kerstin Schwabe & Susanne Winkler (eds.), *The interfaces. Deriving and interpreting omitted structures*, 321–340. Amsterdam: John Benjamins.

Tomioka, Satoshi. 2007. Pragmatics of LF intervention effects: Japanese and Korean wh-interrogatives. *Journal of Pragmatics* 39. 1570–1590.

Torrego, Esther. 1988. *A DP Analysis of Spanish Nominals*. Ms., University of Massachusetts, Boston.

Uriagereka, Juan. 1995. Aspects of the syntax of clitic placement in Western romance. *Linguistic Inquiry* 26. 79–124.

Watanabe, Akira. 1993. *AGR-based case theory and its interaction with the A-Bar system*. Cambridge MA: MIT dissertation.

Zaenen, Annie, Joan Maling & Höskuldur Thráinsson. 1985. Case and grammatical functions: The Icelandic passive. *Natural Language and Linguistic Theory* 3. 441–483.

Chapter 7

First Person Readings of MAN: On semantic and pragmatic restrictions on an impersonal pronoun

Verner Egerland
Lund University

> Cinque (1988) notices that Italian impersonal *si* can be interpreted so as to include the speaker and that such a reading is actually mandatory in certain contexts. A similar conclusion holds for impersonal *man* in a language such as Swedish, with the difference that, in the relevant contexts, *man* takes on the reading of 1st person singular, hence 'I' and not 'we'. In this paper, I argue that Cinque's observation can only be understood in a theory explaining how impersonal readings (generic and existential) are restricted, rather than in a general theory of "inclusiveness". The first part of paper is dedicated to showing how impersonal readings are restricted by the temporal and aspectual specification of the clause. This part summarizes some by now well-known facts concerning the interpretation of *man*. The second part of the paper discusses a further restriction on impersonal readings, stemming from focus and contrastiveness. The relevant effect is shown in cases of topicalization of SELF-anaphora in impersonal constructions in some Germanic languages. To my knowledge, these data have so far gone unobserved in the literature.

1 Introduction: "Inclusive" readings of impersonal pronouns

The literature on impersonal pronouns has grown considerably in the last 20 years. Its findings suggest that "impersonal syntax" is a rather heterogeneous phenomenon which extensively correlates with different parts of grammar, semantics, and pragmatics.

Verner Egerland. 2017. First Person Readings of MAN: On semantic and pragmatic restrictions on an impersonal pronoun. In Michelle Sheehan & Laura R. Bailey (eds.), *Order and structure in syntax II: Subjecthood and argument structure*, 179–195. Berlin: Language Science Press.

In this paper, I intend to discuss two well-known empirical observations. First, in seminal work on impersonal pronouns, Cinque (1988) notices that Italian impersonal *si* can be interpreted so as to include the speaker and that such a reading is actually mandatory in certain contexts. That is to say, while in (1), *si* can be interpreted as 'we', in (2) it has to be interpreted thus:[1]

(1) Italian
 Si è lavorato per due mesi per risolvere il problema.
 SI is worked for two months for solve the problem
 a. 'People have worked for two months to solve the problem.'
 b. 'We have worked for two months to solve the problem.'

(2) Italian
 Ieri si è stati licenziati.
 yesterday SI is been fired
 'yesterday we were fired'

Second, Kratzer (1997; 2000) makes the observation the German impersonal *man* is understood to include the speaker in cases such as (3) and (4):

(3) German
 Als ich klein war, wurde man nur am Freitag gebadet.
 when I little was got MAN only on Friday bathed
 'When I was little, we only had a bath on Fridays.'

(4) German
 Wenn ich Kinder hätte, könnte man zusammen Monopoly spielen.
 If I kids had could man together Monopoly play.
 'If I had children, we could play Monopoly together.'

In the following pages, I will refer to (1–2) as "Cinque's observation", and to (3–4) as "Kratzer's observation". The question arises as to whether the speaker-inclusion-effects observed in (1–4) have a common underlying source. In other words, should we try to formulate a general theory of "inclusiveness" that can account for all of (1–4)? Some such suggestions have been advanced and discussed in the literature (different views are being expressed in e.g. D'Alessandro & Alexiadou 2003; D'Alessandro 2007; Malamud 2006; Zobel 2011). In this paper, however, I argue that a unified account of (1–4) is implausible.

---

[1] There is some regional and dialectal variation concerning the b-reading of (1) and the acceptability of (2). My Italian consultants are speakers of the Tuscan variety.

In fact, the two observations are essentially different in nature: An adequate account of Kratzer's observation should explain why, in certain contexts, an impersonal pronoun *must* be interpreted so as to include the speaker. An account of Cinque's observation, on the other hand, should explain why, in certain contexts, an impersonal pronoun *cannot* be interpreted either as generic or as existential.[2]

The paper is organized as follows: In §2, I list some arguments against a unified approach to (1–4), after which Kratzer's observation is set aside: I assume that Kratzer's claim is correct and, hence, that (3–4) can be successfully accounted for in a theory of logophoricity (as further developed in Kratzer 2009). In §3, I claim that important restrictions on impersonal readings derive from the (interaction between) lexical and grammatical aspect. In §4, I turn to the topicalization of the equivalents of *self* in some Germanic languages. In *self*-topicalization environments, a different restriction on impersonal readings emerges, deriving from the information structural notion of contrastiveness.

2 Against a unified approach to "inclusiveness" phenomena

There are several arguments against a unified account of (1–4). Four of them will be listed in §2.1 – §2.4.

2.1 Inclusive readings vs. specific ones

In Italian (1-2) and German (3-4) alike, impersonal pronouns receive a *we*-reading, but there are languages in which the interpretation differs between the two cases. In Swedish (5), equivalent to Kratzer's example (3), *man* is interpreted as 'we', quite as much as its German counterpart. However, in (6), the equivalent to (2), the reading is 1st singular, 'I':

(5) Swedish
När jag var liten badade man bara på fredagar.
when I was little bathed MAN only on Fridays
'When I was little, we only had a bath on Fridays.'

---

[2] In this paper, the readings of impersonal subjects will be defined as generic or existential (corresponding to generic and episodic time/aspect reference). For present purposes, I will avoid the term "arbitrary" which has frequently been used in the relevant literature.

(6) Swedish
   I går   blev man avskedad.
   yesterday was MAN fired
   'yesterday afternoon I was fired'

Hence, the conclusion that impersonal pronouns in a context such as (2) include the speaker cannot be generalized to Swedish (6), in which the subject does not include, but is *specifically* identified with the speaker.[3]

2.2 The general availability of the 1st singular reading

While Kratzer's inclusiveness effect manifests itself in particular contexts, the 1st singular reading of Swedish *man* is a generally available option. That is to say, *man* can be interpreted as 'I' in virtually any context (although of course the scene setting can make such a reading far-fetched). Thus, an example such as (7) can have at least two interpretations: *People in Spain are in the habit of having dinner late* or *when I'm in Spain, I usually have dinner late*.

(7) Swedish
   I Spanien äter man middag sent.
   In Spain   eats MAN dinner late
   a. 'In Spain people have dinner late'
   b. 'In Spain I have dinner late'

The same holds true for Italian *si* in the relevant varieties. The example (8) has two readings parallel to the Swedish ones, but with the difference that the b-reading corresponds to 1st plural: *When we're in Spain, we usually have dinner late.*

(8) Italian
   In Spagna si mangia tardi.
   In Spain   SI eats   late
   a. 'In Spain people have dinner late'
   b. 'In Spain we have dinner late'

---

[3] Traditionally, the 1st singular usage of *man* has been considered substandard and not all speakers are inclined to accept it. Similar considerations hold true for specific readings of impersonal pronouns in several other languages, including the 1st singular reading of Icelandic *maður* (to which I turn in §4), as well as the 1st plural reading of French *on* and Italian *si*: Such interpretations are sometimes associated with dialectal/substandard registers and, therefore, are often stigmatized by prescriptive grammars.

This state of affairs shows that both Swedish *man* in its 1st singular reading, and Italian *si* in its 1st plural reading, can be under the scope of a generic operator (Chierchia 1995). This, in turn, suggests that such readings are lexicalized options. I will come back to this intuition shortly.

2.3 The sensitivity to aspect

The 1st singular interpretation of Swedish *man* becomes mandatory as a result of the interaction of lexical and grammatical aspect (Egerland 2003b,a). This effect manifests itself in a way which is perfectly parallel to Italian as illustrated in (1–2).

First, consider the generic contexts of (9–10):

(9) Swedish
Man arbetat för mycket nuförtiden.
MAN works too much nowadays
'People/I have work too much nowadays.'

(10) Swedish
Man blir lätt avskedad nufört iden.
MAN is easily fired nowadays
'People / I get fired easily nowadays.'

Let us concentrate on the impersonal reading, setting aside the 1st singular one: In (9–10), the impersonal argument *man* is interpreted generically. *Man* can successfully be raised to subject position, say [Spec, T], regardless of whether it originates as an external argument, as in (9), or as an internal argument, as in (10). The derivations of generic *man* can be illustrated with the structure in (11):

(11) ... [$_{TP}$ *man* [$_{T'}$ T$_{GENERIC}$ [$_{VP}$ (*man*) [$_{V'}$ V (*man*)]]]]

Then, consider the episodic contexts of the examples (12–13):

(12) Swedish
Man har arbetat i två månader för att lösa problemet.
MAN has worked in two months for to solve problem.the
'People/I have been working for two months to solve the problem'

(13) Swedish
I går   blev man avskedad.
yesterday was MAN fired

'yesterday *people were / I was fired.'

In both of (12) and (13), a generic reading of *man* is excluded because of the perfective grammatical aspect.[4] However, in (12), *man* can be interpreted existentially, as 'some (group of) people', whereas in (13), the existential reading too is barred. The derivation of existential *man* can be illustrated with the structure in (14):

(14) ... [TP *man* [T' TEPISODIC [VP (*man*) [v' V (*man*)]]]]

In all of these examples, however, *man* can be interpreted as 1st singular, and this reading actually becomes mandatory in (13). While the generic reading of both (12) and (13) is ruled out by the grammatical aspect, it remains to be established what rules out the existential reading of (13). I turn to this issue in §3.

On the contrary, inclusiveness in Kratzer's theory does not obey any restriction concerning aspect.[5]

2.4 Cross-linguistic variation

Cinque's effect is subject to intricate cross-linguistic variation, also among closely related varieties. While Italian *si* is generally available with the *we*-reading, no such reading is generally associated with Spanish *se*. In Spanish (15), the only available reading is that in which some people have been working for two months, whereas (16) is unacceptable:

(15) Spanish
Se ha trabajado durante dos meses para resolver el problema.
SE has worked   for   two   months to   solve   the problem

'people have worked for two months...'

---

[4] That the crucial notion is grammatical aspect rather than specific time reference was also pointed out by D'Alessandro & Alexiadou (2003).

[5] In fact, the examples offered by Kratzer are typically generic or habitual, as in (3-4), a fact which further underlines the difference between Kratzer's observation and Cinque's observation.

(16) Spanish
Ayer se fue despedido.
yesterday SE was fired.

The variation among Germanic languages is parallel to that between Italian and Spanish. For instance, consider Norwegian and German. In contrast to Swedish, the 1st singular reading of impersonal *man* is not generally available in either of Norwegian or German. That is to say, in (17) and (18), *man* is existentially interpreted as '(some) people', while (19–20) are found unacceptable by my consultants.[6]

(17) Norwegian
Man har arbeidet i to måneder med dette problemet.
MAN has worked in two months with this problem.the

(18) German
Man hat zwei Monate lang gearbeitet, um das Problem zu lösen.
MAN has two months long worked for the problem to solve
'(Some) people have been working for two months to solve the problem.'

(19) Norwegian
?* *I går ble man oppsagt.*
yesterday was MAN fired

(20) German
?* *Gestern wurde man gefeuert.*
yesterday was MAN fired

Kratzer's observation, on the other hand, is not expected to be subject to such cross-linguistic variation. Rather, some basic properties of logophoric reference are expected to be largely constant across languages.

For the purposes of this paper, I assume that Kratzer's logophoricity account for cases of inclusiveness such as (3–4) is correct, and will not further discuss it here. In §3, I turn to the analysis of Cinque's observation.

---

[6]This is not to say that 1st singular or 1st plural readings are all together excluded with Norwegian and German *man*, nor with Spanish *se*. In fact, impersonal readings in all of these languages can be contextually "manipulated" so as to refer to various discourse participants. However, in Norwegian, German, and Spanish, such readings are not generally available, unlike what we see in Swedish and Italian. Recall, however, that in all of these languages, such specific readings emerge as a matter of dialectal variation (see f.n. 3). Therefore, this should not necessarily be understood as a comparison between national "standard" languages, but rather between different varieties of such languages. As for a discussion on the variation within Germanic, see e.g. Malamud (2006); Hoekstra (2010).

3 The aspectual restrictions on impersonal readings

As argued in Egerland 2003b; 2005, Cinque's observation, as well as some of the cross-linguistic variation, can be accounted for on the set of assumptions listed in §3.1 – §3.3

3.1 The 1st person reading is lexical

The *man* pronoun in (the relevant variety of) Swedish can be lexically associated with a 1st singular reading. By this, I mean that 1st singular *man* is an independent lexeme acquired as such and, hence, a homonym to impersonal *man*. I propose the same analysis of the 1st plural reading of (the relevant variety of) Italian *si*. Therefore, such readings are not syntactically constrained but, essentially, always available. For instance, such lexicalized forms can be under the scope of a generic operator, as in (7b) and (8b).

3.2 Impersonal pronouns are featurally deficient

As we have seen, there are environments in which generic as well as existential readings of *man* are excluded. Suppose that the ungrammaticality of Spanish (16), Norwegian (19), and German (20) arises as a result of the interaction between lexical and grammatical aspect: While a generic reading is barred by perfective aspect, the existential reading is barred by a "delimited" lexical aspect, in the sense of Tenny (1987); i.e. the existential reading is excluded by the fact that the surface subject is the internal argument of a delimited event. The generalizations expressed in the structures (11) and (14) can be captured as in (21) (a reformulation of Egerland (2003a: 82):

(21)   *Man* cannot be the impersonal existential subject of a delimited event, if *man* itself corresponds to the argument that limits the event.

There is a natural explanation to (21) on the assumption that, in order to establish whether an argument does or does not limit the event, the argument in question needs to have some inherent content or, informally speaking, a certain degree of referentiality. To be more precise, suppose that a feature corresponding to the Inner Aspect projects a phrase, say EventP (Travis 2000; Borer 2005):

(22)   ... [$_{TP}$ T [$_{vP}$ DP v [$_{EventP}$ Event [$_{VP}$ V DP]]]]

In (22), the internal argument, but not the external one, needs to be matched against the Event. In order to enter into such a relation, the internal argument must carry some specification with regard to specificity and number.[7] As impersonal *man* is underspecified for specificity and number, it is unable to evaluate the Event. The generalization in (21) follows. Therefore, Swedish *man* is interpreted as 1st singular, and Italian *si* as 1st plural, because these are the only remaining options.[8]

3.3 The mandatory 1st person reading is a 'last resort'

If an impersonal pronoun, in a given language, is not lexically associated with such specific readings, and if the context rules out generic and existential readings, the expression is not interpretable. This is what we observe with Spanish *se* (16), Norwegian *man* (19) and German *man* (20).

The intuition behind such an account is that Cinque's observation does not follow from an effect imposing inclusive readings on impersonal pronouns, but rather from independent restrictions on generic and existential readings of such pronouns.

The discussion of this section has taken into consideration restrictions that are aspectual in nature. Clearly, however, generic and existential readings can be restricted by other factors than aspect. In the following section, I turn to a quite different set of data which I believe corroborate the approach outlined in §3.1–§3.3

4 SELF-topicalization

In this section, the hypothesis outlined in §3 will be tested on a different set of data. The following discussion, which concerns information structure, will be limited to the comparison of four Germanic varieties, namely Swedish, Icelandic, Norwegian, and German.[9]

---

[7] Recall that, for instance, the difference between the delimited reading of *Dustin ate an apple* and the non-delimited reading of *Dustin ate apples* depends on the number specification of the object (Carlson 1977, Tenny 1987: 113).

[8] I assume that, in the case of generic *man* as in the structure (11), the semantic content of *man* is provided by the generic operator (Chierchia 1995). Presumably, it is the presence of such an operator that makes it possible for generic *man* to bind anaphors, while existential *man* does not have this property, as pointed out by Cabredo Hofherr (2010).

[9] The hypothesis cannot be tested on Romance data, given that the equivalent elements (French *même*, Italian *stesso*, Spanish *mismo*) cannot be topicalized in a way similar to what we observe in Germanic languages.

4.1 The topicalization of SELF-anaphora

In all of these languages, SELF anaphora can appear in different positions of the clause. Given a setting such as the one stated as Context A, as in (23–26), SELF can appear in a sentence internal position, the exact nature of which is immaterial for the present discussion:[10]

Context A: The coming week everyone in my office is taking a leave...

(23) Swedish
Chefen åker själv på semester.
boss.the goes SELF on holiday

(24) Icelandic
Stjórinn fer sjálfur í frí.
boss.the goes SELF on holiday

(25) Norwegian
Sjefen drar sjøl på ferie.
boss.the goes SELF on holiday

(26) German
Der Chef fährt selbst in Urlaub.
the boss goes SELF on holiday

'...the boss himself / even the boss / the boss too is going on a holiday.'

Furthermore, in all four languages, SELF can be topicalized, as in (27–30). This, however, is pragmatically appropriate in a different kind of setting, as for instance the one suggested in Context B:

---

[10]In all of the languages, SELF can appear in other possible positions as well which will not be considered here. For instance, it can follow the DP (Swedish *chefen själv* 'the boss himself') or even appear sentence-finally. This state of affairs can be taken as evidence that SELF anaphora such as those discussed in the text have "floating" properties (Kayne 1975; Sportiche 1988). On the other hand, an anonymous reviewer suggests that the two instances of German *selbst* in (26) and (30) could be separate lexemes though homonymous. For present purposes, this possibility can remain an open issue.

Context B: Everyone else in my office has to work over the weekend but ...

(27) Swedish
Själv åker chefen på semester.
SELF goes boss.the on holiday

(28) Icelandic
Sjálfur fer stjórinn í frí.
SELF goes boss.the on holiday

(29) Norwegian
Sjøl drar sjefen på ferie.
SELF goes boss.the on holiday

(30) German
Selbst fährt der Chef in Urlaub.
SELF goes the boss on holiday
'... but the boss, on the other hand, is leaving for a holiday.'

Consider that, in the languages in question, SELF creates a contrastive reading. For concreteness, I chose to formulate the information structural notion of contrastiveness in terms of membership in a set, along the lines of e.g. Vilkuna & Vilkuna (1998):[11]

(31) (Vilkuna & Vilkuna 1998: 83)
If an expression **a** is kontrastive, a membership set **M** = {..., a, ...} is generated and becomes available to semantic computation as some sort of quantificational domain ...

In all of (23–30), SELF generates a set reading and picks out one member of the set, the boss: In (23–26), the expression points out that the boss is (unexpectedly) part of the set (while he could have stayed at work, he is leaving together with the others). In (27–30), on the contrary, the boss is interpreted in contrast to the other members of the set (he is leaving while everyone else is staying at work). Now, let us turn to impersonal constructions.

---

[11]Contrastiveness, as in the definition in (31), is presented as a "cover term for several operator-like interpretations of focus that one finds in the literature" (Vilkuna & Vilkuna 1998: 83). That is to say that the generalization we are interested in could be formulated in different terms, as for instance the identificational focus of É. Kiss (1998). For present purposes, (31) will suffice.

4.2 The relevance of SELF-topicalization for the interpretation of impersonal *man*

The reason why Icelandic is taken into consideration at this point is that Icelandic *maður* shares with Swedish *man* the property of being interpretable as 1st singular in a colloquial register. For Icelandic, the effect was first discussed by Jónsson (1992) who gives the example (32) (= his 43): [12]

(32) Icelandic
 Eg vona að maður verði ekki of seinn.
 I hope that MAÐUR will.be not too late
 'I hope I won't be late.'

Given Context A, when SELF appears in the sentence internal position, there are two possible readings as illustrated in Swedish (33) and Icelandic (34):

Context A: In hostels there is sometimes no room cleaning service, so...

(33) Swedish
 Man måste själv städa rummet.
 MAN must SELF clean room.the

(34) Icelandic
 Maður verður sjálfur að þrífa herbergið.
 MAN must SELF to clean room.the
 a. 'People have to clean their rooms themselves / on their own.'
 b. 'I have to clean the room myself / on my own.'

In the a-interpretation of (33–34), the impersonal is referring to people in general. In the b-interpretation (which is colloquial), *man* and *maður* specifically refer to 1st singular. In other words, (33–34) can be taken to mean that whenever I stay in a hostel, I need to clean my room myself.

In Norwegian and German, the same sentence is acceptable in the same kind of context, however only with the generic reading:

---

[12] There are, however, independent differences between Swedish and Icelandic. In particular, unlike Swedish *man*, Icelandic *maður* is not compatible with the existential reading at all in episodic contexts (Jónsson 1992; Egerland 2003b; Sigurðsson & Egerland 2009). This difference need not concern us here.

(35) Norwegian
Man må sjøl rydde rommet.
MAN must SELF clean room.the

(36) German
Man muss das Zimmer selbst aufräumen.
MAN must the room SELF clean
'People have to clean their rooms themselves.'

Thus, (35–36) confirm the earlier observation concerning Norwegian and German: Impersonal *man* is not associated with the 1st singular reading. [13]

Furthermore, under particular circumstances, SELF can be topicalized in both Swedish and Icelandic impersonal sentences. Such a topicalization, however, requires a completely different kind of setting to be pragmatically appropriate. For instance, a child who is grounded while his/her companions are out playing could say something such as (37–38):

Context B: All the other kids are out having fun, but ...

(37) Swedish
Själv måste man städa rummet.
SELF must MAN clean room.the

(38) Icelandic
sjálfur verður maður að þrífa herbergið.
SELF must MAN to clean room.the
'... but I have to stay at home and clean my room.'

The utterance is only acceptable if the subject is identified with 1st singular. I suggest this is so because of the contrastive reading associated with topicalization. Suppose that contrastiveness indeed generates a set reading, as stated in (31). In (31), "**M** is a set of objects matching **a** in semantic type" (Vilkuna & Vilkuna 1998: 84). Arguably, then, contrastiveness can hold between specific individuals or groups of individuals. An impersonal pronoun radically lacks specificity and

---

[13] But recall that it is always the case with generic readings that they encompass all the persons of the paradigm, hence also 1st person.

Verner Egerland

number features. Hence, it cannot be put in contrast with another "object of the same semantic type", quite as much as it cannot delimit the event (see §3).[14]

I believe this restriction on impersonal readings may be illustrated with what is sometimes called generic nouns, such as English *people* (and equivalent expressions in other languages), although an in depth analysis of such nouns goes far beyond the purposes of this study.[15] Consider that *people* cannot be contrasted with a single individual. I can say something like *people around here usually come early to the office, but John doesn't*, but I cannot express this meaning as a contrastive focus:

(39) ??It is *people* who come early to the office (not John).

Under contrastive focus, namely, *people* becomes a kind-denoting expression, as in (40–41) (cf. Chierchia 1998):

(40) It is *people* who do bad things (not God).

(41) Around here, it is *people* who do the work (not machines).

However, unlike impersonal pronouns, *people* is indeed a noun and thus compatible with a lexical restriction, such as a relative clause. Not unexpectedly, a contrastive reading with a non kind-denoting *people* becomes possible if *people* is restricted so as to refer to a specific group of individuals:

(42) It is *people who come early to the office* who get things done (not John).

Impersonal subjects such as *man* are weak pronominal elements: they cannot take restrictions such as the relative clause in (42), neither can they carry stress.[16] Hence, the impersonal pronoun itself cannot be topicalized. However, the associate SELF is generally stressed and can indeed be topicalized.

For concreteness, then, assume that the complex [MAN SELF] originates as a phrase, and that SELF moves out of this phrase during the derivation. The details of such an analysis are not crucial for my line of reasoning, the important thing being that some interpretative dependency holds between the pronoun MAN and the anaphor SELF. The derivation of (37) is illustrated in the structure of (43):

---

[14] The radical featural deficiency of impersonal pronouns such as *man* is also assumed in e.g. Cabredo Hofherr (2010). In Egerland (2003b) this featural deficiency was taken to be directly linked to a certain variability in agreement patterns attested in Swedish. Admittedly, this conclusion may not extend to Germanic languages generally, as pointed out in Malamud (2012).

[15] But in the theory of Hoekstra (2010), impersonal pronouns are taken to be the pronominal counterparts of such generic nouns.

[16] There are exceptions to this rule, such as West Frisian *men* (Hoekstra 2010).

(43) [$_{CP}$ SELF$_i$ [$_{C'}$ måste [$_{TP}$ [MAN SELF]$_i$ ... [$_{vP}$ [MAN SELF]$_i$ VP]]]]

The topicalization creates a reading in which the subject, [MAN SELF], is interpreted in contrast to some other participant of the discourse. As a deficient pronoun cannot be interpreted under contrastive focus, the lexicalized 1st singular option is the only one remaining. Therefore, (37–38) can only be taken to refer to the 1st singular.

Crucially, this line of reasoning gives rise to the prediction that the equivalent sentences are unacceptable in Norwegian and German, given that the 1st singular alternative is not available in these languages. My consultants confirm this prediction:

(44) Norwegian
 * sjøl må man rydde rommet.
 SELF must MAN clean room.the

(45) German
 * selbst muss man das Zimmer aufräumen.
 SELF must MAN the room clean

What we observe in (44–45) is the same kind of effect as in the examples (19) and (20) in §2.4: When the impersonal readings are barred, Norwegian and German cannot recur to a lexicalized specific interpretation.[17]

5 Conclusion

While Kratzer's observation presumably can be successfully analyzed within a theory explaining when a given impersonal must be interpreted as including the speaker, Cinque's observation can only be understood in a theory explaining how impersonal readings are restricted. When they are, some languages can access lexicalized readings of impersonals, such as the 1st singular reading of Swedish *man*, while other languages do not have any such alternative. I conclude from this that Kratzer's observation and Cinque's observation are fundamentally different in nature, despite the superficial similarities.

---

[17] An anonymous reviewer points out the (s)he finds an example such as (44) acceptable in Norwegian, quite unlike my consultants. My only suggestion as to why this could be the case, is that SELF in some Scandinavian varieties can take on the meaning of 'alone'. In fact, Swedish (37) is also interpretable as 'I have to clean the room alone', a possibility which I have chosen to disregard. However, this meaning of SELF is usually taken to be more normal in Swedish than in Norwegian.

Abbreviations

Abbreviations used in this article follow the Leipzig Glossing Rules' instructions for word-by-word transcription, available at: https://www.eva.mpg.de/lingua/pdf/Glossing-Rules.pdf.

References

Borer, Hagit. 2005. *Structuring sense.* Oxford: Oxford University Press.
Cabredo Hofherr, Patricia. 2010. *Binding properties of impersonal human pronouns in generic and episodic contexts.* http://docplayer.net/3847139-Binding-properties-of-impersonal-human-pronouns-in-generic-and-episodic-contexts-1.html. Paper presented at the Workshop on impersonal human pronouns, Université Paris VIII, Paris, France.
Carlson, Greg. 1977. A unified analysis of the English bare plural. *Linguistics and Philosophy* 1. 413–457.
Chierchia, Gennaro. 1995. The variability of impersonal subjects. In Emmon Bach, Eloise Jelinek, Angelika Kratzer & Barbara H. Partee (eds.), *Quantification in natural languages*, 107–143. Dordrecht: Kluwer.
Chierchia, Gennaro. 1998. Reference to kinds across languages. *Natural Language Semantics* 6. 339–405.
Cinque, Guglielmo. 1988. On *Si* constructions and the theory of *Arb*. *Linguistic Inquiry* 19. 521–581.
D'Alessandro, Roberta. 2007. *Impersonal* Si *constructions. Agreement and interpretation.* Berlin: Mouton de Gruyter.
D'Alessandro, Roberta & Artemis Alexiadou. 2003. Inclusive and exclusive impersonal pronouns: A feature-geometrical analysis. *Rivista di Grammatica Generativa* 27. 31–44.
É. Kiss, Katalin. 1998. Identificational focus versus information focus. *Language* 74. 245–273.
Egerland, Verner. 2003a. Impersonal *man* and aspect in swedish. *Venice Working Papers in Linguistics* 13. 73–91.
Egerland, Verner. 2003b. Impersonal pronouns in scandinavian and romance. *Working Papers in Scandinavian Syntax* 71. 75–102.
Egerland, Verner. 2005. *Impersonal Pronouns in Scandinavian and Romance.* Ms. Lund University.
Hoekstra, Jarich. 2010. On the impersonal pronoun *men* in modern West frisian. *Journal of Comparative German Linguistics* 13. 31–59.

Jónsson, Jóhannes Gísli. 1992. *The Pronoun Maður in Icelandic*. Ms. University of Massachusetts, Amherst.

Kayne, Richard S. 1975. *French syntax: The transformational cycle*. Cambridge, Massachusetts: MIT Press.

Kratzer, Angelika. 1997. *German Impersonal Pronouns and Logophoricity*. http://semanticsarchive.net/Archive/WViZTE1M/Impersonal%20Pronouns%20&%20Logophoricity.pdf. Paper presented at *Sinn und Bedeutung*, Berlin 1997, and *Generic Pronouns and Logophoricity*, São Paolo 2000.

Kratzer, Angelika. 2000. *German Impersonal Pronouns and Logophoricity*. http://semanticsarchive.net/Archive/WViZTE1M/Impersonal%20Pronouns%20&%20Logophoricity.pdf. Paper presented at *Generic Pronouns and Logophoricity*, São Paolo 2000.

Kratzer, Angelika. 2009. Making a pronoun: Fake indexicals as windows into the properties of pronouns. *Linguistic Inquiry* 40. 187–237.

Malamud, Sophia. 2006. *Semantics and pragmatics of arbitrariness*. University of Pennsylvania dissertation.

Malamud, Sophia. 2012. Impersonal indexicals: *one*, *you*, *man*, and *du*. *Journal of Comparative Germanic Linguistics* 15. 1–48.

Sigurðsson, Halldór Ármann & Verner Egerland. 2009. Impersonal null-subjects in icelandic and elsewhere. 63(1). 158–185.

Sportiche, Dominique. 1988. A theory of floating quantifiers and its corollaries for constituent structure. *Linguistic Inquiry* 19. 425–449.

Tenny, Carol L. 1987. *Grammaticalizing aspect and affectedness*. Cambridge, MA: MIT dissertation.

Travis, Lisa. 2000. Event structure in syntax. In Carol L. Tenny & James Pustejovsky (eds.), *Events as grammatical objects: The converging perspectives of lexical semantics and syntax*, 145–185. Palo Alto: CSLI.

Vilkuna, Enric & Maria Vilkuna. 1998. On rheme and contrast. In Culicover Peter & Louise McNally (eds.), *The limits of syntax* (Syntax & Semantics 29), 79–108. San Diego: Academic Press.

Zobel, Sarah. 2011. *Against a purely feature based analysis of pronominal meaning*. Poster presented at 34th annual GLOW-colloquium, Vienna, Austria.

Chapter 8

Who are we – and who is I? About Person and SELF

Halldór Ármann Sigurðsson
Lund University

This paper discusses the semantics and syntax of the first person pronouns *we* and *I*, in particular with regard to the Event/Speech Participant Split evidenced in clauses like (i).

(i) **We** finally beat Napoleon at Waterloo two centuries ago.

The propositional event participants (the "Napoleon beaters") are not involved in the speech event (the utterance of (i)), and the speech participants are not involved in the propositional event ("beating of Napoleon"). Nevertheless, the pronoun *we* somehow links the speaker and the theta set ($\{_\theta x_1, \ldots x_n\}$ or simply $\{\theta\}$) of "Napoleon beaters". The paper adopts the idea that person values (1, 2, 3) are computed in syntax, and that the elements entering this computation are: A general abstract Person feature (Pn), vP-internally generated NPs ($\{\theta\}$), and speaker and hearer features (Λ features) at the phase edge. It is this computation that yields the speaker–$\{\theta\}$ linking embodied in *we* (mending the Event/Speech Participant Split). Evidence that Pn can be independently computed for each phase comes from self-talk, first discussed as a linguistically relevant phenomenon by Anders Holmberg (2010). The paper also suggests that the secondary SELF readings seen in logophoric phenomena arise form positive setting of the Pn feature, and that the value +Pn is responsible for the "human bias" of plural pronouns.

1 Introduction

Consider the sentence in (1).

(1) **We** beat them!

Halldór Ármann Sigurðsson. 2017. Who are we – and who is I? About Person and SELF. in Michelle Sheehan & Laura R. Bailey (eds.), *Order and structure in syntax II: Subjecthood and argument structure*, 197–219. Berlin: Language Science Press.

Who are "we" in this sentence? The question might seem to have a simple and an obvious answer: "Well, you and somebody else, of course!" That answer would accord with the common understanding that the first person plural pronoun has the meaning in (2) (see, e.g., Cysouw 2003, Siewierska 2004: 82ff.).

(2) we = 'the speaker augmented by X' ('the speaker + X' for short)

However, this understanding is incorrect. Certainly, *we* is commonly interpreted as 'the person who is speaking and someone else', but it is easy to come up with sentences where this is not the meaning of *we*, such as the one in (3).

(3) I'm a Tottenham fan – and **we** beat Arsenal yesterday!

I have absolutely no relation with Tottenham Hotspurs other than by some coincidence being a fan since I was a kid more than a thousand miles north of London, and yet (3) makes perfect sense to me. Well, in this case you could say: Ok, the pronoun does not actually mean 'the speaker and someone else' but rather 'a set or a group to which the speaker belongs' – in this case the set containing roughly the Tottenham club and its supporters. However, even this broad understanding is too narrow, as suggested by the example in (4).

(4) **We** finally beat Napoleon at Waterloo two centuries ago.

This sentence is not about the speaker – he or she is obviously not included in the set of individuals and forces that finally beat Napoleon and his army at Waterloo on the 18th of June 1815. Rather, it is about a set of actors ('Napoleon beaters'), a THETA SET, with which the speaker identifies himself/herself, for whatever reasons. This is explicitly stated in (5).

(5) a. A THETA SET, $\{_\theta\ x_1, ...\ x_n\}$ (or simply $\{\theta\}$), is the set of individuals/entities that bear or carry out a theta role, θ.

b. The pronoun *we* denotes a theta set with which the speaker identifies himself/herself.

Identifying oneself with some set or group is different from being a member of it. So, if I actually would say the sentence in (3), my friend John, an even more devoted Tottenham fan might respond: "WE who? You never show up on matchdays!" John is in his full right to question my claim to belong to the we-set that beat Arsenal, while I, in turn, am in my full right to empathize or even identify myself with the 'Arsenal beaters'. Crucially, the use of *we* is based on the speaker's own judgment and others do not necessarily share that judgment.

By using *we* I can even empathize with the whole of humanity (across time and space), as in (6).

(6) There can be no doubt that **we** will encounter intelligent beings from other solar systems in the third millennium.

On the other hand, the theta set cannot usually contain anything but humans. Thus, *we* in (7) is normally interpreted as referring to humans only and not to, say, humans and bears. Call this THE HUMAN BIAS.[1]

(7) **We have lived in Europe for at least 40 000 years.**

Many or most of the observations regarding *we* (and *I*) that I will be discussing have parallels for *you*, but, for simplicity, I will for the most part limit my discussion to the first person pronoun. I will also set Number aside. It interacts in intriguing ways with Person in morphological agreement systems, but it does not seem to do so directly in syntax. The pronoun *we* is not the plural of *I*; it does not mean 'many speakers' or many 'Is' (Boas 1911; Benveniste 1966; Lyons 1968; Cysouw 2003; Siewierska 2004; Bobaljik 2008, among many). "Clusivity", as we will see, does not involve Number.

§2 presents initial thoughts on the relation between the speaker and theta sets. §3 discusses the first person singular pronoun, the notion of primary and secondary SELF, and presents a number of secondary SELF contexts, including the context of self-talk (discussed in Holmberg 2010). §4 discusses Person and SELF in a neo-performative perspective, developing the central hypothesis that the speaker–{θ} linking embodied in *we* is brought about by Person computation in syntax, further suggesting that the activation of a secondary SELF arises from a positive setting (+Pn) of the abstract Person feature. In addition, it is suggested that +Pn is responsible for the human bias of plural pronouns.

2 So, more exactly, who are we?

The fact that the theta set represented or expressed by *we* does not need to actually *include* the speaker (although it 'involves' the speaker), and that the meaning of *we* is thus not 'the speaker + X' (or 'the speaker + {θ}'), has not, to my knowledge, been generally noticed or problematized. In the sentence in (4), the speaker

---

[1] Partly non-human readings can be coerced in certain contexts, in particular under partial coreference as in "Bears first came to Europe hundreds of thousand years ago and **we** have been coexisting here for at least the last 40 000 years". The relevant generalization is that *we* must refer to conscious SELFs, either exclusively (the normal case) or at least partly (under coercion).

certainly identifies himself/herself with a theta set of 'Napoleon beaters', but he or she is not one of them – nor are there any 'Napoleon beaters' involved in or responsible for the speech act. Refer to this as the EVENT/SPEECH PARTICIPANT SPLIT, E/SP split, for short.[2]

'The speaker + X' or 'the speaker + {θ}', then, is not an insightful paraphrase of the meaning of *we*. Consider the reverse paraphrase in (8).

(8) we = '{θ} augmented by the speaker' ('{θ}+ speaker' for short)

This is closer to the mark. However, "augmented" in this formula (and the + sign in the short version) is misleading. The relevant relation between the speaker and {θ} is not the logical conjunction, & or ∧, nor is it natural language *and*. Consider the simple (9).

(9) Mary and John got married yesterday.

Here *Mary and John* make up a homogeneous set in the sense that the potential distinction between *Mary* and *John* is irrelevant. This is clearly not the case for the speaker and the 'Napoleon beaters' in (4). The sentence in (4) is not about a set of 'Napoleon beaters' *and* the speaker, as stated in (10).

(10) we in (4) ≠ {Napoleon beaters} & the speaker

Rather, as already noted, (4) is about a set of 'Napoleon beaters' that is somehow related to the speaker in the speaker's own view. This theta set–speaker relation is an instantiation of a more general event/speech participant linking comprising a theta set–hearer relation as well (embodied by plural *you*). Focusing on the speaker side we can call the theta set–speaker relation {θ}-S LINKING and use the sign ↔ to denote it. We thus replace (8) by (11).

(11) we = '{θ} linked to the speaker in his or her own judgment', {{θ} ↔ speaker} for short

The notion of "linking" here is vague, deliberately so, as it is hard to pin down its exact nature: {{θ} ↔ speaker} is often used to express plain additive readings (the additive relation being subsumed under the more general linking relation), but it crucially involves the speaker's own judgement, and, as we have seen, it also expresses non-additive E/SP split readings. In §4, I will suggest that it arises from Person computation.

---

[2] It is also found for plural *you* (as in "You finally beat Napoleon at Waterloo two centuries ago").

{θ}-S linking applies generally to the pronoun *we*, regardless of its position or function, and it does not necessarily involve sympathy (even though it often does), whereas at least some minimal empathy seems to be required. The essentially non-inclusive relation involved defies the idea (Postal 1966; Elbourne 2005) that all personal pronouns are complex DPs, with a pronominal head and a deleted or a reconstructed NP. The pronoun *we*, as we have seen, cannot *generally* be analyzed as [we [NP]], for example as [we [Napoleon beaters]] or [we [unspecified people]]; such a DP would wrongly *include* the speaker in the theta set rather than merely linking the speaker and the theta set. Similarly, as we will see shortly, the pronoun *I* cannot always be paraphrased as 'I, the speaker' (with roughly the structure [I [the speaker]]). Pronouns obviously *can* have reconstructed complex DP interpretations, but the relevant point here is that they *need* not have any such interpretation. I thus adopt the view that plain pronouns can be pure DPs, without an NP complement: [$_{DP}$ we], [$_{DP}$ I], etc.

It is obvious that the special nature of {θ}-S linking does not stem from the theta set (of Napoleon beaters, or whatever) – it must instead be the case that it stems from the speaker category. In the following I will reflect on the nature of the speaker category and on the intriguing question of how it gets activated or involved in the pronoun *we*.

3 On the speaker category: Who is I – and SELF?

The speaker category is normally represented by the first person singular pronoun, *I*, but it is not equivalent with it. There are certain contexts where the pronoun *I* does not relate to or denote the speaker, but to what might be referred to as a secondary SELF, overshadowing the primary SELF of the actual speaker. One such context is regular direct speech, as in (12), where "Christer" is the speaker.

(12)   [Christer speaks:] Halldór said to Anders: "**I** will cite **your** paper again!"

It is evident that direct speech somehow embeds a silent secondary SELF that is referred to by the first person singular pronoun. A related and a much-discussed phenomenon (see Bianchi 2003; Schlenker 2003; Anand 2006) is PERSON SHIFT (indexical shift), as in the Persian clause in (13), where *man* 'I' and *tora* 'you' refer to *Ali* and *Sara*.[3]

---

[3]From Sigurðsson 2004, based on pers. comm. with G h. Karimi Doostan. Thanks also to Alireza Soleimani. The sentence is ambiguous between the shifted reading given in (16) and the regular non-shifted reading 'Ali told Sara that I like you' (irrelevant here).

(13) [Amir speaks:] *Ali be Sara goft [ke* **man tora** *doost* **daram***].*
         Ali to Sara said that I   you friend have.1SG
     'Ali told Sara that **he** likes **her**.'

Yet another case of the first person singular pronoun not really referring to the speaker of the clause involves bound variable readings, as in the subordinate clause in (14).[4]

(14) Only I got a question that I understood.

The natural interpretation of this clause is not 'The speaker of this clause is the only one who got a question that this particular speaker understood'. Rather, it is the bound variable reading 'There was only one person x_i who got a question that x_i understood (and x_i happens to be me, the speaker of this clause)'. That is: The subject of the subordinate clause does not by itself refer to the speaker, only referring to the actual speaker indirectly, by virtue of being a variable bound by the matrix subject (which in turn does refer to the speaker). Bound first (and second) person variables of this sort are sometimes called "fake indexicals" (Kratzer 2009).

These well-known observations show that the first person singular pronoun does not equal the actual speaker. The pronoun *I* canonically denotes the speaker but that is evidently not all *I* can do. In certain contexts, it can represent a SELF that is different from, albeit somehow dependent on that of the actual speaker's. In indexical shift and direct speech contexts, as in (12) and (13), the distinction between the primary SELF of the actual speaker and the secondary SELF represented by *I* is quite clear. It is less distinct but also discernable in bound variable readings, as in (14).[5]

A secondary SELF can also hide behind a third person pronoun. This is the case in *de se* (lit. 'of oneself') readings of bound third person pronouns, as *she* in (15).

(15) Mary looked into the mirror and thought she looked good.

---

[4] See Rullmann 2004 for a clear discussion of bound variable readings of first and second person pronouns.

[5] Typical IMPOSTERS are third person expressions, such as *Daddy, Mom, my boy*, that are used to express a first or a second person relation to the speaker (see Collins & Postal 2012; Wood & Sigurðsson 2011), as in "Daddy already told you that" or "How is my boy?" The first person singular pronoun in the direct speech, indexical shift, and the bound variable contexts in (12–14) is an inverse imposter of sorts. That is: The pronoun expresses a third person relation (to the actual speaker) in spite of its first person camouflage.

The salient reading of the subordinate clause is the *de se* reading that Mary thought of herself "I look good". The *de re* reading 'she looks good' is far-fetched but not in principle excluded (in case Mary for some reason, such as insanity or drunkenness, thought she was looking at someone distinct from herself). *De se* is the only possible reading of PRO in control infinitives such as the one in (16) (Chierchia 1989).[6]

(16) Mary hoped to look good.

Here Mary cannot possibly, not even by accident, have someone else's looks in mind (*de re*). There is no possible world where Mary could be thinking: "I_i hope she$_k$ will be looking good".

The presence of a secondary SELF is also discernable in contexts that are commonly referred to as "logophoric", where the "speech, thoughts, feelings, or general state of consciousness" of someone distinct from the speaker are reported (Clements 1975: 141). I will instead use the term SECONDARY SELFHOOD, reserving "logophoric" and "logophoricity" for other purposes (see §4). It seems that most languages do not overtly signal secondary selfhood, but some do, either by using special markers for this purpose (see Sells 1987 and the references there) or by some specific use of pronouns that are also used for other purposes, commonly reflexive pronouns. Icelandic is a language of this latter type, using long-distance reflexives, LDRs, to mark secondary selfhood, as described by Thráinsson (1976; 1990; 2007); see also Maling 1984 and Sigurðsson 1990.[7] The contrast in (17) illustrates this, as will be explained below.

(17) Aðeins forsetinn$_i$ heldur að öll þjóðin   elski sig$_i$/hann$_i$.
 only   president.the believes that all country love self/him
 'Only the president believes that all the people love him.'

LDR is optional, coreference of the matrix subject and the subordinate object being expressed by either the reflexive *sig* or the pronoun *hann*. There is a subtle difference, though, such that only the reflexive reflects the matrix subject's point of view or consciousness. While the pronominal reading is that the president is the only one who believes that all the people love the president,[8] the reflexive

---

[6]Potential *de re* readings in adverbial PRO infinitives (discussed in Landau 2013: 32–33) are irrelevant in the present context.

[7]Similar facts are found in other languages. See for example Giorgi 2006 on Italian.

[8]We can disregard the reading, irrelevant here, where *hann* refers to somebody other than the president. Local coreference of the object with the subordinate subject is usually expressed by the complex reflexive *sjálf- sig* (*sjálfan sig, sjálfa sig,* etc.); see Sigurjónsdóttir 1992: 56 (and Thráinsson 2007: 464 and further references there).

reading is the bound variable *de se* reading that the president is the only person who believes of himself that the whole people love him, as explicitly stated in (18).

(18) a. HANN: the president is the only one who believes that all the people love the president

b. SIG: the president (x_i) is the only person who believes of himself that all the people love him (x_i)

Notice that the English translation in (17) is ambiguous between the two readings. English does not have means to lexically distinguish between these readings – but they are both there, just as in languages with overt markers of secondary selfhood.

The capacity to linguistically reflect someone else's mind or internal world is a remarkable phenomenon. Let us refer to it as the SYNTACTIC EMPATHY CAPACITY (cf. Kuno & Kaburaki 1977).[9] In the examples we have been looking at so far, the syntactic empathy is, so to speak, external, reflecting secondary SELFs (represented by first or third person pronouns or by PRO) that are distinct from the speaker. However, perhaps not surprisingly, the syntactic empathy can also be internal, directed towards the speaker himself or herself. That is: Speakers can simultaneously (i.e., in a single utterance) talk about their present speech event SELF and another potential SELF of theirs, not present in the speech event. This SELF-SPLIT is nicely illustrated by the indicative/subjunctive contrast in the Icelandic (19) (see Sigurðsson 1990: 325–326).

(19) a. *Ég vissi að María **kom** heim.*
I knew that Mary came.IND home
'I knew that Mary came home.'

b. *Ég vissi að María **kæmi** heim.*
I knew that Mary came.SUBJ home
'I knew that Mary would come home.'

While (19a) simply reports that the speaker was aware of the fact that 'Mary came home' at some time point in the past, the subjunctive clause in (19b) reflects on the speaker's past (secondary) SELF, saying that his or her past SELF was confident (rather than actually knew) that 'Mary would come home' at some time

---

[9] This is sufficiently accurate for my present purposes, but it is an oversimplification. As argued elsewhere (see Sigurðsson 2010a: 49), the relevant notion is a "negative" one, namely ABSENT SPEAKER TRUTHFULNESS RESPONSIBILITY (signaled by the subjunctive mood in Icelandic).

8 Who are we – and who is I? About Person and SELF

point later than his or her past time of consciousness. Notice that the existence of the two readings is not dependent on the morphological mood distinction; it is only made extra visible by it.[10]

SELF-TALK is another context with a self-split: a SECONDARY SPEAKER SELF, in addition to the primary speaker SELF. Anders Holmberg has written an essay (2010) about the interesting but hitherto unnoticed properties of self-talk, where self-talk "[is] speaking to yourself, the self being speaker as well as addressee" (2010: 57). Thus, as Holmberg shows, you can refer to yourself either as "I" or as "you" in the context of self-talk. A few of Holmberg's examples are given below.

(20) a. You're an idiot.
    b. I'm an idiot.

(21) a. You're hopeless.
    b. I'm hopeless.

(22) a. What's wrong with you?
    b. What's wrong with me?

(23) a. I think I've/you've had it
    b. *You think I've/you've had it. [* in self-talk]

(24) a. You're driving me mad.
    b. *I'm driving you mad. [* in self-talk]

On the basis of contrasts such as the ones in (23) and (24) between the "I mode" and the "you mode" Holmberg concludes that self-talk "*you* can't [usually] refer to the self as holder of thoughts or beliefs, in self-talk", nor can it "refer to the self as an experiencer of feelings or holder of intentions or plans" (2010: 59–60). This is further demonstrated by the sharp contrast in (25).

(25) a. I hate you!
    b. *You hate me!

All these observations show that language can operate with at least two distinct SELFs, the primary SELF of the speaker and a secondary SELF of either the

---

[10]Languages that lack inflectional subjunctive have the same semantics, often morphologically unmarked but sometimes marked by other means than mood distinctions, for example by modals as in the English translation of (19b).

speaker or of someone else. Holmberg (2010: 60) observes that *you* in (normal) self-talk "never answers back, however much he is insulted ... because he can't think; he is a mindless self. The property shared by the referent of *you* in self-talk and the referent of *you* in dialogue is that they are not controlled by the mind of the speaker: dialogue-you because it has a different mind, self-talk-you doesn't have a mind".

I agree, of course, that self-talk *you* has a more limited mind than the speaker and self-talk *I*, but I suspect that Holmberg overstates its "mindlessness". It cannot be the agent or controller of speech, thought, feelings – cannot answer back as Holmberg notes – but it is not like a lifeless thing. I believe it is more like the other types of secondary SELFs we have been looking at: an incomplete and an inactive SELF with no executive power, verbally or otherwise, but with the capacity of perceiving. Insulting or encouraging it is thus not pointless or an expression of madness, as insulting or encouraging a table or a pen would be in most situations in most cultures. It is thus warranted, I believe, to make a distinction between the fully active primary SELF of the speaker and a less active secondary SELF of either the speaker or someone else.

While the distinction between a primary and a secondary speaker SELF is upheld in normal self-talk, this distinction seems to break down in abnormal self-talk, symptomatic of dementia and madness, such that *you* gains the status of an entirely separate SELF (of an addressee), and "may, for example, answer back when being reproached" (Holmberg 2010: 63, building on Crow's theory (1998; 2004) of schizophrenia as a linguistic disorder).

4 Person and selfhood: a neo-performative approach

There is no way of expressing the word *you* without that being the "responsibility" of some *I*. Holmberg points out (2010: 60–61) that "when addressing yourself as *you*, there is still an *I* linguistically represented in the sentence, covertly if not overtly", suggesting that the PERFORMATIVE HYPOTHESIS was on the right track, after all. According to this (much reviled) hypothesis, any declarative sentence is embedded under a silent performative clause, roughly, "I hereby say to you". Ross famously advocated for this understanding, roughly as sketched in (26) for the simple clause "Prices slumped" (see 1970: 224).

(26) [I hereby say to you] Prices slumped.

Translated into modern generative theory this amounts to saying that the C-edge of the clause contains (among other features) a silent speaker feature or operator that takes scope over the clause (Sigurðsson 2004; 2014). However, it cannot really be the case that this edge feature gets directly spelled out as the pronoun *I*. Consider the "Ross formula" in (27).

(27) [I hereby say to you] I know that prices will slump.

The spelled-out *I* could not be a plain copy of the silent edge *I* or vice versa. That is: these two "*I*s" cannot be just two occurrences of the same element, or else all occurrences of *I* would simply refer to the actual speaker (precluding person shift as in 12–14), and also yielding an insoluble infinite regress problem). Rather, the silent "edge *I*" and the overt *I* are distinct but computationally related elements. And when you think about it, it is actually rather obvious that "first person" is a computed value, normally assigned to an NP (a theta set) that somehow relates to the speaker, much as "second person" is normally assigned to an NP that somehow relates to the hearer or the addressee. In other words, "first person" and "second person" are not primitives of language, whereas (roughly) "speaker" and (roughly) "hearer" arguably are basic notions.

In the a neo-performative and neo-Reichenbachian approach developed in previous work (e.g., Sigurðsson 2004; 2011; 2014; 2016), any phase edge contains a number of silent features, EDGE LINKERS, that link the inner phase to the next phase up or to the speech act context.[11] I will not go deep into the details of this approach here. Suffice it to say that abstract speaker and hearer features, referred to as the logophoric agent and the logophoric patient, Λ_A and Λ_P, are among the edge linkers and enter the computation of Person (Pn). Any phase that licenses an NP (subject, object, indirect object, etc.) has such linkers as well as an abstract Pn head (and a separate Number head, see Sigurðsson & Holmberg 2008). For expository ease, this is sketched in (28) for only the simple case of a clause with a defective v (in the sense of Chomsky 2001); as defective vP is not a strong phase, the edge linkers are only operative in the C edge in cases of this sort.[12]

---

[11] Cf. Chomsky 2004: 125, n. 17. This is inspired by Rizzi's theory of the left periphery (1997, etc.) and by the work of Bianchi (2003; 2006); Schlenker (2003); Frascarelli (2007), and others. The literature on this is rapidly growing; see for instance Giorgi 2010; Sundaresan 2012; Haddad 2014; Martín & Hinzen 2014. The approach adopted here differs from other structural neo-performative approaches (e.g. Tenny & Speas 2003) in that it claims, in the spirit of Ross 1970, that the speaker/hearer categories are themselves silent *by necessity*, even though they often have overt correlates somewhere else in the structure (providing indirect evidence for their activeness).

[12] On this approach, as indicated, abstract Agree is a computational valuing process (distinct from, albeit related to, morphological agreement).

(28) [$_{CP}$ Λ$_A$ - Λ$_P$ ... Pn ... [$_{vP}$ NP$_{αPn}$]]
       ↑_____↑↑_____↑
         Agree   Agree
       (valuing) (valuing)

Under Agree with the Pn head an NP (NP$_{αPn}$) is valued as either a "personal" or a "non-personal" argument, NP$_{+Pn}$ or NP$_{-Pn}$. A "personal" NP (NP$_{+Pn}$), in turn, must get valued in relation to the Λ linkers, as sketched in (29) (where the arrow reads 'gets valued as').[13]

(29)   a1. NP$_{+Pn}$ → NP$_{+Pn/+ΛA, -ΛP}$ = 1st person by computation
       a2. NP$_{+Pn}$ → NP$_{+Pn/-ΛA, +ΛP}$ = 2nd person by computation
       a3. NP$_{+Pn}$ → NP$_{+Pn/-ΛA, -ΛP}$ = 3rd person by computation
       b. NP$_{-Pn}$ = 3rd person by default ("no person")

In passing it is worth noticing that the computation of Person largely parallels that of Tense (cf. Partee 1973). Much as Event Time is computed in relation to Speech Time via Reference Time (Reichenbach 1947), so is an event participant (NP$_{αPn}$ or {θ}) computed in relation to a speech act participant via abstract Person (Sigurðsson 2004; 2016). Although I will not do so here, the parallelism could be underlined by talking about Speech Person, Event Person and Reference Person.

The spelled-out pronoun *I*, then, in for example (27), is not (at all) identical with the abstract speaker category. Instead, like the other "truly personal" pronouns, it is the spell out of a relation between an NP$_{αPn}$ (or a theta set), a general Person category (Pn), and the Λ features. Thus, the "speaker" in the "we-formula" in (11) is the abstract value +Λ$_A$, and its linking to NP$_{αPn}$ or {θ} yields its theta relatedness. The theta set can also be linked to the hearer feature, +Λ$_P$, or to both +Λ$_A$ and +Λ$_P$, as sketched in (30) and (31) below. It is the computation of the person value (the NP$_{αPn}$/Pn/Λ relation) that "mends" the Event/Speech Participant Split, thereby yielding the speaker–{θ} linking embodied in *we*.

The theta set is primary in relation to the speaker and hearer features. Given an event there is always a theta set that saturates it whereas there may or may not be

---

[13] The distinction between DPs and NPs is irrelevant in this context, so I am using "NP" as a cover term for both. As seen in (29), NPs may be in the third person either by computation, valued as +Pn, or by default, in which case they are valued as −Pn ("no person" in Benveniste 1966). The former typically applies to "personal" definite NPs, while the latter typically applies to indefinite and "non-personal" NPs (see Sigurðsson 2010b: 168–169). So-called "impersonal" pronouns, such as English *one*, French *on*, etc., are not "non-personal". Instead, they are (usually) "non-specifically personal", valued as +Pn. This extends to arbitrary and generic PRO (inheriting the +Pn valuation under control, see shortly).

positive speaker or hearer relatedness. This accords with the standard minimalist bottom-to-top approach to the derivation: vP is merged lowest, then TP, then CP (vP > TP > CP). While a theta role and therefore some (at least unspecific) theta set is given as soon as the vP predicate has been merged, the speaker and hearer categories are not accessible until at the edge of a phi-complete phase (i.e., not until at the C level in defective v structures like (28)). The theta set is open to any interpretation ('John and Mary', 'boat', 'God', etc.) that does not involve the speech participants, including the empty set interpretation {∅}. For the empty set interpretation, the options are as listed in (30) (recall that the double pointed arrow denotes the linking between a theta set and a speech participant category, see (11)).[14]

(30) a. $\{\{_\theta\ \emptyset\} \leftrightarrow \{+\Lambda_A, -\Lambda_P\}\}$ *I*
    b. $\{\{_\theta\ \emptyset\} \leftrightarrow \{-\Lambda_A, +\Lambda_P\}\}$ singular *you*
    c. $\{\{_\theta\ \emptyset\} \leftrightarrow \{+\Lambda_A, +\Lambda_P\}\}$ exhaustively hearer inclusive *we*
    d. $\{\{_\theta\ \emptyset\} \leftrightarrow \{-\Lambda_A, -\Lambda_P\}\}$ expletives

The options for non-empty theta set interpretations are listed in (31).

(31) a. $\{\{_\theta\ x_1, ... x_n\} \leftrightarrow \{+\Lambda_A, -\Lambda_P\}\}$ hearer exclusive *we*
    b. $\{\{_\theta\ x_1, ... x_n\} \leftrightarrow \{-\Lambda_A, +\Lambda_P\}\}$ regular plural *you*
    c. $\{\{_\theta\ x_1, ... x_n\} \leftrightarrow \{+\Lambda_A, +\Lambda_P\}\}$ general hearer inclusive *we*
    d. $\{\{_\theta\ x_1, ... x_n\} \leftrightarrow \{-\Lambda_A, -\Lambda_P\}\}$ computed third person

This exhausts the syntactic options – the speaker and hearer features are thus crucially involved in the computation of both person and "clusivity".[15] Notice that both inclusive and exclusive readings of *we* are available even in languages like English that do not overtly mark the inclusive/exclusive distinction, as illustrated in (32) and (33).

(32) Exclusive *we*
    [X speaks]: Peter, **we** have decided to help you (Anna and I).

---

[14] The theta role itself is of course not empty, only the set of individuals or entities (other than the speech act participants) that bear it. Thus, in the sentence "I beat Napoleon" there is the role of a 'Napoleon beater' that is carried by $\{\{_\theta\ \emptyset\} \leftrightarrow \{+\Lambda_A, -\Lambda_P\}\}$.

[15] For typological overviews of person and "clusivity", see Siewierska (2004) and Cysouw (2003). Semantic interpretation at the conceptual-intentional interface is based on both the syntactic computation and post-syntactic pragmatics. I claim that the analysis in (30)–(31) exhausts the syntactic options, but not all the pragmatically possible ones (cf. Bobaljik 2008).

(33) Inclusive *we*
 [X speaks]: Peter, **we** should go to the movies tonight (the two of us).

The representations in (30) and (31) are descriptions of pronominal meanings, showing the outcome of pronominal computation (and not the computation process itself). Syntactically, the Λ features at the phase edge normally enter an identity or a control relation with the actual speech event participants (Sigurðsson 2004; 2011). In certain cases, however, they can instead be controlled by overt arguments in a preceding clause. This is what happens in direct speech or quotations, as in (12), and in indexical or person shift examples like (13), as illustrated (for only the C edges) in (34) and (35). For simplicity, the Number and Pn features involved in argument computations are not shown (but, as stated in (28) and (29), only NP_{+Pn} feed valuation of $Λ_A, Λ_P$).

(34) [Christer speaks]: *Halldor said to Anders: "I will cite **your** paper again!"*
 $[_{CP} ... \{Λ_A\}_i ... \{Λ_P\}_k ... [_{TP} ...$ Halldor$_j$ ... Anders$_l$ ... $[_{CP} ... \{Λ_A\}_j ... \{Λ_P\}_l ...$ $[_{TP} ...$ I$_j$ ... you$_l$ ...

(35) [Amir speaks]: *Ali be Sara goft [ke **man tora** doost daram].*
 Ali to Sara said that I you friend have.1SG
 'Ali told Sara that **he** likes **her**.'
 $[_{CP} ... \{Λ_A\}_i ... \{Λ_P\}_k ... [_{TP} ...$ Ali$_j$ ... Sara$_l$ ... $[_{CP} ... \{Λ_A\}_j ... \{Λ_P\}_l ... [_{TP} ...$ I$_j$ ... you$_l$ ...

The pronouns themselves are not shifted. Just as in regular unshifted readings they relate to their local Λ features: The meaning of the pronouns *I* and singular *you* is invariably $NP_{+Pn/+ΛA, -ΛP}$ and $NP_{+Pn/-ΛA, +ΛP}$, respectively, as stated in (29).[16]

Activation or promotion of a secondary SELF is dependent on positive setting of the person category, +Pn (in the *matrix* clause, see shortly). In contrast, positive setting of the speaker and hearer features is not directly involved (although

---

[16] Contrary to common assumptions, person shift of this sort is cross-linguistically widespread (see for example the general discussion in Sigurðsson 2014 and the discussion of Norwegian in Julien 2015); indeed, indexical shift is plausibly a universal syntactic option (based on universally available secondary selfhood). It should be noted, though, that quotations have properties that set them apart from regular clauses; they can for instance be pure sound or gesture imitations (see Anand 2006: 80ff.). However, the mechanism of person shift as such is the same in quotations as in other person shift contexts: The Λ features at the phase edge are shifted under control by matrix arguments (and *not* in some "semantically free" manner or by discourse antecedents farther away, suggesting that this is a syntactic process subject to locality restrictions).

8 Who are we – and who is I? About Person and SELF

secondary SELFs may be represented by arguments that are valued as +Λ_A or +Λ_P, in addition to +Pn, as in 34 and 35).[17] We can obviously say (or think) a first or a second person pronoun from the point of view of the speaker without activating a secondary SELF, and it is also possible to activate a secondary third person SELF in the presence of a first person or a second person pronoun that simply refers to the speaker vs. the hearer. This is illustrated for the first person in Icelandic in (36), where the reflexive *sig* reflects the secondary SELF's (Anna's) perspective (the reading being *de se* 'Anna thought: "X sees me"').[18]

(36) *Anna hélt   að ég sæi   sig.*
     Anna tought that I saw.SUBJ SIG
     'Anna thought/believed that I saw her.'

The matrix clause subject *Anna* is NP$_{+Pn/-\Lambda A,-\Lambda P}$ and the SELF of this NP takes scope over the event and (the past) tense perspective in the subjunctive subordinate clause, despite the presence of *ég* 'I'. The activation of a secondary SELF thus requires +Pn, whereas positive setting of the Λ features is not necessarily involved.

Notice that the relevant +Pn valuation takes place in the matrix clause but takes scope over only the subordinate clause (the perspective in the matrix clause being exclusively the speaker's) – much as the long-distance reflexive is bound in the matrix clause but does not show until in the subordinate clause. In a similar fashion, the past subjunctive of *sæi* 'saw' is triggered by the matrix predicate *hélt* 'thought, believed'. Thus, both the long-distance reflexive and the subjunctive in the subordinate clause are sanctioned or licensed by factors in the matrix clause (see Thráinsson 1976; 2007; Sigurðsson 2010a). Compare (36) to (37), where indicative *sá* and the regular third person pronoun *hana* are required (*sæi sig* being ungrammatical).

(37) *Anna veit ekki að ég sá   hana.*
     Anna knows not that I saw.IND her.
     'Anna does not know that I saw her.'

---

[17] But given that negative as well as positive Λ-valuation is fed by +Pn, see (29), *some* valuation of the Λ features (usually a negative one) is indirectly involved.

[18] The parallel holds for the second person ("Anna thought that *you* saw SIG"). It is even possible to construe examples with a first or a second person pronoun in both the matrix and the subordinate clause, nevertheless letting a matrix third person SELF through. In some languages, though, long-distance secondary selfhood relations are blocked by an intervening first or second person. See Jayaseelan 1998 on Malayalam and Giorgi 2006 on Chinese.

As in (36), the matrix subject *Anna* in (37) is valued as NP$_{+Pn/-\Lambda A, -\Lambda P}$, but here the factive semantics of the matrix predicate *veit ekki* 'knows not' blocks the SELF of *Anna* from overshadowing the primary SELF of the speaker (hence not only the main clause but also the subordinate one reflects the perspective of the actual speaker).

Now, consider the *de se* reading of (15), and of the simplified (38), and recall that on this reading Mary thought of herself "I look good".

(38) Mary thought she looked good.

Again, the relevant +Pn valuation takes place in the matrix clause, taking scope over the subordinate clause. There is of course another +Pn valuation in the subordinate clause, yielding the NP$_{+Pn/-\Lambda A, -\Lambda P}$ subordinate subject *she*, but this second +Pn valuation has no intervening effects (as also seen in 36). It is evident, (i), that at most one secondary SELF is licensed at the time, and (ii), that it can only have discernible effects in a lower clause (under c-command by a matrix subject). It is remarkable that a secondary SELF can neither have any discernible effects in a main clause, nor, more generally, locally in the clause where it has its +Pn source, be it at matrix clause or a subordinate one (cf. Thráinsson 1976). It thus seems that a non-speaker perspective must be mediated via a C-edge that is in the scope of (c-commanded by) an argument that is distinct from the primary, speech event speaker SELF. It also seems that the +Pn valuation of a c-commanding matrix subject (*Mary* in 38) is the factor that activates its secondary SELF (provided that the matrix predicate is an attitude predicate).

The hypothesis that +Pn valuation of a matrix subject is the factor that activates its secondary SELF gains support from the fact that *de se* is the only possible reading of PRO in control infinitives like the one in (16) = (39).

(39) Mary hoped to look good.

The reason for this, I believe, is that PRO infinitives differ from finite clauses in lacking a subject Pn head, thus lacking "independent" subject person. They can have independent non-subject (e.g. object) person and they can have subject person interpretation under control, as illustrated in (40).

(40) I$_i$ will try [PRO$_i$ to convince you].

What PRO infinitives cannot have is independently or locally person-valued PRO (see Sigurðsson 2008: 424–425). In contrast, a person value can be transmitted to PRO under control, as in (40). Similarly, the third person value of generic PRO, as in (41), is arguably transferred from a silent *one* (plural in some languages) in the matrix clause, as indicated.

(41) It is always interesting [PRO to discover things about oneself].
= It is always interesting {for one$_i$} [PRO$_i$ to discover things about oneself$_i$] [19]

Consider a subordinate clause as the one in (42), stated by, say, Anna.

(42) [Anna speaks]: John knew that Mary was sick.

On the prominent reading of (42) the subordinate clause is a regular factive clause (*de re*), stated from the speaker's (Anna's) point of view, not reflecting the perspective or SELF of John (cf. also 37). The reason why this is an option, I believe, is that the subordinate clause contains an independent +Pn subject valuation, capable of shielding it from the matrix clause +Pn valuation, hence from the perspective of the secondary SELF of John's. This perspective shielding is not forced (as seen in 36 and 38), but it is commonly possible in the presence of a local +Pn valuation. There is no such subject valuation in PRO infinitives like the one in (39), hence the inescapable *de se* reading.

Person shift, as in (34) and (35), and indexical shift more generally, usually works such that all indexicals or deictic elements in a given speech context domain must shift together. Anand & Nevins (2004) even argue that indexical shift is subject to a general Shift-Together Constraint. A wholesale shift-together is exemplified in (43) (modelled on Banfield 1982: 25).

(43) [Peter speaks at time X and location Y]: Mary told me yesterday at the station: "I will meet you here tomorrow."

While the introductory clause ("Mary told me yesterday at the station") is stated from the speaker's (Peter's) perspective, the perspective in the quotation is completely shifted to that of Mary's. However, despite the commonness of shift together, there are certain discourse modes that allow split selfhood or two centers of consciousness simultaneously (as discussed in Banfield 1982 and Sigurðsson 1990). Consider REPRESENTED SPEECH AND THOUGHT (sometimes called "free indirect discourse"), exemplified in (44).

(44) *John was* upset. **That fool of an actor** always *treated him* badly and **now this idiot** *was* even yelling at **mama**.

---

[19] This analysis implies that there is no non-controlled +human PRO, the +human reading boiling down to control by +Pn of an overt or a silent controller.

This passage contains both split temporal and anaphoric deixis. The adverbial *now* is anchored in "the moment of the act of consciousness" (Banfield 1982: 99), in which the SELF of John is thinking. The verbal past tense, on the other hand, is anchored with the primary SELF of the author (speaker, in our terms) – it lies in the past relative to the moment of utterance or writing of the passage. Similarly, *that fool of a teacher, this idiot* and *mama* all represent John's view, are anchored in his consciousness, whereas John himself is referred to from outside, in the third person (as *John, him*), from the point of view of the author. Represented speech and thought is a literary phenomenon, but it nevertheless illustrates that split selfhood (split *origo* in the sense of Bühler 1934) is compatible with natural language grammar.

As we have seen, self-talk is another discourse mode that allows split selfhood, the difference being that the split is speaker internal in self-talk. Importantly also, self-talk, as in "I hate you!", illustrates that person values can be computed separately for each phase. Nevertheless, shift-together is a pervasive phenomenon, in particular in direct speech or quotations. It would thus seem that the C-edge is more prominent than the v-edge and other "small" phase edges, such that the smaller phase edge computations are usually "coordinated" at the C-edge, by what might be called C-EDGE COORDINATION.

5 Concluding remarks

An exact analysis of C-edge coordination, just mentioned, has yet to be developed, but self-talk throws some light on what its opposite, absent C-edge coordination, involves. There is a RELATION OF SAMENESS between both the DPs in self-talk examples like "I hate you!", but not a relation of binding in the sense of (any) binding theory.[20] A common sameness integer (cf. Baker 2003: 104) is sufficient to link both the subject and the object DP to the speaker, while their separate +Pn valuations activate two distinct SELFs, a primary and a secondary speaker SELF. Double linking to the speaker is reminiscent of temporal Double Access Readings, DAR (see, e.g., Giorgi 2010; Sigurðsson 2016) – but I will not go into that here.

Finally, recall that there is a human bias in *we* such that it usually refers to humans only, see (7) = (45).

(45) We have lived in Europe for at least 40 000 years.

---

[20] A reviewer asks what the difference between "I hate myself" and self-talk "I hate you" might be. Given the present approach, the reflexive-containing clause involves C-edge coordination, as opposed to the self-talk clause.

The human bias is shared by plural *you* (and partly also by *they*). Plausibly, the +Pn valuation involved in the computation of "truly personal" pronouns is the factor that triggers this bias as well as secondary SELF interpretations.

Central issues arise. If the notions of Universal Grammar and narrow syntax are understood as narrowly as in much recent minimalist work (including my own work), then there is every reason to assume that "natural language syntax" is a much broader system, based on but not confined to UG and narrow syntax, in turn raising the question of what other conceptual systems are involved in broad syntax. The speaker and the hearer categories and even the central Person category might stem from some other subsystem than syntax in the narrowest sense (a plausible thought if the machinery of syntax, Merge and abstract Agree in recent terms, is "autonomous and independent of meaning" as famously stated by Chomsky 1957: 17; the speaker/hearer categories and Person are not independent of or unrelated to meaning). These issues, as well as the moot issue of C-edge coordination, will hopefully be subject to much future research that will deepen our understanding of the internal–external language correlation. What seems clear is that the Event/Speech Participant Split as well as the "mending" speaker-{θ} linking embodied in *we* are central properties of the human mind and of language in at least the broad sense.

Abbreviations

Abbreviations used in this article follow the Leipzig Glossing Rules' instructions for word-by-word transcription, available at: https://www.eva.mpg.de/lingua/pdf/Glossing-Rules.pdf.

Acknowledgements

The research for this paper is part of a project on pronouns and pronoun features, partly funded by a grant from Riksbankens Jubelumsfond, P15-0389:1. The ideas pursued here were presented at Università Ca'Foscari and Università degli Studi Roma Tre in November 2015. I am grateful to Massimiliano Bampi, Mara Frascarelli, Giuliana Giusti, Roland Hinterhölzl, Nicola Munaro, and other friends and colleagues in Venice and Rome for their hospitality and for their questions and comments. For valuable remarks and discussions, many thanks also to two anonymous reviewers and to Verner Egerland, Jim Wood, and, last but not least, Anders Holmberg himself.

References

Anand, Pranav. 2006. *De de se*. MIT Doctoral dissertation.
Anand, Pranav & Andrew Nevins. 2004. Shifty operators in changing contexts. In Kazuha Watanabe & Robert B. Young (eds.), *Proceedings of the 14th Conference on Semantics and Linguistic Theory*, 20–37. Ithaca, NY: CLC Publications.
Baker, Mark. 2003. *Lexical categories: Verbs, nouns, and adjectives*. Cambridge University Press: Cambridge.
Banfield, Ann. 1982. *Unspeakable sentences*. Boston: Routledge & Kegan Paul.
Benveniste, Émile. 1966. *Problèmes de linguistique générale*. Vol. 1. Paris: Gallimard. [English translation by Mary E. Meek published 1971 as *Problems in general linguistics*. Cora Gables, FA].
Bianchi, Valentina. 2003. *On the syntax of personal arguments*. Paper presented at XXIX Incontro di Grammatica Generativa, Urbino, February 13–15, 2003.
Bianchi, Valentina. 2006. On the syntax of personal arguments. *Lingua* 116. 2023–2067.
Boas, Franz. 1911. Introduction. In Franz Boas (ed.), *Handbook of American indian languages* (Bureau of American Ethnology Bulletin 40), 1–83. Washington, D.C.: Government Printing Office. http://hdl.handle.net/10088/15507.
Bobaljik, Jonathan D. 2008. Where's φ? Agreement as a post-syntactic operation. In Daniel Harbour, David Adger & Susana Béjar (eds.), *Phi-Theory: Phi features across interfaces and modules*, 295–328. Oxford: Oxford University Press.
Bühler, Karl. 1934. *Sprachtheorie: Die Darstellungsfunktion der Sprache*. Jena: G. Fischer. [English translation by Donald Goodwin published 1990 as *Theory of language: The representational function of language*.
Chierchia, Gennaro. 1989. Anaphora and attitudes de se. In Johan van Benthem Renate Bartsch & Peter van Emde Boas (eds.), *Semantics and contextual expressions*, 1–31. Dordrecht: Foris.
Chomsky, Noam. 1957. *Syntactic structures*. The Hague: Mouton.
Chomsky, Noam. 2001. Derivation by phase. In Michael Kenstowicz (ed.), *Ken Hale: A life in language*, 1–52. Cambridge, MA: The MIT Press.
Chomsky, Noam. 2004. Beyond explanatory adequacy. In Adriana Belletti (ed.), *Structures and beyond: The cartography of syntactic structure*, vol. 3, 104–131. Oxford: Oxford University Press.
Clements, George N. 1975. The logophoric pronoun in Ewe: Its role in discourse. *Journal of West African Languages* 10. 141–177.
Collins, Chris & Paul Postal. 2012. *Imposters: A study of pronominal agreement*. Cambridge, MA: MIT Press.

Crow, Timothy J. 1998. Nuclear schizophrenic symptoms as a window on the relationship between thought and speech. *British Journal of Psychiatry* 173. 303–309.

Crow, Timothy J. 2004. Auditory hallucinations as primary disorders of syntax: An evolutionary theory of the origins of language. *Cognitive Neuropsychiatry* 9. 125–145.

Cysouw, Michael. 2003. *The paradigmatic structure of person marking.* Oxford: Oxford University Press.

Elbourne, Paul D. 2005. *Situations and individuals.* Cambridge, MA: MIT Press.

Frascarelli, Mara. 2007. Subjects, topics and the interpretation of referential pro. An interface approach to the linking of (null) pronouns. *Natural Language & Linguistic Theory* 25. 691–734.

Giorgi, Alessandra. 2006. From temporal anchoring to long distance anaphors. *Natural Language & Linguistic Theory* 24. 1009–1047.

Giorgi, Alessandra. 2010. *About the speaker: Towards a syntax of indexicality.* Oxford: Oxford University Press.

Haddad, Youssef A. 2014. Attitude datives in Lebanese Arabic and the interplay of syntax and pragmatics. *Lingua* 145. 65–103.

Holmberg, Anders. 2010. How to refer to yourself when talking to yourself. *Newcastle Working Papers in Linguistics* 16. 57–65.

Jayaseelan, K. A. 1998. Blocking effects and the syntax of Malayalam *Taan*. *The Yearbook of South Asian Languages and Linguistics* 1998. 11–27.

Julien, Marit. 2015. The force of v2 revisited. *Journal of Comparative Germanic Linguistics* 18. 139–181.

Kratzer, Angelika. 2009. Making a pronoun: Fake indexicals as windows into the properties of pronouns. *Linguistic Inquiry* 40. 187–237.

Kuno, Susumu & Etsuku Kaburaki. 1977. Empathy and syntax. *Linguistic Inquiry* 8. 627–672.

Landau, Idan. 2013. *Control in generative grammar: A research companion.* Cambridge: Cambridge University Press.

Lyons, John. 1968. *Introduction to theoretical linguistics.* Cambridge: Cambridge University Press.

Maling, Joan. 1984. Non-clause bounded reflexives in Icelandic. *Linguistics and Philosophy* 7. 211–241.

Martín, Txsuss & Wolfram Hinzen. 2014. The grammar of the essential indexical. *Lingua* 148. 95–117.

Partee, Barbara. 1973. Some structural analogies between tenses and pronouns in English. *The Journal of Philosophy* 70. 601–609.

Postal, Paul. 1966. On so-called 'pronouns' in English. In Francis P. Dinneen (ed.), *Report on the seventeenth annual round table meeting on linguistics and language studies*, 177–206. Washington, D. C.: Georgetown University Press.

Reichenbach, Hans. 1947. *Elements of symbolic logic.* New York: Macmillan Co.

Rizzi, Luigi. 1997. The fine structure of the left periphery. In Liliane Haegeman (ed.), *Elements of grammar: Handbook in generative syntax*, 281–337. Dordrecht: Kluwer.

Ross, John R. 1970. On declarative sentences. In Roderick Jacobs & Peter Rosenbaum (eds.), *Readings in English transformational grammar*, 222–277. Waltham, MA: Ginn & Co.

Rullmann, Hotze. 2004. First and second person pronouns as bound variables. *Linguistic Inquiry* 35. 159–168.

Schlenker, Philippe. 2003. A plea for monsters. *Linguistics and Philosophy* 26. 29–120.

Sells, Peter. 1987. Aspects of logophoricity. *Linguistic Inquiry* 18. 445–479.

Siewierska, Anna. 2004. *Person.* Cambridge: Cambridge University Press.

Sigurðsson, Halldór Ármann. 1990. Long distance reflexives and moods in Icelandic. In Joan Maling & Annie Zaenen (eds.), *Modern Icelandic syntax*, 309–346. San Diego: Academic Press.

Sigurðsson, Halldór Ármann. 2004. The syntax of person, tense, and speech features. *Italian Journal of Linguistics* 16. 219–251.

Sigurðsson, Halldór Ármann. 2008. The case of PRO. *Natural Language & Linguistic Theory* 26. 403–450.

Sigurðsson, Halldór Ármann. 2010a. Mood in Icelandic. In Björn Rothstein & Rolf Thieroff (eds.), *Mood systems in the languages of Europe*, 33–55. Amsterdam: John Benjamins.

Sigurðsson, Halldór Ármann. 2010b. On EPP effects. *Studia Linguistica* 64. 159–189.

Sigurðsson, Halldór Ármann. 2011. Conditions on argument drop. *Linguistic Inquiry* 42. 267–304.

Sigurðsson, Halldór Ármann. 2014. Context-linked grammar. *Language Sciences* 43. 175–188.

Sigurðsson, Halldór Ármann. 2016. The Split T Analysis. In Kristine Melum Eide (ed.), *Finiteness matters*, 79–92. Amsterdam: John Benjamins.

Sigurðsson, Halldór Ármann & Anders Holmberg. 2008. Icelandic dative intervention: Person and number are separate probes. In Roberta D'Alessandro, Susann Fischer & Gunnar Hrafnbjargarson (eds.), *Agreement restrictions*, 251–279. Berlin: Mouton de Gruyter.

Sigurjónsdóttir, Sigríður. 1992. *Binding in Icelandic: Evidence from language acquisition*. UCLA dissertation.
Sundaresan, Sandhya. 2012. *Context and co(referene) in syntax and its interfaces*. University of Tromsø & Universität Stuttgart Doctoral dissertation.
Tenny, Carol L. & Margaret Speas. 2003. Configurational properties of point of view roles. In Anna Maria Di Sciullo (ed.), *Asymmetry in grammar: Syntax and semantics*, vol. 1, 315–344. Amsterdam: John Benjamins.
Thráinsson, Höskuldur. 1976. Reflexives and subjunctives in Icelandic. In Alan Ford, John Reighard & Rajendra Singh (eds.), *Papers from the sixth meeting of the North eastern linguistic society* (Montreal Working Papers in Linguistics 6), 225–239. Montreal: McGill University.
Thráinsson, Höskuldur. 1990. A semantic reflexive in Icelandic. In Joan Maling & Annie Zaenen (eds.), *Modern Icelandic syntax*, 289–307. San Diego: Academic Press.
Thráinsson, Höskuldur. 2007. *The syntax of Icelandic*. Cambridge: Cambridge University Press.
Wood, Jim & Einar Freyr Sigurðsson. 2011. Icelandic verbal agreement and pronoun-antecedent relations. *Working Papers in Scandinavian Syntax* 88. 81–130.

Chapter 9

New roles for Gender: Evidence from Arabic, Semitic, Berber, and Romance

Abdelkader Fassi Fehri

Mohammed V University

> Contrary to a widespread sex-based typology/theory of Gen(der), where it is essentially construed as (a) a *nominal class marking* device, (b) semantically *sex-based*, and (c) syntactically *reflected in gender agreement* through sexed-animate controllers, I argue instead that Gen is (a) *polysemous*, (b) *multi-layeredly distributed* in the DP, CP, or SAP architecture, and (c) it exhibits a variety of distinct controllers and properties of agreement. Consequently, its grammar, semantics/pragmatics, and representation turn out to be radically different from what is standardly assumed. The analysis is implemented in a minimalist Distributed Morphology model.

1 Introduction

Up until very recently, both typologists and theoretical linguists have entertained a rather simplistic (and exclusive) view of Gender and its role in the grammar, despite its well-acknowledged complexity. Hence back to (at least) Grimm (1822) for Indo-European, or Caspari (1859) for Semitic, a wide-spread typology/theory sees Gen(der) as (a) essentially a nominal class marking device, (b) semantically sex-based (e.g. Corbett 1991; Kibort & Corbett 2008), or animacy-based (Dahl 2000), in addition to (c) being reflected in gender agreement (Kibort & Corbett 2008) with sexed controllers (or goals). But back to Brugmann (1897) for Indo-European, or Brockelmann (1910) for Semitic (among other sources), Gen (and typically the feminine) has been associated with diverse meanings including *individuation, collectivity, abstractness, quantity, size*, etc. Old or new grammarians have added even more new meanings and structures, including qualitative *evaluation* ('depreciative', 'affective', 'endearing', etc.), *perspectivization* (of plurality,

Abdelkader Fassi Fehri. 2017. New roles for Gender: Evidence from Arabic, Semitic, Berber, and Romance. In Michelle Sheehan & Laura R. Bailey (eds.), *Order and structure in syntax II: Subjecthood and argument structure*, 221–256. Berlin: Language Science Press.

'attenuation', etc.), and *speech act role modification* or *performativity* in expressive contexts (as I will show). This polysemy and the differentiated multitude of structures are not expected if Gen is confined to the *n* (and 'lexical') domain, construed as sex, and gender agreement limited to sexed configurations rather than appropriately distributed over various layers of the DP structure, or even the more higher CP and Speech Act role cartography (as in Speas & Tenny 2003; Hill 2014), with productive non-sex interpretations and interrelations.

Overall, the contribution aims at providing a more *integrative* description of the *gender polysemy* than the 'orthodox' sex/animate view can allow for. It is meant to be *constructional*, and hence providing room for more 'unorthodox' syntax (such as that of CP, or the higher SAP). The various *distributed* positions of Gen, and its plausibly related orthodox and unorthodox meanings make Gen potentially and semantically *hyperonymic* (i.e. general enough to embrace more diverse and structurally organized and related meanings found cross-linguistically), and sex/animacy only a *hyponym* (or special) case. Our polysemic treatment and representation is inspired partly by Jurafsky (1996) and Grandi (2015) analysis of evaluative meanings, and it receives further support from work on neural correlates of semantic ambiguity, offering behavioral and neurophysiological support for a single-entry model of polysemy (in contrast to homonymic separate entries), in line with Beretta et al. (2005); Pylkkänen et al. (2006), or Marantz (2005). The article is organized as follows. In §2, I present various instances of the rich semantic diversity of Gender, as illustrated by Standard and Moroccan Arabic varieties. In §3, I investigate the properties of two unorthodox gendered constructions: the *singulative* and the *plurative*, and their forms of agreement alternations. In §4, I motivate the identification of *five layers* of Gen architecture which produce essential interpretations of Gen (including conceptual Gen, and 'performative' Gen). Multiple distinct valued features (including $\pm$ fem, $\pm$ indiv, $\pm$ group, $\pm$ small/big, $\pm$ bad/good, $\pm$ endearing, etc.) are made use of, when interpretable. §5 is dedicated to investigate size and performative evaluation. The latter interpretation is implemented in a Speech Act Cartography à la Speas & Tenny (2003) and Hill (2014). In §6, I turn to more cross- linguistic motivation of the polysemic distributed view of Gen by identifying and investigating some relevant gender patterns in Berber, Hebrew, and Romance. In §7, I discuss the issue of semantics-pragmatics and morpho-syntax interfaces, and the representation of Gen polysemy. §8 provides a conclusion. Throughout the paper, I will be assuming a minimalist distributed-morphology model of grammar based on Chomsky (1995); Halle & Marantz (1993); Marantz (1997); Harley (2014), among others.

2 The many various facets and uses of Gen

2.1 Sex-based and formal Gen

'Natural' sex gender (interpretable as FEMALE/MALE) plays only a partially productive role in the grammar of Arabic 'inflection' (the -*at* suffix often marking the feminine, a general property of Semitic). In (1), the feminine suffix -*at* is added to the 'masculine' form to derive the feminine:[1]

(1) *kalb* dog 'he-dog' → *kalb-at* dog-FEM 'she-dog'

But the feminine is also largely expressed as an (inherently) 'lexical' gender, as in (2):

(2) a. *qird* monkey 'he-monkey' → *qišš-at* monkey-FEM 'she-monkey'
    b. *ḥimaar* donkey 'he-donkey' → *ʔataan* donkey-FEM 'she-donkey'

Note, however, that the morphological feminine tends to replace the 'lexical' counterpart in modern standard usage, as exemplified in (3). In the colloquials, only the regular morphological formation tends to be used in these cases, as exemplified by the Moroccan Arabic pairs in (4):

(3) Standard Arabic
    a. *qird* monkey 'he-monkey' → *qird-at* monkey-FEM 'she-monkey'
    b. *ḥimaar* donkey 'he-donkey' → *ḥimaar-at* donkey-FEM 'she-donkey'

(4) Moroccan Arabic
    a. *qard* monkey 'he-monkey' → *qard-a* monkey-FEM 'she-monkey'
    b. *ḥmaar* donkey 'he-donkey' → *ḥmaar-a* donkey-FEM 'she-donkey'

Formal 'idiosyncratic' gender has been claimed to be a property of nouns like the following:

(5) a. *šams* 'sun', FEM (compare with French *soleil*, MASC)
    b. *qamar* 'moon', MASC (cf. French *lune*, FEM)
    c. *nahr* 'river', MASC (cf. French *rivière*, FEM)

---

[1] Unless stated otherwise, the examples given are from Standard Arabic.

2.2 Less 'orthodox' meanings

What is more important is the long list of 'unorthodox' gender meanings. I will exemplify only some instances here, with no pretention to be exhaustive.

2.2.1 Singulative

In singulative expressions (traditionally called *ism waḥd-ah* 'nouns of unit' by Arabic traditional grammarians), a 'feminine' suffix (-*at*) forms a singular nP denoting a discrete *unit* from a kind base. It also controls a feminine agreement (although the controller is not a female):

(6) a. *naḥl* bee 'bees' → *naḥl-at* bee-UNIT 'a bee'
 b. *štaray-tu samak-at-an kabiir-at-an*
   bought-I fish-UNIT-ACC big-FEM-ACC
   'I bought a big fish.'
 c. *štaray-tu samak-an kabiir-an*
   bought-I fish-ACC big-ACC
   'I bought big fish.'

The suffix -*at* here is known as 'singulative' in the literature. It has been qualified as playing essentially the same role as an individualizing classifier (Greenberg 1972, after the Arabic tradition, back to Sibawayhi 1938; Fassi Fehri 2004; 2012; Mathieu 2012; Zabbal 2002, among others). Typologically in fact, the singulative is closer to a noun Class than to a Classifier, although it fulfils essentially the same role.[2]

2.2.2 Plurative

In plurative expressions (in my terminology), the same gender morpheme -*at* forms a *group* or a collection individual from a singular or a plural of individuals (see Fassi Fehri 1988; 2012):

(7) a. *saakin* 'inhabitant' → *saakin-at* 'inhabitants, population'
 b. *muʕtazil(-ii)* solitary 'a member of the (so-named) theologian thinker group' → *muʕtazil-at* 'the (so-named) theologian thinker group'

---

[2] The comparison has been made between Gender, Class, and Classifier by Seifart (2010), as well as Crisma et al. (2011), among others, using distinctive criteria. They both conclude that the Chinese classifier type is singled out as not implicating agreement, in contrast to the other two (in Romance and Bantu), which appear to be closer to Gen manifestations.

9 New roles for Gender: Evidence from Arabic, Semitic, Berber, and Romance

    c. *kaafir* 'unbeliever' → *kafar* 'unbelievers' → *kafar-at* 'unbelievers (as a group)'

In the relevant cases, the constructed nP denotes an *integrated whole*, and the morpheme contributes to shape this whole. It can be thought of as a sort of classifier (or a "grouper"). I return later on to its exact contribution. Note that the plurative, like the singulative, controllers feminine singular agreement, as illustrated by the following construction:

(8) s-saakin-at-u   ḥtajj-at
     the-inhabitant-FEM-NOM protested-FEM
     'The inhabitants (as a group) protested.'

2.2.3 Gendered augmentative

Augmentatives are internally formed first, then *-at* can be affixed to them. The affix then functions as intensive or evaluative:

(9) *raaḥil* 'travelling, traveller' → *raḥḥaal* 'a big traveller'
    → *raḥḥaal-at* 'traveller + augmentative + FEM'
    a. intensive: 'an extremely big traveller'
    b. evaluative: 'an acknowledged big traveller'

2.2.4 Gendered diminutive

When a diminutive is internally formed, and the morpheme *-at* is suffixed to it, it expresses 'intensive' decrease in size, affectivity, or eventually a 'unit reading', as is exemplified by the various meanings of (10):

(10) *zayt* 'oil' → *zuwayt* oil.DIM 'small quantity of oil' → *zuwayt-at* oil.DIM-FEM
    a. intensive: 'an extremely small quantity of oil'
    b. evaluative: 'a beloved small quantity of oil'
    c. unit reading: 'a discrete small quantity of oil'

2.2.5 Gendered event units

An event nominal acting as a cognate object can express a *kind event*, as in (11a), where it denotes that one or more dances have been performed, or a countable *event unit* (or instance) as in (11b):

(11) a. *raqaṣa raqṣ-an*
 danced dance-ACC
 'He danced some dancing.'

 b. *raqaṣa raqṣ-at-an;   raqṣ-at-ayn*
 danced dance-UNIT-ACC dance-UNIT-DUAL
 'He danced a dance; two dances.'

The formation of event units here parallels that of concrete nouns formed in (6); see Fassi Fehri (2005; 2012) for detail.

2.2.6 Gendered abstract nouns

Abstract nouns or concepts which name qualities, doctrines, sects, etc. also behave syntactically like feminine nPs, and they are affixed with the feminine marker:

(12) a. *suhuul-at-un   kabiir-at-un*
 easy-FEM-NOM big-FEM-NOM
 'A great easiness.'

 b. *ʕuruub-at* 'arabity'; *zunuuj-at* 'negritude'

In most cases, these nouns are formed from an adjectival base to denote the name of the property or quality, or abstract concept. Nouns such as those are often feminine in other languages as well, as in French *facile* 'easy' → *facilité* 'easy-ness'.

2.3 A new picture

In Indo-European studies, Brugmann (1897) observed that the same marker is employed for collectives, abstractions, and the feminine, which suggests questioning the "sexual content" of the feminine, rather than "feminizing" collectives and abstractions. Leiss (1994) reformulated Brugmann's insight in terms of *perspectivization*, in the sense that the function of gender is to provide a "different perspective to represent a multitude of entities" (203).[3]

---

[3] Perspective, construal, point of view, or subjectivity have been used as terms to designate the speaker's perception of the entity involved. According to Unterbeck (2000), quantity is the feature that connects the two categories Num and Gen: Num expresses a multitude, and Gen different perspectives of multitudes (see also Hachimi 2007). I adopt the perspectivization view of Gen below, and provide a representation of its place in the DP.

9 New roles for Gender: Evidence from Arabic, Semitic, Berber, and Romance

In the Arabic grammatical and philological tradition, regular descriptions of Gen connect feminine, collectives, abstractions, plurals, intensives, etc. I derive these connections through the architecture of quantity (#, as in Borer 2005), sex (± fem), and size (± big / small). Evaluation is especially included in the Arabic tradition for the diminutive, and only marginally for the augmentative.[4]

3 Singulativity and plurativity

3.1 Singulativity

3.1.1 Essential properties

Fassi Fehri (2016) provides a list of the most salient properties of the singulative:

1. It is a process by which a collective (and less frequently a mass noun) is turned into a single individual or unit.

2. It is commonly marked via Gender (or the feminine) cross-linguistically (Arabic, Berber, Breton, Welsh, Somali, Hebrew, Russian, etc.; see e.g. Mathieu 2013).

3. It triggers feminine singular agreement on its target.

4. It has the interpretation of a singularity (not that of an 'inclusive' or 'week' plural, as in (14c) below).

5. It can be dualized, pluralized, or counted by numerals.

In (13), the feminine appears to individualize a mass noun:

(13) a. *xašab* 'wood' (mass) → *xašab-at* 'piece of wood'
      b. *šamʕ* 'wax' (mass) → *šamʕ-at* wax-UNIT 'a candle'

In (14a), the singulative is singular, in (14b), it is dual; but in (14c), the general noun is rather interpreted as 'weak plural' (i.e. as singular or plural):

---

[4] Regarding Western sources, I refer to Ibrahim (1973) for an early synopsis of the traditions of thoughts, Hachimi (2007) for a good overview of the patterns and issues involved, in addition to Fleisch (1961); Roman (1990), and Wright (1971; originally written in German by Caspari (1859), with many Arabic sources included).

(14) a. *ʔakal-tu tamr-at-an*
 ate-I date-UNIT-ACC
 'I ate a date.'

b. *ʔakal-tu tamr-at-ayn*
 ate-I date-UNIT-DUAL.ACC
 'I ate two dates.'

c. *ʔakal-tu tamr-an*
 ate-I date-ACC
 'I ate (one or more) dates.'

By contrast, the plural of the singulative in (15) can only be 'strong' or 'exclusive' (which means that only more than one date can be involved):

(15) *ʔakal-tu tamar-aat-in*
 ate-I date-UNIT.PLURAL-ACC
 'I ate (many) dates.'

3.1.2 Structure

We can see from (14) and (15) that there is no complementary distribution between the individualizer (Div or Cl) and Num (#), the dual, or the multiplying plural. I postulate (16) as a structure of (15), in which the singular (Cl) and the plural (Num) co-occur:[5]

(16)

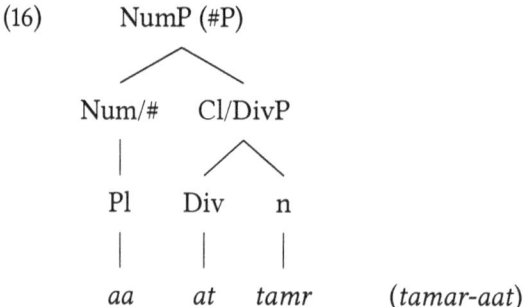

---

[5]Ouwayda (2014), although arguing that Num and Gen are separate categories in this sound plural construction, maintains the view that the plural here is a mere agreement marker (with a hidden numeral). But there is enough evidence to reject this complementarity view. See Fassi Fehri (2012; 2016) for detail.

3.2 The plurative

Contrary to the singulative, the *plurative* is only marginally mentioned in the literature, identified, or investigated. Few rather informal uses of this term are found in the Africanist literature (see e.g. Dimmendaal 1983, or Mous 2008), basically seeing it as the opposite process of the singulative. Discussing Hayward's (1984) observation that in the Cushitic language Arbore, many nouns have a general form (which is non-specified as to the singular/plural distinction), although they can be pluralized, as in:

(17) *kér* 'dog(s)' → *ker-ó* 'dogs'

Corbett (2000: 17, fn. 11) made the following comment: "If one uses 'singulative' consistently for singular forms which correspond to a more basic plural form, then it would be logical to use the term 'plurative' for plural forms which correspond to a more basic singular, as in *kér* 'dog' ~ *ker-ó* 'dogs' above, as suggested by Dimmendaal (1983: 224)".

Compared to the singulative, the plurative appears to be taking an opposite path to be derived, as schematized in (18):

(18) a. 'collective' → singulative
 b. plurative ← 'collective'

In the Africanist literature, the plurative appears to be a process by which a strong or distributive plural is derived from a base which is a general noun (see Mous 2008). The exact Arabic counterpart of such a process would then be the plural of a collective, which is rather exclusive. The following derivation illustrates such a process:

(19) a. *samak* 'fish' (collective) → *ʔasmaak* 'many fish' (plurative)
 b. *štaray-tu ʔasmaak-an mulawwan-at-an*
 bought-I fish.PL-ACC coloured-FEM-ACC
 'I bought (many) coloured fish.'
 c. *štaray-tu samak-an mulawwan-an*
 bought-I fish-ACC coloured-ACC
 'I bought (one or more) coloured fish.'

Compared to (19c), which can be felicitous even if only one fish is bought, (19b) cannot be so interpreted, and the number of fish must be more than one, comparable to the interpretation of the strong interpretation associated with the plural of the singulative in (15) above. But because (19b) might be seen as pluralizing a weak plural (the so-called general noun), it is often thought to be a 'double plural'; although the plural of the singulative cannot be so conceived (see Fassi Fehri 2012 for detail).

According to Mous (2012, p.c.), the most important property of the Cushitic plurative is that it triggers a 'third gender' agreement, which takes the form of a plural. But note that the Arabic plurative, as I construe it, is not the plural of the collective, as in Cushitic, but rather the closest counterpart to the singulative. Both control a 'feminine' (singulative) agreement, and the plurative is also forming a unit, or a group. Like the singulative, the Arabic plurative can be seen as closer to noun Class and Gender, unlike the Cushitic plurative, which may be, if it is really a 'gender', as Mous put it, closer to the gender found with Arabic non-human plurals.[6]

3.2.1 Essential properties

The most salient properties of the plurative include the following:

1. The plurative derivation is a process by which a collective, a singular, or a plural nP is turned into a group unit (or a collection unit).

2. It is morphologically marked by the same feminine suffix, on the controller and/or the target.

3. Syntactically, it takes part in feminine singular agreement.

4. When the plurative marked nP participates in (or controls) normal plural agreement, it 'looses' its group meaning.

5. Semantically, it expresses a plurality, or more precisely a 'perspective' on plurality. It controls reciprocity, or plural predication, etc.

6. The plurative is potentially countable, and can undergo dualization or pluralization in relevant contexts (see Fassi Fehri 2016 for detail).

7. The plurative is in complementary distribution with both Number and other Gen (including the singulative).

The group or collection unit is formed from various classes of nouns, only few of which are exemplified here.

---

[6] See Fassi Fehri (2016) for examples of non-human plurals controlling feminine singular agreement. My proposal for the Cushitic plurative is only speculative at this stage, as it is still very poorly understood.

9 New roles for Gender: Evidence from Arabic, Semitic, Berber, and Romance

3.2.2 Professional groups, corporations, property sharing, or collections units

Standard Arabic uses -*at*, and Moroccan Arabic –*a* as exponents:

(20) Standard Arabic
najjaar 'carpenter' → *najjaar-at* 'the corps of carpenters'

(21) Moroccan Arabic
šeffaar 'thief' → *šeffaar-a* 'thieves (as a group)'

(22) Moroccan Arabic
jebl-ii mountain-sing 'an inhabitant of the mountain' → *jbal-a* 'inhabitants of the mountain'

Groups based on property sharing are normally derived from adjectives or participles:

(23) a. *kaafir* 'unbeliever' → *kafar-at* 'unbelievers (as a group)'
 b. *saaḥir* 'magician' → *saḥar-at* 'magicians (as a group)'

With feminine singular agreement, pluratives behave more like 'kind/collective' nouns when the latter are read as collection units:

(24) a. *al-fursu   wa-r-rum-u   štarak-at-aa   fii ḥarb-in*
 the-Persians and-the-Romans participated-FEM-DUAL in war-GEN
 ḍidda   l-ʕarabi
 against the-Arabs
 'Persians and Romans participated together (as a group) in a war against Arabs.'

 b. *al-fursu   wa-r-rumu   štarakuu   fii ḥarb-in*
 the-Persians and-the-Romans participated-PL.MASC in war-GEN
 ḍidda   l-ʕarabi
 against the-Arabs
 'Persians and Romans participated together in a war against Arabs.'

Likewise, pluratives can control a dual (or a plural) target:

(25) *al-muʕtazil-at-u   wa-l-ʔašʕariyy-at-u   tawaḥḥad-at-aa   fii*
 the-Mutazilite-FEM-NOM and-the-Asharite-FEM-NOM unified-FEM-DUAL in
 haaḏaa
 this
 'Mutazilites and Asharites have unified (their view) on this.'

The dualization of the plurative suggests that pluratives are potentially countable.

Note that simple collective nouns, plurative nPs/DPs can either trigger a plurative agreement, as in (8) above, or 'normal' plural agreement as in (26):

(26)   s-saakinat-u   ḥtajj-uu
       the-inhabitant-FEM protested-PL.MASC
       'The inhabitants protested.'

This 'hybridity' in agreement points to a duality in behavior of the plurative DP, being denoting either a group, as in (8), or a sum, as in (26); see Fassi Fehri (2012; 2016) for detail.

3.2.3 The "hybrid" plurative

The plurative then appears to be neither a pure Gen, nor a pure Num (as in the Mous/Corbett dispute), but rather a sort of hybrid complex of both:

(a) It is not (a low) Gen, since it cannot be interpreted semantically on the scale of sex;

(b) Unlike Gen in other contexts, the plurative Gen feature is not compatible with variation in Num values (being invariably in the form of the feminine singular), as illustrated by the contrast in interpretation above.

Another important property is that the plurative is a *syntactic plurality*, rather than a singularity. For example, it controls syntactic reciprocity:

(27)   š-šiiʕ-at-u   t-antaqidu   baʕḍ-a-haa baʕḍ-an
       the-Shiite-FEM-NOM FEM-criticize some-her   some-ACC-HER
       'The Shiites criticize each other.'

It is used with plural predicates, unlike singulars:

(28)   takaṯṯal-at š-šiiʕatu   ḍidda daaiš-a
       united-FEM the-Shiites against Daesh-ACC
       'The Shiites made a coalition against ISIS.'

But note also that the hybridity of the plurative comes from the fact that it can be treated as a singular. For example, the dual used in the construction (25) above counts the two groups.

Finally, with respect to its semantics, the hybridity of the plurative is confirmed by the fact that it shares the semantics of groups (or "collective" nouns), as described e.g. by Barker (1992), typically their twofold potential of being atoms/individuals or sums/sets, as reflected by agreement alternations. See also Pearson (2011). But its hybridity is even stronger than normal group since it appears to be both a plurality (at some low layer) and a singularity (at a higher layer), as reflected by its structure given below in (29); see Fassi Fehri (2016) for more detail and references.

3.3 Structure of the "perspectivizing" Gen

Various options for the structure of pluratives are explored there, but shown to be inadequate. The following structure is motivated by various considerations, taking into account the fact that pluratives are collection units formed in syntax (or "particulars" in the perspective of the speaker), rather than normal plurals (or simple atomic groups). For the sake of illustration, I propose then that the structure of the DP in (8) is as in (29):

(29) GroupP (= GenP)

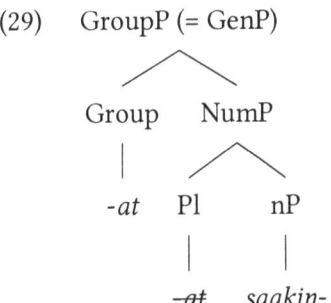

The structure represents the view that a plurative is formed as a plural of a specific sort first, then *perspectivized* as a unit (or group) through Gen, assuming that it is Gen which provides the perspectivization of plurality, then Gen (or Group) is placed higher, to "scope over" Plural, or Num.[7]

4 Gender layers and architecture

To account for the various meanings of the feminine (or Gender), I depart from the view that Gen is confined to a dedicated syntactic position, be it GenP (as in Picallo 2008), or nP (as in Kihm 2005, Lowenstamm 2008, or Kramer 2014, among

---

[7]For concreteness sake, I assume that -*at* is placed first in the Num position, and then moves higher to Group/Gen. N also moves there, and then higher to D as in the usual N-to-D movement (see Longobardi 2001; Fassi Fehri 1993).

others), and it is interpreted as basically male/female (Percus 2011). Gen is rather distributed over the various layers of the nP/DP, in the spirit of Steriopolo & Wiltschko (2010); Pesetsky (2013), or Ritter (1993), and even higher in the CP, or SAP. Gen and its meanings then turn out to be essentially *constructional*, contra lexicalist or natural views. Furthermore, at least *five distinct layers* (or sources) of Gen are postulated and motivated in the grammatical nP/DP architecture: (a) conceptual Gen; (b) n Gen; (c) Cl Gen; (d) Num Gen; (e) D/C Gen, or even higher, SAP Gen.

4.1 Conceptual and n Gender

Consider first cases of nominalized abstract feminine nouns, compared to their (gendered) bases:

(30) a. *ʔab* 'father' → *ʔubuww-at* 'fatherhood'

   b. *ʔumm* 'mother' → *ʔumuum-at* 'motherhood'

   c. *rajul* 'man' → *rujuul-at* 'manliness'

(31) a. *ʕamm* 'paternal uncle' → *ʕamm-at* 'paternal aunt' → *ʕumuum-at* 'paternal auntness or uncleness'

   b. *xaal* 'maternal uncle' → *xaal-at* 'maternal aunt' → *xuʔuul-at* 'maternal auntness'

The gender complexity of these forms point to the existence of (at least) two distinct layers of Gen, needed for interpretation: one is *conceptually-based* (i.e. a 'father' is masculine, a 'mother' is feminine, a 'maternal uncle or aunt' has two genders, and the same is true for a 'paternal uncle or aunt').[8] Call this "lower" gender *conceptual Gen*. The second grammatical upper gender (marked by -*at*) forms an *n* (entity or concept) from a property. Call it *n Gen*. The need for conceptual Gen has been pointed out by e.g. Köpcke et al. (2010), who have argued that "... much of the German grammatical gender is *conceptually* motivated in that certain semantic fields tend to be marked by some specific gender [italics mine; FF]", despite "the widespread view among autonomist grammarians that [...] gender in German is most purely grammatical [totally arbitrary] category,

---

[8]Note that Arabic kinship terms are more specific than those of Germanic or Romance, in that there is no such a "vague" kinship relationship like 'cousin', 'uncle', 'aunt', etc. Rather, each of these relationships in Arabic must indicate whether it connects to the mother or the father (e.g. cousin from the mother, or aunt from the father), as the examples and their translations illustrate.

9 New roles for Gender: Evidence from Arabic, Semitic, Berber, and Romance

not motivated in any way by conceptual factors" (172). Various other motivations have also been more recently brought in by McConnell-Ginet (2015) for the equivalent "notional" gender, or Mithun (2015) for "cultural" gender, among others.

4.1.1 Various conceptual sources of female/male pairs

Sources of gender may be conceptually or "culturally" different (even in the same language), and derivations from these sources may lead to various results. Consider the following pairs of feminization:

(32) *rajul* 'man' → *mraʔ-at* 'woman'
(33) *qiṭṭ* 'he-cat' → *qiṭṭ-at* 'she-cat'
(34) *mruʔ* 'man, male person' → *mraʔ-at* 'woman'
(35) *rajul* 'man' → *rajul-at* 'a property of a strong woman' (an adjective)

The first pair in (32) is conceptually/semantically the minimal pair to name the female/male human pair, although the members of the pair do not share any common morpho-phonological base. In contrast, *mraʔ-at* and *mruʔ* in (34) are grammatically and morpho-phonologically related, although they are not the genuine counterparts of 'man' and 'woman' in English; the first member means 'male person' rather than 'man'. As for the (35) pair, it shows that although *rajul* can be made feminine, the only feminine it can form is a manner adjective, not a noun.

Note that contrary to what happens in the examples (30a & 30b) above, where the feminine affix *-at* can be taken as a *categorizer*, or part of the categorizing *n* process, the morpheme in the examples (32–34) can hardly be taken as a nominalizer. First, the 'masculine' base is already nominal or adjectival (or coerced to be so) as the contrast between (34) and (35) suggests. If this is so, then the base of the derivation may be seen as providing a conceptual ground for forming a feminine (or masculine) of an entity or a property. If gender is only taken as a feature of the category *n*, and no distinction is made between the contribution of the conceptual (or root) gender and that of the functional gender, it is hard to see how such contrasts can be accounted for.

4.1.2 The placement of n Gen

Let assume that the suffix *-at* in (30) is a *categorizer* (n Gen), forming the abstract noun. Let us also take it to be a *head* feature of the category *n*, by virtue of contributing to its abstract (rather than concrete) nouniness, in addition to is interpretation as naming a property (rather than an object). Such a 'category change' property is clearer in cases of (abstract) property nouns deriving from adjectives, as has been seen in examples (12) above. I assume that Gen there is interpretable, contributing to name an abstract property.

As for Gen in cases like (33), it may be in a different position. It is not a head categorizer, since the derivation operates on what is already a noun, and the affix does not operate any "category change" or "mutation" here. It is rather a *modifier* feature.

Other cases may be included in the categorizing case. Consider the following pair:

(36)   *maktab* 'office' → *maktab-at* 'library'

Although a (formal) derivational relation can be established between the two nouns, the semantics of the second member is in no way compositional (with respect to the first member). We can account for these properties by postulating that Gen is a categorizing head feature in this case, since its contributes to shaping the content of the noun.

4.2 Cl Gen and Num Gen

The singulative/individuative Gen investigated above instantiates a classifier/-Class gender, as explained there. The plurative gender, on the other hand, instantiates the case of Number that is "gendered", or Num Gen, as an expression of perspectivization, as explained earlier.

5 Size and evaluative modification

5.1 Diminuitive Gen

Diminutive and augmentative Arabic morphemes behave mostly as modifiers, denoting either decrease/increase in size, or expressive/evaluative meanings. They occasionally behave as heads (and individualizers), with a portioning out that produces countable units, as has been established for some languages, but only when they are gendered in Arabic.[9] It is then the feminine suffix that can be held responsible for this potential meaning.

---

[9]See Wiltschko (2008); de Belder (2008); Mathieu (2012); Steriopolo (2013), among others.

9 New roles for Gender: Evidence from Arabic, Semitic, Berber, and Romance

Three different meanings of the morpheme can then be distinguished, and represented structurally: (a) ClP (or DivP in Borer's sense), (b) SizeP (DimP or AugmentP, as in Cinque 2014), and (c) EvalP for the evaluative (endearing, pejorative, etc.). The following example from Moroccan Arabic instantiates the multiple role of diminutive Gen:

(37) Moroccan Arabic
 lben 'buttermilk' → lbeyy-in buttermilk-DIM 'a small quantity of buttermilk' → lbin-a buttermilk.DIM-FEM
 a. intensive: 'a very small quantity of buttermilk'
 b. evaluative: 'an appreciated small quantity of buttermilk'
 c. individuative: 'a discrete small portion of buttermilk'

Two distinct structures can be proposed for the intensive (modifier) and the individualizing (head) readings of *lbin-a*, respectively:[10]

(38)   (intensive modifier)

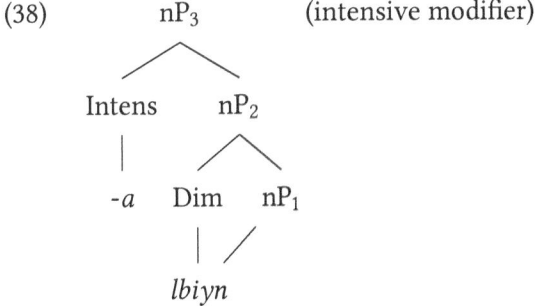

---

[10] A reviewer wonders whether there are two morphemes involved here (-*i* as diminutive, and –*a* as feminine), or just one 'feminine' -*a*, which can be used as diminutive. The first option is motivated by the fact that the two morphologies distribute separately, the diminutive being regularly internal to the stem, whereas the evaluative is regularly external to the stem. The realizations of the diminutive as -*y*- or -*i*- are morpho-phonologically conditioned, being a glide or a short vowel, depending on whether the syllable is open or closed. Moreover, there is no independent evidence that the two morphemes are fused.

(39)   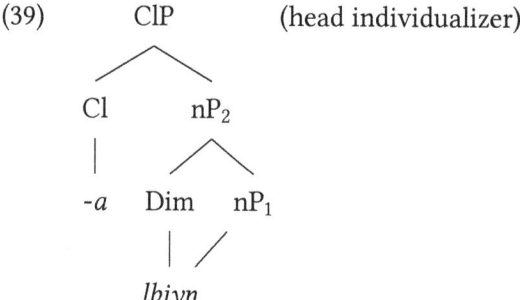   (head individualizer)

5.2 Augmentative Gen

Augmentatives can get intensive and evaluative readings through augmentative morphemes and Gender. I can think of no case where the augmentative is an individualizing head. In (40), a participle adjective undergoes both augmentative and Gender affixation, to yield either an intensive reading or an evaluative:

(40) *raaḥil* 'traveler' → *raḥḥaal* (traveler + augmentative) 'big traveler' → *raḥḥaal-at* traveler + augmentative + FEM 'famous big traveler'

5.3 Evaluative Gen

In the "appreciative" diminutive in (37), I assume that Eval is placed inside the DP (as a sort of degree phrase), and interpreted in DP:

(41)   DP   (diminutive modifier)

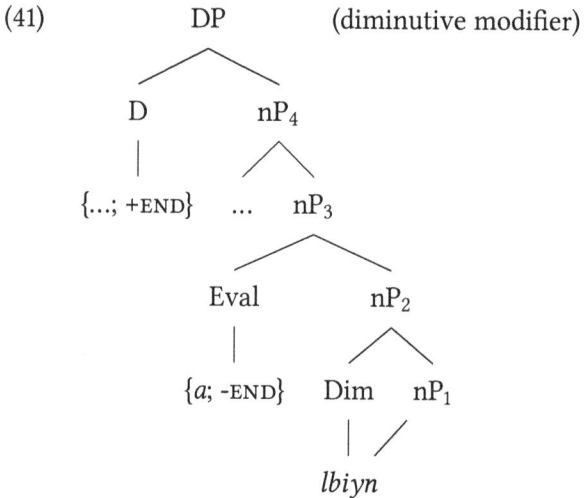

(END = endearing; - for uninterpretable, + for interpretable)

9 New roles for Gender: Evidence from Arabic, Semitic, Berber, and Romance

For the sake of simplicity, I leave aside the details of the granularity of Eval, and the issue of whether more cartography needs to be involved here.[11]

As for the augmentative evaluative in (40), I assume that its Eval here is similar to the diminutive Eval, and should be represented in a strictly parallel way, inside DP:

(42)   DP   (augmentative modifier)

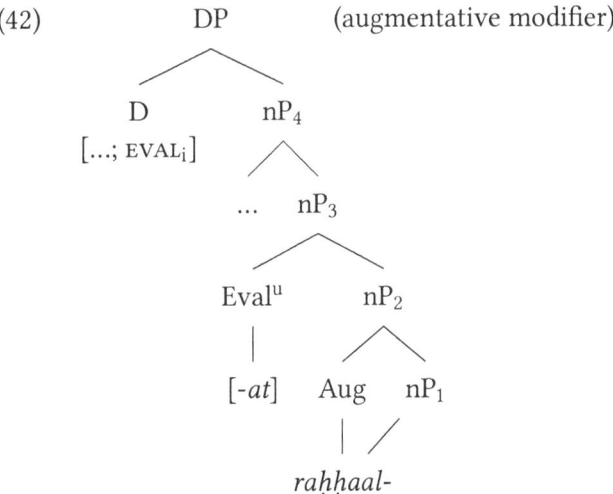

5.4 'Performative' expressive Gen

Previous evaluative Gen occurred in contexts where a quantitative size modification can obtain, with an internal DP source. I turn here to cases where Gen lacks both such a quantitative option, and internal DP interpretive source. These cases are unique, in that they are devoted to qualitative evaluation or expressivity, with specific external characteristics.

Consider e.g. the following constructions (END for endearing):[12]

---

[11]Cinque (2014: 8; Table 1) proposes a cartographic hierarchization of expressives, as in (i):

  (i) augmentative > pejorative > diminuitive > endearment

With respect to such a hierarchization, Arabic seems to go in inverse order, given that EndP appears higher than both both DimP and AugP. I have no explanation at this point for this reversal. Further research is needed to clarify the nature of such variation.

[12]Note that the third person pronoun $-h$ is used here for the speaker (or 'first' person), as is usually the case in some European language styles.

239

(43) *yaa ʔab-at-i!*
oh father-END-mine
'Oh my beloved father!'

(44) *waa ʔumm-at-aa-h!*
oh mother-END-EXCLAM-his
'Oh my beloved mother!'

(45) a. *yaa wayl-at-i!*
oh misery-distress-mine
'Oh my terrible woe!'

b. Moroccan Arabic
waa saʕd-at-i!
oh chance-END-mine
'Oh my great chance!'

In none of these expressions, can the 'feminine' noun (or morpheme) be associated with a female, a singulative, or an intensive interpretation. There is obviously no 'female father' interpretation in (43), neither a 'female mother' in (44); there is no 'individuative' involved in (45), and no 'intensive' anywhere. The only available "meaning" here is an expression of the speaker's emotional feelings (endearment, distress, etc.). What is even more appealing is that these 'feminine' forms cannot be used outside these illocutionary marked contexts. It is also striking that the existence of this rather original expression and meaning of gender has hardly been acknowledged in the Arabic or orientalist literature, and it did not generate any preliminary account, as far as I can tell.[13]

There is evidence that these evaluatives are clause-dependent, or interpreted in the CP (or some level higher), unlike those examined above (which are DP dependent). First, contrary to the previous evaluatives, the constructions under investigation do not occur as normal DPs in contexts where the sentence force is not crucial for interpretation, as in e.g. declarative clauses:

(46) a. *najaa ʔab-ii mina l-ġaraq-i*
escaped father-mine from the-drowning-GEN
'My father escaped from drowning.'

---

[13]Wright (1971: II, 87–88) did mention the constructions in (43) and (44) in the context of expressives, but he did not indicate what is the content of *-at* there, describing them as 'peculiar forms'! Likewise, Hämeen-Anttila (2000: 601) qualifies the case of (43) as 'obscure'! In the early Arabic grammatical tradition, the morpheme *-at* is seen as fulfilling a morpho-phonological role, i.e. "replacing" the possessive mark (*-y* 'mine'), or "compensating" (*taʕwii*) its absence.

b. *najaa   ʔab-at-i   mina l-ġaraq-i
    escaped father-END-mine from the-drowning-GEN

c. *najat   ʔumm-at-aa-hu   mina l-ġaraq-i
    escaped mother-END-EXCLAM-his from the-drowning-GEN

The contrast between the ill-formedness of (46b & 46c) and the well-formedness of (43) and (44) point to a DP/CP divide in the syntax/semantics of evaluatives. In the latter case, evaluatives can only be interpreted outside the DP, in a position higher in the CP, or even higher and outside the CP, in a clearly performative context (the vocative here).

What are the bases and motivations of such a divide, and how are outer evaluatives anchored in the CP? For the sake of concreteness, let us assume some cartographic representation of the CP a la Cinque/Rizzi/Moro, enriched with Speech Act role cartography (SAP) a la Hill (2014), among others. In the expanded CP cartography, vocatives tend to be associated with a high functional projection located in the CP, possibly above Force (as in Moro 2003). Hill proposed that they be associated with a SAP projected above (and outside) the CP, in line with Speas & Tenny (2003). Moreover, the structure of vocatives is sensitive to the speaker/hearer hierarchization.[14]

There are reasons to take the gender in the vocative phrase examined to be speaker-oriented, and interpreted in the speaker field. First, the evaluative gender in (43) is exclusively interpreted as a modifier of (the subjectivity of) the speaker. It cannot be associated with the hearer, as the ungrammaticality of (47) indicates:[15]

---

[14]Thus, Hill (2014: 207) distinguishes among speech acts between *speaker-oriented clause types* like exclamations (which convey the speaker's point of view about situations), and *hearer-oriented* ones like direct addresses (which convey the speaker's manipulation of the interlocutor). Since the structural placement of the speaker and the hearer is distinct, it is the lower segment of the SAP which is dedicated to (the merger of) the vocative. However, the existence of the upper segment in the SAP of the vocative is not superfluous, because the speaker's field may interact with the hearer's (direct address) field in speaker-oriented vocatives and other vocative contexts. See Hill (2014) for detail, and relevant references cited there.

[15]A reviewer wonders what is the status of a parallel of (44) in this case, i.e. the following construction:

(i) *yaa ʔumm-at-aa-k!
    oh mother-END-EXCLAM-your
    Intended: 'Oh your beloved mother!'

Its ungrammaticality indicates that the same observations can be extended to 'mother' as well (or, in fact, to any other relational noun).

(47) * *yaa ʔab-at-aa-k!*
    oh father-END-EXCLAM-your
    Intended: 'Oh your beloved father!'

What the judgement indicates is that the gender of VocP can only probe for the higher SA role, the Speaker (which c-commands it), not the lower SA hearer. Second, note that the gender on the imperative verb (agreeing with the second person hearer) is exclusively dedicated to the hearer in the lower segment (which also c-commands it), as the following construction illustrates:[16]

(48) *yaa ʔumm-at-aa-hu   ṭmaʔinn-ii!*
    oh mother-END-EXCLAM-his reassure-FEM
    'Oh beloved mother, be reassured!'

Two genders are involved here, the endearing evaluative *-at* on the vocative DP expression, and the feminine *-ii* on the imperative verb. In both cases, the gender realized can be assumed to be "displaced", or uninterpretable in situ. The lower gender on the verb is interpretable higher, its goal being the 2nd Person of the SA hearer. As for Gen on the vocative DP, it is neither interpretable in the DP, as already established through the (46) contrasts, nor by the lower SA hearer. It is only interpretable higher in the SA cartography, in the speaker "field" (as part of the speaker subjectivity). These contrasts give credence to the speaker vs. hearer differentiation in SAPs, as postulated by Hill (2014), among others. I tentatively represent the relevant part of the structure of (43) as follows (s for speaker, h for hearer):

---

[16] In the embedded imperative inside the vocative, the verb agrees in Num and Gen with the (hidden) addressee, and only covertly in 2nd Pers:

  (i) *ṭmaʔinn-ii!*
      reassure-FEM
      'Be reassured!' (for a single female)
  (ii) *ṭmaʔinn-uu!*
      reassure-PL
      'Be reassured!' (for a plurality of males)

These patterns can be taken as forms of allocutary agreement (as in Miyagawa 2012). See Fassi Fehri (2016) for other details.

9 *New roles for Gender: Evidence from Arabic, Semitic, Berber, and Romance*

(49)

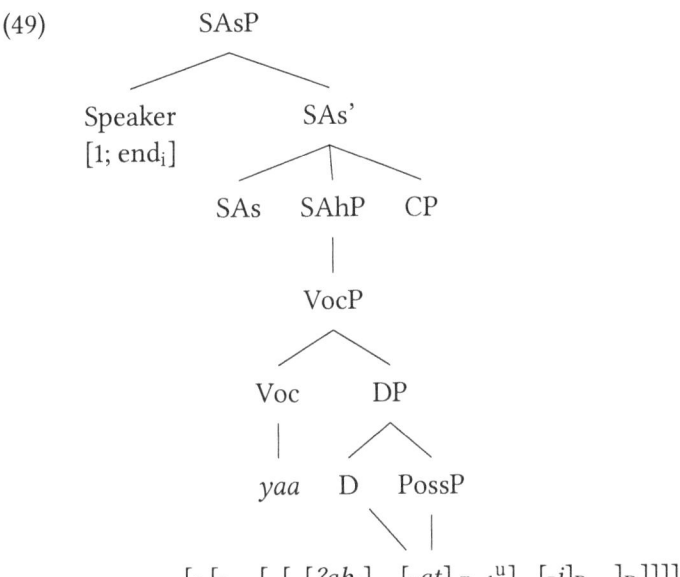

$[_D[_{Poss}[_n[_n[ʔab\text{-}]\ _n\ [\text{-}at]\ _{End^u}]_n\ [\text{-}i]_{Poss}]_D]]]$

I assume that the head noun *ʔab* here has moved to D, after having integrated the endearing 'feminine', and the cliticized possessor. If the hidden Speaker has an interpretable 1Pers feature, and an interpretable End feature, then both are targeted in the probe-goal (or indexing) relationship needed for interpretation.

As for (48), its structure is as follows:

(50)

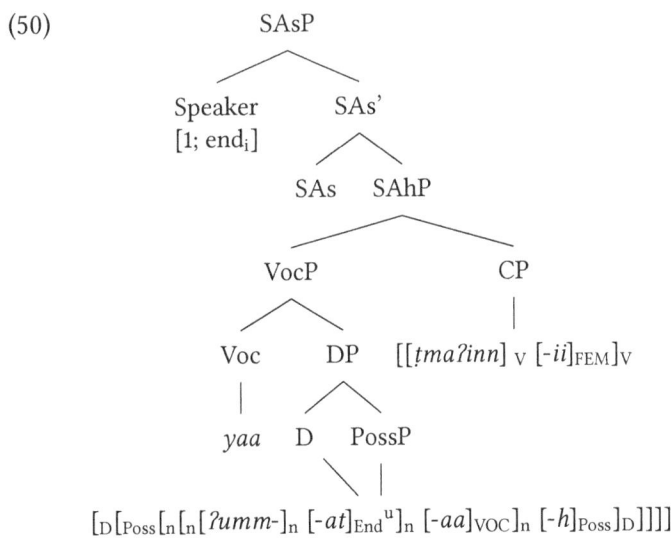

$[_D[_{Poss}[_n[_n[ʔumm\text{-}]_n\ [\text{-}at]_{End^u}]_n\ [\text{-}aa]_{VOC}]_n\ [\text{-}h]_{Poss}]_D]]]$

243

Note that the endearing agreement involves only coindexation in person (for the speaker or utterer). There is no formal gender agreement here, compared to the agreement found with the singulative or the plurative (see Fassi Fehri 2016 for detail).

6 Cross-linguistic extensions

This section does not intend to describe the vast number of gendered languages that instantiate similar patterns and correlations, but only give some examples for the sake of identification and comparison. The list includes Berber (Afroasiatic), Hebrew (Semitic), and Romance.

6.1 Berber

Berber has a two-gender opposition, expressing natural gender, abstracts, units, size, expressive evaluation, and it interacts with "enunciation" (Mettouchi 1999). The morpheme -*t* (occurring as a reduplicating discontinuous morpheme, or "circumfix") provides the formal means to express these various meanings which compete for the same slot on the noun, without any possibility of being added to each other (being in "complementary distribution"; Kossmann 2014), while the augmentative is expressed via a form of (uncommon) "substractive" morphology (Grandi 2015). In the descriptions provided, there are systematic relationships between gender forms and meaning forms, e.g. between feminine and diminutive, or between masculine and augmentative. There are also expressions of endearment, contempt, "in relation to the speaker", etc.

First, -*t* expresses *sex* for animates:

(51) Kabyle (Mettouchi 1999)
   a. *agyul* 'donkey' → *t-agyul-t* 'she-donkey'
   b. *aganduz* 'veal' → *t-aganduz* 'heifer'

(52) Ayt Seghrouchen (Kossmann 2014)
   a. *arba* 'male child' → *t-arba-t* 'female child'
   b. *afrux* 'boy' → *t-afrux-t* 'girl'
   c. *afunas* 'ox' → *t-afunas-t* 'cow'

Second, *unity* nouns are formed by the feminine:

(53) a. *nnamus* 'mosquitoes' → *tanamust* 'a single mosquito'
      b. *l-mašmaš* 'apricots' → *tamšmašt* 'a single apricot'

Third, a *quantitative diminutive* is expressed by the feminine:

(54) a. *afus* 'hand' → *t-fus-tt* 'little hand'; variant: *afus* → *t-afus-t*
      b. *t-aherdan-t* 'small lizard' (also 'female lizard')
      c. *t-aslem-t* 'small fish' (Kossmann 2014; Grandi 2015)
      d. *lkursi* 'chair' → *takursitt* 'little chair'
      e. *muka* 'owl' → *tamukatt* 'little owl' (Kossmann 2014)

Fourth, *abstract* nouns can be formed as feminine, expressing qualities, professions, names of languages, etc.:

(55) a. *aryaz* (m) 'man' → *taryazt* 'manliness (courage)'
      b. *aslmati* (m) 'fisherman' → *taslmatit* (f) 'profession of fisherman'
      c. *ašəlḥi* 'Berber' → *tašəlḥit* 'Berber language' (Kossmann 2014)

As for *augmentative*, it is said to be expressed by the 'masculine':

(56) a. *t-a-bhir-t* 'garden' → *a-bhir* 'big garden'
      b. *tamṣaṭṭ* 'thigh' → *amṣaḍ* 'very big thigh' (Kossmann 2014)
      c. *amuka* 'big owl'

Abdel-Massih (1971) observes that "certain feminine nouns give augmentatives by a process that is the reverse of diminutive formation", and hence, only feminine nouns can be augmentativized (-*t* if present is then 'deleted', in "a typologically unusual instance of subtractive morphology", as Grandi (2015: 10). As for masculine nouns, they can only be diminutivized. A triplet of normal, singulative, and augmentative are given in the following example:

(57) *lḥumṣ* 'chickpeas' → *taḥumṣtt* 'one chickpea' → *aḥumṣ* 'big individual chickpea'

As for *evaluative* endearment and contempt, Mettouchi (1999: 219) observes that "both diminutives and augmentatives can be reinterpreted as depreciative", or else appreciative. Hence it is apparently possible to depreciate/appreciate from the masculine to the feminine, or vice versa, as in (58) and (59), respectively:

(58) *argaz* 'man' → *t-argaz-t* 'mannish female'

(59) *tamtut* 'woman' → *amtu* 'a wimp woman'

Endearment is also expressed via the diminutive feminine, as in (60):

(60) *baba* (m) 'my father' → *tababatt* (f) 'little father; endeared father' (Kossmann 2014; second translation mine)

As for the *expressive performative* (in my terms), I have found what appears to be one of instantiation of it in an example brought up by Kossmann (2014), where the feminine establishes a relation (of low age), in relation to the speaker:

(61) *ʕəmm-i* 'my paternal uncle' → *t-aʕəmmi-tt* 'paternal uncle (younger than the speaker)'

6.2 Hebrew

Early Semitic had a common feminine marker -*at*, which was found before it split into East and West Semitic (Hasselbach 2014, and references cited there). When compared to Akkadian, Classical Arabic, and Géez, Hebrew appears to have a short list of meanings. The feminine suffix -*a* appears to be the most productive, compared to other morphemes (including -*t* or its variants -*et*, -*at*, *ot*, etc.). Here are some patterns of semantic diversity.

Female sex can be expressed by -*a* or -*it*:

(62) a. *more* 'teacher' → *more-a* 'female teacher'
b. *kélev* 'dog' → *kalv-a* 'she-dog'

(63) *tanah* 'cook' → *tanah-it* 'female cook'

The feminine can mark abstracts:

(64) *neqam-a* 'vengeance'

It forms singulatives:

(65) *oni* 'fleet' → *oniyy-a* 'a ship'

The 'collective' can be marked by the feminine, and the unit singular unmarked, just as is the case in the Arabic plurative:[17]

(66) a. *daag* 'a fish' → *dagg-a* 'fish (as a collection)'
b. *yoseb-et* 'inhabitants as a group; population'

---

[17] See Hasselbach (ibid.), among others, and relevant references cited there.

6.3 Romance

De la Grasserie (1904) notes that gender as a sex appears only very late in the historical grammatical hierarchical strata associated with gender, in fact the last one. But languages like Bantu has non-hierarchical multiple genders. In a second stage from this state, there is development of a hierarchical animate/inamimate opposition, rather than sex. In a third stage, sex is allotted to nouns, even without reason, although construed by subjectivity, and interlocution (De la Grasserie 1904: 226–227). It is then 'big/small', 'important/less important', 'strong/weak' etc., or rather an opposition of 'wide, vague, or generic' (for the feminine) and 'specific, precise' for the masculine. There is also a tendency to feminize nouns in languages that have no neuter, "which is in the middle".

As an illustration, Kahane & Kahane (1949: 135) observe that "… in the Romance languages the *feminine* form of a noun may have an *augmentative* value in relation to the corresponding masculine", e.g. *sacca* 'large sack', compared to *saccu* 'sack'. The augmentative use of the feminine is further illustrated in a number of Italian dialect constructions, including the following examples Kahane & Kahane (1949: 138):

(67) a. *kavana* 'big basket' (*kavan* 'basket')
 b. *kortella* 'large kitchen knife' (*kortello* 'knife')
 c. *pavela* 'large butterfly' (*pavel* 'small butterfly')

By gender change, diminutive or intensive are also expressed (Kahane & Kahane 1949: 139–141):

(68) a. *padellina* 'small frying pan' → *padellino* 'very small frying pan'
 b. *trombettina* 'small trumpet' → *trombettino* 'very small trumpet'
 c. *barchina* 'small bark' → *barchino* 'tiny hunting boat'
 d. *cassetta* 'drawer' → *cassetto* 'small drawer'

In a similar vein, Bergen (1980) argues that there are various semantic uses of gender in (dialects of) Spanish, including natural sex, unitization, small or large size, etc., built on the feminine suffix -*a* (Bergen 1980: 49–50; 53; 56):

(69) a. *gato* 'cat' → *gat-a* 'female cat' (sex)
 b. *Rafael* → *Rafael-a* (female proper name)

(70) *aceituno* 'olive tree' → *aceituna* 'olive'

(71) *barco* → *barca* 'small ship' (diminuitive)

(72) *panero* → *panera* 'large basket' (augmentative)

In sum, a gender polysemy can be established across languages, which corroborates the Arabic picture, and which supports the multi-layered approach adopted here.[18]

7 Semantics-pragmatics, morpho-syntax, and representation

Having established that the Gender functional affix is polysemous, and that its morpho-syntax is distributed (rather than unique), I first discuss some preliminary proposals made in the literature to account for regular polysemy and sense extensions of similar morpho-syntax and semantics. I then postulate a single representation of the various senses of the affix.

7.1 Semantics, discourse, and interface with morpho-syntactic peculiarities

Grandi (2015), building on previous work by Dressler and Jurafsky in particular, argue for various semantic and pragmatic interpretations formally dependent on the peculiarities of language-specific evaluative word-formation strategies (including affixation, gender shift, compounding, reduplication, etc.). Cross-linguistically, evaluative constructions can express either (a) descriptive/quantitative or (b) qualitative/expressive evaluation. In the case of (a), the description relies on real/objective properties (of objects, persons, actions, etc.), which are measured with respect to a standard/default value, and seen as a deviation with respect to the norm (culturally or socially determined). In the case of (b), the evaluative and subjective is concerned with personal feelings or opinions. For example, *cagnolino* in Italian can objectively describe a small dog, and *cagnone* a big one, in relation to a standardly sized one, using objective dimensional parameters. But if someone calls his Great Dane *cagnolino*, she/he would be expressing her/his affection towards it, or feelings, which depend crucially on pragmatics or discourse factors. The semantic-formal correlation is often unpredictable, but there are numerous instances of regular morphological qualitative evaluation (e.g. Slovak *mam-isko* 'mother-AUG' expresses a pejorative, whereas *mam-ička* 'mother-DIM' expresses an affectionate evaluative). See also Cinque (2014).

---

[18]See Fassi Fehri (2016) for more extensions to German, Dutch, Spanish, and more relevant references.

Wierzbicka (1989) proposes to consider the evaluative functions as instantiations of typological or universal prototypes, based on semantic primitives: the quantitative SMALL/BIG, and the qualitative GOOD/BAD. Jurafsky (1996) offers an in-depth view of the polysemy of diminutives and their semantic complexities via a "radial model" (inspired by Lakoff's 1987 radial category). According to him, the central (semantic) category of the diminutive is CHILD. Other diminutive senses come about through a process of *semantic change,* which uses various important mechanisms, including the *creation of metaphors, bleaching,* and the *conventionalization of inference.* Finally, in Körtvélyessy's 2014 model of evaluative formation, the semantic pragmatic functions of quantitative and qualitative evaluation are reflected in the form of two alternative paths of evaluative formation. The semantics of evaluation takes evaluative constructions as part of a continuum of QUANTITY (under or above) the default value, or a 'supercategory' including other categories.[19]

7.2 A unique hierarchical representation of Gen polysemy

In a polysemic analysis of Gen, its multi-layered distributed architecture and its distributed morphology model concur to provide an integrative view of regularities, correlations, and patterns found in Arabic varieties, and other languages as well. The variety of meanings and morpho-syntactic features or categories are interrelated and often regularly interfaced, rather than being accidental. As regard meanings, it is possible to see Gen as a semantic 'supercategory' or *hyperonym* of Quantity (or Quality), with a hierarchization (or a tree geometry), in which a *hyponym* Gen would be sex, taking into account historical stages of gender evolutions, various gender origins, as well as language-specific semantic and formal gender uses. Providing such a global and integrative model of Gen is far beyond the scope of this work, although such a model is possible to construct, typically based on empirical formal-semantic/pragmatic regular correlations. By correlating a unique (feminine) Gen morpheme to these various meanings and layers, we avoid an unmotivated exclusion of numerous meanings and configurations in which Gen is found.[20]

---

[19] According to her, the categories subsumed include Plurality or Aktionsart, with concepts of multiplicity, iterativity, distributiveness, attenuation, etc., which are of quantitative nature. See Körtvélyessy (2014) for detail, and the relevant references there.

[20] The Distributed morphology model is precisely designed to represent such complex and hierarchical semantic and morpho-syntactic mappings. Properties of traditional lexical terms are actually distributed across separate lists in the model, each of which is relevant only to a subset of functions of the traditional lexicon. Syntactic primitives (functional or contentful) are ± interpretable feature bundles, and Vocabulary Items pronounce terminal nodes in context only late in the derivation (given their "Late insertion" property). See Halle & Marantz (1993); Harley (2014), among others, for details.

Given that Gen is neither mono-semic (but rather having the potential to express many senses), nor mono-functional (not being limited e.g. to 'referential-tracking', but also expressing perspectivization of referents or shifts, expressiveness, or illocutionary/speech act modification), an associated semantics/pragmatics of Gender based on its alleged "natural" sex/animacy appears to be highly inappropriate. By contrast, our minimalist/distributed treatment is designed to take into account both its polysemy (with no homonymic alternative) and its polyfunctionality, in a motivated constructional and integrative approach.

Building on various contributions in the literature to account for regular polysemy, or sense extensions, and its representation or generation, I assume a single geometric representation in which Gen can be (distributively) *hyperonymic*, embracing the diverse and structurally organized and related meanings or functions found cross-linguistically, the sex (or animate) meaning being only a *hyponym*. This view builds on insightful relevant work by Dressler & Barbaresi (1994); Jurafsky (1996); Körtvélyessy (2014); Grandi & Körtvélyessy (2015) with regard to the semantic treatment of evaluatives, Lakoff's (1987) "radial" categorization, as well as work on neural correlates of semantic ambiguity, offering behavioral and neurophysiological support for a single-entry model of polysemy, in line with Beretta et al. (2005); Marantz (2005); Pylkkänen et al. (2006).

8 Conclusion

I have shown that Gender is more central and active in the nP/DP architecture, as well as in the (upper and parallel) CP structure or higher SAP than has been thought so far. It is found in multiple layers of the grammar, and it employs much more semantic features. An integrative treatment of its polysemy and its distributed syntax has been proposed. This multi-layered integrated account of Gender has relevant and broad consequences for both the typology and the theory of Gender, as well as other interrelated categories (namely Number), and processes such as Gender agreement (which also turns out to be a cover for various types, with different properties).

Acknowledgements

Parts of this work have been presented at various academic events and places during the academic year 2014–2015, including Paris VII University ling-lunch on February 2015, Qatar University Linguistic Gulf 5 Conference Keynote address in March 2015, the Syntax Workshop of Arabic Varieties in Geneva in August 2015, the SLE Conference in Leiden in September 2015, and the Ottawa workshop on Gender in October 2015, the Linguistic Society of Morocco Workshop in April 2014. I would like to thank the audiences there, and acknowledge helpful discussions, remarks and comments by Bernard Fradin, Peter Hallman, Anna Maria Di Sciullo, Noam Chomsky, Sylvain Bromberger, David Pesetsky, Marten Mous, Frederic Hoyt, Ur Shlonsky, Ahmad Rizwan, Maathir Al-Rawii, Margherita Pallottino, Pascal Amisli, Danièle Godard, Eric Mathieu, Saleh al-Qahtani, Miryam Dali, and two anonymous reviewers of the volume. Special thanks are due to Anders Holmberg for commenting on part of this work, and providing insightful feedback. His original contributions have always been a source of inspiration for various topics in my research, as well as innovative work in generative theory. The usual disclaimers apply.

References

Abdel-Massih, Ernest T. 1971. *A reference grammar of Tamazight*. Ann Arbor, MI: Center for Eastern & North African Studies, The University of Michigan.

Barker, Chris. 1992. Group terms in English: Representing groups as atoms. *Journal of Semantics* 9. 69–93.

Beretta, Alan, Robert Fiorentino & David Poeppel. 2005. The effects of homonymy and polysemy on lexical access: An MEG study. *Cognitive Brain Research* 24(1). 57–65.

Bergen, John. 1980. The semantics of gender contrasts in Spanish. *Hispania* 63(1). 48–57.

Borer, Hagit. 2005. *Structuring sense*. Oxford: Oxford University Press.

Brockelmann, Karl. 1910. *Précis de linguistique sémitique*. Paris: Geuthner.

Brugmann, Karl. 1897. *The Nature and Origin of the Noun Genders in the Indo-European Languages*. Lecture. Princeton University.

Caspari, Carl Paul. 1859. *Grammatik der arabischen Sprache für akademische Vorlesungen*. Leipzig: Verlag von C. F. Schmidt. (translated by William Wright 1971).

Chomsky, Noam. 1995. *The minimalist program*. Cambridge, MA: MIT Press.

Cinque, Guglielmo. 2014. Augmentative, pejorative, diminuitive, and endearing heads in the extended nominal projection. Ms. University of Venice.

Corbett, Greville. 1991. *Gender*. Cambridge: Cambridge University Press.

Corbett, Greville. 2000. *Number*. Cambridge: Cambridge Unviersity Press.

Crisma, Paola, Lutz Marten & Rint Sybesma. 2011. The point of Bantu, Chinese, and Romance nominal classification. *Rivista di Linguistica* 23(2). 251–299.

Dahl, Östen. 2000. Elementary Gender distinctions. In Barbara Unterbeck & Matti Rissanen (eds.), *Gender in grammar and cognition* (Trends in Linguistics. Studies and Monographs 124), 577–593. Berlin: Mouton De Gruyter.

de Belder, Marijke. 2008. Size matters: towards a syntactic decomposition of countability. In Natasha Abner & Jason Bishop (eds.), *Proceedings of the 27th West Coast Conference on Formal Linguistics*, 116–122. Somerville, MA: Cascadilla Proceedings Project.

De la Grasserie, Raoul. 1904. De l'expression de l'idée de sexualité dans le langage. *Revue philosophique de la France et de l'étranger* 58. 225–246.

Dimmendaal, Gerrit. 1983. *The Turkana language*. Dordrecht: Foris.

Dressler, Wolfgang U. & Lavinia M. Barbaresi. 1994. *Morphopragmatics: Diminutives and intensifiers in Italian, German, and other languages* (Trends in Linguistics, Studies and Monographs 76). Berlin: De Gruyter Mouton. DOI:10.1515/9783110877052

Fassi Fehri, Abdelkader. 1988. Agreement, binding, and coherence. In Michael Barlow & Charles Ferguson (eds.), *Agreement in natural language*, 107–158. Stanford, CA: CSLI.

Fassi Fehri, Abdelkader. 1993. *Issues in the structure of Arabic clauses and words*. Dordrecht: Kluwer Academic Publishers.

Fassi Fehri, Abdelkader. 2004. Nominal classes and parameters across interfaces and levels, with particular reference to Arabic. *Linguistic Variation Yearbook* 4. 41–108.

Fassi Fehri, Abdelkader. 2005. *Verbal and nominal parallelisms* (Documents & Reports 8). Rabat: IERA. 1–22.

Fassi Fehri, Abdelkader. 2012. *Key features and parameters in Arabic grammar*. Amsterdam: John Benjamins. DOI:10.1075/la.182

Fassi Fehri, Abdelkader. 2016. Semantic gender diversity and its architecture in the grammar of Arabic. *Brill's Journal of Afroasiatic Languages and Linguistics* 8(1). 154–199. DOI:10.1163/18776930-00801007

Fleisch, Henri. 1961. *Traité de philologie arabe*. Vol. 1. Beirut: Imprimerie Catholique.

Grandi, Nicola. 2015. Berber. In Nicola Grandi & Livia Körtvélyessy (eds.), *Edinburgh handbook of evaluative morphology*, 453–460. Edinburgh: Edinburgh University Press.

Grandi, Nicola & Livia Körtvélyessy (eds.). 2015. *Edinburgh handbook of evaluative morphology*. Edinburgh: Edinburgh University Press.

Greenberg, Joseph. 1972. Numeral classifiers and substantival number. *Working Papers on Language Universals* 9. 1–39.

Grimm, Jacob. 1822. *Deutsche Grammatik*. Göttingen: Der Dieterichen Buchhandlung.

Hachimi, Atiqa. 2007. Gender. In Kees Versteegh, Mushira Eid, Alaa Elgibali, Manfred Woidich & Andrzej Zaborski (eds.), *Encyclopedia of Arabic languages and linguistics*, vol. 1, 155–164. Leiden: Brill.

Halle, Morris & Alec Marantz. 1993. Distributed morphology and the pieces of inflection. In Kenneth Hale & Jay Keyser (eds.), *The view from building 20*, 111–176. Cambridge, MA: MIT Press.

Hämeen-Anttila, Jaakko. 2000. Grammatical gender and its development in classical arabic. In Barbara Unterbeck, Matti Rissanen, Terttu Nevalainen & Mirja Saari (eds.), *Gender in grammar and cognition*, 595–608. Berlin: De Gruyter.

Harley, Heidi. 2014. On the identity of roots. *Theoretical Linguistics* 40(3-4). 225–276.

Hasselbach, Rebecca. 2014. Agreement and the development of gender in Semitic. *ZDMG* 164. 33–64.

Hayward, Richard J. 1984. *The Abore language: A first investigation including a vocabulary* (Kuschitische Sprachstudien 2). Hamburg: Helmut Buske.

Hill, Virginia. 2014. *Vocatives: How syntax meets with pragmatics*. Leiden: Brill.

Ibrahim, Muhammad. 1973. *Grammatical gender: Its origin and development*. The Hague: Mouton.

Jurafsky, Daniel. 1996. Universal tendencies in the semantics of the diminuitive. *Language* 72(3). 533–578.

Kahane, Henry & Renée Kahane. 1949. The augmentative feminine in the Romance languages. *Romance Philology* 2. 135–175.

Kibort, Anna & Greville Corbett. 2008. Gender. Grammatical Features. www.grammaticalfeatures.net/features/gender.html.

Kihm, Alain. 2005. Noun class, gender and the Lexicon-Syntax-Morphology interfaces: A comparative study of Niger-Congo and Romance languages. In Guglielmo Cinque & Richard S. Kayne (eds.), *The handbook of comparative syntax*, 459–512. Oxford: Oxford University Press.

Köpcke, Klaus-Michael, Klause-Uwe Panther & David A. Zubin. 2010. Motivating grammatical and conceptual gender agreement in German. In Hans-Jörg Schmid & Susanne Handl (eds.), *Cognitive foundations of linguistic usage patterns*, 171–194. Berlin: Mouton de Gruyter.

Körtvélyessy, Livia. 2014. Evaluative derivation. In Rochelle Lieber & Peter Štekauer (eds.), *The Oxford handbook of derivational morphology*, 296–316. Oxford: Oxford University Press.

Kossmann, Maarten. 2014. Derivational gender in Moroccan Berber: Examples from Ayt Seghrushen. *STUF – Language Typology and Universals* 67(1). 21–33. DOI:10.1515/stuf-2014-0003

Kramer, Ruth. 2014. Gender in Amharic: a morphosyntactic approach to natural and grammatical gender. *Language Sciences* 43. 102–115.

Lakoff, George. 1987. *Women, fire, and dangerous things: What categories reveal about minds*. Chicago: University of Chicago Press.

Leiss, Elisabeth. 1994. Genus und sexus: Kritische anmerkungen zur sexualisierung von grammatik. *Linguistische Berichte* 152. 281–300.

Longobardi, Guiseppe. 2001. The structure of DPs: Some principles, parameters, and problems. In Mark Baltin & Chris Collins (eds.), *The handbook of contemporary syntactic theory*, 562–603. Oxford: Blackwell.

Lowenstamm, Jean. 2008. On little n, √, and types of nouns. In Jutta Hartmann, Veronika Hegedüs & Henk van Riemsdijk (eds.), *Sounds of silence*, 105–144. Amsterdam: Elsevier.

Marantz, Alec. 1997. No escape from syntax: Don't try morphological analysis in the privacy of your own lexicon. *University of Pennsylvania Working Papers in Linguistics* 4(2). 201–225.

Marantz, Alec. 2005. Generative linguistics within the cognitive neuroscience of language. *The Linguistic Review* 22(2–4). 429–445.

Mathieu, Eric. 2012. Flavors of division. *Linguistic Inquiry* 43(4). 650–679. DOI:10.1162/ling_a_00110

Mathieu, Eric. 2013. The plural of the singulative. *McGill Working Papers in Linguistics* 23. 1–12.

McConnell-Ginet, Sally. 2015. Gender and its relation to sex: The myth of 'natural' gender. In Greville Corbett (ed.), *The expression of gender*, 3–38. Berlin: Walter de Gruyter.

Mettouchi, Amina. 1999. Le "t" n'est-il qu'une marque de féminin en berbère (kabyle)? *Faits de langues* 7(14). 217–225.

Mithun, Marianne. 2015. Gender and culture. In Greville Corbett (ed.), *The expression of gender*, 131–160. Berlin: Walter de Gruyter.

Miyagawa, Shigeru. 2012. Agreements that occur mainly in the main clause. In Lobke Aelbrecht, Liliane Haegeman & Rachel Nye (eds.), *Main clause phenomena*, 79–111. Amsterdam: John Benjamins.

Moro, Andrea. 2003. Notes on vocative case: a case study in clause structure. In Josep Quer et al. (ed.), *Romance languages and linguistic theory 2001*, 251–264. Amsterdam: John Benjamins.

Mous, Marten. 2008. Number as an exponent of gender in Cushitic. Ms. RCLT.

Mous, Marten. 2012. Cushitic. In Zygmunt Frajzyngier & Erin Shay (eds.), *Interaction of morphology and syntax: case studies in afroasiatic (typological studies in language 75)*, 137–160. Amsterdam: John Benjamins.

Ouwayda, Sarah. 2014. *Where number lies*. Los Angeles, CA: University of Southern California dissertation.

Pearson, Hazel. 2011. A new semantics for group nouns. In Mary Byram Washburn, Katherine McKinney-Bock, Erika Varis, Ann Sawyer & Barbara Tomaszewicz (eds.), *Proceedings of the 28th West Coast Conference on Formal Linguistics*, 160–168. Somerville, MA: Cascadilla Proceedings Project.

Percus, Orin. 2011. Gender features and interpretation: A case study. *Morphology* 21(2). 167–196.

Pesetsky, David. 2013. *Russian case morphology and the syntactic categories*. Cambridge, MA: The MIT Press.

Picallo, Carme. 2008. Gender and number in Romance. *Lingue e Linguaggio* 7(1). 47–66.

Pylkkänen, Liina, Rodolfo Llinás & Gregory Murphy. 2006. The representation of polysemy: MEG evidence. *Journal of Cognitive Neuroscience* 18(1). 97–109.

Ritter, Elizabeth. 1993. Where's gender? *Linguistic Inquiry* 24(4). 795–803.

Roman, André. 1990. De l'accord et du pseudo-accord du féminin en arabe. *Annales Islamologiques* 25. 27–56.

Seifart, Frank. 2010. Nominal classification. *Language and Linguistics Compass* 4(8). 719–736.

Sibawayhi, Amr. 1938. *Al-Kitaab*. Cairo: Buulaaq.

Speas, Margaret & Carol L. Tenny. 2003. Configurational properties of point of view roles. In Anna Maria Di Sciullo (ed.), *Asymmetry in grammar*, 315–344. Amsterdam: John Benjamins.

Steriopolo, Olga. 2013. Diminutive affixes in the number domain: a syntactic variation. *Questions and Answers in Linguistics* 1(2). 33–56.

Steriopolo, Olga & Martina Wiltschko. 2010. Distributed gender hypothesis. In Gerhild Zybatow, Philip Dudchuk, Serge Minor & Ekaterina Pshehotskaya (eds.), *Formal studies in Slavic linguistics* (Linguistik International 25), 155–172. Frankfurt: Peter Lang.

Unterbeck, Barbara. 2000. Gender: New light on an old category. In Barbara Unterbeck (ed.), *Gender in grammar and cognition*, xv–xxv. Berlin: Mouton de Gruyter.

Wierzbicka, Anna. 1989. Soul and mind: Linguistic evidence for ethnopsychology and cultural history. *American Anthropologist* 91(1). 41–58.

Wiltschko, Martina. 2008. The syntax of non-inflectional plural marking. *Natural Language and Linguistic Theory* 26(3). 639–694.

Wright, William. 1971. *A grammar of the Arabic language.* Third edition. Cambridge: Cambridge University Press. Translated from Caspari 1859, with additions and corrections.

Zabbal, Youri. 2002. *The semantics of number in the Arabic noun phrase.* Calgary: University of Calgary MA thesis.

Chapter 10

Puzzling parasynthetic compounds in Norwegian

Janne Bondi Johannessen
MultiLing, Department of Linguistics and Scandinavian Studies, University of Oslo

> This paper describes parasynthetic compounds in Norwegian and questions some recent claims made in the literature about this kind of word formation. In particular, it will be argued that they are not marginal, but productive, and that they are semantically compositional.

1 Introduction

The existence of parasynthetic compounds provides linguistics with some puzzles that I shall discuss, though not solve, in this paper. Parasynthetic compounds are compounds that consist of three parts, where any combination of just two of the parts would be ungrammatical, and where there is a bracketing paradox, see the Norwegian example in (1). They can be found in many other Indo-European languages, such as the other mainland North Germanic languages Swedish (Teleman et al. 1999) and Danish (Hansen & Heltoft 2011), English (Hirtle 1970), Greek, Slavic and Romance (Melloni & Bisetto 2010).[1]

---

[1] Some examples from other languages are given below.

    (i) *in+busta *bust(a)+are → im+bust+are 'to put in an envelope' (Italian)

   (ii) *red-blood *blooded → red-blooded (English)

  (iii) *blauwog+ig *blauw+ogig → blauwogig 'blue-eyed' (Dutch)

  (iv) *kokkino+mal *mal+is → kokkinomalis 'red-haired' (Greek)

   (v) *obc(o)kraj+oc obc(o)+*krajoc → obcokrajowiec 'foreigner' (Polish) (Melloni & Bisetto 2010: 199–201)

Janne Bondi Johannessen. 2017. Puzzling parasynthetic compounds in Norwegian. In Michelle Sheehan & Laura R. Bailey (eds.), *Order and structure in syntax II: Subjecthood and argument structure*, 257–273. Berlin: Language Science Press.

Janne Bondi Johannessen

(1) a. *rødøyd*
 red-eyed
 'red-eyed'
 b. Three parts: *rød*$_{adj}$ + *øye*$_{noun}$ + *d*$_{adj\text{-suffix}}$
 red eye d
 c. Ungrammatical combinations of two: **rødøye*, **øyd*
 d. Bracketing paradox:
 Semantically: [[*rød*+*øye*]*d*]
 Morphologically: [*rød*+[[*øye*]*d*]]²

My perspective will be that of Norwegian, and the puzzles, some of which have been raised as claims in the literature, are these: What do the strict requirements for the parts of speech of the individual compound members mean for syntactic theory? How strict is the category of inalienable possession? Why do they behave morphophonologically as past participles? Why are they often non-compositional semantically? Are they marginal?

The paper is structured in the following way. An empirical investigation is carried out in §2, using a special compound search interface to the dictionaries and one big corpus. This section also comments on the usability of these empirical resources. §3 discusses several aspects of parasynthetic compounds, partly based on claims in the literature. It is discussed whether parasynthetic compounds are a marginal phenomenon, whether they are semantically compositional, why they have the same morphophonological suffix as past participles, to what extent there is a relationship of inalienable possession, and finally their strict categorial restrictions. §4 concludes the paper. Using these rich empirical data collections it will be demonstrated that not all claims in the literature can be defended.

2 Empirical investigation

Parasynthetic compounds in Norwegian have been briefly discussed in Johannessen (2001) and more thoroughly, with a semantic focus, in Grov (2009). In order to test claims and get a further basis for the questions posed in §1, a thorough empirical investigation is necessary. There are two types of sources of data that seem particularly appropriate for finding such compounds in Norwegian. Both

---

²When a lexical stem ends in –*e*, it is deleted under certain morphophonological conditions, thus *øye*, but *øyd*. This process is general and applies in many other contexts than parasynthetic compounding.

are large electronic data collections, where there is a special option for searching for compounds. One type of data is dictionaries, more specifically, the reference dictionaries *Bokmålsordboka* (Wangensteen 2005) and *Nynorskordboka* (Hovdenak 2001). These books are the official dictionaries of the two written varieties of Norwegian (Bokmål and Nynorsk). The other type of empirical source is the NoWaC-corpus (*Norwegian Web as a Corpus*) (Guevara 2010).

These two types of empirical source complement each other. The dictionaries only contain compounds that are sufficiently established for the lexicographers to accept them as worthy of entries or subentries. The corpus, on the other hand, includes all the compounds that have been coined by the authors of the texts it contains.

2.1 Parasynthetic compounds in the two dictionaries

A special search interface for compounds exists for the dictionaries. The compounds in the dictionaries have all been manually annotated, based on the original compounds in the dictionary (Bjørghild Kjelsvik, p.c.). This means that all the compounds are well-formed (in that they represent Norwegian words) and have a correct analysis.

The simple search interface makes it possible to express a search such as: return all compounds that end in *−t* (one of the common adjectival derivational suffixes for parasynthetic compounds), and that are adjectives. The type of results that are returned are illustrated in Figure 1, which also illustrates the compound analysis returned by the search interface.

The list in Figure 1 shows that we do not only get parasynthetic compounds. There is also a substantial number of a similar kind of compound where the second member is derived from a verb (and in effect is a past participle). These are not parasynthetic, since past participles can occur on their own. The analysis in Figure 1 shows that the lexicographers have chosen not to include the original part of speech of the second member (i.e. noun), and have only included the resulting part of speech of the whole second member including the adjectival derivational suffix. To illustrate, the parasynthetic compound *brei-kinnet* 'broad-cheeked' has been (wrongly) given the same structure as the past participle *bort-glømt* 'away-forgotten':

(2) a. *brei*+Adj+Seg+-*kinnet*+Adj+Pos+Sg+Indef
 broad cheeked
 'broad-cheeked'

	Leddanalyse
	blek+Adj+Seg+fet+Adj+Pos+MF+Sg+Indef
blek*fet	bevegelse+Noun+SJuncture+Seg+-hemmet+Adj+Pos+Sg+Indef
bevegelses*hemmet	bibel+Noun+Seg+-sprengt+Adj+Pos+Sg+Indef
bibel*sprengt	bort+Adv+Seg+-bestilt+Adj+Pos+Sg+Indef
bort*bestilt	bort+Adv+Seg+-glemt+Adj+Pos+Sg+Indef
bort*glemt	bort+Adv+Seg+-glømt+Adj+Pos+Sg+Indef
bort*glømt	bort+Adv+Seg+-kommet+Adj+Pos+Sg+Indef
bort*kommet	bort+Adv+Seg+-reist+Adj+Pos+Sg+Indef
bort*reist	blå+Adj+Seg+fiolett+Adj+Pos+Sg+Indef
blå*fiolett	bløt+Adj+Seg+-hjertet+Adj+Pos+Sg+Indef
bløt*hjertet	boge+Noun+Seg+-formet+Adj+Pos+Sg+Indef
boge*formet	brei+Adj+Seg+-skuldret+Adj+Pos+Sg+Indef
brei*skuldret	brott+Noun+Seg+fast+Adj+Pos+Sg+Indef
brott*fast	brudd+Noun+Seg+fast+Adj+Pos+Sg+Indef
brudd*fast	bratt+Adj+Seg+-lendt+Adj+Pos
bratt*lendt	bred+Adj+Seg+-kinnet+Adj+Pos+Sg+Indef
bred*kinnet	bred+Adj+Seg+-skuldret+Adj+Pos+Sg+Indef
bred*skuldret	brei+Adj+Seg+-akslet+Adj+Pos+Sg+Indef
brei*akslet	brei+Adj+Seg+-kinnet+Adj+Pos+Sg+Indef
brei*kinnet	brei+Adj+Seg+-kjeftet+Adj+Pos+Sg+Indef
brei*kjeftet	

Figure 1: Results of a search for compounds that are adjective and that end in –t.

b. *bort*+Adv+Seg+-*glømt*+Adj+Pos+Sg+Indef
away forgotten
'totally forgotten'

It would have been better for our purpose if the analysis had included the part of speech of their original second member, as suggested in (3):

(3) *brei*+Adj+Seg+-*kinn*+**Noun**-*et*+Adj+Pos+Sg+Indef
bort+Adv+Seg+-*gløm*+**Verb**-*t*+Adj+Pos+Sg+Indef

For this reason we will not know exactly how many parasynthetic compounds there are in the dictionaries. Some examples of the irrelevant past participles are given in (4) and (5). Some of the many parasynthetic compounds are given in (6).

(4) Compound past participles

    a. *bevegelses-hemmet*
    movement-impaired
    'movement-impaired'

    b. *bort-bestilt*
    away-booked
    'booked by somebody else'

(5) a. *bort-glømt*
    away-forgotten
    'totally forgotten'

    b. *bort-reist*
    away-gone
    'gone away'

(6) Parasynthetic compounds

    a. *bløt-hjertet*
    soft-hearted
    'soft-hearted'

    b. *brei-skuldret*
    broad-shouldered
    'broad-shouldered'

    c. *bred-kinnet*
    broad-cheeked
    'broad-cheeked'

d. *brei-kjeftet*
wide-mouthed
'wide-mouthed'

e. *bar-føtt*
bare-footed
'bare-foot'

f. *blank-øyd*
shiny-eyed
'shiny-eyed'

g. *blid-lynt*
happy-tempered
'happy-tempered'

h. *blid-mælt*
happy-voiced
'happy-voiced'

i. *brå-lynt*
quick-tempered
'quick-tempered'

j. *djup-gjengt*
deep-threaded
'deep-threaded'

k. *en-cellet*
one-celled
'one-celled'

l. *fir-beint*
four-legged
'four-legged'

2.2 Parasynthetic compounds in the NoWaC Corpus

The NoWaC text corpus of the Norwegian Bokmål variety (Guevara 2010) contains around 700 million words, and its compounds are tagged. This corpus complements the dictionaries. While the latter contain compounds that lexicographers have chosen to include due to frequency and other factors, the compounds that are marked as such in the NoWaC corpus are those that 1) are not recognized as compounds in the dictionaries, thereby triggering the compound recognizer in the tagger module, 2) satisfy certain characteristics, for example that they have a last member that can be recognized as a word, and at least a couple of letters before that. The search interface allows the user to specify that the result should be a compound, and that it should end in *–t* (for example). However, unlike the dictionaries, the NoWaC corpus has been annotated automatically and the words marked as compounds therefore also include spelling errors (*difust* 'vague', should have been spelt with two f's), foreign words (*treatment*, English loan) and new words (*ukomprimert* 'uncompressed'), or rightly as compounds, but not parasynthetic ones: *pårygget* 'on-backed', *sesongbetinget* 'season-dependent'.

While it is possible to find the appropriate examples in the dictionaries given their careful manual annotation, which includes the grammatical category of the first compound member, the corpus is more difficult to use for somebody interested in the parasynthetic subgroup of compounds. The compounds are only marked by the resulting grammatical category, viz. the adjectival one given by the derivational suffix. A better use of the corpus is searching for a longer sequence, such as a full last member of a parasynthetic compound. The corpus contains compounds that have been used in texts independently of the judgement of lexicographers, and therefore present more and potentially interesting data, and complement the dictionaries. As an example, we have searched for the last member *–beint* '–legged', which gave 10 results in the Bokmål dictionary, and 15 in NoWaC, (7–8).

(7) From the dictionaries
firebeint 'four-legged'
likebeint 'ambi-legged'
lettbeint 'light-footed'
stivbeint 'stiff-legged'
sårbeint 'sore-legged'
tobeint 'two-legged'
kalvbeint 'calf-legged'
(knock-kneed)
langbeint 'long-legged'
trebeint 'three-legged'
kjappbeint 'quick-legged'
(swift-footed)

(8) From NoWaC
venstrebeint 'left-legged'
stivbeint 'stiff-legged'
langbeint 'long-legged'
firbeint 'four-legged'
breibeint 'wide-legged'
kortbeint 'short-legged'
høyrebeint 'right-legged'
tungbeint 'heavy-legged'
lavbeint 'low-legged'
tibeint 'ten-legged'
lettbeint 'light-legged'
(light-footed)
jevnbeint 'even-legged'
snublebeint 'stumble-legged'
(clumsy-footed)
åttebeint 'eight-legged'
hjulbeint 'wheel-legged'
(bow-legged)

Janne Bondi Johannessen

We see that both sources are useful for finding examples of this phenomenon. In order to be able to say something general about this kind of compounds, we need to have a wide selection of examples, which we have now.

3 Some aspects of parasynthetic compounds

3.1 A marginal phenomenon?

Melloni & Bisetto (2010: 200) claim that parasynthetic compounds represent "a marginal phenomenon in most Germanic and Romance languages", in contrast to the Slavic languages. This claim is not further substantiated, so it is not clear what they mean by marginal. However, Johannessen (2001: 77) seems to say the opposite[3], she claims that this compound type is productive, and that new words are made all the time.

If "marginal" refers to quantity, the total number of compounds, we should find an answer by counting. There are altogether 3795 cases of Bokmål hits and 1594 of Nynorsk in the dictionaries. Without going into each case individually, we do not know how many are genuine examples (recall the list in Figure 1), but if we guess that half of them are, this is still a high number, though how to evaluate what it takes to be a high number is not obvious.

If it refers to the strict morpho-syntactic requirements as to their make-up, one could justify calling them marginal. Unlike other compounds, they must have a number or an adjective as their first member, a noun as their second member, and an adjective-deriving suffix as their last member.

However, within those grammatical constraints, there is quite a bit of variation. Extracting the second member of the parasynthetic compounds in the dictionary, there are quite a few and they come from different semantic fields, see (9), including the human body, animal bodies, vehicles, weapons, poems, clothes etc.

(9) *aksla* 'shouldered', *aldra* 'aged', *arma* 'armed', *auga* 'eyed', *barma* 'breasted', *barka* 'barked', *beina* 'legged', *blada* 'leaved', *bottna* 'bottomed', *bremma* 'brimmed', *bringa* 'chested', *brysta* 'breasted', *buka* 'stomached', *cella* 'celled', *egga* 'edged', *erma* 'sleaved', *farga* 'coloured', *fingra* 'fingered', *fibra* 'fibred', *felta* 'filed', *finna* 'finned', *folka* 'peopled', *forma* 'shaped', *fota* 'footed', *greina* 'branched', *halsa* 'throated', *hjarta* 'hearted', *hjula* 'wheeled', *horna* 'horned', *huda* 'skinned', *hæla* 'healed', *høgda*

---

[3]"Denne typen er produktiv – nye ord lages stadig" (Johannessen 2001: 77).

'heighted', *håra* 'haired', *kalibra* 'calibred', *kanta* 'edged', *kinna* ' cheeked' , *kjaka* 'jawed', *kjefta* 'mouthed', *kjønna* 'gendered', *knea* 'kneed', *korna* 'grained', *lemma* 'limbed', *leppa* 'lipped', *lesta* 'lasted', *leta* 'coloured', *liva* 'lived', *linja* 'lined', *lugga* 'haired', *løpa* 'barrelled', *maga* 'stomached', *masta* 'masted', *munna* 'mouthed', *mønstra* 'patterned', *nakka* 'necked', *nasa* 'nosed', *nebba* 'beaked', *nerva* 'nerved', *pigga* 'spiked', *panna* 'foreheaded', *rada* 'rowed', *rauva* 'bottomed', *rumpa* 'bottomed', *rygga* 'backed', *røsta* 'voiced', *seila* 'sailed', *sida* 'sided', *sifra* 'numbered', *sinna* 'minded', *skafta* 'shafted', *skala* 'shelled', *skinna* 'skinned', *skjefta* 'shafted', *skjegga* 'bearded', *snuta* 'snouted', *spalta* 'slitted', *spora* 'spored', *stamma* 'stemmed', *streak* 'lined', *strenga* 'stringed', *strofa* 'versed', *sylindra* 'cylindered', *tagga* 'spiked', *tanna* 'toothed', *vegga* 'walled', *venga* 'winged', *vinkla* 'angled', *vomma* 'stomached', *ætta* 'familied', *øra* 'eared', *mælt* 'voiced'...

There is also a semantic requirement for parasynthetic compounds, as the relationship between the parasynthetic compound and what it modifies, must be inalienable (see §3.4). Within the constraints given in this section, parasynthetic compounding is productive (see §3.4 for this, too). It seems fair to conclude that parasynthetic compounds are both marginal and not marginal, depending on the definition of this word.

3.2 Parasynthetic compounds and (non-)compositionality

Melloni & Bisetto (2010: 209) refer to Ackema & Neeleman's (2004) theory to argue that some types of parasynthetic compounds are non-compositional. It is quite obvious, though, that whenever we can find productively made compounds, they must have compositional semantics, at least to start out with. The self-made parasynthetic compounds in (10) all have a completely transparent meaning.

(10) a. *spisshanket* 'pointed-handled', *rundhanket* 'round-handled', *ovalhanket* 'oval-handled' (about jugs)

b. *femlommet* 'five-pocketed', *sjulommet* 'seven-pocketed', *firkantlommet* 'square-pocketed' (about coats)

c. *tohyllet* 'two-shelved', *smalhyllet* 'narrow-shelved' (about book-cases)

However, just as the Slavic [A+N]$_N$ compounds Melloni & Bisetto (2010: 209) discuss, there is a group of parasynthetic compounds that could perhaps be argued to be non-compositional, some examples are given in (11).

(11)   *mørkhudet*: lit. 'dark-skinned', 'person who originates from Africa or Asia'
   hardhudet: lit. 'hard-skinned', 'person who endures criticism'
   tykkhudet: lit. 'thick-skinned', meaning: as above
   gullkantet: lit. 'gold-edged', 'will give somebody wealth'

However, rather than claiming non-compositionality for these, a better classification is probably as compounds with a metaphorical meaning. They are after all compositional when taking the metaphorical aspect into account: A thick-skinned person has such a thick metaphorical skin that the criticisms cannot get through and influence her.

It wouldn't be surprising, though, if some parasynthetic compounds were non-compositional. All compounds, not just the parasynthetic ones, can be lexicalized and then freeze in a meaning that has appeared at some stage. Many compounds contain words that are no longer in use apart from inside those compounds, and others are impossible to analyse semantically in spite of the known individual members. Some examples are given in (12).

(12)   *putevar* 'pillow-case' (the word *var* is not known any longer)
   tyttebær 'x-berry' (the word *tytte* is unknown today)
   tøffelhelt lit. 'slipper-hero', 'man who has no power in his own home'

The conclusion here is that parasynthetic compounds are compositional when they are productively made and when they are used metaphorically, but it would be surprising if not a few, at least, were also non-compositional.

3.3 The phonological form of the parasynthetic compound suffix

The derivational suffix that changes the noun of the parasynthetic compound into an adjective has the same form as that of the past participle. Their shape depends on the phonological form of the stem they attach to. When the stem ends in a vowel, the suffix is obligatorily –*d*. When it ends in a lamino-dental stop or labial consonant, the suffix must be either –*et* or –*a* depending on dialect, and finally, after other consonants, –*t* . These are all exemplified in (13).

(13) a. After a vowel stem: *–d*
　　　Verb stem: *bøy* 'bend', participle: *bøyd* 'bent'
　　　Noun stem: *øy* 'eye', parasynthetic compound: *rødøyd* 'red-eyed'
　　　i. After a lamino-dental or labial plosive stem: *–et* (some dialects)
　　　　Verb stem: *stopp* 'stop', participle: *stoppet* 'stopped'
　　　　Verb stem: *varm* 'warm', participle: *varmet* 'warmed'
　　　　Noun stem: *hud* 'skin', parasynthetic compound: *mørkhudet* 'dark-skinned'
　　　　Noun stem: *arm* 'arm', parasynthetic compound: *toarmet* 'two-armed'
　　　ii. After a lamino-dental or labial plosive stem: *–a* (other dialects)
　　　　Verb stem: *stopp* 'stop', participle: *stoppa* 'stopped'
　　　　Verb stem: *varm* 'warm', participle: *varma* 'warmed'
　　　　Noun stem: *hud* 'skin', parasynthetic compound: *mørkhuda* 'dark-skinned'
　　　　Noun stem: *arm* 'arm', parasynthetic compound: *toarma* 'two-armed'
　　b. **After other consonant stems:** *–t*
　　　Verb stem: *spis* 'eat', participle: *spist* 'eaten'
　　　Noun stem: *bein* 'leg', parasynthetic compound: *tobeint* 'two-legged'

The parasynthetic compound suffix clearly does not make the noun into a past participle; there is nothing agentive or verbal about these words. However, both classes of words end up with a word that is or (in the case of participles) can be turned into a different part of speech, and in both cases this is an adjective. Some researchers have tried to find a deeper semantic connection between the two. Koontz-Garboden (2012) suggests that the meaning of the English *–ed* has the meaning of 'difference'. For nominals that would entail a possessive relation.

Maybe related to this is the question why it is impossible to use the noun + derivational suffix without a preposed adjective or number. Thus, why is it okay to say about somebody that they are *langbeint* 'long-legged', while it is impossible to say that they are **beint* 'legged'? Booij (2005: 218–219) claims that such constructions are grammatical, but that they are pragmatically odd, since humans are expected to have the property of legs. There are some problems with such pragmatic constraints, though. One problem is that other pragmatic redundancies are perfectly grammatical, such as *tobeint* 'two-legged'. Another problem is that we find inalienable possession also in cases where the property is not something to be expected. So we find *tremasta* 'three-masted', even if boats are not all expected to have masts. In fact, for small boats it would be more unexpected to find masts at all, yet it would be strange or impossible to say about a small boat with masts that it is **masta* 'masted'.

3.4 Inalienable possession

It is known that parasynthetic compounds must be part of a relationship of inalienable possession with the noun that they modify, as is also pointed out by Grov (2009). Melloni & Bisetto (2010: 210) further claim that the nouns of the compound must not only be inalienably possessed, but must be body-parts of humans or animals.[4] Looking at examples of parasynthetic compounds, it is obviously true that they must involve a relationship of inalienable possession between the compound and the owner. For Norwegian, however, it is very clear that any noun from any semantic field can occur as long as the special relationship is fulfilled. Some examples of words that use the second member in parasynthetic compounds from (9) are given in (14), together with the kind of possessor they would have:

(14)   *Clothes:* *blåfarga* 'blue-coloured', *mangefibra* 'many-fibred'
       Containers: *dobbelbottna* 'double-bottomed'
       Hats: *vidbremma* 'wide-rimmed'
       Humans: *breiaksla* 'broad-shouldered', *berrarma* 'bare-armed', *gråøyd* 'grey-eyed', *breibarma* 'broad-breasted', *kjappbeint* 'quick-legged', *breibringa* 'broad-chested', *trongbrysta* 'narrow-breasted'
       Knives: *tviblada* 'two-bladed', *kvassegga* 'sharp-edged'
       Numbers: *fleirsifra* 'several-digited'
       Poems: *einstrofa* 'one-versed'
       Trees: *råbarka* 'raw-barked'

There does seem to be full productivity. I found some examples in NoWaC that seemed rare, and googled them, (15). There were from one to three hits for these, indicating that they have been productively made. I include some self-made ones as well, (16), to illustrate that this is possible and the result grammatical.

(15)   *trangkjefta* 'narrow-mouthed'
       skakkjefta 'skew-mouthed'
       rødkjefta 'red-mouthed'

---

[4]It is unclear whether they apply this generalisation to all parasynthetic compounds or to Russian or Slavic ones only.

(16) *kortnegla* 'short-nailed'
grønnesa 'green-nosed'
smalpanna 'narrow-foreheaded'

The examples all show that parasynthetic compounds require inalienable possession, but the kind of possessor can belong to any semantic field, not just human or animate. Why they have to obey the inalienability condition remains a puzzle.[5]

3.5 Parasynthetic compounds and syntactic theory

The fact that parasynthetic compounds have very strict categorial requirements makes them very interesting. Consider an example like (17a), *seksbeinte* 'six-legged.PL'. It contains the noun *bein* 'leg' modified by the number *seks* 'six' and the adjectival derivational suffix *–t*. The compound is inflected in the plural. Other parts of speech are not possible (apart from the first member, that could also be an adjective), see (17b–d).

(17) a. *seksbeinte* 'six-legged.PL' (first member: adjective/number)
b. * *plastikkbeint* 'plastic-legged' (noun instead of adjective/number)
c. * *haltebeint* 'limp-legged' (verb instead of adjective/number)
d. * *dårligbeint* 'badly-legged' (adverb instead of adjective/number)

The second member could be substituted with a verb, in which case all the characteristics of the parasynthetic compounds disappear, consider (18a) vs. (18b–d).

(18) a. *blåøyd* 'blue-eyed' (second member: adjective, followed by derivational suffix)
b. *blåmalt krus* 'blue-painted cup' (second member: past participle instead of adj and *–t*)
c. *børstemalt* 'brush-painted' (first member: noun, not adjective)
d. *hurtigmalt* 'quickly-painted' (first member: adverb, not adjective)

---

[5]One reviewer, referring to Myler & Nevins (2014) asks about phrases such as *ragged-trousered philanthropists*, *top-hatted gentleman*, which seem to run contra to the requirement of inalienability for this construction. I don't know whether these are productive in English, but their equivalents do not seem right in Norwegian. One could explain them, perhaps, by claiming that the top hat is an inalienable possession of a gentleman, et cetera, and that *top* is analysed as an adjective.

(18b–d) cannot be considered to be parasynthetic compounding, just ordinary synthetic compounding. First, there is no inalienable possession. In (18b), *blåmalt krus* 'blue-painted mug', the possessor would be *krus* 'mug', but there is no noun to be possessed. Second, it has only two members, *blå-malt*, i.e. adjective+past participle, as *malt* 'painted' is also a possible word of its own. Third, this entails that there is no bracketing paradox either. Fourth, it does not have any other restrictions w.r.t. part of speech of the first member, so *børstemalt* 'brush-painted' with a noun and *hurtigmalt* 'quickly-painted' with an adverb are both ok.

Johannessen (2001: 79) suggested the analysis in (19), in which the adjectival derivational suffix *–t* is attached to the compound stem number/adjective+noun. The idea is that this compound stem has a compound feature with information about the individual members, which is percolated up to the combined compound stem. The derivational suffix selects this kind of stem, giving a parasynthetic compound.

(19)

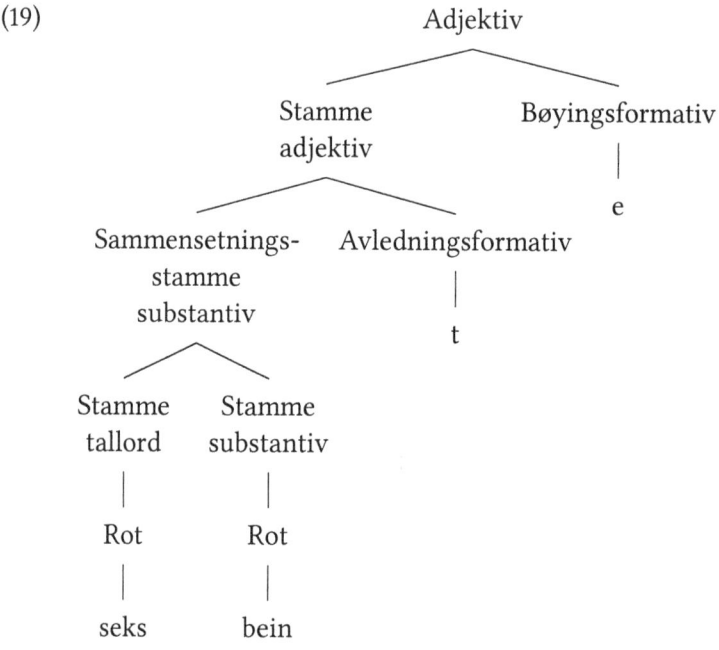

A similar analysis is suggested by Melloni & Bisetto (2010: 216), building on Ackema & Neeleman (2004), for words like *bisillabo* 'bisyllabic', see (20).

(20)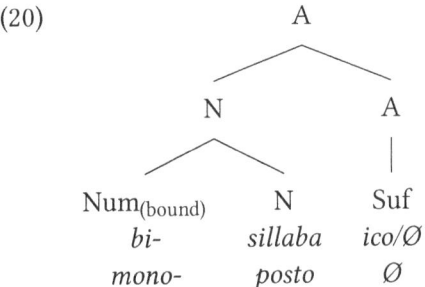

A syntactic theory that has received some interest in recent years is the exoskeletal theory proposed by Borer (2003) and implemented for Norwegian in work such as Åfarli (2007) and Grimstad et al. (2014). In this theory syntactic categories are properties of the structure, not of the items themselves. Borer (2003: 34–40) illustrates the theory by taking roots such as *dog*, *sink* and *boat*, and inserting them freely in the syntactic structure yielding sentences such as *The boat will dog three sinks*, as well as *The boat will sink three dogs* etc.

If the theory is applied to parasynthetic compounds, the skeleton might look like (19), but with empty terminals, waiting to be filled. We have already seen in (17) that there are very strict categorial restrictions on parasynthetic compounds.

Further, if we substitute the second member, the lexical item *øye* 'eye' (usually used in a noun structure) of a parasynthetic compound such as *blåøyd* 'blue-eyed' with a lexical item often used as a verb *male* 'paint', like we have done in (18a–b), the result is not a parasynthetic compound with an item previously used as a verb now interpreted as a (new) noun. It seems impossible to force a parasynthetic compound reading onto *blåmalt* 'blue-painted', such that for example *blåmalt krus* 'blue-painted mug' would be a mug possessing paint that is blue. This would also have made the prediction that the bracketing paradox would be observed, so that the second item with the suffix should be unacceptable. Again, forcing an unacceptable interpretation onto *malt* 'painted' is beyond what a language user can do. Johannessen (under development) currently investigates a different way of looking at the data; one in which there are semantic parallels between parasynthetic compounds and past participles.

4 Conclusion

The paper has investigated parasynthetic compounds using large empirical resources: a searchable dictionary database especially marked for compounds and a big web-corpus. These turned out to be very useful to garner large amounts of relevant data quickly. It was also discussed whether parasynthetic compounds are a marginal phenomenon, as claimed in the literature. This can hardly be the case since, though there are some syntactico-semantic restrictions on their formation, they are productive. Since many are productively made, they clearly cannot be non-compositional, as has also been claimed. One of the clear semantic restrictions is that there must be a relationship of inalienable possession, but it is not true that it must only be restricted to body parts of humans and animals, as has been claimed. Finally, with the very strict categorial restrictions on the formation of parasynthetic compounds, syntactic theories that dismiss the idea that lexical items have categorial features have been shown to face a challenge.

Acknowledgements

I would like to thank Bjørghild Kjelsvik and Oddrun Grønvik for inviting me to their workshop on compounds at MONS (Møter om norsk språk) 16, 25th–27th November 2015, University of Agder, Kristiansand. This made me start thinking about the exciting topic of compounding again.

I would like to thank two anonymous reviewers for very good comments and Kolbe, Steve Pepper and George Walkden for thorough proof reading.

Web resources

Compound analysis search interface, Bokmålsordboka: http://www.edd.uio.no/perl/search/search.cgi?appid=72&tabid=3174
Compound analysis search interface, Nynorskordboka: http://www.edd.uio.no/perl/search/search.cgi?appid=73&tabid=2562
NoWaC corpus (Norwegian Web as a Corpus): http://hf-tekstlab.uio.no/glossa2/?corpus=nowac_1_1

References

Ackema, Peter & Ad Neeleman. 2004. *Beyond morphology: Interface conditions on word formation.* Oxford: Oxford University Press.
Åfarli, Tor A. 2007. Do verbs have argument structure? In Eric J. Reuland, Tanmoy Bhattacharya & Giorgos Spathas (eds.), *Argument structure*, 1–16. Amsterdam: John Benjamins Publishing Company.

Booij, Gert. 2005. Compounding and derivation: Evidence for construction morphology. In Wolfgang U. Dressler, Franz Rainer, Dieter Kastovsky & Oskar Pfeiffer (eds.), *Morphology and its demarcations*, 109–132. Amsterdam/Philadelphia: John Benjamins.

Borer, Hagit. 2003. Exo-skeletal vs. endo-skeletal explanations: Syntactic projections. In Maria Polinsky & John Moore (eds.), *The nature of explanation in linguistic theory*. Stanford: CSLI.

Grimstad, Maren Berg, Terje Lohndal & Tor A. Åfarli. 2014. Language mixing and exoskeletal theory: A case study of word-internal mixing in American Norwegian. *Nordlyd* 41(2). 213–237.

Grov, Astrid Marie. 2009. *For venstrehendte er det dei høgrehendte som er feilhendte: Ein studie av uavhendelege samansetjingar i norsk*. MA thesis.

Guevara, Emiliano Raul. 2010. NoWaC: A large web-based corpus for Norwegian. In *Proceedings of the NAACL HLT 2010 Sixth Web as Corpus Workshop. Association for Computational Linguistics page*, 1–7. http://www.aclweb.org/anthology/W10-1501.

Hansen, Erik & Lars Heltoft. 2011. *Grammatik over det Danske Sprog. Det Danske Sprog- og Litteraturselskab*. København: Syddansk Universitetsforlag.

Hirtle, Walter H. 1970. *Ed* adjectives like 'verandahed' and 'blue-eyed'. *Journal of Linguistics* 6. 19–36.

Hovdenak, Marit (ed.). 2001. *Nynorskordboka – definisjons- og rettskrivingsordbok*. Oslo: Det Norske Samlaget.

Johannessen, Janne Bondi. 2001. Sammensatte ord. *Norsk Lingvistisk Tidsskrift*. 59–92. http://urn.nb.no/URN:NBN:no-46106.

Koontz-Garboden, Andrew. 2012. *The morphosemantics of –ed*. Paper presented at Workshop on Aspect and Argument Structure of Adjectives and Participles. 22-23 June 2012. University of Greenwich.

Melloni, Chiara & Antonietta Bisetto. 2010. Parasynthetic compounds. In Sergio Scalise & Irene Vogel (eds.), *Cross-Disciplinary issues in compounding*, 199–218. Amsterdam: John Benjamins Publishing Company.

Myler, Neil & Andrew Nevins. 2014. *Inalienable Possession and the Morphosyntax of 'Brown-Eyed'*, abstract.

Teleman, Ulf, Staffan Hellberg & Erik Andersson. 1999. *Svenska Akademiens grammatik*. Stockholm: Norstedts.

Wangensteen, Boye (ed.). 2005. *Bokmålsordboka – definisjons- og rettskrivingsordbok*. Oslo: Kunnskapsforlaget.

Part II

Squibs

Chapter 11

On a "make-believe" argument for Case Theory

Jonathan David Bobaljik
University of Connecticut

> I argue here that evidence from Icelandic challenges one argument for Case Theory given in Chomsky's seminal paper *On Binding*. Chomsky suggested that a locality (adjacency) condition on structural case assignment explains the systematic absence of ditransitive ECM verbs. I argue here that Icelandic lacks this adjacency condition: structural Case in Icelandic is available to the second argument of a ditransitive in Icelandic. The Case-theoretic account would predict that Icelandic should therefore contrast with English and allow ditransitive ECM constructions. It does not. The absence of ditransitive ECM predicates is thus part of a broader generalization than Case Theory can explain.

1 The *make-believe* argument

Chomsky (1980: 29), in the paper introducing GB Case Theory, notes the absence of ditransitive ECM verbs, and suggests that Case provides a straightforward account of this lexical gap. While there are double object constructions like (1) and ECM (equivalently Raising-to-Object) predicates like (2), the two properties do not cooccur with a single predicate. There are no ditransitive ECM predicates, neither of the double object type (3a) nor with a matrix PP internal argument (3c).

(1)   Leo gave Julia a book.

(2)   Leo believes Julia$_j$ [t$_j$ to have won].

(3)   a. *Leo convinced Sarah Julia$_j$ [t$_j$ to have won].
        b. *Leo persuaded Sarah Julia$_j$ [t$_j$ to win].
        c. *Leo appealed to Sarah Julia$_j$ [t$_j$ to be nominated].

Jonathan David Bobaljik. 2017. On a "make-believe" argument for Case Theory. In Michelle Sheehan & Laura R. Bailey (eds.), *Order and structure in syntax II: Subjecthood and argument structure*, 277–283. Berlin: Language Science Press.

Jonathan David Bobaljik

Verbs that select an infinitive and two other arguments are systematically control predicates, or allow a *for* complement:

(4) a. Leo convinced Sarah$_i$ [PRO$_i$ to win].
    b. Leo appealed to Sarah$_i$ [PRO$_i$ to (let him) win].
    c. Leo appealed to Sarah [for Julia to be nominated].

This is a curious gap, inasmuch as semantically, verbs like *convince* and *persuade* seem to mean roughly a kind of causative of *believe* (thus 5 implies 6). There is no obvious reason why a verb meaning *make-believe* should not be able to have the range of arguments available to *believe*, plus a causer.

(5) Sarah convinced/persuaded Leo [that Julia won].

(6) Leo believes [that Julia won].

Chomsky argues that Case Theory accounts straightforwardly for this gap: structural case assignment is only possible to the adjacent complement of the verb, and the higher internal argument, whether an NP or PP, will invariably disrupt the adjacency between the verb and the infinitival subject required for structural case assignment.[1]

The recent ascendance of Dependent Case Theory [DCT] (Marantz 1991; Baker 2015) as an alternative to (L)GB Case Theory invites a reconsideration of established arguments for the latter. Under the strongest version of DCT, the syntactic distribution of NPs is not regulated by case (or Case), rather, NPs are assigned a particular morphological case as a function of the grammatical structure in which they are found. As such, the explanation of the contrast in (2–3) originally sketched by Chomsky is unavailable under DCT, and thus constitutes a prima facie argument against a strong DCT. In this squib, I argue that Chomsky's argument that Case is implicated does not withstand scrutiny. Specifically, the contrast in (2–3) is replicated in Icelandic, although it can be shown that there is no intervention (or adjacency) effect on structural accusative case assignment in that language. This yields two conclusions: the absence of ditransitive ECM constructions is not a language-particular quirk of English, but at the same time, GB/MP-style Case Theory is not a viable explanation of the gap. After presenting

---

[1] This argument is revived in Boeckx & Hornstein (2005) with more modern technology: in place of adjacency, Boeckx & Hornstein (2005) follow Bošković (2002) in claiming that structural case requires movement, and posit a structure under which movement across the higher NP in examples parallel to (3a) violates relativized minimality (they do not mention the PP cases). Boeckx & Hornstein (2005) claim that the case on the theme in (1) is inherent and thus not subject to minimality/adjacency. This is implausible in Icelandic, see note 2.

11 On a "make-believe" argument for Case Theory

this argument, I will speculate that the absence of ditransitive ECM predicates is plausibly a special case of the oft-cited generalization that a single underived predicate may take no more than three obligatory arguments (see e.g., Pesetsky 1995).

2 Icelandic

Icelandic has played a significant role in discussions of case across multiple generative frameworks, especially since the seminal article by Zaenen et al. (1985). A central finding is that Icelandic (descriptively) lacks the adjacency or intervention condition on structural (accusative) case which plays the key role in Chomsky's account of why (3a) is excluded. The main observation comes from double-object constructions in Icelandic of the *give* type, illustrated in (7):

(7) a. Jón   gaf Ólafi   bókina.
    Jon.NOM gave Olaf.DAT book.the.ACC
    'Jon gave Olaf the book.' (Holmberg & Platzack 1995: 187)

   b. Ólafi   var gefin bókin.
      Olaf.DAT was given book.the.NOM
      'Olaf was given the book.' (Falk 1990)

   c. Það hafa einhverjum strák   verið gefnar gjafir.
      EXPL have some.DAT boy.DAT been given.PL gifts.NOM.
      'Some boy has been given presents.' (Holmberg & Nikanne 2002: 99)

Of the two internal arguments of ditransitive construction in Icelandic, the higher one (the dative NP in 7a) becomes the subject in the passive, but the lower one in the configuration in (7a) undergoes the case alternation which is diagnostic of structural case: accusative in the active, but nominative in the passive.[2]

---

[2] One might question whether the case alternation in passive is sufficient evidence that the accusative on the theme is structural case. The literature at least since Andrews (1982) has noted that Icelandic has both inherent and structural accusative, and these are distinguished precisely by this diagnostic. For example, inherent accusative (as on the subject of *vanta* 'lack'), unlike structural accusative, is preserved in the passive of an ECM complement, as shown in the following:

(i) Han telur mig   vanta peninga.
    he believes me.ACC lack money
    'He believes me to lack money.'

(ii) Mig   er talið   vanta peninga.
     me.ACC is believed lack money
     'I am believed to lack money.' (Andrews 1982)

These examples have received extensive scrutiny in the literature since Zaenen et al. (1985), and it is very firmly established that the dative is the subject in (7b) (for example, it constitutes the associate in the transitive expletive construction 7c) and the nominative is an object.[3] Whatever the analysis, these examples establish the baseline: in Icelandic, structural case is available to the lower of two internal arguments in a ditransitive construction. If accusative is assigned by (a functional projection associated with) the verb, then (7a) and related examples show that this assignment is not subject to an adjacency or intervention condition.[4]

Like English, Icelandic also has ECM verbs, like 'believe':

(8) *Ég tel   Harald   hafa   unnið.*
    I   believe Harald.ACC have.WIN won
    'I believe Harald to have won.'

And like English, the 'convince' type verbs, taking an upstairs internal argument, may take a finite or an infinitive (object control) complement, but disallow ECM:[5]

(9) a. *Ég sannfærði þá   um [að Harald-ur   hefði unnið].*
       I   convinced them P   that Harald-NOM had   won
       'I convinced them that Harald had won.'
   b. *Ég sannfærði Harald   um [að PRO vinna].*
       I   convinced Harald.ACC P   to   win.INF
       'I convinced Harald to win.'
   c. * *Ég sannfærði þá   um [Harald   hafa   unnið].*
       I   convinced them P   Harald.ACC have.INF won
       'I convinced them Harald to have won.'

---

[3] As Holmberg (1994) and Holmberg & Platzack (1995) discuss, an 'inverted' order is also possible: the nominative theme may raise to subject position with this class of verbs, but this stems from an 'inverted' order in the active, in which the theme precedes and c-commands the goal.

[4] Holmberg & Nikanne (2002) argue that nominative case is subject to an intervention effect, accounting for the absence of impersonal passives of double-object constructions. In theory, one could maintain an intervention-like locality condition on all structural case in Icelandic, but then posit an additional case-assigning head below the indirect object in examples like (7a); see Svenonius (2006). The source of structural accusative does not bear on the argument made in this squib; the important fact is that it is available to the lower NP in a ditransitive construction. As noted above, the accusative in (7a) patterns with structural, rather than inherent, case in Icelandic, where the distinction is sharper than in English: inherent case in Icelandic, unlike structural case, fails to alternate in the periphrastic passive, and other contexts.

[5] The verb meaning 'convince' in this context happens to be a particle verb, but this is not relevant to the generalization as just stated – there are evidently no verbs with the frame in (9c) with or without a particle.

Note finally, that Icelandic has predicates like *virðast* 'seem' which (i) select an infinitive complement, (ii) treat the subject of that complement (*María* in 10) as a matrix object in an ECM-like fashion, and (iii) select a second internal NP argument, distinct from the embedded subject (*Haraldi* in 10). Crucially, though, all such verbs lack an external argument of the matrix predicate, and thus have a dative-nominative case array: the embedded subject behaves in the matrix clause as a nominative object (and not as a matrix subject).

(10)   Harald-i   virðist María   vera   þreytt.
       Harald-DAT seems Maria.NOM be.INF tired
       'Maria seems to Harald to be tired.'

Icelandic has more options than can be seen in English, but in key respects, Icelandic is like English, lacking ditransitive ECM predicates. However, since Icelandic allows structural accusative to be assigned 'across' an intervening NP or PP, the account given by Chomsky (and Boeckx & Hornstein 2005) does not extend to Icelandic.

3 Conclusion

Chomsky's intriguing observation that there are no ditransitive ECM verbs holds of Icelandic as well, a language with an English-like ECM construction. This is in and of itself interesting, since it affirms Chomsky's suggestion that this gap in the lexicon is systematic, and not accidental. At the same time, Icelandic undermines the proposed analysis of this gap in terms of Case Theory (and thus the corresponding argument for Case Theory). Since Icelandic evidently lacks the adjacency requirement that English (supposedly) has, that requirement cannot be the source of the absence of ditransitive ECM verbs across both languages.

What direction might an alternative account take? I suggest that it is not implausible to see the absence of ditransitive ECM verbs as part of the broader generalization that there is an apparent upper bound on the number of arguments a non-derived predicate may take as part of its argument structure.[6] Although there is some dissent, general opinion seems to place that limit at three.[7] A ditransitive verb like *give* or *put* takes the maximum, with three arguments. So too do object control predicates *convince* and *appeal* likewise take three arguments

---

[6] Derived predicates, such as causatives, applicative, and other types of complex predicates, may take more.

[7] Lisa Travis points me to Carter (1976) for the suggestion that the limit is four, on the basis of verbs like *trade*: *John traded his cobra to Mary for something.*

apiece: an external NP, an internal NP or PP argument, and the infinitival complement. If the non-thematic position associated with raising predicates counts as one argument towards the maximum, then Chomsky's generalization is subsumed under this larger one: one argument of the raising verb is the infinitive complement (LFG's XCOMP), and a second the athematic position that is the landing site of raising (whether to subject or object). This leaves only one 'free' slot, which may be an external argument (as in *believe*) or an internal one, as in *seem* (with a PP experiencer). But crucially not both. I leave open here the explanation for the apparent limit to three arguments per predicate, noting, though, that as NPs, PPs, CPs and infinitival clauses (whether those are CP or IP) all contribute towards the maximum, but only a subset of these bear Case, any attempt to account for these effects in terms of Case will necessarily cover only a subset of the generalization.

Acknowledgments

This squib arose out of a discussion with Susi Wurmbrand, Željko Bošković, and Mark Baker. I thank Gísli Rúnar Harðarson, Höskuldur Þráinsson, and Jim Wood, for discussion of Icelandic (and for the examples). For other feedback, I thank two anonymous reviewers, as well as Lisa Travis, Richard Larson and other audience members at McGill, EGG Brno, UConn, ReCoS Villa Salmi, and Stony Brook University.

References

Andrews, Avery. 1982. The representation of case in Modern Icelandic. In Joan Bresnan (ed.), *The mental representation of grammatical relations*, 424–503. Cambridge, Mass: MIT Press.
Baker, Mark. 2015. *Case: Its principles and parameters.* Cambridge: Cambridge University Press.
Boeckx, Cedric & Norbert Hornstein. 2005. A gap in the ECM paradigm. *Linguistic Inquiry* 36. 437–441.
Bošković, Željko. 2002. A-Movement and the EPP. *Syntax* 5. 167–218.
Carter, Richard. 1976. Some constraints on possible words. *Semantikos* 1. 27–66.
Chomsky, Noam. 1980. On binding. *Linguistic Inquiry* 11. 1–46.
Falk, Cecilia. 1990. On double object constructions. *Working Papers in Scandinavian Syntax* 46. 53–100.

Holmberg, Anders. 1994. The pros and cons of agreement in Scandinavian impersonals. In Guglielmo Cinque, Jan Koster, Jean-Yves Pollock, Luigi Rizzi & Raffaella Zanuttini (eds.), *Paths toward Universal Grammar: Studies in honor of Richard S. Kayne*, 217–336. Washington: Georgetown University Press.

Holmberg, Anders & Urpo Nikanne. 2002. Expletives, subjects, and topics in Finnish. In Peter Svenonius (ed.), *Subjects, expletives, and the EPP*, 71–105. Oxford: Oxford University Press.

Holmberg, Anders & Christer Platzack. 1995. *The role of inflection in the syntax of the Scandinavian languages*. Oxford: Oxford University Press.

Marantz, Alec. 1991. Case and licensing. In German Westphal and Benjamin Ao and Hee-Rahk Chae (ed.), *Proceedings of ESCOL 91*, 234–253. Cornell Linguistics Club.

Pesetsky, David. 1995. *Zero syntax: Experiencers and cascades*. Cambridge, MA: The MIT Press.

Svenonius, Peter. 2006. Case alternations and the Icelandic passive and middle. In Satu Manninen, Diane Nelson, Katrin Hiietam, Elsi Kaiser & Virve Vihman (eds.), *Passives and impersonals in European languages*. Amsterdam: John Benjamins.

Zaenen, Annie, Joan Maling & Höskuldur Thráinsson. 1985. Case and grammatical functions: The Icelandic passive. *Natural Language and Linguistic Theory* 3. 441–483.

Chapter 12

Semantic characteristics of recursive compounds

Makiko Mukai
University of Kochi

> In this paper I propose a structure for recursive compounds, such as peanut butter sandwich in Phase Theory (Chomsky 2008). I propose that a root without a categorical feature is merged with a category-determining feature (Marantz 1997) in the narrow syntax and another root is merged to form a compound word. I also argue that another root without categorical feature is merged to form a right-branching recursive compound. On the other hand, a linking element is there for the sake of asymmetry (cf. Okubo 2014): it checks the head of the two-member compound and another [√ROOT n] can be merged. As a result the final categorising nominal head is the head of the whole compound word.

1 Introduction

(1) [mail [delivery service]]
 'delivery service of mails'

(2) [[chocolate chip] cookie]
 'cookie cooked with flakes of chocolate'

(3) Swedish
 [barn-[bok-klub]]
 [child-[book-club]]
 'book club for children'

(4) Swedish
[[röd-vins-s]-flaska]
[[red-wine-LE]-bottle]
'bottle for red wine'

(5) Japanese
[doitsu [bungaku kyookai]]
[Germany [literature association]]
'literature association in Germany'

(6) Japanese
[[nyuugaku shiken] taisaku]
[[entrance exam] study]
'study for entrance exam'

The interpretation of the whole compounds, is, for example, *book club for children*, not *club for children's books* in (5). This recursive compound is called right-branching recursive compounds. In contrast, in the examples (2,4,6) the modifier at the right hand expands the already-made compound. This type is called left-branching recursive compounds.

2 Proposed structure

According to Miyagawa & Nóbrega (2015) merge is the recursive operation of the language faculty. I follow this claim and use Phase Theory (Chomsky 2008; Marantz 1997) for a structure of compounds. I propose structures for right-branching and left-branching recursive compounds in Phase Theory.

(7)

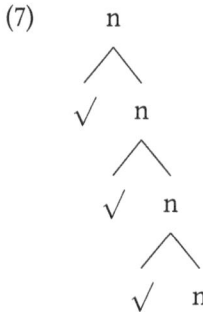

12 Semantic characteristics of recursive compounds

The structure (7) is derived as follows. Once the two-member compound is derived, another derivation can take place. Another root without any features is merged. This is the derivation of the right-branching recursive compounds, like (1,3,5). If one assumes that both constituents of the compound are merged with category-defining element, the LF does not see which element is the head, and the derivation crashes at the LF level. So in my proposed structure, only one root is merged with a cateogory-defining head, turning the root into an *n*. This is labelling in terms of Chomsky (2008). The head of the whole compound is the category-defining element. The whole compound is transferred to the interpretational representation and spelled out as a phase (Chomsky 2008).

(8)

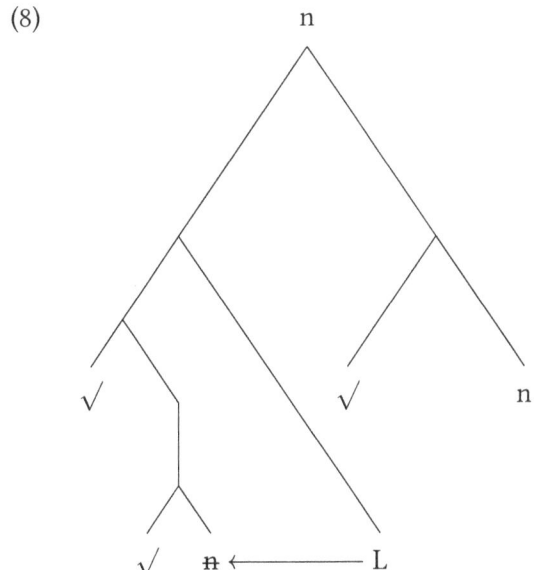

For left-branching recursive compounds, there is a linking element in left-branching recursive compounds, phonetically realised in Mainland Scandinavian but not in Japanese or English (see 4). I propose that the linking element has an uninterpretable feature (cf. Okubo 2014) and checks the category-defining feature. The resulting structure is sent to the interpretational component and spelled out as phase.

The resulting structure is merged with another root, which is merged with a category-defining head in parallel. As a result the head of the whole compound is the right-most category-defining head and this compound is transferred to the interpretational representation and spelled out as phase.

287

3 Conclusion

In this paper, the author proposed a structure for recursive compounds in Phase Theory. If the linking morpheme does not check the categorical features of the non-head, the structure will be impossible, having two heads. Thus, in the languages without recursive compounding, there is no linking element. Assuming that the two-member is a phase we can capture the word-like accent characteristic, as opposed to phrase-like right-branching recursive compounds.

I would like to thank Anders Holmberg, Hideki Kishimoto, and Shigeru Miyagawa for their discussions on this topic. Also, I would like to thank the 8 English native speakers on their judgments for the data.

References

Chomsky, Noam. 2008. On phases. In Roberto Freidin, Carlos P. Otero & Maria L. Zubizarreta (eds.), *Foundational issues in linguistic theory: Essays in honor of Jean-Roger Vergnaud*, 133–166. Cambridge, MA: MIT Press.

Marantz, Alec. 1997. No escape from syntax: Don't try morphological analysis in the privacy of your own lexicon. *University of Pennsylvania Working Papers in Linguistics* 4(2). 201–225.

Miyagawa, Shigeru & Vitor A. Nóbrega. 2015. The precedence of syntax in the rapid emergence of human language in evolution as defined by the integration hypothesis. *Frontiers in Psychology* 271(6).

Okubo, Tatsuhiro. 2014. Linking elements as expletives in distributed morphology. In *Proceedings of the 31st Annual Meeting of the English Linguistic Society of Japan*, 130–136.

Chapter 13

Expletive passives in Scandinavian – with and without objects

Elisabet Engdahl
University of Gothenburg

> Holmberg (2002) proposes an account for the variation concerning expletives, participial agreement and word order in periphrastic passives in the Mainland Scandinavian languages in terms of parameters. In this short article, the predictions of Holmberg's proposal are evaluated against a corpus study of expletive passives. It turns out that only Norwegian 1 (*bokmål*) behaves as expected given Holmberg's parameter settings; it lacks participle agreement and only displays the PCP DO word order, with few exceptions. Danish, which has the same parameter settings as Norwegian 1, is shown to have had the DO PCP order in earlier stages and this order is still used in many dialects. Norwegian 2 (*nynorsk*) and Swedish are predicted to allow both the PCP DO order and the DO PCP order, but it is shown that Norwegian 2 uses the same order as Norwegian 1, PCP DO, whereas Swedish – to the limited extent that the periphrastic passive is actually used in expletive passives – uses the DO PCP order. In both Danish and Swedish, the DO PCP order is facilitated by an incorporated negation in the DO, just as in active clauses, a fact that should presumably be reflected in the analysis.

1 Introduction

The interplay between agreement and word order in expletive passive constructions in Mainland Scandinavian has received considerable attention starting with Christensen & Taraldsen (1989). At first glance, the pattern seems quite clear: when the direct object (DO) precedes the participle (PCP), the latter shows agreement, but when the PCP precedes the DO, the form of the PCP is consistently neuter singular, as shown by the Swedish examples in (1).[1]

---

[1] I follow Holmberg (2002: 104) in glossing the expletive subject as EX and non-agreeing participles simply as PCP. Agreeing participles are glossed as C for common gender singular, N for neuter singular. The gender distinction is neutralised in the plural, glossed PL.

Elisabet Engdahl. 2017. Expletive passives in Scandinavian – with and without objects. In Michelle Sheehan & Laura R. Bailey (eds.), *Order and structure in syntax II: Subjecthood and argument structure*, 289–306. Berlin: Language Science Press.

Elisabet Engdahl

(1) Swedish (Holmberg & Nikanne 2002: 86)

a. Det **blev** **skrivet** / *****skrivna** tre böcker om detta.
   EX became written.N / written.PL three books about this
   'Three books were written about this.'

b. Det **blev** tre böcker ***skrivet** / **skrivna** om detta.
   EX became three books written.N / written.PL about this
   'Three books were written about this.'

In his detailed study of these constructions, Holmberg (2002) proposes several parameters in order to account for the variation. One parameter determines whether or not the expletive and the participle have ɸ-features.[2] In Swedish, both the expletive *det* ('it', neut. sing.) and the participle are assumed to have ɸ-features. Consequently the participle can agree either with the expletive or with the DO and both orders are possible, as shown in (1). In Danish, both the expletive *der* ('there') and the participle lack ɸ-features and only the PCP DO order should be possible, see (2) (cf. Holmberg p. 104). Norwegian displays more variation; the *bokmål* varieties (Holmberg's Norwegian 1) use *det* as expletive and lack participle agreement (3), whereas the *nynorsk* varieties (Holmberg's Norwegian 2) have agreeing participles (4) and hence are predicted to allow the order DO PCP.[3]

(2) Danish (Holmberg & Nikanne 2002: 104)

a. Der **blev** **skrivet** tre bøger om dette.
   EX became written.PCP three books about this
   'Three books were written about this.'

b. * Der **blev** tre bøger **skrivet** om dette.
   EX became three books written.PCP about this

(3) Norwegian 1 (cf. Holmberg & Nikanne 2002: 104)

a. Det **ble** **skrevet** tre bøker om dette.
   EX became written.PCP three books about this
   'Three books were written about this.'

b. * Det **ble** tre bøker **skrevet** om dette.
   EX became three books written.PCP about this

---

[2] See the helpful survey in the Appendix (Holmberg 2002: 125f).
[3] In addition Holmberg identifies a third variety, Norwegian 3, which uses the locative expletive *der* but has participle agreement. He also notes that there is actually more dialectal variation in Norway. This is confirmed in a recent study by Aa et al. (2014).

13 Expletive passives in Scandinavian – with and without objects

(4) Norwegian 2 (cf. Holmberg & Nikanne 2002: 104)

    a. *Det **vart** skrive / *skrivne tre bøker um dette.*
       EX became written.N / written.PL three books about this
       'Three books were written about this.'

    b. *Det **vart** tre bøker *skrive / skrivne um dette.*
       EX became three books written.N / written.PL about this
       'Three books were written about this.'

Another parameter proposed by Holmberg (2002: 106f) is whether the Participle Phrase (PrtP) is a phase or not, in the sense of Chomsky (2001).[4] In Norwegian 2 and Swedish, where PrtP is assumed to be a phase, the participle is "formally stronger" and the PrtP is "more sentence-like" than in Danish and Norwegian 1. If the PrtP is not a separate phase, examples like (3a) in Norwegian 1 will consist of a single array with the expletive merged with VP, shown in (5a) before spell-out and spelled out as (5b).

(5) Norwegian 1 (Holmberg & Nikanne 2002: 106)

    a. C [$_{TP}$ det T [$_{AuxP}$ bli [$_{PrtP}$ t Prt [$_{vP}$ V DP]]]]

    b. *Det **ble** skrevet mange bøker.*
       EX became written.PCP many books
       'Many books were written.'

If PrtP is a separate phase, as in Swedish, the lexical array is divided into two subarrays, according to Holmberg (2002: 106). One contains C, T and the auxiliary and the other contains the participle, V and the DP. The expletive may belong to either array, which accounts for the two word orders. If the expletive belongs to the second subarray, the derivation will be as in (5), but if it belongs to the first subarray, the DP object has to move to SpecPrtP in order to satisfy the EPP-feature on the head. Holmberg's illustration is given in (6) (cf. the Swedish example in (1b)).

(6) Swedish (Holmberg & Nikanne 2002: 107)

    a. C [$_{TP}$ det T [$_{AuxP}$ t bli [$_{PrtP}$ DP Prt [$_{vP}$ V t]]]]

    b. *Det **blev** många böcker **skrivna**.*
       EX became many books written.PL
       'Many books were written.'

---

[4] This parameter is necessary in order to account for the word order and agreement patterns in corresponding structures in English and Icelandic, see Holmberg (2002: 105).

Elisabet Engdahl

In this article I show that the pattern of variation is more complex than assumed by Holmberg and that other factors need to be taken into account, in particular whether or not the object has an incorporated negation.

2 Transitive expletive constructions, word order and agreement

Before discussing to what extent the patterns shown in (1)–(4) reflect the ways expletive passives are used, a few words about the distribution of the two passive forms in Mainland Scandinavian are in order, viz. the periphrastic and the morphological passive. For obvious reasons, Holmberg (2002) limits his discussion to periphrastic passives, i.e. passives formed with an auxiliary and a participle, as shown in (1)–(4).[5] The morphological passive is formed by adding -s to the infinitive or the tensed form of the verb. The choice of passive form – periphrastic passive or *s*-passive – depends on several factors such as genre, tense, mood, animacy of the subject, control, event structure and to some extent lexical preferences (see Sundman 1987, Engdahl 1999; 2006 and Laanemets 2012: 47–61 for overviews and De Cuypere et al. 2014 for a multivariate statistical analysis). The data in the next three subsections come from the extensive corpus study in Laanemets (2012), complemented by some specific searches for impersonal passives.[6]

2.1 Swedish

In Swedish there is a clear preference for the *s*-passive in general; *s*-passive is used in 97% of all passive verb phrases in written texts (newspapers and novels) and in 85% of all passive phrases in informal conversations (Laanemets 2012: 92). This also applies to transitive expletive passives; only 1–3% are *bli*-passives, varying somewhat with genre.[7] This means that Holmberg's examples in (1) are rather unusual. The normal way of conveying this message in Swedish would be with an *s*-passive as in (7).

---

[5]In Danish, Norwegian 1 and Swedish, the auxiliary is *bli* 'become' (*blive* in Danish); in Norwegian 2 and some Swedish dialects, the preferred auxiliary is *varda* 'become'.

[6]Laanemets (2012) extracted *s*- and *bli(ve)*-passives from comparable written and spoken corpora in Danish, Norwegian (*bokmål*) and Swedish and annotated around 11 300 passive examples.

[7]Hedlund (1992: Chapter 3) discusses *bli*-passives without mentioning their limited distribution. Periphrastic passives with *få* 'get' are discussed in Larsson (2012).

13 Expletive passives in Scandinavian – with and without objects

(7) Swedish
*Det har **skrivits** tre böcker om detta.*
EX has written.s three books about this
'Three books have been written about this.'

Among the 3176 Swedish passive examples analysed by Laanemets, there were 108 impersonal passives with expletive subjects and of these only three were transitive *bli*-passives. One example from spoken Swedish is shown in (8).

(8) Swedish, spoken (Laanemets 2012)
*men jag har en känsla av att det **blir** inte någonting **gjort** där ändå*
but I have a feeling of that EX becomes not something done.N there still
'but I have a feeling that still nothing gets done there'

All three examples had the word order DO PCP. They resemble the authentic examples in (9).

(9) Swedish (Engdahl 1999: 31)
 a. *Det **blev** inte så mycket **sagt** kanske.*
 EX became not so much.N said.N maybe
 'Not much was said, maybe'.
 b. *Men då **blev** det ingenting **gjort**.*
 but then became EX nothing.N done.N
 'But nothing got done then.'

The examples in (8) and (9) sound quite natural, unlike (1). Note that they all contain a negative element, either the negation *inte* 'not' or *ingenting* 'nothing'. In order to find a wider range of examples, Anu Laanemets and I carried out a search in an 800 million subcorpus of *Korp*, looking for instances of this pattern, i.e. *det*, followed or preceded by a form of the lemma BLI, with an optional adverb or negation, a quantifying pronoun or numeral, a noun and a participle.[8] The search produced 283 examples which gives us a relative frequency of 0.4 per

---
[8]We searched in newspapers, novels and blogs using the schematic search string in (i):

(i) {det BLI | BLI det} []{0,1} {INGEN | MYCKEN | MÅNGEN | NÅGON | artikel | pronomen | grundtal } []{0,1} PCP ej-NN

See Engdahl & Laanemets (2015a) for details about the corpus searches.

million words. This can be compared to transitive expletive *s*-passives as in (7) which were used around 50 times per million words in the same corpora, i.e. a hundred times more often.

Some representative examples from the corpus search are given in (10).[9] The participle agrees with the preceding DO, as predicted.

(10) Swedish (*Korp*)

a. *Det **blev** ingen post **utdelad** alls igår.*
   EX became no post.C distributed.C at-all yesterday
   'No post whatsoever was distributed yesterday.'

b. *Jag sitter där vid datorn och ska skriva, jag vet vad jag*
   I sit there by computer.DEF and shall write I know what I
   *ska göra men det **blir** ändå inget **gjort**.*
   shall do but EX becomes still nothing.N done.N
   'I sit there in front of the computer, about to write, I know what I should do, but still nothing gets done.'

c. *Utan deras försörjning och rimliga villkor, **blir** det inga*
   without their support and reasonable conditions become EX no
   *filmer **gjorda**, inga böcker **skrivna**, inga låtar **komponerade**.*
   films made.PL no books written.PL no songs composed.PL
   'Without their support and reasonable conditions, there won't be any films made, books written or songs composed.'

This type of expletive passive is used primarily when an expected result does not occur: about two thirds of the hits are negated. The construction is also used to emphasize that a result was obtained, (11a), often with a numeric specification, as in (11b,c), cf. (1b).

(11) Swedish (*Korp*)

a. *"så hit med en skyffel så det **blir** något **gjort**."*
   so here with a shovel so EX becomes something.N done.N
   'Hand me a shovel so that something gets done.'

b. *I går **blev** det bara två mål **insläppta**,*
   yesterday became EX only two goals let-in.PL
   'Yesterday only two goals were let in.'

---

[9] The whole dataset with our annotations is available: https://svn.spraakbanken.gu.se/sb-arkiv/pub/engdahl/Opersonlig_passiv.

c. *Allt som allt **blev** det fem hus **byggda**.*
   all as all became EX five houses built.PL
   'Altogether there were five houses built.'

We also searched for the order PCP DO and found one example, see (12a), where the participle is in the neuter singular form.

(12) Swedish (*Korp*)
   a. *Så det **blev** inte **skrivet** någon berättelse om loppet.*
      so EX became not written.PCP any story.C about race.DEF
      'So no story about the race was written.'
   b. *? Så det **blev** ingen berättelse om loppet **skriven**.*
      so EX became no story.C about race.DEF written.C
   c. *Så det **blev** ingen berättelse **skriven** om loppet.*
      so EX became no story.C written.C about race.DEF

This example is actually quite similar to Holmberg's (1a); note the complex noun phrase placed after the participle. Placing the entire noun phrase before the participle is less felicitous (12b), whereas splitting it up is OK (12c), just as in Holmberg's (1b).

We can conclude that practically all the authentic examples in Swedish have the DO PCP order and that the DO is very often negated. The opposite order is grammatical, but used very sparingly, primarily when some other factor such as weight influences the word order. One way of integrating this finding with Holmberg's analysis would be to assume something along the following lines: whether the expletive belongs to the first or the second subarray depends on the complexity of the DP and whether or not there is a negation present.

3 Danish

In Danish, the *blive*-passive and the *s*-passive are distributed more evenly than in Swedish. *s*-passive is primarily used in the present tense and with infinitives, especially following modal verbs. The periphrastic *blive*-passive dominates all the other tenses. Heltoft & Falster Jakobsen (1996) claim that the choice of passive form reflects a mood distinction in Danish; *s*-passive is used in objective statements whose validity is independent of the speaker, whereas *blive*-passive is preferred when the speaker makes a subjective judgment about some event that s/he has first hand knowledge about.[10] Among the 4765 Danish passive examples analysed by Laanemets (2012), roughly 10% (474) were impersonal passives and of these 185 were transitive *blive*-passives, as illustrated in (13).

(13) a. Danish, spoken (Laanemets 2012)
 der **bliver** næsten ikke **optaget** nye elever
 EX becomes almost not admitted.PCP new pupils
 'Hardly any new pupils are admitted.'

 b. Danish, written (Laanemets 2012)
 Der er **blevet produceret** flere terrorister i de sidste år
 EX is become produced.PCP more terrorists in the last years
 pga. den politik,
 because-of that policy
 'More terrorists have been produced in recent years because of that policy.'

All of these examples had the word order PCP DO, without participle agreement, as expected on Holmberg's analysis. In order to find out if the DO PCP order is used at all, we carried out a similar search to the one in Swedish in the 56 million word corpus *KorpusDK*. We found altogether eleven examples, eight of which were negated, see (14b,c).

(14) Danish (*KorpusDK*)
 a. Hver gang der **bliver** en ny **indlagt**, skal man sætte sig
 every time EX becomes a new admitted.PCP shall one put REFL
 ind i patientens journaler.
 into in patient.DEF.POSS notes
 'Every time a new patient is admitted, one has to familiarize oneself with his/her notes.'

 b. Der **blev** ingenting **sagt**, før det ringede på døren,
 EX became nothing said.PCP before EX rang on door.DEF
 'Nothing was said before the door bell rang.'

 c. Ifølge SAS **blev** der ingen fejl **fundet** på nogle af
 according SAS became EX no fault found.PCP on any of

---

[10] This view is also put forward in the Danish reference grammar (Hansen & Heltoft 2011: 747ff). See Laanemets (2012: 101ff) for a critical assessment.

flyene,
planes.DEF

'According to SAS, no fault was found on any of the planes.'

These examples resemble the Swedish ones except that the participles lack agreement. The DO PCP order is also used in spoken Danish, as shown in (15). The examples come from the *Nordic Dialect Corpus* (*NDC*).

(15) a. Danish (*NDC*, østjylland2)
 *der **blev** inte noget **gjort** ved det_der*
 EX became not anything done.PCP with that
 'Nothing was done with that.'

 b. Danish (*NDC*, fyn2)
 *klokken fem om morgenen der **blev** der én **skudt** ned*
 clock.DEF five in morning there became EX one.C shot.PCP down
 'At 5 o'clock in the morning one person was shot down there.'

According to Pedersen (2017), the DO PCP order is, or has been, possible in all Danish dialects and is still the preferred order in Sønderjylland (North Schleswig) as shown in (16).

(16) Danish, Sønderjylland (K. M. Pedersen, p.c.)
 *da **blev** der en stor gryde grød **kogt** hver dag*
 then became EX a large pot porridge.C cooked.PCP every day
 'Then a large pot of porridge was cooked every day.'

Note that the participle has the neuter singular form even when placed after a non-neuter object in (15b) and (16). In older Danish, when the DO PCP order was more common, agreeing participles were used, as shown in the following examples from Høysgaard (1752[1979]), supplied by K. M. Pedersen (e-mail, April 2015). Later grammars such as Mikkelsen (1894; 1911[1975]) do not have any examples with agreeing participles.

(17) Danish (Høysgaard 1752[1979]: 327)
 *Der **blev** en sølvske **staalen**.*
 EX became a silverspoon.C stolen.C
 'A silver spoon was stolen.'

(18) Danish (Høysgaard 1752[1979]: 345)
*Der **blev** en Död **udbaaren**.*
EX became a dead.C out-carried.C
'A dead person was carried out.'

In contemporary Danish, only the dialect spoken in the island of Bornholm has agreeing participles, see the example in (19).[11]

(19) Danish, Bornholm (K. M. Pedersen, e-mail, April 2015)
*Dær **ble** ejnj værja **tesatter**.*
EX became a sword.MASC added.MASC
'A sword was added.'

We conclude that although the dominant word order pattern in modern Danish is PCP DO, the DO PCP order, without participle agreement, is available for many dialect speakers and is often used with quantified, especially negated objects like *ingenting*. It would be interesting to look closer at the diachronic development of the modern Danish system.

4 Norwegian

The distribution of *s*- and *bli*-passive in Norwegian *bokmål* (Holmberg's Norwegian 1) resembles the situation in Danish. *S*-passive is only used in the present tense and infinitives. Among the 3096 examples analysed by Laanemets (2012), 238 were impersonal passives, of which 87 transitive *bli*-passives, see the examples in (20).

(20) Norwegian 1 (Laanemets 2012)

    a. *for det **ble** **bygd** veldig mye akkurat den tida*
       because EX became built.PCP very much exactly that time.DEF
       'because a lot was built right at that time'

    b. *Det **ble** ikke **funnet** tekniske bevis i kvinnens leilighet.*
       EX became not found.PCP technical evidence in woman.DEF.POSS flat
       'No technical evidence was found in the womans flat.'

---

[11]Pedersen (2013) shows that the use of *s*-passive in Bornholm also resembles the Swedish pattern.

13 Expletive passives in Scandinavian – with and without objects

All the examples in Laanemets (2012) had the order PCP DO, again as expected, and quantified objects were common. Using the same procedure as for Swedish and Danish, we investigated if the word order DO PCP is used in Norwegian 1. We searched in a 41.4 million word subcorpus of *Leksikografisk bokmålskorpus* (LBK) but only found a few examples.

(21) Norwegian (*LBK*)

a. *Dermed* **blir** *det mye vanndamp* **fordelt** *på hver*
with-this becomes EX much steam distributed.PCP on every
dråpe.
drop
'This way a lot of steam is distributed over each drop.'

b. *Ifølge Amnesty International* **ble** *det 5.000 uskyldige*
according Amnesty International became EX 5000 innocent
drept.
killed.PCP
'According to Amnesty International, 5000 innocent people were killed.'

We did not find any examples with negated pronouns or other quantified expressions, like *ingenting*, before the participle, i.e. Norwegian counterparts to (10) in Swedish or (14b) in Danish. This is presumably linked to the fact that Norwegian speakers are much less likely to prepose negated objects than Danish and Swedish speakers (see below).

With respect to *nynorsk*, Holmberg's Norwegian 2, there is variation in the choice of expletive and whether or not the participle shows agreement, but apparently not much variation with respect to word order (see Åfarli 2009; Aa et al. 2014: 218ff). The order PCP DO dominates strongly, just as in Norwegian 1. Only one example with a preposed negated DO was found in the Oslo corpus of *nynorsk* (3.8 million words), see (22). It is not possible to tell whether the participle agrees with *det* or *ingenting*, since both are neuter.

(22) Norwegian 2 (*Oslo corpus*)
Ei lang stund **vart** *det ingenting* **sagt.**
a long while became EX nothing.N said.N
'For a long while nothing was said.'

This resembles the examples found in Swedish and Danish. However, speakers of Norwegian 2 are less willing to accept preposed objects with numerical attributes, as in (11b,c) and (21b). The fact that Norwegian 2 speakers accept the DO PCP order when the DO is negated distinguishes them from Norwegian 1 speakers, but more informant studies are clearly needed here.

4.1 The NEG-DO PCP order

We have seen that when a direct object precedes the participle in expletive transitive *bli(ve)*-passives in Swedish and Danish, it is very often negated. This pattern is also used with active participles in Danish and Swedish, see (23).

(23) a. Danish (Engels 2012, example (6))
Manden havde måske ingenting sagt.
man.DEF had maybe nothing said.PCP
'Maybe the man hadn't said anything.'

b. Swedish (Engels 2012, example (6))
Mannen hade kanske ingenting sagt.
man.DEF had maybe nothing said.PCP
'Maybe the man hadn't said anything.'

This word order is often described as stylistically marked and reserved for formal and literary genres. However, Engels (2012) found that it is used both in spoken language and in blog texts on Google. She investigated the positioning of negated objects with five frequent verbs (the Scandinavian counterparts of *say, hear, see, get* and *do*) and found that 33% preceded the participle in Danish and 15% in Swedish, compared to 0% in Norwegian (see Engels 2012: Table 1).[12] It thus seems that one additional factor that affects the word order options is whether the language allows for incorporated negative objects to precede the participle. In Swedish, where *bli*-passives are unusual, they are primarily used with negated objects. In Danish, where expletive transitive *blive*-passives normally have the

---

[12] In Swedish, preposing of negated objects is also possible in *s*-passive.

(i) *Det har ingenting sagts (*ingenting) om detta.*
EX has nothing said.S about this
'Nothing has been said about this.'

(ii) *Det har (??mycket) sagts (ᵒᵏmycket) om detta.*
EX has said.S much about this
'Much has been said about this.'

word order PCP DO, most of the exceptions involve negated objects. And in Norwegian 1, where preposed negated objects are rare, we hardly find any deviations from the PCP DO order.

5 Double object constructions

Holmberg (2002) also discusses the word order options in double object constructions. For Swedish, he gives examples where either both objects follow the participle (24a) or where the indirect object (IO) precedes and the direct object follows the participle, (24b).

(24) a. Swedish (Holmberg 2002: 87)
*Det **blev** givet pojken presenter.*
EX became given.N boy.C.DEF presents
'The boy was given presents.'

b. Swedish (Holmberg 2002: 114)
*Det **blev** inte många barn **givna** presenter den julen.*
EX became not many children given.PL presents that Christmas.DEF
'Not may children were given presents that Christmas.'

The orders shown in (24) are grammatical, but hardly used. It is somewhat more common for both objects to precede the participle, especially if the indirect object is a pronoun, as also pointed out in Börjars & Vincent (2005). In that case the participle agrees with the direct object.

(25) Swedish (Teleman et al. 1999: 4:387)

a. *Det skulle **bli** oss en belöning **tilldelad**.*
EX should become us a reward.C awarded.C
'We were supposed to receive an award.'

b. *Det **blev** oss inte mycket **anförtrott**.*
EX became us not much.N confided.N
'Not much was confided to us.'

c. *Det **blev** ingen särskilt mycket **anförtrott**.*
EX became nobody very much.N confided.N
'Not much was confided to anybody.'

Note that the pronominal indirect object is shifted across the negation in (25b). In (25c) the negation is incorporated into the indirect object *ingen* ('nobody').[13] In both Norwegian 1 and 2, it seems that only the order PCP IO DO is used, see (26).[14]

(26) Norwegian 2 (Faarlund et al. 1997: 845)
 Det **blei nekta** oss adgang.
 EX became denied.PCP us admittance
 'We were denied admittance.'

Also in Danish, the preferred order is PCP IO DO, as in the following examples from *KorpusDK*.

(27) Danish (*KorpusDK*)

 a. Jeg skulle være naturlig, der **blev** ikke **pålagt** mig
  I should be natural EX beccame not imposed.PCP me
  noget.
  anything
  'I was supposed to be natural, nothing was imposed on me.'

---

[13]In this respect, the expletive double object passives differ from active versions. Whereas negated direct objects can be preposed, as shown in (23b), preposing a negated indirect object is not felicitous in Swedish.

(i) ?* Vi har ingen anförtrott särskilt mycket.
  we have nobody confided very much
  Intended: 'We have not confided very much to anybody.'

This was brought to my attention by Björn Lundqvist (e-mail, May 2016) who mentioned a similar observation concerning Norwegian in Lødrup (1989: 22).

[14]The order IO PCP is found in Norwegian *bli*-passives with extraposed clauses, as shown in (i).

(i) Norwegian (*LBK*)
 Det **blir** meg ofte **fortalt** at israelske soldater scorer så høyt på motivasjon.
 EX beccomes me often told.PCP that Israeli soldiers score so high on motivation
 'I am often told that Israeli soldiers score high on motivation.'

Engdahl & Laanemets (2015a) argue that this type should not be analysed as expletive passives, one reason being that they are grammatical in English, (ii), where expletive passives are ungrammatical (cf. Carnie & Harley 2005).

(ii) It has to be said that the budget proposal is unlikely to pass.

b. *Der **bliver** **pålagt** børn et alt for stort ansvar i*
EX becomes imposed.PCP children a too for big responsibility in
dag.
day
'A too big responsibility is imposed on children today.'

Our corpus searches also produced some examples with IO preceding PCP, as in the examples in (28).

(28) Danish (*KorpusDK*)

a. *De udførte blot de opgaver, der **blev** dem **pålagt** af*
they carried-out just the tasks that became them imposed.PCP by
folketinget,
parliament.DEF
'They only carried out the tasks that had been imposed on them by the parliament.'

b. *Vent og se, hvem der **bliver** dig **tildelt**.*
wait and see who that becomes you assigned.PCP.
'Wait and see who is asssigned to you.'

However, these are not expletive transitive constructions but ordinary passives where the DO has been relativized or questioned. In modern Danish, the expletive pro-form *der* is also used as relativizer ('that') in subject relatives and questions. Consequently examples may be ambiguous between an expletive and a personal passive, as discussed in Engdahl & Laanemets (2015b). An example is given in (29a) which can be analysed as a relative clause with either an expletive passive (29b), or a personal passive (29c).

(29) Danish (Engdahl & Laanemets 2015b: 314)

a. *Det er det forlig, der **bliver** refereret til.*
EX is this settlement DER becomes referred.PCP to

b. *Det er det forlig$_i$,* [$_{CP}$ [Ø][$_{IP}$ *der* bliver refereret til e_i]]
'It is this settlement there are references to.'

c. *Det er det forlig$_i$,* [$_{CP}$[*der*][$_{IP}$ e_i bliver refereret til]]
'It is this settlement that is being referred to.'

Elisabet Engdahl

6 Concluding remarks

Of the investigated language varieties, Norwegian 1 (*bokmål*) stands out as the only one that behaves as expected given Holmberg's parameters; it lacks participle agreement and only displays the PCP DO word order, with few exceptions. Danish, which has the same parameter settings as Norwegian 1, apparently had the DO PCP word order in earlier stages and this still shows up in many dialects. The assumed parameter settings for Swedish and Norwegian 2 (*nynorsk*) predict that these languages should allow both word orders. Nevertheless, there is very little evidence for this in actual use. The languages differ furthermore in which pattern is preferred; the PCP DO order is hardly used in Swedish, but is the preferred order in Norwegian 2, just as in Norwegian 1.

Although expletive *bli*-passives are very infrequent in Swedish compared with expletive *s*-passives, corpus studies have revealed a characteristic pattern where a quantified, often negated, DO precedes the participles, as illustrated in (10). The same type of DO occasionally appears preceding the participle in Danish which suggests that there may be a correlation between the availability of NEG-DO PCP order in expletive passives and in active clauses.

Acknowledgments

I am grateful to Anu Laanemets for discussions and for help with the corpus searches for this article. I would also like to thank Filippa Lindahl and Henrik Rosenkvist for comments on an earlier draft and members of the Grammar seminars in Gothenburg and Lund for stimulating questions and comments, in particular Lars-Olof Delsing, Verner Egerland, Gunlög Josefsson, Erik Petzell, Halldór Sigurðsson and Øystein Vangsnes.

Corpora

Korp: http://spraakbanken.gu.se/korp/
KorpusDK: http://ordnet.dk/korpusdk
Leksikografisk bokmålskorpus: http://www.hf.uio.no/iln/tjenester/kunnskap/sprak korpus/skriftsprakskorpus/lbk
Nordic Dialect Corpus http://www.tekstlab.uio.no/nota/scandiasyn/
Oslo Corpus of Tagged Norwegian Texts http://www.tekstlab.uio.no/norsk/nynorsk/ index.html

References

Aa, Leiv Inge, Kristin Eide & Tor A. Åfarli. 2014. Somme mytar er fort avkledde: perfektum partisipp i dialektkorpuset [Some myths are easily seen through: perfect participle in the dialect corpus]. In Janne B. Johannessen & Kristin Hagen (eds.), *Språk i norge og nabolanda*, 217–239. Oslo: Novus.

Åfarli, Tor A. 2009. Passive participle agreement in Norwegian dialects. *Groninger Arbeiten zur Germanistischen Linguistik* 49. 167–181.

Börjars, Kersti & Nigel Vincent. 2005. Position versus function in Scandinavian presentational constructions. In Miriam Butt & Tracy King (eds.), *Proceedings of the LFG05 conference*, 54–72.

Carnie, Andrew & Heidi Harley. 2005. Existential impersonals. *Studia Linguistica* 59. 46–65.

Chomsky, Noam. 2001. Derivation by phase. In Michael Kenstowicz (ed.), *Ken Hale: A life in language*, 1–52. Cambridge, MA: The MIT Press.

Christensen, Kirsti Koch & Tarald Knut Taraldsen. 1989. Expletive chain formation and past participle agreement in Scandinavian dialects. In Paola Benincà (ed.), *Dialect variation in the theory of grammar*, 53–84. Dordrecht: Foris.

De Cuypere, Ludovic, Kristof Baten & Gudrun Rawoens. 2014. A corpus-based analysis of the Swedish passive alternation. *Nordic Journal of Linguistics* 37. 199–223.

Engdahl, Elisabet. 1999. *The choice between* bli-*passive and* s-*passive in Danish, Norwegian and Swedish*. http://www.svenska.gu.se/digitalAssets/1336/1336829_engdahl-nordsem-passivechoice-1999.pdf.

Engdahl, Elisabet. 2006. Semantic and syntactic patterns in Swedish passives. In Lyngfelt Benjamin & Torgrim Solstad (eds.), *Demoting the Agent. Passive, middle and other voice phenomena*, 21–45. Amsterdam & Philadelphia: John Benjamins.

Engdahl, Elisabet & Anu Laanemets. 2015a. Opersonlig passiv i danska, norska och svenska – en korpusstudie. *Norsk Lingvistisk Tidsskrift* 33(2). 129–156.

Engdahl, Elisabet & Anu Laanemets. 2015b. Prepositional passives in Danish, Norwegian and Swedish. A corpus analysis. *Nordic Journal of Linguistics* 38. 285–337.

Engels, Eva. 2012. Scandinavian negative indefinites and cyclic linearization. *Syntax* 15. 109–141.

Faarlund, Jan Terje, Svein Lie & Kjell Ivar Vannebo. 1997. *Norsk referansegrammatikk*. Oslo: Universitetsforlaget.

Hansen, Erik & Lars Heltoft. 2011. *Grammatik over det Danske Sprog*. København: Det Danske Sprog- og Litteraturselskab.

Hedlund, Cecilia. 1992. *On participles.* Department of Linguistics, University of Stockholm dissertation.

Heltoft, Lars & Lisbeth Falster Jakobsen. 1996. Danish passives and subject positions as a mood system. A content analysis. In Elisabeth Engberg-Pedersen, Michael Fortescue, Peter Harder, Lars Heltoft & Lisbeth Falster Jakobsen (eds.), *Content, expression and structure: Studies in Danish Functional grammar,* 199–234. Amsterdam & Philadelphia: John Benjamins.

Holmberg, Anders & Urpo Nikanne. 2002. Expletives, subjects, and topics in Finnish. In Peter Svenonius (ed.), *Subjects, expletives, and the EPP,* 71–105. Oxford: Oxford University Press.

Holmberg, Anders. 2002. Expletives and agreement in Scandinavian passives. *Journal of Comparative Germanic Linguistics* 4. 85–128.

Høysgaard, Jens. 1752[1979]. Metodisk forsøg til en fuldstændig dansk syntax. In *Danske grammatikere,* vol. V. København: Det Danske Sprog- og Litteraturselskab.

Laanemets, Anu. 2012. *Passiv i moderne dansk, norsk og svensk. Et korpusbaseret studie af tale- og skriftsprog.* Tartu Universitet dissertation. http://dspace.utlib.ee/dspace/bitstream/handle/10062/27711/laanemets_anu.pdf.

Larsson, Ida. 2012. Inte helt passiv: Konstruktion med *få* + particip i tal och skrift [Not completely passive: Constructions with *få* + participle in speech and writing]. *Språk och stil* 22(2). 27–61.

Lødrup, Helge. 1989. Indirekte objekter i LFG. *Norskrift* 60. 19–36. https://www.duo.uio.no/handle/10852/37827.

Mikkelsen, Kristian. 1894. *Dansk Sproglære med sproghistoriske Tillæg. Haandbog for Lærere og Viderekomne.* København: Lehmann & Stage.

Mikkelsen, Kristian. 1911[1975]. *Dansk Ordföjningslære.* København: Hans Reitzels forlag.

Pedersen, Karen Margrethe. 2013. Brugen av *s*-passiv i traditionelt bornholmsk [The use of *s*-passive in the traditional Bornholm dialect]. In Henrik Jørgensen & Simon Borchmann (eds.), *Gode ord er bedre end guld. Festskrift til Henrik Jørgensen,* 337–355. Aarhus: Aarhus universitet.

Pedersen, Karen Margrethe. 2017. Simple *der*-konstruktioner. In *Dansk sproghistorie [History of the Danish language].* København: Det Danske Sprog- og Litteraturselskab. in preparation.

Sundman, Marketta. 1987. *Subjektsval och diates i svenskan [Subject choice and diathesis in Swedish].* Åbo: Åbo Akademis förlag.

Teleman, Ulf, Staffan Hellberg & Erik Andersson. 1999. *Svenska Akademiens grammatik.* Stockholm: Norstedts.

Chapter 14

The null subject parameter meets the Polish impersonal -NO/-TO construction

Małgorzata Krzek
Newcastle University

> This squib argues that null generic inclusive subjects are found in consistent null subject languages not only in the passive voice, as maintained by Fassi Fehri (2009), but also in the active voice – in the so-called -NO/-TO construction. However, the null subject of the -NO/-TO construction is not logophoric, so it does not receive its inclusive reading by being anchored to the Speech Act, where the [Speaker] and the [Addressee] features are located (D'Alessandro 2007; Sigurðsson 2004; Bianchi 2003). It is proposed that the interpretation of the null subject of the -NO/-TO construction is dependent on a binding relation with a null Topic (Frascarelli & Hinterhölzl 2007) that is merged in the C-domain.

1 Introduction

According to Roberts & Holmberg (2010: 12), there are four types of null subject languages (NSL):

1. Expletive null subject languages (German, Dutch)
2. Partial null subject languages (Finnish, Russian)
3. Consistent null subject languages (Italian, Greek)
4. Discourse pro-drop languages (Chinese, Indonesian)

Expletive null subject languages allow for subject expletives to be null. Partial null subject languages allow for a generic subject to be null, as in (2), but 3rd person subjects have to be overt, as in (3).

Małgorzata Krzek. 2017. The null subject parameter meets the Polish impersonal -NO/-TO construction. In Michelle Sheehan & Laura R. Bailey (eds.), *Order and structure in syntax II: Subjecthood and argument structure*, 307–318. Berlin: Language Science Press.

(1) Finnish (Holmberg 2010b: 200)
 Tässä istuu mukavasti.
 here sits comfortably
 'One can sit comfortably here.'

(2) Finnish (Holmberg 2005: 539)
 **(Hän) puhuu englantia.*
 S/he speak.3sc English
 'S/he speaks English.'

In consistent NSL all subject pronouns regardless of the person and tense can be null. Indefinite null subjects, on the other hand, have to be overt. Holmberg (2010a: 92) illustrates this difference by contrasting Brazilian Portuguese (BP), a partial NSL, with European Portuguese (EP), a consistent NSL.

(3) Brazilian Portuguese (Holmberg 2010a: 92)
 É assim que faz o doce.
 is thus that makes the sweet
 'This is how one makes the dessert.'

(4) European Portuguese (Holmberg 2010a: 92)
 É assim que __se__ faz o doce.
 is thus that __SE__ makes the sweet
 'This is how one makes the dessert.'

In BP the subject pronoun corresponding to the English *one* is null. In EP the overt pronoun *se* is used. Holmberg (2010a) notes that this generalization only concerns those generic pronouns that have an inclusive reading; that is, they denote people in general including speaker and the addressee. On the other hand, pronouns that express exclusive generic reading, which is equivalent to generic *they* in English (as in *They eat a lot of cheese in France*), can be null in consistent NSL.

The reason why this is the case is that, according to Holmberg (2005; 2010a), consistent NSL have an unvalued D-feature in T(ense), which is valued by an A-Topic (Frascarelli 2007). This means when a null ΦP ('phi-phrase'; 3rd person deficient pronoun) enters into an Agree relation with T and, as a result of this, is incorporated in T, it can be interpreted as definite, referring to an individual or a group. But it also means that a null subject cannot have a generic interpretation; is, it cannot refer to people in general. Therefore, in order to express a generic meaning, consistent NSL have to resort to a variety of 'overt strategies'. Thus, they may express it with an overt pronoun of *SI/SE*-type. Partial NSL, on the other hand, do not have an uD in T that could be valued by an A-Topic. As a result, an incorporated ΦP can only receive an indefinite interpretation.

More recently, Fassi Fehri (2009) has argued for a qualification of these generalizations, claiming that generic inclusive null pronouns are actually found in consistent NSL, contra Holmberg (2005; 2010a), but only in the passive voice.

In this squib, I present evidence from Polish, a consistent NSL (Sigurðsson & Egerland 2009), that null generic inclusive subjects are found in the active voice – in the so-called -NO/-TO construction. I also show that the passive construction identified in Fassi Fehri (2009) shares a number of morphosyntactic properties with the -NO/-TO construction, suggesting that the construction in question may need to be actually reanalyzed as an active construction. The observation that null generic subjects can be found in consistent NSL suggests that a more fine-grained typology of null subjects is needed.

First, I present a brief overview of morphosyntactic properties of the Polish -NO/-TO construction and compare them to those of an Arabic passive construction identified in Fassi Fehri (2009). Next, I discuss possible interpretations of the null pronoun in the -NO/-TO construction and touch upon some of the possible consequences it may have for the internal structure of pronouns (Harley & Ritter 2002).

2 The morphosyntactic properties of the -NO/-TO construction in Polish

The -NO/-TO construction uses an uninflected verb form with a -NO/-TO suffix and can only refer to the past. It has been classified as 'active indefinite', and not passive (Kibort 2004; Dziwirek 1994; Śpiewak 2000) [1]. The reason for this is that it can occur with transitive and intransitive verb types and with accusative case on the direct object argument. It is illustrated by the examples in (5)

(5) a. *Bywano tam często.*
 were.IMP there often
 '[One/They] used to come/be there often.'

---

[1] The passive analysis of the -NO/-TO construction has been supported by the diachronic argument; that is, the -NO/-TO form was historically a neuter nominal passive participle used with neuter passive subjects (Siewierska 1988; Kibort 2004).

b. *Dopiero w 1988 roku odczuto ponownie potrzebę odtworzenia*
only in 1988 year felt.IMP again need reconstitution,
Towarzystwa Przyjaciół 'Ossolineum'.
Society Friends 'Ossolineum'

'It wasn't until 1988 that [one/they] felt the need to reconstitute the Society of the Friends of "Ossolineum".' (adapted from Kibort 2004: 259)

c. *Kupowano tutaj dużo chleba.*
bought.IMP here a-lot-of bread

'[One/They] bought a lot of bread here.'

What is more, the construction in question is ungrammatical with a passive auxiliary and a passive by-phrase (Lavine 2005), as given in (6).[2]

(6) (*Zostało) znaleziono pieniądze w restauracji (*przez kelnera).
(AUX.PASS) found.IMP money in restaurant (by waiter)

'[One/They] found money in the restaurant.'

As for the null subject of the -NO/-TO construction, the fact that it is projected is confirmed by the fact that it participates in control and binding.[3] Bondaruk & Charzyńska-Wójcik (2003) observe that the -NO/-TO impersonals can share their subjects with embedded infinitive clauses (7), with present and past participle forms, and in subject-raising constructions.

(7) *Próbowano zrozumieć ten problem.*
tried.IMP understand.INF this.ACC problem.ACC

'[One/They] tried to understand this problem.'

With regard to binding, Kibort (2004) observes that the covert subject of the -NO/-TO is also capable of binding reflexive and reflexive-possessive pronouns that need to be bound by the subject. The former is illustrated by the example in (8).

---

[2] For a full overview of the differences between the -NO/-TO construction and the passive, see Kibort (2004).

[3] Babby (1998) maintains that there is no subject in the -NO/-TO construction at any level of representation. The affixation of the passive morpheme ensures the dethematisation of the subject whereas the impersonal inflectional ending -o is used only when the external argument (i.e. subject) is not selected. This, according to Babby (1998), confirms that the sentence is truly subjectless. Babby (1998) argues that the canonical subject position non-obligatory, and suggests that in the -NO/-TO construction it is simply not projected.

(8) Polish (Kibort 2004: 273)
   Oglądano siebie/się w lustrze.[4]
   looked.IMP self/SIĘ in mirror
   '[One/They] looked at oneself/themselves in the mirror.'

The null subject of the -NO/-TO construction has been argued to be either pro_arb (Dziwirek 1994) or PRO_arb (e.g. Maling 1993; Lavine 2005). However, contrary to PRO found in infinitival clauses, the null pronoun in the subject position in the -NO/-TO is always interpreted as human. Secondly, the null subject of the -NO/-TO does not require control (Kibort 2004), contrary to PRO. Finally, the subject of the -NO/-TO construction is only compatible with adjectival predicates that are MASC.PL whereas the PRO_arb in Polish uncontrolled infinitivals patterns with adjectival predicates that are MASC.SG, as in (9) (Lavine 2005: footnote 26).

(9) a. *Jest ważne [PRO być szczęśliwym / *szczęśliwymi].*
      is important PRO to.be happy.INSTR.SG / *happy.INSTR.PL
      'It is important to be happy.'

   b. *PRO wyglądano na *szczęśliwego/ szczęśliwych.*
      PRO look for *happy.MASC.ACC.SG/ happy.MASC.ACC.PL
      'They looked happy.'

3 Fassi Fehri (2009)

Fassi Fehri (2009), focusing on data from Arabic, confirms that in Arabic, just as in Italian, null 3rd person pronouns can only receive a definite/referential reading (i.e. *she/he*). They cannot be interpreted as non-referential or generic. A generic or arbitrary interpretation can, however, be found, as Fassi Fehri (2009) observes, when a verb appears in its passive form, as in (10) and (11).

(10) Arabic (Fassi Fehri 2009: 4)
    Y-u-jlas-u hunaa waqt-a l-istiraahat-i.
    3-PASS-sit-IND here time-ACC the-brake-GEN
    'One sits here at brake time.'

---

[4]In Polish the reflexive pronoun *siebie* 'self_ACC' is, in very restricted contexts, interchangeable with a multifunctional enclitic form *się* (see Nagórko 1998 and Kibort 2004).

(11) Arabic (Fassi Fehri 2009: 6)
Wa-y-u-xraj-u   la-hu   yawm-a l-qiyaamat-i   kitaab-an.
and-3-PASS-bring-IND to-him day-ACC the-resurrection-GEN book-ACC
'And someone will bring to him a book the day of the resurrection.'

As illustrated by (10) and (11), the kind of passive construction discussed by Fassi Fehri (2009) can occur with both transitive and intransitive verbs, and it does not support a *by*-phrase. Contrary to personal passives, in the passive construction in question objects are not promoted to the subject position, and they retain their accusative case, as in (11) above. What is more, the null subject of the Arabic construction binds reflexives/reciprocals, and it controls the subject of a participial clause. This is illustrated by the examples in (12) from Fassi Fehri (2009: 17).

(12) Arabic (Fassi Fehri 2009: 17)
Y-u-ġ-t-asal-u   hunaa.
3-PASS-ref-wash-IND here
'One washes oneself here.'

(13) *Y-u-tasallalu   ard-an   fard-an   ʕabra l-hawaajizi*
3-PASS-infiltrate individual-ACC individual-ACC across the-barriers
daʕimiina   baʕ   d-un   baʕd-an.
supporting.PL.ACC each-NOM each-ACC
'People will infiltrate through barriers, supporting each other.'

A very brief overview of the morphosyntactic properties of this Arabic passive suggests that the properties displayed are not those typical of canonical passives, as identified Blevins (2003)[5], but rather strikingly similar to those of the Polish -NO/-TO construction, which has been traditionally analysed by Slavic linguists as 'active indefinite' (Wierzbicka 1966; Doros 1975; Brajerski 1979; Bogusławski 1984; Siewierska 1988; and Rozwadowska 1992). It may be then that this Arabic construction should be reanalysed as active. Space limitations, however, do not allow for a more in-depth analysis of this issue to be carried out here.

---

[5] For Blevins (2003: 512) 'passivisation is a detransitivising operation that deletes a subject term in the argument structure of a verb'. The logical subject can then be reintroduced into the structure by means of an oblique phrase. Impersonalised verb forms, on the other hand, 'preserve the lexical transitivity of their input retain an unexpressed subject that characteristically determines an active indefinite interpretation and may even provide an antecedent for reflexive pronouns' (Blevins 2003: 508).

4 The interpretation of the subject in the -NO/-TO construction in Polish

The covert subject of the -NO/-TO impersonal triggers masculine plural marking on adjectival and nominal predicative complements, suggesting that the null subject is specified as 3PL.MASC. Despite its specification, however, it can be used with reference to participants that are other than masculine, plural or speaker and addressee exclusive (Kibort 2004). Kibort (2004) notes that as long as the inflectional criteria are fulfilled, the construction can be found in a variety of contexts, implying that the referent of the agent is non-masculine, as in (14); or that it is other than 3rd person or plural, as in (15a).

(14) Polish (Kibort 2004: 284)
 Kochano swoich mężów.
 loved.IMP own.ACC husbands.ACC
 '[They] loved [their] husbands.'

(15) a. Polish (Siewierska 1988: 284, footnote 19)
 Mówiono o tym wyżej.
 talked.IMP about this higher
 '[One] discussed this above.' (meaning: 'As I/we said above')

 b. Polish (Kibort 2004: 285)
 Proszę pani, ja się nie awanturuję, tylko proszę, żeby mi
 please madam, I REFL NEG brawl.1SG only ask.1SG that me.DAT
 wydano zaświadczenie.
 issued.IMP certificate.ACC
 'Madam, I am not brawling, but only asking that [one] would issue the certificate to me.' (meaning: '... I am only asking you to issue the certificate to me', said by a customer to an uncooperative clerk)

 c. *A w tym roku na co wydaliśmy najwięcej?*
 and in this year on what spent.1PL the-most
 'And what did we spent the most on this year?'

 d. *W tym roku najwięcej wydawano na czynsz.*
 in this year the-most spent.IMP on rent
 'This year [we] spent the most on rent.'

The sentences in (15a) demonstrate that the subject of the -NO/-TO construction can refer to a group of people that includes the speaker and the addressee, suggesting that generic inclusive reading of the null subject pronoun is possible in the -NO/-TO. This observation has further consequences. Firstly, it shows that null inclusive generic subjects are available in consistent NSL in active sentences. If this is the case, then the typology of null subject languages should be revisited. Another point worth mentioning with respect to the subject of the -NO/-TO is a possible bearing it may have on the feature geometry of pronouns (Harley & Ritter 2002). Contrary to the subject of the Italian impersonal SI construction (16) or Polish SIĘ construction, the subject of the -NO/-TO construction is not logophoric. It means that it does not refer back to the 'reporting' speaker (in 17).

(16) (D'Alessandro 2007: 173)
<u>Maria e Gianni</u>   hanno raccontato che <u>si</u> era   mangiato bene in quel
<u>Maria and Gianni</u> have   told   that <u>si</u> was eaten   well in that
locale.
place
'Maria and Gianni have told that they had eaten well at that place.'

(17) Maria i   Paweł   powiedzieli że   oglądano   te   filmy
[Maria and Paweł]$_i$ said.3PL   that pro$_{j/*i}$ watched.IMP these movies
często.
often
(Intended) 'Maria and Paweł said that they watched these movies often.'

D'Alessandro (2007) reports that *si* in (16) is logophoric. This means that it refers back to the person who reports what happens, rather than to the person who utters the whole sentence. *si* then receives its inclusive interpretation by being anchored to the Speech Act, where the [Speaker] and the [Addressee] features are located (D'Alessandro 2007; Sigurðsson 2004; Bianchi 2003). It is, however, not clear how an inclusive interpretation is achieved with the subject of the -NO/-TO, as it does not refer back to the reporting speaker. It is possible that one of the reasons why the null subject of the Polish construction cannot refer to the 'reporting' speaker may have to do with a more general ban on it being bound. Consider the examples in (18) below.

(18)   a. *Marysia   słuchała   muzyki kiedy [pro$_i$] gotowano.*
          Marysia$_{j/*i}$ listented.3SG.FEM music   when [pro$_i$]   cooked.IMP
          'Marysia listened to music when [they/people] cooked.'

b. *Marysia słucha muzyki kiedy [pro$_j$] gotuje.*
   Marysia$_j$ listens.3SG music when [pro$_j$] cooks.3SG
   'Marysia listens to music when she cooks.'

In (18b) the main clause subject *Marysia* is coreferential with the null subject of the subordinate clause. In (18a), on the other hand, such coreferentiality between *Marysia* and a null subject in the subordinate clause is not possible. I propose that this may well be caused by the difference in the feature-geometry make-up of pronouns (Harley & Ritter 2002).[6] To be more specific, it may be that the [Participant] feature in the geometry is underspecified with respect to the [Speaker] and the [Addressee] features, such that the [Participant] feature cannot be specified any further. Alternatively, it may be that the [Participant] feature is deleted altogether. This null pronoun is then similar to 3rd person pronouns for which the [Participant] feature either does not exist in their featural make-up or is present but underspecified, and as such they can only be bound by Topics and not by logophoric features. Now in order to explain how the inclusive interpretation is attained, I propose that the interpretation of the null subject of the -NO/-TO construction will depend on a binding relation with the null Topic[7] (Frascarelli & Hinterhölzl 2007) that is merged in the C-domain. Consider the extract in (19). The examples (19ii) and (19iii) are answers to (19i).

(19) (i) *Na co my Polacy wydawaliśmy najwięcej w ubiegłym roku?*
       on what we Poles spent.1PL most in last year
       'What did we spent on most last year?'

---

[6]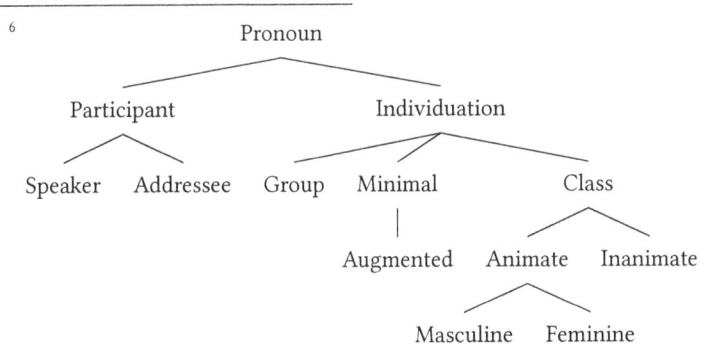

(Harley & Ritter 2002)

[7] An initial investigation suggests that it may be an Aboutness Topic (Frascarelli 2007), but more research is needed to establish whether this is really the case.

(ii) *My sądzimy, że   wydawano najwięcej na czynsz.*
we$_i$ think.1PL that [pro$_{j/?i}$] spent.IMP most   on rent
'We think that [people living in Poland/they/we?] spent most on rent.'

(iii) *Eksperci sądzą,   że   wydawano najwięcej na czynsz.*
experts$_i$ think.3PL that [pro$_{j/*i}$] spent.IMP most   on rent
'Experts think that [people living in Poland] spent most on rent.'

In (19) speaker (i) introduces *my Polacy* 'we Poles' as a Topic. This Topic is then re-merged as a silent copy in the C-domain in (ii). The null subject (*pro*) in (ii) refers back *my Polacy* 'we Poles' as it is an established Topic. If *my* 'we' in (ii) has the same referent as *my* 'we' in (i), which is a Topic, then the *pro* in (ii) may accidentally be coreferential with *my* 'we' in (ii). Crucially, however, for my informants *my* 'we' in (ii) does not have to be coreferential with *pro*, and for some of them it cannot. In other words, those who think do not have to be/cannot be those who spent most on rent in (19ii). In (19iii) again, the Topic *my Polacy* 'we Poles' is remerged in the C-domain, and the null subject *pro* refers back to that Topic, and it cannot be coreferential with the subject *eksperci* 'experts'. These data suggest that for the null subject in the -NO/-TO construction to receive a generic interpretation, it needs to be bound by a Topic.

5 Conclusion

This squib presented evidence that Polish, a consistent NSL, has an impersonal active construction whose subject can receive an inclusive interpretation. The Polish construction shares a number of morphosyntactic properties with a type of a passive construction in Arabic (Fassi Fehri 2009) – a consistent NSL as well – the subject of which can also receive a generic interpretation. It is, however, clear that the range of occurrence of inclusive generic subjects in these languages is very restricted. In the -NO/-TO construction the generic interpretation arises only when the null subject is bound by a Topic that has a generic referent.[8] It remains to be investigated whether there is any relation between the uninflected verb form used in the -NO/-TO construction and the availability of a generic interpretation that a null subject occurring in it can receive.

---

[8] According to Frascarelli (2007: 707), an indefinite DP can be a Topic when it is intended as specific indefinite; that is, when it is used to refer to specific type of referent.

Abbreviations

Abbreviations used in this article follow the Leipzig Glossing Rules' instructions for word-by-word transcription, available at: https://www.eva.mpg.de/lingua/pdf/Glossing-Rules.pdf.

References

Babby, Leonard H. 1998. *Voice and diathesis in Slavic.* Position paper at the Comparative Slavic Morphosyntax conference in Bloomington, Indiana, 5-7 June 1998.

Bianchi, Valentina. 2003. On finiteness as logophoric anchoring. In Jacqueline Guéron & Liliane Tasmovski (eds.), *Tense and point of view*, 213–246. Nanterre: Université Paris X.

Blevins, James P. 2003. Passives and impersonals. *Journal of Linguistics* 39(3). 473–520.

Bogusławski, Andrzej. 1984. Polskie nieidentyfikacyjne wyrażenia osobowo-referencjalne. *Polonica* 10. 49–71.

Bondaruk, Anna & Magdalena Charzyńska-Wójcik. 2003. Expletive pro in impersonals passives in Irish, Polish and Old English. *Linguistische Berichte* 195. 325–362.

Brajerski, Tadeusz. 1979. Geneza orzeczen typu (z)jedzono i (wy)pito. *Język polski* 59(2). 84–98.

D'Alessandro, Roberta. 2007. *Impersonal Si constructions. Agreement and interpretation.* Berlin: Mouton de Gruyter.

Doros, Aleksander. 1975. *Werbalne konstrukcje bezosobowe w językach rosyjskim i polskim na tle innych języków słowiańskich.* Wrocław: Ossolineum.

Dziwirek, Katarzyna. 1994. *Polish subjects.* New York: Gardland.

Fassi Fehri, Abdelkader. 2009. Arabic silent pronouns, person and voice. *Brill's Annual of Afroasiatic Languages and Linguistics* 1. 1–38.

Frascarelli, Mara. 2007. Subjects, topics and the interpretation of referential pro. An interface approach to the linking of (null) pronouns. *Natural Language & Linguistic Theory* 25. 691–734.

Frascarelli, Mara & Roland Hinterhölzl. 2007. Types of topics in German and Italian. In Kerstin Schwade & Susanne Winkler (eds.), *On information structure, meaning and form*, 87–116. Amsterdam: John Benjamins.

Harley, Heidi & Elizabeth Ritter. 2002. Person and number in pronouns: A feature-geometric analysis. *Language* 78(3). 482–526.

Holmberg, Anders. 2005. Is there a little pro? Evidence from Finnish. *Linguistic Inquiry* 36(4). 533–564.

Holmberg, Anders. 2010a. Null subject parameters. In Theresa Biberauer, Anders Holmberg, Ian Roberts & Michelle Sheehan (eds.), *Parametric variation: Null subjects in minimalist theory*, 88–124. Cambridge: Cambridge University Press.

Holmberg, Anders. 2010b. The null generic pronoun in Finnish: A case of incorporation in T. In Theresa Biberauer, Anders Holmberg, Ian Roberts & Michelle Sheehan (eds.), *Parametric variation: Null subjects in minimalist theory*, 200–230. Oxford: Oxford University Press.

Kibort, Anna. 2004. *Passive and passive-like constructions in English and Polish*. Cambridge: University of Cambridge dissertation.

Lavine, James E. 2005. The morphosyntax of Polish and Ukrainian -NO/-TO. *Journal of Slavic Linguistics* 13(1). 75–117.

Maling, Joan. 1993. *Unpassives of unaccusatives.* Handout to talks given at Univ. of California Irvine (Jan), Univ. of Massachusetts-Amherst (April), Helsinki Univ. (May), Univ. of Iceland (June).

Nagórko, Alicja. 1998. *Zarys gramatyki polskiej [Polish grammar. An outline].* 2nd edn. Warszawa: PWN.

Roberts, Ian & Anders Holmberg. 2010. Introduction: Parameters in minimalist theory. In Theresa Biberauer, Anders Holmberg, Ian Roberts & Michelle Sheehan (eds.), *Parametric variation. Null subjects in minimalist theory*, 1–57. Cambridge: Cambridge University Press.

Rozwadowska, Bożena. 1992. *Thematic constraints on selected constructions in English and Polish* (Anglica Wratislaviensia 20). Wrocław: Wydawnictwo Uniwersytetu Wrocławskiego.

Siewierska, Anna. 1988. The passive in Slavic. In Masayoshi Shibatani (ed.), *Passive and voice*, 243–289. Amsterdam: John Benjamins.

Sigurðsson, Halldór Ármann. 2004. The syntax of person, tense, and speech features. *Italian Journal of Linguistics* 16. 219–251.

Sigurðsson, Halldór Ármann & Verner Egerland. 2009. Impersonal null-subjects in Icelandic and elsewhere. *Studia Linguistica* 63(1). 158–185.

Śpiewak, Grzegorz. 2000. *The lexical-conceptual structure of nominativeless constructions Polish. Towards a unified account.* Lublin: M. Curie-Skłodowska University Doctoral Dissertation.

Wierzbicka, Anna. 1966. Czy istnieja zdania bezpodmiotowe. *Język polski* 46(3). 177–196.

Chapter 15

Ellipsis in Arabic fragment answers

Ali Algryani
The Libyan Academy

> Fragment answers are short answers to questions consisting of non-sentential XPs that convey the same propositional content as complete sentential answers. This squib discusses the syntax of ellipsis in Arabic fragments answers focusing on whether or not ellipsis in fragmentary utterances contains syntactic structure and whether, if so, such fragmentary XPs can be derived via A-bar movement to a clause-initial position plus TP deletion at PF in a way similar to that of Merchant (2004). It is argued that ellipsis in Arabic fragment answers contains syntactic structure and therefore can be analysed as TP ellipsis derived by focus movement of the remnant to a left peripheral position followed by deletion of the TP constituting the background information. Such an analysis captures some morpho-syntactic effects such as morphological case-matching, preposition-stranding, and islands effects.

1 The syntax of ellipsis in fragment answers

Fragment answers are short answers to questions consisting of non-sentential XPs. Such XPs, however, convey the same propositional content as full sentential answers (Merchant 2004). Fragmentary utterances, such as (1B), have been analysed according to non-structural and structural approaches. While the former argue against positing a structure in ellipsis at any level of representation, that is, there is no more structure than what is pronounced (see Progovac 2006; Casielles 2006), the latter assume that ellipsis in such utterances contains invisible syntactic structure (Merchant 2004; 2006; Krifka 2006; van Craenenbroeck 2010).

(1) A: Who did she see?
    B: John.

Ali Algryani. 2017. Ellipsis in Arabic fragment answers. In Michelle Sheehan & Laura R. Bailey (eds.), *Order and structure in syntax II: Subjecthood and argument structure*, 319–328. Berlin: Language Science Press.

There are several arguments that seem to speak in favour of the non-elliptical approach. One comes from the facts seen in (2a,b).

(2) Who ate the pizza?
    a. Me/him/them.
    b. *I/he/they.

Progovac (2006) takes the absence in (2a) of structural nominative case, which is assigned in T, as an indication that such fragments are complete syntactic objects (NPs), not TPs. The lack of a tense projection in the structure explains why the NPs *me/him/them* surface in the (default) accusative case. The ungrammaticality of (2b) is ascribed to the fact that the pronouns *I/he/them* contain unchecked nominative Case features. In contrast, a subject pronoun in an answer such as *I did* surfaces in the nominative case, as is expected given that nominative case assignment requires a tense projection.

Another arguments given by Progovac (2006) against the ellipsis analysis of fragment answers comes from verbal utterances. These too can be analysed as base-generated phrases. The verb in (3B) surfaces in the bare infinitive form which is not expected if such a verbal answer is derived from a full sentential source, as in (4). The absence of tense and verbal agreement on the verb *play* in (3B) is ascribed to the lack of a tense node, which in turn suggests that such an utterance is better analysed as a base-generated VP (see Progovac 2006 and Casielles 2006 for further discussion).

(3) A: What did Andres do?
    B: Play volleyball.

(4) Andres plays volleyball.

In the structural approach, utterances like (1) are analysed as the result of a deletion process. Merchant (2004), for instance, provides an analysis of fragment answers in which the fragment answer is fronted to a clause-peripheral position and the remainder of the sentence is deleted. Accordingly, the fragment answer in (1), i.e. *John*, originates as an object of the verb *saw* and it moves to a clause initial position while the rest of the clause is elided, that is, not pronounced. This is illustrated in the tree diagram in (5).

(5)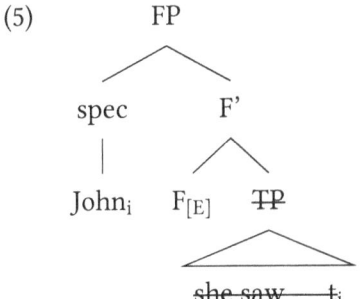

There is evidence for such an analysis based on morphological case marking, preposition stranding, and binding effects. For instance, in languages where case is marked morphologically, it has been argued that the remnant in short answers can bear only the same case as it would display in full answers, as in (6) from Greek. The short answer in (6a) can be explained as follow: the remnant DP fragment answer starts as a subject bearing the nominative case, as is expected in full answers prior to ellipsis. The short answer in (6b) is ungrammatical due to its accusative case.

(6) Greek (Merchant 2006: 75)

    Q: *Pjos   idhe tin Maria?*
       who.NOM saw the Maria?
    'Who saw Maria?'

  a. A: *O Giannis.*
       The Giannis.NOM

  b. A: **Ton Gianni.*
       The Giannis.ACC

The p-stranding phenomenon also argues in favour of the ellipsis analysis. P-stranding is permitted in fragment answers only if it is permitted in sentential answers. In (7), preposition stranding is unacceptable since Greek is a non-p-stranding language; the preposition in such cases has to be pied-piped. In a p-stranding language such as Norwegian, both options are available, as in (8), indicating that only constituents that are independently able to move in a language can be fragment answers in that language.

(7) Greek (Merchant 2004: 685–686)

    a. *Me pjon milise i Anna?*
       with whom spoke the Anna?
       'Who did Anna speak with?'

    b. *Me ton Kosta.*
       with the Kostas

    c. **Ton Kosta.*

(8) Norwegian (Merchant 2004: 685–686)

    a. *Hvem har Per snakket med?*
       Who has Per talked with?

    b. *Mary.*

Finally, DP fragments show the distribution regulated by the Binding Theory just like their sentential counterparts. The anaphor *himself* in (9a) is acceptable as a fragment answer despite the absence of any antecedent. This can be explained under the assumption that there is a clausal structure in the ellipsis site hosting the antecedent, which in such a case satisfies Condition A of the Binding Theory, which stipulates that an anaphor has to be bound in its governing category (see Merchant 2004; 2006).

(9) Who does John like?

    a. Himself.

    b. John$_i$ likes himself$_i$.

This squib provides an overview of the syntax of ellipsis in Arabic fragment answers. It is organised as follows: §2 presents fragment answers in Standard Arabic and discusses the interaction between ellipsis and information structure. §3 puts forward an analysis for fragment answers in Arabic. Finally, §4 presents the conclusion.

2 Fragment answers in Arabic

Fragment answers exist in Arabic. Speakers of the language often answer a question with a phrase, a fragment of a sentence, rather than with a full sentence. Such non-sentential fragments are, however, interpreted as full sentential structures. Fragment answers can be DPs, PPs or VP, as in (10–12).

(10) A: *Maða ištarat   Hind-un?*
    what bought.3FS Hind-NOM
    'What did Hind buy?'

  B: *Kitaab-an.*
    book-ACC
    'A book.'

(11) A: *Maʕa man   ðahabat Hind-un?*
    with whom went.3FS Hind-NOM
    'With whom did Hind go?'

  B: *Maʕa Zayd-en.*
    with Zayd-GEN
    'With Zayd.'

(12) A: *Maða faʕalat Hind-un   b-ssayyarat-i?*
    what did.3FS Hind-NOM with-the-car-GEN
    'What did Hind with the car?'

  B: *baʕat-ha.*
    sold.3FS-it

Ellipsis in fragment answers is linked to information structure, since the remnant is interpreted in terms of focus which can be informational or identificational (see Brunetti 2003; Busquets 2006; Kolokonte 2008). Focus can be expressed in Arabic in two different means: a focused constituent can appear in situ or in a left peripheral position, as in (13). The former is perceived as new informational focus, while the latter is normally interpreted as contrastive/identificational focus (see Moutaouakil 1989; Aoun et al. 2010 for discussion).

(13) Standard Arabic (Aoun et al. 2010: 202)

  a. *šariba   zayd-un ŠAY-AN.*
    drank.3MS zayd-NOM tea-ACC
    'Zayd drank TEA.'

  b. *ŠAY-AN šariba   zayd-un.*
    tea-ACC drank.3MS zayd-NOM
    'It was tea that Zayd drank.'

3 Analysis of Arabic fragment answers

Fragment answers in Arabic display some morpho-syntactic effects that are also found in their full sentential counterparts. For instance, the morphological case-marking effect is evident in Arabic as in (14), where the fragment answer can only bear accusative case it would bear in a sentential answer (14C).

(14) A: *Maðaištarat   Hind-un?*
     what bought.3FS Hind-NOM
     'What did Hind buy?'

   B: *kitaab-an. / *kitaab-un*
      book-ACC   book-NOM

   C: *Hind-un   ištarat   kitaab-an.*
      Hind-NOM bought.3FS book-ACC

The remnant in (14) bears the accusative case, indicating that it originates as an object of the verb *ištarat* 'bought', where it is assigned accusative case. The remnant undergoes focus movement to a left peripheral position followed by TP deletion at PF, as illustrated in the tree diagram in (15).[1] As for the interpretation of the remnant, it is interpreted as new informational focus given that it is not in contrast with any existing information but rather it expresses new information that is not shared by the speaker and the addressee.[2]

---

[1] An alternative idea could be that the remnant, e.g. in (14), might be in situ, that is, in the TP, and that all of the TP except for the constituent that surfaces as a remnant elides, as in (i), is unacceptable since it would entail that a syntactic operation can apply to a string of words that do not make up a constituent.

   (i) ~~*ištarat*~~ ~~*Hind-un*~~ *kitaab-an.*
       bought.3FS Hind-NOM book-ACC
       'a book'

[2] The same is true of English examples like (1) and similar cases in Italian and Greek (Brunetti 2003; Kolokonte 2008).

(15)

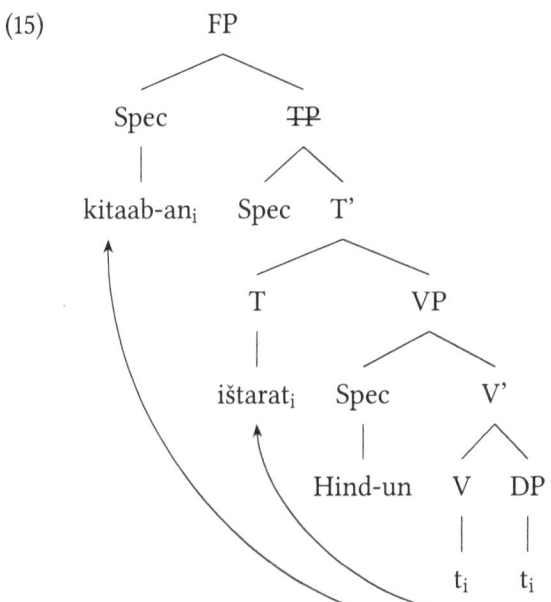

The preposition stranding argument of Merchant (2004) can also be extended to Arabic. Arabic is a non-p-stranding language; p-stranding is not permitted in fragment/short answers, as in (16A1) nor in full answers (16A3). The p-stranding effect can be accounted for by the movement-plus-deletion analysis, according to which the remnant PP *maʕa Zayd-en* 'with Zayd' starts as a complement of the verb *taḥadaθat* 'talked' and moves up to the left periphery before the entire TP gets deleted, as shown in (17). The ungrammaticality of (A1) can be ascribed to the ban on p-stranding in the language.

(16) *maʕa man taḥadaθat Hind-un?*
with who talked.3FS Hind-NOM
'With whom did Hind talk?'

  a. **Zayd.*
    Zayd

  b. *maʕa Zayd-en.*
    with   Zayd-GEN.

  c. **Zayd-en taḥadaθat Hind-un maʕa.*
    Zayd-GEN talked.3FS Hind-NOM with

(17)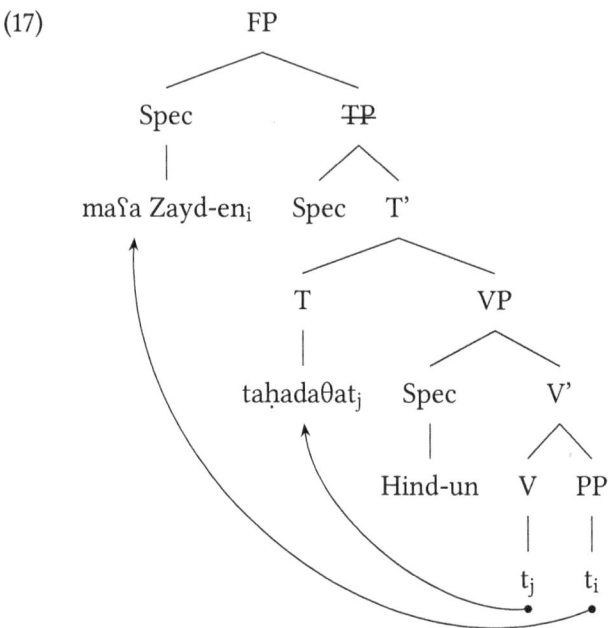

Finally, a third argument in favour of the assumption that the remnant undergoes A-bar movement to the left periphery is the fact that the remnant in fragment answers is sensitive to island domains. Merchant (2004) shows for English that if the correlate to a fragment answer is within an island, then only the sentential answer is possible. The same is true in Arabic, as shown in (18–19).

(18) Adjunct island

    A: Hal ʔatat   liʔana-ka   lam tadʕu   Hind-an?
       Q   came.3FS because-you NEG invited.2MS Hind-ACC
       'Did she come because you didn't invite Hind?'

    B: *la, Omar-an.
       no, Omar-ACC.

    C: la, ʔatat   liʔana-ka   lam tadʕu   Omar-an.
       no came.3FS because-you NEG invited.2MS Omar-ACC
       'No, she came because you didn't invite Omar.'

(19) Relative clause island

    A: *hal istalamat   al-ressalat-a   allati kataba-ha   li-Zaynab?*
        Q   received.3FS the-letter-ACC that   wrote.3MS-it to-Zaynab
        'Did she receive the letter that he wrote to Zaynab?'

    B: **la, li-Zayd-en.*
        no to-Zayd-GEN.

    C: *la, istalamat   al-ressalat-a   allati kataba-ha   li-Zayd-en.*
        no received.3FS the-letter-acc that   wrote.3MS-it to-Zayd-GEN
        'No, she received that the letter that he wrote to Zayd.'

The ungrammaticality of (18B) and (19B) is expected if we assume that the fragment DPs derive from the structures in (C) and that they have moved across island domains to the left periphery.

4 Conclusion

Arabic fragment answers contain syntactic structure and can be derived by focus movement of the remnant to the left periphery followed by TP ellipsis. Such a movement-plus-deletion analysis is based on evidence from morphological case-matching, preposition-stranding as well as island effects. The remnant is interpreted as new informational focus, indicating that new information focus can appear in the left periphery in the context of ellipsis.

References

Aoun, Joseph E., Elabbas Benmamoun & Lina Choueiri. 2010. *The syntax of Arabic*. Cambridge: Cambridge University Press.

Brunetti, Lisa. 2003. Information focus movement in Italian and contextual constraints on ellipsis. In Mimu Tsujimura & Gina Garding (eds.), *Proceedings of 22nd West Conference on Formal Linguistics*, 95–108. Somerville, MA: Cascadilla Press.

Busquets, Joan. 2006. Stripping vs. VP-ellipsis in Catalan: What is deleted and when. *Probus* 18. 159–187.

Casielles, Eugenia. 2006. Big questions, small answers. In Ljiljana Progovac, Kate Paesani, Eugenia Casielles & Ellen Barton (eds.), *The syntax of non-sententials: Multidisciplinary perspectives*, 118–145. Amsterdam: John Benjamins.

van Craenenbroeck, Jeroen. 2010. *The syntax of ellipsis: Evidence from Dutch dialects*. Oxford: Oxford University Press.

Kolokonte, Marina. 2008. *Bare argument ellipsis and information structure*. Newcastle University dissertation.

Krifka, Manfred. 2006. Association with focus phrases. In Valéria Molnár & Suzanne Winkler (eds.), *The architecture of focus*, 105–136. Berlin: Mouton de Gruyter.

Merchant, Jason. 2004. Fragments and ellipsis. *Linguistics and Philosophy* 27. 661–738.

Merchant, Jason. 2006. Small structures. A sententialist perspective. In Ljiljana Progovac, Eugenia Casielles Kate Paesani & Ellen Barton (eds.), *The syntax of non-sententials: Multidisciplinary perspectives*, 73–91. Amsterdam: John Benjamins.

Moutaouakil, Ahmed. 1989. *Pragmatic functions in a functional grammar of Arabic*. Dordrecht: Foris Publications.

Progovac, Ljiljana. 2006. The syntax of nonsententials: Small clauses and phrases at the root. In Ljiljana Progovac, Kate Paesani, Eugenia Casielles & Ellen Barton (eds.), *The syntax of non-sententials: Multidisciplinary perspectives*, 33–71. Amsterdam: John Benjamins.

Chapter 16

Anaphoric object drop in Chinese

Patrick Chi-wai Lee

Caritas Institute of Higher Education, Hong Kong

> This squib proposes a novel means of solving the problem of non-specific null object with an indefinite antecedent in Chinese whereas Huang (1982; 1984; 1989) argued that a dropped object is bound by a topic which must be definite. This squib proposes a formal representation that develops Holmberg's (2005) and Roberts & Holmberg's (2010) analysis of radical pro-drop as [uD] (unvalued determiner-feature). Null object arguments in Chinese are argued to have the same featural composition: [uD]. They can be valued from an antecedent, but it is with a referential index or a referential variable. It is hoped that this squib can make a valuable contribution to our understanding of anaphoric specific and non-specific object drop in Chinese, particularly in the simplicity of its theoretical machinery.

1 Introduction

This squib aims to offer a concise description of the interpretation of null objects in Chinese, and further proposes a formal representation that develops Holmberg's (2005) and Roberts & Holmberg's (2010) analysis of radical pro-drop as [uD] (unvalued determiner-feature). It is hoped that the proposal can shed some light in the context of classical analyses of null objects, especially in the Chinese syntax literature, which early on argued that the null object is a variable bound by an empty topic (Huang 1982; 1984; 1989). For this variable analysis, a significant problem is that the dropped object in Chinese can have an indefinite interpretation, even though a topic must be definite.[1] This squib proposes a novel means

---

[1] Besides indefinite object-drop, the second classic problem with Huang's (1982; 1984; 1989) variable analysis of null object drop is the availability of null object arguments coindexed with an antecedent across an island boundary. Li & Wei (2014: 277) argue that "a missing object can occur within islands co-indexed with their antecedent across island boundaries". They (2014:

of solving this problem through its descriptive and analytic distinction between specific and non-specific object drop.

To start with, anaphoric object drop means an object is dropped when there is an antecedent, and anaphoric object drop is characteristic of Chinese. Consider (1) from Huang (1984: 533),

(1) a. *Zhangsan kanjian Lisi le ma?*
    Zhangsan see   Lisi ASP Q
    'Did Zhangsan see Lisi?'

  b. *Ta kanjian e   le.*
    he see   [Lisi/him] ASP
    'He saw (him).' (ASP = aspect marker; *e* = empty category; Q = question particle)

(1b) shows that the empty category refers to *Lisi*, that is, the specific null object is bound by the definite topic in the discourse. Huang (1982; 1984; 1989) argued that an empty object is a variable bound by an empty topic, and topics can be null given that they can be identified with a topic in a topic chain. I now look at another example with a non-specific null object with an indefinite topic. Consider (2),

(2) Mandarin
    Zhang yao yi bu che Mali ye yao.
    Zhang want one CL car Mali also want
    'Zhang wants a car. Mary also wants one.' (CL = Classifier)

In (2) the null object *yi bu che* 'one car' is non-specific. It does not mean that there is a car and he or she wants it. Huang (1984) argued that a dropped object is bound by a topic which must be definite; however, the antecedent in this case is indefinite. Hence, this squib attempts to propose a novel means of solving this problem.

---

282) explain that "empty objects can be within islands bound by an A or A'-antecedent across island boundaries, unlike topicalization cases, which are subject to island constraints and only involve A'-antecedents". It should be noted that this squib does not attempt to address the issues about the null object and island boundaries, but those issues are also well-noted (see Li & Wei 2014 and Li 2014).

2 Types of anaphoric object drop

I now begin by examining various types of anaphoric object drop. They are distinguished by types of antecedent and by types of object dropped.[2] Briefly, a null object with specific reference has a definite antecedent, and a null object with specific reference is allowed where the antecedent does not have to be definite. In addition, a null object with non-specific reference has an indefinite antecedent.

2.1 Specific object drop

In (3) a null object with specific reference has a definite antecedent *zhe zhi xiong* 'this bear', with a demonstrative *zhe* 'this'.

(3) Mandarin
Zhang kanjian zhe zhi xiong le Mali ye kanjian.
Zhang see this CL bear ASP Mali also see
'Zhang saw this bear. Mary also saw it.' (The context is that they are looking at the same bear.)

Chinese also allows specific object drop where the antecedent does not have to be definite, and in fact, does not have to be specific as in (4).

(4) Mandarin
Zhang kanjian yi zhi xiong le Mali ye kanjian.
Zhang see one CL bear ASP Mali also see
'Zhang saw a bear. Mary also saw it.' (the same bear)

Here it can be specific in (4), so that it means 'Zhang and Mary saw a specific bear' (it's the one in the zoo), but it can also have a non-specific reading (see 5).

2.2 Non-specific object drop

2.2.1 Non-specific existential

In (5) a null object with non-specific reference has an indefinite antecedent *yi zhi xiong* 'one bear'.

---

[2] It should be noted that the verb-types play a role in the thematic assignment to the arguments, and the semantic properties of verbs are also significant when interpreting a missing object (see Huang et al. 2009 and Li & Wei 2014).

(5) Mandarin
Zhang kanjian yi zhi xiong le Mali ye kanjian.
Zhang see one CL bear ASP Mali also see

'Zhang saw a bear. Mary also saw one.' (meaning 'Mary saw a bear'. It can be a different bear.)

Here it can also have a non-specific existential reading in (5): 'There is a bear such that Mary saw it', and a sloppy interpretation is available to a missing object in Chinese (see (4) and (5)).

2.2.2 Non-specific generic

In (6) a null object with non-specific reference has a 'generic reading': Zhang likes anything which belongs to the *kind* or *species* 'bear'.

(6) Mandarin
Zhang xihuan xiong Mali ye xihuan.
Zhang like bear Mali also like

'Zhang likes bears. Mary also likes them.'

2.2.3 Non-specific attributive ('attributive reading of NP')

Consider non-specific object drop in Chinese as in (2), repeated here as (7).

(7) Mandarin
Zhang yao yi bu che Mali ye yao.
Zhang want one CL car Mali also want

'Zhang wants a car. Mary also wants one.'

In (7) a null object with non-specific reference is non-specific in a different sense, and I will call this the 'attributive reading of NP'. It is non-existential; it might be called a non-referential reading, but in a sense it is still referential.

In summary, based on the above data, anaphoric object drop can be classified into two main types: (1) specific object drop and (2) non-specific object drop which is further divided into: (a) non-specific existential, (b) non-specific generic and (c) non-specific attributive.

3 Argument ellipsis and the derivation of object drop

There are many works on discussion of ellipsis. Among many others, Saito (2007) suggests that radical pro-drop is a kind of argument ellipsis. He (2007: 25) argues that "those languages that have argument ellipsis can use LF objects provided by the discourse in the derivation of a new sentence". Sigurðsson (2011: 269) proposes "a unified minimalist approach to referential null arguments, where all types of (overt and silent) definite arguments require C/edge linking". Duguine (2014) is in favour of a unitary approach, and she proposes to reduce both types of pro-drop to ellipsis of full-fledged argument DPs. Li (2014) also contributes her idea of True Empty Categories (TEC) on argument ellipsis. She (2014: 65) explains that "a topic in the discourse not mentioned in the sentences containing the TEC can also be an antecedent (empty topic). It can also have a linguistic antecedent in the previous discourse by a different speaker or a preceding clause of a complex sentence by the same speaker".

As for the derivation of object drop, I now turn to examine how specific and non-specific null objects are licensed. Following Holmberg (2005; 2010)),[3] I firstly assume that null object arguments in Chinese (discourse pro-drop language) have the same featural composition: [uD, N]. The null arguments have an unvalued D-feature which needs to be assigned a value in the course of the derivation, and a nominal feature which means they can occur in all positions where nominal constituents are found. I explain that [uD] in Chinese can be valued from an antecedent, but it is with a referential index $[D_i\ N]$ or a referential variable $[D_x\ N]$. The valuation can be depicted as in (8), where DP needs to be in a local relation to the null pronoun.

(8) $DP_i\ ...\ [uD, N] \rightarrow DP_i\ ...\ [D_i, N]$

Consider (9) and (10) as illustrations of both $[Di\ N]$ and $[Dx\ N]$.

---

[3]Holmberg (2005) argues that in the context of a feature theory like the one in Chomsky (1995: Ch. 4, 2001) the phi-features of I (or T) are themselves uninterpretable (or unvalued), being assigned interpretation (or value) by agreement with the subject, so they cannot specify the value of the subject. Instead, he argues, the null subject pronoun has features just like an overt pronoun. "Following the Chomskyan approach to agreement, the null pronoun has interpretable phi-features and assigns values to the inherently unvalued features of Agr" (Holmberg 2005: 548). Holmberg further discusses a difference between two types of null subject languages (NSLs): consistent NSLs and partial NSLs. As for consistent NSLs like Italian, they have referential agreement, i.e. the phi-features in I/T include the feature [D(efinite)]. As for partial NSLs like Finnish, they have agreement, but it is not referential, i.e. there is no [D] feature in I/T. As for discourse pro-drop languages like Chinese, they have no unvalued phi-features in I/T (no subject-verb agreement) (Holmberg 2005: 559).

(9) Referential index (specific interpretation)
Mandarin
Zhang kanjian yi   zhi xiong le   Mali ye   kanjian e.
Zhang see   one CL bear$_i$ ASP Mali also see   [D$_i$ N]
'Zhang saw a bear. Mary also saw it.'

(10) Referential variable (non-specific interpretation)
Mandarin
Zhang kanjian yi   zhi xiong le   Mali ye   kanjian e.
Zhang see   one CL bear   ASP Mali also see   [D$_x$ N]
'Zhang saw a bear. Mary also saw one.'

3.1 An Aboutness topic feature accounts for specific object drop in Chinese

Holmberg & Nikanne (2002: 78) also point out that "a language is topic-prominent when the argument which is externalized need not be the subject, but can be any category capable of functioning as topic. English is generally taken as the perfect representative of subject-prominent languages, while representatives of topic-prominent languages include Chinese, Tagalog, and Hungarian". As for Chinese, declarative sentences have a feature in C which requires a topic specifier, and I will call this feature [Aboutness topic] (see Frascarelli & Hinterhölzl 2007 on the typology of topics; see Badan & Del Gobbo 2011 on types of topics in Mandarin[4]). According to Lambrecht (1994), aboutness topic represents what the sentence is about. An aboutness topic is an XP referring to the entity which the sentence is about. As such it is always referential, always definite, and often has the function of subject. This topic can be an overt phrase or a null pronoun. Typically this specifier will be the result of movement from IP, leaving a copy behind (a 'trace' in theories prior to Chomsky 1995), where this copy is 'deleted', i.e. not pronounced. The specifier may be a null pronoun, with a null pronoun copy in IP. The null pronoun in spec, CP needs to receive a referential index from a topic antecedent, and the copy in IP will share this index. There is also an 'EPP-feature' postulated with the Topic feature in Chinese C, which is the formal trigger of the movement (see Chomsky 1995; 2001). Chinese also has the option

---

[4]Badan & Del Gobbo (2011) discuss three different types of Topics in Mandarin: Aboutness Topics, Hanging Topics (HT) and Left Dislocated (LD) ones. They state that those types are organized hierarchically and they precede the only Focus projection that occurs above IP, the lian-Focus: Aboutness Topic › HT › LD › lian-Focus › IP.

of base-generating a topic in spec, CP with no copy in IP. The following is an example to illustrate a topic derived by base-generation.

(11) Mandarin (Huang et al. 2009: 202)
 shuiguo wo zui xihuan xiangjiao
 fruit, I most like banana
 '(As for) fruits, I like bananas most.'

Chinese has a topic feature in C (coupled with an EPP-feature). The interpretation of a null topic in terms of a topic chain follows from general, universal properties of null topics: a null topic will pick up the index of a local, salient topic in the immediately preceding discourse context, if there is an immediately preceding linguistic context, non-linguistic otherwise (see Frascarelli & Hinterhölzl 2007). This makes null definite object pronouns possible in Chinese. Chinese has movement of different types of topics to spec, CP which can be null if it has an antecedent.

3.2 NP-deletion with (null) determiner stranding accounts for non-specific object drop

As discussed in §2.2 *non-specific object drop*, the indefinite case cannot be topic drop because an indefinite DP cannot be topic. Therefore, the remaining question is how anaphoric non-specific object drop is to be licensed. First, Jackendoff (1971) described a rule which he called N'-deletion, which strands a genitive phrase, but cannot strand an indefinite or definite article. In the more current framework of the DP-hypothesis (Abney 1987), the rule can be redefined as NP-deletion, deleting the complement of D under certain conditions. Hoji (1998)[5] and Tomioka (2003) argue that discourse pro-drop languages have bare, D-less NP arguments.

---

[5]Hoji (1998) further explains that a bare nominal in Japanese such as *kuruma* 'car' can be translated as any of 'a car', 'the car', 'cars', or 'the cars', and argues that this is because a nominal projection whose sole content is its head N can be interpreted in various ways as just indicated. He 1998: 142 proposes that "the content of the N head of the null argument is supplied by the context of discourse. If the N head that is supplied by the context is a Name, then it can participate in a coreference relation with another Name". In addition, the supplied N head can be *kuruma* 'car' and it can function on a par with an indefinite in English. He points out that the null argument in Japanese behaves either like a definite or an indefinite. Tomioka (2003) agrees in part with Hoji's approach to null arguments in Japanese. Tomioka argues that Japanese lacks obligatory marking of definiteness and plurality on NPs, and therefore bare NP arguments get a variety of interpretations. His main claim is that null pronouns in discourse pro-drop languages like Japanese and Chinese are the result of NP-deletion with null determiner stranding.

If NP-ellipsis is applied in such a language, the result is a null argument. For Chinese, it is controversial whether overtly article-less arguments are bare NPs or DPs with a null article. In either case, if NP-ellipsis applies, the result will be a null argument. In the case of (10), the null object will be a deleted NP, where I assume that there is a null [uD]: [$_{DP}$ [$_{D'}$ uD [$_{NP}$ Ø]]], and a DP can have an index without a pronounced D (i.e. [uD] gets a value from an antecedent).

As for non-specific and specific object drop, I further assume that [uD] in Chinese can be valued from an antecedent, but it is with a referential index [D_i N] or a referential variable [D_x N]. A specific interpretation is the result when [uD] is valued by a referential index, whereas a non-specific interpretation is the result when it is valued by a referential variable. In both cases (9) and (10) the N of null [uD, N] is recovered by virtue of the overt noun of the antecedent.

After the above discussion of NP-ellipsis, I will assume that Tomioka is right. Huang (1984) argues that there is a null topic mediating between the antecedent and the null object, but that cannot be so in the indefinite cases (because an indefinite DP cannot be a topic). In the cases of non-specific object drop, they are derived by NP-ellipsis, stranding a null D. In the cases of specific object drop, they are derived by movement, as under Huang's theory of topic drop.

4 Conclusion

This squib proposes a novel means of solving the problem of non-specific null object with a definite topic. Null object arguments in Chinese are argued to have the same featural composition: [uD]. They can be valued from an antecedent, but it is with a referential index [Di N] or a referential variable [Dx N]. In addition, two types of anaphoric object drop in Chinese were studied: specific and non-specific object drop, and they were analyzed to be due to the existential state of an antecedent. Lastly, it is hoped that this squib can make a valuable contribution to our understanding of anaphoric specific and non-specific object drop in Chinese, particularly in the simplicity of its theoretical machinery.

References

Abney, Steven Paul. 1987. *The English noun phrase in its sentential aspect.* Cambridge: MIT dissertation.

Badan, Linda & Francesca Del Gobbo. 2011. On the syntax of topic and focus in Chinese. In Paola Benincà & Nicola Munaro (eds.), *Mapping the left periphery*, 63–91. Oxford: Oxford University Press.

Chomsky, Noam. 1995. *The minimalist program.* Cambridge, MA: MIT Press.
Chomsky, Noam. 2001. Derivation by phase. In Michael Kenstowicz (ed.), *Ken Hale: A life in language*, 1–52. Cambridge, MA: The MIT Press.
Duguine, Maia. 2014. Argument ellipsis: A unitary approach to pro-drop. *The Linguistic Review.* 31. 515–549.
Frascarelli, Mara & Roland Hinterhölzl. 2007. Types of topics in German and Italian. In Kerstin Schwade & Susanne Winkler (eds.), *On information structure, meaning and form*, 87–116. Amsterdam: John Benjamins.
Hoji, Hajime. 1998. Null object and sloppy identity in Japanese. *Linguistics Inquiry* 29. 127–152.
Holmberg, Anders. 2005. Is there a little pro? Evidence from Finnish. *Linguistic Inquiry* 36(4). 533–564.
Holmberg, Anders. 2010. Null subject parameters. In Theresa Biberauer, Anders Holmberg, Ian Roberts & Michelle Sheehan (eds.), *Parametric variation: Null subjects in minimalist theory*, 88–124. Cambridge: Cambridge University Press.
Holmberg, Anders & Urpo Nikanne. 2002. Expletives, subjects, and topics in Finnish. In Peter Svenonius (ed.), *Subjects, expletives, and the EPP*, 71–106. Oxford: Oxford University Press.
Huang, C. T. James. 1982. *Logical relations in Chinese and the theory of grammar.* MIT dissertation.
Huang, C. T. James. 1984. On the distribution and reference of empty pronouns. *Linguistic Inquiry* 15. 531–574.
Huang, C. T. James. 1989. Pro-drop in chinese: A generalized control theory. In O. Jaeggli & K. Safir (eds.), *The null subject parameter*, 185–214. Dordrecht: Kluwer.
Huang, C. T. James, Y.-H. Audrey Li & Yafei Li. 2009. *The syntax of chinese.* Cambridge: Cambridge University Press.
Jackendoff, Ray S. 1971. Gapping and related rules. *Linguistic Inquiry* 2. 21–35.
Lambrecht, Knud. 1994. *Information structure and sentence form: Topic, focus, and the mental representations of discourse referents.* Cambridge: Cambridge University Press.
Li, Y.-H. Audrey. 2014. Born empty. *Lingua* 151. 43–68.
Li, Y.-H. Audrey & Ting-Chi Wei. 2014. Ellipsis. In C.-T. James Huang, Li Y.-H. Audrey & Andrew Simpson (eds.), *The handbook of Chinese linguistics*, 275–310. Oxford: John Wiley & Sons.
Roberts, Ian & Anders Holmberg. 2010. Introduction: Parameters in minimalist theory. In Theresa Biberauer, Anders Holmberg, Ian Roberts & Michelle Sheehan (eds.), *Parametric variation. Null subjects in minimalist theory*, 1–57. Cambridge: Cambridge University Press.

Saito, Mamoru. 2007. Notes on East Asian argument ellipsis. *Language research* 43. 203–227.

Sigurðsson, Halldór Ármann. 2011. Conditions on argument drop. *Linguistic Inquiry* 42(2). 267–304.

Tomioka, Satoshi. 2003. The semantics of Japanese null pronouns and its cross-linguistic implications. In Kerstin Schwabe & Susanne Winkler (eds.), *The interfaces. Deriving and interpreting omitted structures*, 321–340. Amsterdam: John Benjamins.

Chapter 17

Icelandic as a partial null subject language: Evidence from fake indexicals

Susi Wurmbrand
University of Connecticut

> The distribution and licensing of null subjects has been a much debated topic in generative grammar. In many recent works, Anders Holmberg has proposed an enlightening typology that distinguishes between three types of null subject languages (see Holmberg 2005; 2010b,a; Holmberg & Sheehan 2010): consistent null subject languages such as Spanish, discourse *pro*-drop languages such as Chinese, and partial null subject languages. Among the latter are Finnish, Brazilian Portuguese, Marathi, and Icelandic. In this short note, I provide some new data from binding, in particular fake indexicals in Icelandic, that support Holmberg's view that Icelandic is a partial null subject language.

> One of the core defining characteristics of partial null subject languages is that 3rd person subjects can be unexpressed when they receive a non-referential generic interpretation or when they are a bound variable. Non-null subject languages such as German, in contrast, do not allow null subjects of any kind.

(1) a. Icelandic (Holmberg 2010a: 106, (27a))
   Nú má Ø fara að dansa.
   now may Ø go to dance
   'One may begin to dance now.'

   b. German
   Jetzt kann ✓ man/*Ø tanzen gehen.
   now can ✓ one/*Ø dance go
   'Now, one can go dancing.'

The account offered by Holmberg is that in partial null subject languages, null third person pronouns are weak deficient pronouns which contain φ-features

Susi Wurmbrand. 2017. Icelandic as a partial null subject language: Evidence from fake indexicals. In Michelle Sheehan & Laura R. Bailey (eds.), *Order and structure in syntax II: Subjecthood and argument structure*, 339–345. Berlin: Language Science Press.

(hence displaying agreement with the verb) but no referential D-feature. The only way such φPs can be interpreted is via binding by a higher DP, or as default generic pronouns.

Partial null subject languages differ regarding whether 1st and 2nd person pronouns can be null when they are used as indexicals: Finnish and Hebrew allow null indexical subjects, Marathi only allows a 2nd person indexical, and Brazilian Portuguese and Icelandic allow neither. According to Holmberg, indexical subjects (i.e., referential 1st and 2nd person pronouns) in partial null subject languages are always full definite pronouns including a referential D head, and languages differ regarding whether these subjects can be non-pronounced at PF. In consistent null subject languages, on the other hand, null indexicals are weak deficient pronouns lacking a DP, and the referential interpretation is contributed via a D-feature in I/T.

A prediction this account makes is that in partial null subject languages, even 1st and 2nd person pronouns should be allowed to be null (bare φPs) when they are not interpreted referentially—i.e., not as indexicals but as bound pronouns. As shown in (2), 1st and 2nd person pronouns in English, German, and Icelandic can be interpreted as bound variables.[1] As indicated by the paraphrase, in these contexts, the person features of indexicals are not interpreted (e.g., the 1st person pronoun *my* is not interpreted as the speaker in the set of alternatives, but as a variable), hence the term fake indexicals.

(2) All: I/You did my/your best and no one else did their best.
    a. English
       Only I did my/*her best.
    b. German
       Only you did your/*his best.
    c. German
       Nur ich habe mein/*ihr Bestes gegeben.
       only I have.1.SG my/*her best given
    d. German
       Nur du hast dein/*sein Bestes gegeben.
       only you have.2.SG your/*his best given

---

[1] The tenses are varied in some of the examples to avoid syncretism. This has no influence on fake indexicals.

17 Icelandic as a partial null subject language: Evidence from fake indexicals

e. Icelandic[2]
Aðeins ég geri   mitt/*hennar besta.
only   I do.1.SG my/*her   best

f. Icelandic
Aðeins þú gerðir   þitt/*hans besta.
only   you did.2.SG your/*his best

Turning to fake indexicals in subject position, an interesting difference arises between Icelandic and German. Let us start with the Icelandic examples in (3). In these cases, the 1st and 2nd person possessive pronouns are interpreted as bound variables (one cannot do someone else's best). The embedded verbs obligatorily agree with the matrix subjects, and this agreement, I propose, is controlled by a null subject in the embedded clause as indicated (an overt subject is not possible).

(3) Icelandic

a. *Ég er   sá   eini sem Ø.1.SG geri   mitt besta.*
   I am.1.SG DEM one that Ø.1.SG do.1.SG my   best
   'I am the only one who is doing my best.'

b. *Þú ert   sá   eini sem Ø.2.SG gerðir þitt besta.*
   you are.2.SG DEM one that Ø.2.SG did.2.SG your best
   'You (SG) are the only one who did your best.'

One may object that the null elements in (3) are simply null relative operators and not (true) null subjects. While this is in part correct, the existence of a true null subject in (3) can nevertheless be motivated by two properties. First, as shown in (4a), German does not allow fake indexicals in contexts where the embedded verb agrees with the matrix subject. German does, however, exhibit a special form of relative pronoun 'doubling' where the *d-* pronoun is paired with a regular personal pronoun (see Ito & Mester 2000). For some speakers this is only possible in non-restrictive relative clauses, but for others it is also possible in cases such as (4b). When such a pronoun is added, the embedded verb must agree with the additional subject, and, crucially, a bound variable interpretation then becomes possible for the possessive pronoun.

(4) a. German (Kratzer 2009: 206; (36a))
    *Ich bin die   einzige,   die   meinen Sohn versorge.
    I   am the.F.SG only.one who.F.SG my   son take.care.of.1.SG
    'I am the only one who is taking care of my son.'

---
[2] All of the following Icelandic examples are provided by Gísli Rúnar Harðarson.

b. German
   %Ich bin die   einzige,   die   ich meinen Sohn versorge.
   I   am the.F.SG only.one who.F.SG I   my   son take.care.of.1.SG
   'I am the only one who is taking care of my son.'

Under Holmberg's typology of null subjects, the differences between (3) and (4) follow if it is assumed that the possessive pronoun requires a featurally identical antecedent in subject position, in order to be interpreted as a fake indexical (see Wurmbrand 2015 for a detailed account of fake indexicals along these lines). Since Icelandic is a partial null subject language, subjects can be unexpressed, but only if they are bound by a higher DP. This is the case in (3), illustrated in (5a): the matrix (true) indexical pronoun binds the embedded null subject, which in turn binds the possessive pronoun—thus both the embedded subject and the possessive pronoun are bound fake indexicals. In the German varieties that allow relative pronoun doubling in restrictive relative clauses, the same configuration is possible, however, since German is a non-null subject language, the only option is to overtly realize the embedded subject.[3]

(5) a. DP.1.SG [$_{CP}$ OP.3.SG [$_{TP}$ Ø.φP.1.SG T.1.SG]] Icelandic
    b. DP.1.SG [$_{CP}$ OP.3.SG [$_{TP}$ φP1.SG T.1.SG]] German

The second piece of evidence for a null subject in (3) comes from constructions in which the embedded fake indexical subject cannot be bound. Note first that the examples in (3) also have a counterpart in which the null operator corresponds to the head of the relative clause, the 3rd person DP *the only one*. In these cases, the embedded verb shows 3rd person agreement and only the reflexive possessives are possible, as shown in (6).

(6) Icelandic

   a. *Ég er   sá eini sem gerir   sitt besta.*
      I am.1.SG DEM one that do.3.SG REFL best
      'I am the only one who is doing her best.'

   b. *Þú ert   sá eini sem gerði   sitt besta.*
      you are.2.SG dem one that did.3.SG refl best
      'You (sg) are the only one who did her best.'

---

[3]This account has interesting consequences for the structure of relative clauses and DPs in general. Since the relative operator and the additional subject pronoun correspond to one argument, a DP structure is necessary that allows splitting, for instance, the D-part (the relative operator/pronoun) and the φ-part (the additional pronoun).

17 Icelandic as a partial null subject language: Evidence from fake indexicals

An important difference regarding binding arises in the inverted (specificational) sentences in (7). As shown in (7a,b), the analogues of (3) are impossible—fake indexical possessives, and as I suggest, fake indexical null subjects are not licensed in these configurations. Crucially, as shown in (7c,d), bound variable interpretations of the possessive are still possible, however, only when both the verb and the possessive show 3rd person agreement. If all that is involved in (3) is a relative operator, it would not be obvious why in cases such as (3)/(6) both 3rd person bound pronouns and fake indexicals are possible, whereas in cases such as (7) only the 3rd person variant is available. An account based on the existence of null subjects, which are only licensed in Icelandic when bound by a higher DP, covers this difference very well. While the matrix DPs in (3)/(5) can bind and license an embedded null subject, this is not possible in (7) due to the lack of c-command in the inverted order.

(7) Icelandic

    a. *?*Sá eini sem geri   mitt besta er   ég.*
       DEM one that do.1.SG my best am.1.SG I.NOM
       'The only one who is doing my best is me.'

    b. **Sá eini sem gerðir þitt besta varst   Þú.*
       DEM one that did.2.SG your best was.2.SG you.NOM
       'The only one who did your best is you.'

    c. *Sá eini sem gerir   sitt besta er   ég.*
       DEM one that do.3.SG REFL best am.1.SG I.NOM
       'The only one who is doing his/her best am I.'

    d. *Sá eini sem gerði   sitt besta varst   Þú.*
       DEM one that did.3.SG REFL best was.2.SG you.NOM
       'The only one who did his/her best is you.'

Finally, the assumption that the additional subject in German cases such as (4b), like the null subject in Icelandic, is licensed by a higher c-commanding antecedent, predicts that this option should also disappear in inverted specificational sentences. The examples in (8) show that this is correct—(8a) is impossible for all speakers of German, and only a 3rd person possessive as in (8b) is possible to express a bound variable interpretation.

(8) German

    a. *Die einzige die ich mein Bestes gegeben habe bin ich.
       the only.one who I my best given have.1.SG am.1.SG I
       'The only one who did her (lit. my) best is me.'

    b. Die einzige die ihr Bestes gegeben hat bin ich.
       the only.one who her best given have.1.SG am.1.SG I
       'The only one who did her best is me.'

While the behavior of fake indexicals in relative clauses provides nice evidence for Holmberg's null subject typology, the conclusions have to also be taken with a grain of salt. As shown in (9), null fake indexicals are not possible in complement clauses. Even under the bound variable interpretation, the pronoun must be realized overtly.[4]

(9) Icelandic

    a. Aðeins ég held að *(ég) tali íslensku.
       only í think.1.SG that *(I) talk.1.SG.SUBJ Icelandic
       'Only I think that I can speak Icelandic.'

    b. Aðeins þú hélst að *(þú) talaðir íslensku.
       only you thought.2.SG that *(you) talked.2.SG.SUBJ Icelandic
       'Only you thought that you could speak Icelandic.'

    c. Aðeins hann hélt að *(hann) talaði íslensku.
       only he thought.3.SG that *(he) talked.3.SG.SUBJ Icelandic

Holmberg's proposal which treats Icelandic as a partial null subject language makes surprising, but correct, predictions about subtle differences between Icelandic and German (and English) in the distribution of fake indexicals, yet leaves as still open the difference between relative clauses and complement clauses. The question remains whether Holmberg will think that I am the only one who likes my extension of his analysis.

---

[4] A reviewer mentions that control contexts, under certain assumptions, may constitute another case of an obligatorily null bound variable subject. Since infinitival subjects in Icelandic have Case (Sigurðsson 1991) and φ-features (in particular in partial control contexts), the reviewer suggests that one could perhaps treat those subjects as *pro* rather than PRO.

Acknowledgments

Thanks to Jonathan Bobaljik, Gísli Rúnar Harðarson, and Ian Roberts for comments and feedback.

References

Holmberg, Anders. 2005. Is there a little pro? Evidence from Finnish. *Linguistic Inquiry* 36(4). 533–564.

Holmberg, Anders. 2010a. Null subject parameters. In Theresa Biberauer, Anders Holmberg, Ian Roberts & Michelle Sheehan (eds.), *Parametric variation: Null subjects in minimalist theory*, 88–124. Cambridge: Cambridge University Press.

Holmberg, Anders. 2010b. The null generic pronoun in Finnish: A case of incorporation in T. In Theresa Biberauer, Anders Holmberg, Ian Roberts & Michelle Sheehan (eds.), *Parametric variation: Null subjects in minimalist theory*, 200–230. Oxford: Oxford University Press.

Holmberg, Anders & Michelle Sheehan. 2010. Control into finite clauses in partial null-subject languages. In Theresa Biberauer, Anders Holmberg, Ian Roberts & Michelle Sheehan (eds.), *Parametric variation: null subjects in minimalist theory*, 125–152. Cambridge: Cambridge University Press.

Ito, Junko & Armin Mester. 2000. "ich, der ich sechzig bin": An agreement puzzle. In Sandra Chung, James McCloskey & Nathan Sanders (eds.), *Jorge hankamer webfest*. Santa Cruz: University of California Santa Cruz. http://babel.ucsc.edu/Jorge/.

Kratzer, Angelika. 2009. Making a pronoun: Fake indexicals as windows into the properties of pronouns. *Linguistic Inquiry* 40. 187–237.

Sigurðsson, Halldór Ármann. 1991. Icelandic case-marked PRO and the licensing of lexical arguments. *Natural Language and Linguistic Theory* 9. 327–364.

Wurmbrand, Susi. 2015. *Fake indexicals, feature sharing, and the importance of gendered relatives*. Colloquium talk, MIT, Cambridge, MA.

Name index

Aa, Leiv Inge, 290, 299
Abdel-Massih, Ernest T., 245
Abels, Klaus, 129
Abney, Steven Paul, 335
Ackema, Peter, 265, 270
Adams, Nikki B., 116, 134, 135, 142
Adger, David, 132, 133
Åfarli, Tor A., 271, 299
Alexiadou, Artemis, 41, 42, 54, 71, 169, 170, 172, 173, 175, 180, 184
Alsina, Alex, 116, 144
Anagnostopoulou, Elena, 41, 42, 54, 71, 127, 128, 131, 157, 158, 160–162, 169–173, 175
Anand, Pranav, 201, 210, 213
Andrews, Avery, 279
Angantýsson, Ásgrímur, 15, 18, 22, 24
Aoun, Joseph E., 323
Avelar, Juanito, 49, 51

Babby, Leonard H., 310
Badan, Linda, 334
Baker, Mark, 115, 116, 119, 126, 128, 143, 144, 155, 173, 214, 278
Banfield, Ann, 213, 214
Bárány, András, 126
Barbaresi, Lavinia M., 250
Barbosa, Pilar, 49, 167, 168
Barker, Chris, 233
Barnes, Michael P., 15

Bartra-Kaufmann, Anna, 74
Bastin, Yvonne, 140
Bax, Anna, 135
Beaudoin-Lietz, Christa, 131
Beck, Sigrid, 155
Belletti, Adriana, 48, 159
Bennis, Hans, 83
Benveniste, Émile, 199, 208
Beretta, Alan, 222, 250
Bergen, John, 247
Berlinck, Rosane, 51
Berwick, Robert C., 4
Bianchi, Valentina, 201, 207, 307, 314
Biberauer, Theresa, 137
Bisetto, Antonietta, 257, 264–266, 268, 270
Blevins, James P., 312
Boas, Franz, 199
Bobaljik, Jonathan D., 22, 131, 156, 199, 209
Boeckx, Cedric, 4, 6, 278, 281
Bogusławski, Andrzej, 312
Bolinger, Dwight, 70
Bondaruk, Anna, 310
Bonet, Eulalia, 162
Booij, Gert, 267
Borer, Hagit, 54, 186, 227, 271
Börjars, Kersti, 301
Bošković, Željko, 278
Bostoen, Koen, 135
Brajerski, Tadeusz, 312

Name index

Bresnan, Joan, 115
Brockelmann, Karl, 221
Brody, Michael, 50
Bruening, Benjamin, 131, 144
Brugmann, Karl, 221, 226
Brunetti, Lisa, 323, 324
Buell, Leston C., 115
Bühler, Karl, 214
Bullock, Barbara, 75
Busquets, Joan, 323
Buthers, Christiane, 49

Cabredo Hofherr, Patricia, 187, 192
Cann, Ronnie, 135
Cardinaletti, Anna, 72, 82, 167
Carlson, Greg, 187
Carnie, Andrew, 302
Carrilho, Ernestina, 88
Carter, Richard, 281
Carvalho, Janayna, 51
Casielles, Eugenia, 319, 320
Caspari, Carl Paul, 221, 227
Cavalcante, Sílvia, 42
Charzyńska-Wójcik, Magdalena, 310
Chierchia, Gennaro, 183, 187, 192, 203
Chomsky, Noam, 4, 5, 42, 70, 126, 137, 142, 154, 155, 162, 168, 207, 215, 222, 277, 281, 285–287, 291, 333[3], 333, 334
Christensen, Kirsti Koch, 289
Cinque, Guglielmo, 49, 179, 180, 237, 239, 248
Clements, George N., 203
Cohen, Ariel, 54
Collins, Chris, 126, 143, 202
Condoravdi, Cleo, 159
Corbett, Greville, 221, 229

Cowart, Wayne, 161
Craenenbroeck, Jeroen van, 86, 87, 319
Creissels, Denis, 135, 136
Crisma, Paola, 224
Cyrino, Sônia, 49, 51, 57
Cysouw, Michael, 198, 199, 209

Dahl, Östen, 221
Dao, Huy Linh, 77
de Belder, Marijke, 236
De Caluwe, Johan, 83
De Cuypere, Ludovic, 292
de Kind, Jasper, 135
De la Grasserie, Raoul, 247
De Vogelaer, Gunther, 83, 84, 88
Deal, Amy Rose, 42
Déchaine, Rose-Marie, 55
Del Gobbo, Francesca, 334
Den Dikken, Marcel, 157
Devos, Magda, 83, 84, 88
Diercks, Michael, 126, 135
Dimitriadis, Alexis, 160
Dimmendaal, Gerrit, 229
Doggett, Teal Bissell, 127
Doros, Aleksander, 312
Dressler, Wolfgang U., 250
Duarte, Maria Eugênia, 42
Duffield, Nigel, 79
Duguine, Maia, 333
Duranti, Alessandro, 119
Dziwirek, Katarzyna, 309, 311
D'Alessandro, Roberta, 173, 180, 184, 307, 314

É. Kiss, Katalin, 189
Egerland, Verner, 183, 186, 190, 192, 309
Eilam, Aviad, 155

Elbourne, Paul D., 201
Engdahl, Elisabet, 292, 293, 302, 303
Engels, Eva, 300
Erteschik-Shir, Nomi, 54
Eythórsson, Thórhallur, 11, 32, 34

Faarlund, Jan Terje, 302
Falk, Cecilia, 279
Falster Jakobsen, Lisbeth, 295
Farkas, Donka, 79
Fassi Fehri, Abdelkader, 224, 226–228, 230, 232, 233, 242, 244, 248, 307, 309, 311, 312, 316
Ferreira, Marcelo, 57
Figueiredo-Silva, Maria Cristina, 42
Fleisch, Henri, 227
Frascarelli, Mara, 207, 307, 308, 315, 316, 334, 335
Freeze, Ray, 42, 50

Gagliardi, Annie, 35
Galves, Charlotte, 42, 47, 51, 52
Georgala, Effi, 161
Gerdts, Donna B., 144
Gibson, Edward, 4, 7
Giorgi, Alessandra, 203, 207, 211, 214
Githinji, Peter, 140
Givón, Talmy, 135
Grandi, Nicola, 222, 244, 245, 248, 250
Greco, Ciro, 77, 79
Greenberg, Joseph, 224
Grimm, Jacob, 221
Grimstad, Maren Berg, 271
Grohmann, Kleanthes, 72, 88
Grov, Astrid Marie, 258, 268
Guéron, Jacqueline, 60, 83, 87
Guevara, Emiliano Raul, 259, 262
Gupton, Timothy, 75, 76, 81

Gurman, Bard Ellen, 161

Hachimi, Atiqa, 226, 227
Haddad, Youssef A., 207
Haddican, William, 115, 129, 130, 132
Haegeman, Liliane, 82, 83, 86, 87
Halle, Morris, 222, 249
Hämeen-Anttila, Jaakko, 240
Hansen, Erik, 257, 296
Harbour, Daniel, 132, 133
Harizanov, Boris, 128, 173
Harley, Heidi, 144, 222, 249, 302, 309, 314, 315
Haspelmath, Martin, 4, 6
Hasselbach, Rebecca, 246
Hayward, Richard J., 229
Hedlund, Cecilia, 292
Helgadóttir, Sigrún, 7
Hellan, Lars, 79
Heltoft, Lars, 257, 295, 296
Henderson, Brent, 135
Hill, Virginia, 222, 241, 242
Hinterhölzl, Roland, 307, 315, 334, 335
Hinzelin, Marc-Oliver, 76
Hinzen, Wolfram, 207
Hirtle, Walter H., 257
Hodges, Kathryn S., 119
Hoekstra, Jarich, 185, 192
Hoji, Hajime, 335
Holmberg, Anders, 3–8, 33, 35, 42–45, 51, 53, 55, 56, 59, 71–74, 76, 115, 116, 129, 130, 132, 137, 153–155, 159, 166, 167, 173, 197, 199, 206, 207, 279, 280, 289–292, 301, 307–309, 329, 333, 334, 339
Hornstein, Norbert, 278, 281
Hovdenak, Marit, 259

Name index

Høysgaard, Jens, 297, 298
Hróarsdóttir, Thorbjörg, 155
Huang, C. T. James, 76, 329–331, 335, 336
Hyman, Larry M., 119, 133, 144

Ibrahim, Muhammad, 227
Iorio, David, 126
Ito, Junko, 341

Jackendoff, Ray S., 335
Jayaseelan, K. A., 211
Jeong, Youngmi, 127, 144
Jerro, Kyle, 116, 144
Johannessen, Janne Bondi, 258, 264, 270
Jónsson, Jóhannes Gísli, 11, 32, 34, 156, 190
Julien, Marit, 132, 210
Jurafsky, Daniel, 222, 249, 250

Kaburaki, Etsuku, 204
Kahane, Henry, 247
Kahane, Renée, 247
Kaiser, Georg, 76
Kato, Mary, 42
Kayne, Richard S., 42, 102, 107, 110, 112, 188
Keller, Frank, 161
Kibort, Anna, 221, 309–311, 313
Kihm, Alain, 233
Kiss, Katalin, 72, 74, 82
Kolokonte, Marina, 323, 324
Koontz-Garboden, Andrew, 267
Köpcke, Klaus-Michael, 234
Koppen, Marjo van, 87
Körtvélyessy, Livia, 249, 250
Kossmann, Maarten, 244–246
Kramer, Ruth, 128, 144, 173, 233

Kratzer, Angelika, 50, 180, 181, 202, 341
Krifka, Manfred, 319
Kroch, Anthony S., 3, 4, 34
Kula, Nancy C., 121
Kuno, Susumu, 204

Laanemets, Anu, 292, 293, 296, 298, 299, 302, 303
Ladusaw, William, 78
Lakoff, George, 249, 250
Lambrecht, Knud, 334
Landau, Idan, 203
Larsson, Ida, 292
Lavine, James E., 310, 311
Lechner, Winfried, 154, 155
Legate, Julie Anne, 35, 142
Leiss, Elisabeth, 226
Li, Y.-H. Audrey, 329–331, 333
Lidz, Jeffrey, 35
Lightfoot, David, 4, 7
Lødrup, Helge, 302
Longobardi, Guiseppe, 233
Lowenstamm, Jean, 233
Lowman, Sarah, 75, 76, 81
Lunguinho, Marcus, 52, 58, 59
Lyons, John, 199

Mabugu, Patricia, 135
Machobane, 'Malillo, 120
Malamud, Sophia, 180, 185, 192
Malchukov, Andrej L., 138
Maling, Joan, 15, 27, 203, 311
Marantz, Alec, 51, 116, 144, 222, 249, 250, 278, 285, 286
Marten, Lutz, 121, 122, 135
Martín Zorraquino, Maria Antonia, 75
Martín, Txsuss, 207

Name index

Martínez Sanz, Cristina, 75
Mathangwane, Joyce T., 119
Mathieu, Eric, 224, 227, 236
Matushansky, Ora, 170
McConnell-Ginet, Sally, 235
McGinnis, Martha, 129, 131
Mchombo, Sam, 116, 144
Medeiros Junior, Paulo, 58, 59
Melloni, Chiara, 257, 264–266, 268, 270
Merchant, Jason, 319–322, 325, 326
Mester, Armin, 341
Mettouchi, Amina, 244, 245
Mikkelsen, Kristian, 297
Mithun, Marianne, 235
Miyagawa, Shigeru, 242, 286
Mohr, Sabine, 70
Morimoto, Yukiko, 135
Moro, Andrea, 241
Morolong, 'Malillo, 119, 133, 144
Moshi, Lioba, 115, 116
Mous, Marten, 229, 230
Moutaouakil, Ahmed, 323
Mugari, Victor, 119
Muñoz Pérez, Carlos, 75
Muriungi, Peter, 119, 139, 140
Myler, Neil, 269

Nagórko, Alicja, 311
Nakamura, Masanori, 144
Naves, Rozana, 52
Neeleman, Ad, 265, 270
Nevins, Andrew, 170, 173, 174, 213, 269
Newmeyer, Frederick J., 4, 6, 8, 32, 33, 35, 37, 71
Ngoboka, Jean Paul, 116, 119, 141, 144
Ngonyani, Deo, 115, 116, 140, 144
Nguyen, Hoang Thuy, 77

Nguyen, Van Hiep, 77
Nikanne, Urpo, 51, 72–74, 76, 279, 280, 290, 291, 334
Nóbrega, Vitor A., 286
Nomura, Masashi, 156
Nowenstein, Iris, 5, 32, 34
Nunes, Jairo, 42, 52, 57, 126

Oehrle, Richard. T., 125
Okubo, Tatsuhiro, 285, 287
Osam, E. Kweku, 119
Otheguy, Ricardo, 75
Ouwayda, Sarah, 228

Partee, Barbara, 208
Pearson, Hazel, 233
Pedersen, Karen Margrethe, 297, 298
Percus, Orin, 234
Pesetsky, David, 144, 159, 234, 279
Phan, Trang, 79
Phimsawat, On-Usa, 42, 59
Picallo, Carme, 233
Pilati, Eloísa, 52
Platzack, Christer, 3, 6, 33, 279, 280
Pontes, Eunice, 52
Portóles Lázaro, José, 75
Postal, Paul, 201, 202
Poulsen, Jóhan Hendrik W., 14
Preminger, Omer, 126, 162, 173
Progovac, Ljiljana, 319, 320
Pylkkänen, Liina, 124, 125, 127, 222, 250

Ramadhani, Deograsia, 122
Ranero, Rodrigo, 141
Reichenbach, Hans, 208
Revithiadou, Anthi, 168
Richards, Marc, 42
Riedel, Kristina, 116, 132

Name index

Rigau, German, 54
Ritter, Elizabeth, 57, 58, 234, 309, 314, 315
Rizzi, Luigi, 41, 42, 48, 54, 70–72, 80, 82, 87, 159, 167
Roberts, Ian, 4, 5, 33, 35, 48, 71, 73, 126, 134, 137, 153, 154, 166, 167, 307, 329
Rodrigues, Cilene, 52, 56, 57
Rögnvaldsson, Eiríkur, 7
Roman, André, 227
Ross, John R., 207
Roussou, Anna, 137
Rozwadowska, Bożena, 312
Rugemalira, Josephat M., 116
Rullmann, Hotze, 202

Saito, Mamoru, 333
Schadeberg, Thilo C., 116
Schäfer, Florian, 42
Schlenker, Philippe, 201, 207
Schneider-Zioga, Patricia, 143
Schütze, Carson, 155
Seifart, Frank, 224
Sells, Peter, 203
Sevdali, Christina, 160
Sheehan, Michelle, 126, 137, 138, 339
Shlonsky, Ur, 42, 70–72
Sibawayhi, Amr, 224
Siewierska, Anna, 198, 199, 209, 309, 312, 313
Sigurðsson, Einar Freyr, 28, 202
Sigurðsson, Halldór Ármann, 4, 19, 34, 167, 190, 201, 203, 204, 207, 208, 210–214, 307, 309, 314, 333, 344
Sigurjónsdóttir, Sigríður, 27, 203
Simango, Silvester Ron, 116, 144
Speas, Margaret, 207, 222, 241

Śpiewak, Grzegorz, 309
Sportiche, Dominique, 170, 174, 188
Spyropoulos, Vassilios, 168
Ssekiryango, Jackson, 128, 129
Starke, Michal, 167
Steriopolo, Olga, 234, 236
Stowell, Tim, 42
Sundaresan, Sandhya, 207
Sundman, Marketta, 292
Svenonius, Peter, 51, 280

Taraldsen, Tarald Knut, 167, 289
Teleman, Ulf, 257, 301
Tenny, Carol L., 186, 187, 207, 222, 241
Thráinsson, Höskuldur, 5, 7, 10, 11, 15, 18, 19, 22, 32, 34, 203, 211, 212
Thwala, Nhlanhla, 116
Tomioka, Satoshi, 155, 167, 335
Toribio, Almeida Jacqueline, 75
Torrego, Esther, 54, 174
Travis, Lisa, 186

Unterbeck, Barbara, 226
Ura, Hiroyuki, 128
Uriagereka, Juan, 72, 74, 76, 88, 174

van der Wal, Jenneke, 117, 126, 132, 133, 135
Vergnaud, Jean-Roger, 107
Vikner, Sten, 15, 19, 22
Vilkuna, Enric, 189, 191
Vilkuna, Maria, 189, 191
Vincent, Nigel, 301

Wangensteen, Boye, 259
Watanabe, Akira, 155
Wei, Ting-Chi, 329–331

Wexler, Kenneth, 4, 7
Whaley, Lindsay, 144
Wierzbicka, Anna, 249, 312
Wiltschko, Martina, 55, 57, 58, 234, 236
Wood, Jim, 51, 202
Wright, William, 240
Wurmbrand, Susi, 342

Yang, Charles, 3–5, 7, 35
Yoneda, Nobuko, 135

Zabbal, Youri, 224
Zaenen, Annie, 11, 156, 279, 280
Zeller, Jochen, 116, 118, 119, 133–135, 139, 144
Zerbian, Sabine, 135
Zobel, Sarah, 180

Language index

Akkadian, 246

Arabic, viii, 222, 223, 223[1], 224, 227, 227[4], 229–231, 234[8], 236, 237, 239[11], 240, 240[13], 246, 248–250, 309, 311, 312, 316, 322–327

Bantu, viii, 115–117, 124, 126, 126[4], 126[5], 130[8], 132, 135, 143, 224[2], 247

Berber, 222, 227, 244

Brazilian Portuguese, 42–44, 46–48, 51–53, 56–59, 168, 308, 340

Breton, 227

Danish, 9, 14, 257, 290, 291, 292[5], 292[6], 295, 296, 296[10], 297–300, 302–304

Dutch, 70[1], 154, 156–158, 161, 166, 167, 171, 172, 172[10], 174, 248[18], 257[1], 307

European Portuguese, 308

Faroese, vii, 5–7, 10, 11, 11[4], 14, 14[5], 15, 18[6], 19, 22, 24[7], 26, 29, 31, 34, 36, 37

Finnish, 42–45, 45[2], 47, 48, 48[9], 49–51, 53, 54, 56, 57, 59–62, 71–73, 73[3], 73[4], 74, 76, 77, 82, 86, 89, 90, 307, 308, 333[3], 340

French, 35, 168, 182[3], 187[9], 208[13], 223, 226

German, viii, 180, 181, 185, 185[6], 186–188, 188[10], 189–191, 193, 227[4], 234, 248[18], 307, 339–344

Greek, 42, 43, 43[1], 53, 54, 61, 62, 154, 158–161, 161[3], 162, 163, 163[4], 164, 165, 165[5], 166, 167[7], 168, 169, 169[8], 170[9], 171, 172, 172[10], 173[12], 174, 175, 257, 257[1], 307, 321, 322, 324[2]

Géez, 246

Hebrew, 222, 227, 244, 246, 340

Hungarian, 334

Icelandic, viii, 7, 8, 11, 18[6], 19, 22, 27, 28, 36, 37, 154–156, 158, 166, 167, 167[7], 171, 172, 172[10], 174, 182[3], 187–190, 190[12], 191, 203, 204, 204[9], 211, 278, 278[1], 279, 279[2], 280, 280[4], 281, 282, 291[4], 339–341, 341[2], 342–344, 344[4]

Italian, viii, 49[11], 71, 130[8], 138, 168, 169, 172[10], 180, 180[1], 181, 182, 182[3], 183–185, 185[6], 186, 187, 187[9], 203[7], 247, 248, 257[1], 307, 311, 314, 324[2], 333[3]

Japanese, 286

Kimeru, 119, 124

Language index

Kîîtharaka, 119, 124, 139, 140

Lubukusu, 119, 124, 141, 142
Luguru, 121, 122, 124, 137, 138, 143

Mainland Scandinavian, 6, 287, 289, 292
Mandarin, 330–332, 334, 334^4, 335

Norse, 7, 26
Norwegian, viii, 9, 95, 97^4, 113, 129, 142, 185, 185^6, 186–191, 193, 193^{17}, 210^{16}, 257–259, 262, 268, 269^5, 271, 272, 290, 290^3, 291, 292^5, 292^6, 298–302, 302^{13}, 302^{14}, 304, 322

Otjiherero, 121, 124

Polish, viii, 257^1, 309, 311, 311^4, 312–314, 316

Romance, 46, 74, 76, 187^9, 222, 224^2, 234^8, 244, 247, 257, 264
Russian, 227

Scandinavian, viii, 3–5, 22, 31, 37, 193^{17}, 300
    Insular, 3, 6
    Mainland, 3, 6
Semitic, 221, 223, 244
Shona, 119, 124
Slavic, 257, 264, 266, 268^4, 312
Somali, 227
Southern Sotho, 119, 120, 124
Swahili, 123, 124
Swedish, 9, 129, 181–185, 185^6, 186–188, 188^{10}, 189, 190, 190^{12}, 191, 192^{14}, 193, 193^{17}, 257, 285, 286, 289–292, 292^5, 292^6, 293–297, 298^{11}, 299, 300, 300^{12}, 301, 302^{13}, 304

Thai, 59, 76

Welsh, 227

Zulu, 115, 116, 118, 124, 133–135, 137–139, 141, 142

Subject index

A-bar movement, 143, 326, see A'-movement, see wh-movement
A-movement, 111, 112, 144, 168
Accusative, 11
Addressee, 314, 315, 315^6
Adv, 261
Adverb, see Adv
Agr, 5, 333^3
Agree, viii, 126, 126^4, 127, 133, 142, 154, 155, 155^2, 156–158, 164, 166, 167, 167^7, 171, 174, 207^{12}, 208, 215, 308
    see also agreeing,
    see also agreement
agreeing, 85, 126, 131, 173^{12}, 242, 289^1, 290, 297, 298
agreement, 7, 28, 74, 76, 83^8, 126, 127, 132, 135, 142, 143, 154, 155, 155^2, 156, 167, 167^7, 168, 169^8, 171, 172, 172^{10}, 173, 173^{11}, 174, 174^{13}, 192^{14}, 199, 207^{12}, 221, 222, 224, 224^2, 225, 227, 228^5, 230, 230^6, 231–233, 242^{16}, 244, 250, 289, 290, 290^3, 291^4, 296–299, 304, 320, 333^3, 340–343
Appl, 134^{10}, 115–144, 167, 172^{10}
Asp, see aspect
aspect, 129, 181, 181^2, 183, 184, 184^4, 186, 187, 266, 330

Aux, 168, 169, 169^8
    see also auxiliary
auxiliary, 23, 24^7, 73, 97, 99, 154, 169, 169^8, 291, 292, 292^5, 310
A'-movement, 70, 111, 112

Cartography, 222
Case, viii, 45, 45^3, 52^{13}, 53, 126, 126^5, 127, 130, 131, 135, 158, 171, 277, 278, 281, 282, 320, 344^4
causative, 115–144, 278, 281^6
Clitic, 168
Clitic left dislocation, see CLLD
cliticization, 158, 162, 170, 170^9, 171
CLLD, 168
Competing grammars, see grammar competition
complementizer, 85, 87, 87^9, see complementizer
compound, viii, 248, 286–288
CP, 42, 54, 55, 62, 88, 107–109, 110^9, 112, 209, 222, 234, 240, 241, 243, 250, 282, 334, 335

Dem, see demonstrative
demonstrative, 331
DOC, 122, 125, 125^3, 126, 129, 130, 136, 143, 144, 277, 301
Double object construction, see DOC

EPP, 42, 43, 47^8, 48, 49, 51–54, 56, 57,

Subject index

61, 62, 70–72, 82, 158, 166, 168, 169^8, 170, 171
Experimental, 161
expletive, 19, 26

finite, 19, 24, 70, 82, 84, 86, 87, 87^9, 154, 159, 170, 212, 280
FinP, 88
Focus, 73, 323, 334^4
Force, 241

gender, viii, 88, 221–224, 224^2, 226, 227, 230, 234–236, 238, 240–242, 244, 247–251, 289^1
Generic, 78
grammar competition, 34

impersonal, 27, 42–61, 191, 192
impersonal passive, 19, 20, 280^4, 292, 293, 296, 298
impersonals, 41, 42, 44–46
INFL, 57, 58, 60, 61
Intra-speaker variation, 32

Merge, 215
merger, 169, 170, 173, 241^{14}
merges, 51^{12}, 55, 57, 169^8

Neg, *see* negation
negation, 132, 292, 293, 295, 302
Nominative, 11, 160
null expletive, 3, 5–9, 19–21, 25–27, 29–33, 36
Null pronoun, *see* pro-drop
null subject, vii–ix, 43, 44, 48, 71, 73, 83^8, 153^1, 165, 166, 169, 169^8, 170, 173, 173^{12}, 174^{13}, 175, 307–316, 333^3, 339–344

Num, 226^3, 228, 228^5, 232, 233, 233^7, 234, 236, 242^{16}, 271
see also number
number, vii, viii, 88, 155, 156, 167^7, 187, 187^7, 192, 199, 207, 210, 230, 236, 250, 264, 267, 269, 270

Oblique subjects, 7, 8, 25, 26

P-stranding, 321
Participle, 291
Pass, *see* passive
passive, viii, 28, 116, 135, 139, 141–144, 161, 169^8, 279, 279^2, 280^4, 289, 292, 292^6, 293–296, 298, 298^{11}, 300^{12}, 303, 309, 309^1, 310, 310^2, 310^3, 311, 312, 316
PCC, 132, 133, 167^7
Person, 133, 199, 200, 207, 208, 213, 215, 242
Person Case Constraint, *see* PCC
Phase, 286, 288
see also phasehood
phasehood, 143
Poss, *see* possessor
possessor, 52, 52^{13}, 53, 144, 243, 268–270
preposition, 96^2, 98, 98^5, 99–102, 104–106, 108, 110, 321, 325
Preposition stranding, *see* P-stranding
pro-drop, vii, 42, 46, 53–55, 55^{14}, 56, 59, 61, 71–77, 82, 83, 88, 89, 153, 164–167, 167^7, 168, 172, 173^{12}, 174^{13}, 307, 329, 333, 333^3, 335, 335^5

358

Subject index

Quantity, 249
Question, 165, 166

recursive, viii, 286–288
reference, 46, 60, 159, 181[2], 184[4], 185, 199[1], 203, 208, 259, 331, 332, 335[5]
relative, 16, 17, 96, 96[2], 97, 98, 98[5], 99, 102–105, 109, 110[9], 111, 112, 192, 303, 327, 341, 342, 342[3], 343, 344
Relativized Minimality, 111

semantic, 50, 60, 70[1], 71, 71[2], 72, 76, 78, 81, 86, 101, 155[2], 187[8], 189, 191, 192, 222, 234, 246–249, 249[20], 250, 258, 264, 265, 267–269, 271, 272, 331[2]
Speaker, 242, 243, 314, 315, 315[6]
spell out, 83[8], 127, 131, 171, 173, 208
spells out, 134[10], 143
Stylistic Fronting, 5, 7–9, 15, 19, 25–27, 32, 33, 36

Tense, 35, 208
    see also TP
Topic, 81, 308, 309, 315, 315[7], 316, 316[8], 334, 334[4]
    see also Top
TP, viii, 51, 53–55, 57, 62, 73, 76, 87, 88, 125, 128, 130, 154, 157, 158, 162, 167, 168, 209, 324, 324[1], 325, 327
Transitive expletives, 7–9

universal, 34, 35, 210[16], 249, 335
Universal Grammar, 4, 215

V movement, 87
V2, ix, 84, 86, 87, 87[9], 106[8]

verb movement, 171
    see also V-movement
Vfin, *see* finite

wh-movement, 155[2]

359

www.ingramcontent.com/pod-product-compliance
Lightning Source LLC
Chambersburg PA
CBHW080917100426
42812CB00007B/2305